Toufic Haddad holds a PhD from SOAS, University of London. He is co-author of *Between the Lines: Israel, the Palestinians and the US 'War on Terror'* (2007), and previously worked as a journalist, editor and researcher in Jerusalem, including for different UN bodies.

'A crisply written, painstakingly researched study that puts Palestine in a much-needed global economic context, laying out the harrowing consequences of market fundamentalism and disaster capitalism in particular. Amid growing worldwide rejection of neoliberalism, this terrific and timely book will be a key resource for anyone fighting for justice in the region.'

Naomi Klein, author of *This Changes Everything*
and *The Shock Doctrine*

'This is truly an exceptional study of the Oslo process and Western donor intervention therein. Meticulously and rigorously researched, Toufic Haddad's book represents an invaluable contribution to a literature that still requires the kind of critical scrutiny and analysis that Haddad provides. While the book carefully examines and exposes the role of the West in Palestine's debility – a role that was deliberate and considered – none of Oslo's protagonists are spared. *Palestine Ltd.* is compelling and should be required reading for anyone seeking to understand what the Oslo process was really about and why it has proved so disastrous for Palestinians.'

Sara Roy, Senior Research Scholar,
Center for Middle Eastern Studies, Harvard University

'Evidence is emerging across the spectrum of development, peace and statebuilding settings of the last 25 years that neoliberalism is not a silver bullet that speeds development, facilitates peace, and creates an efficient state. Instead, it enables predatory geopolitical and geoeconomic behaviour to corrupt these processes. Increasingly, it has become apparent that neoliberalism has had terrible consequences for peace processes and conflict- or development-affected societies' prospects. It undermines justice and emancipation while claiming to facilitate it, allowing oppressive power relations to flourish and appear legitimate. This is nowhere more evident than in the Occupied Territories, as this brilliant and incisive book by Toufic Haddad outlines.'

Oliver Richmond, Professor of International Relations,
Peace & Conflict Studies, University of Manchester

'Ever since co-authoring one of the earlier forays into the question of the trade-offs between neoliberalism and national liberation in the Palestinian context, I have closely followed the work of a range of new Palestinian political economists and social scientists who have widened and deepened this field of enquiry, and Toufic Haddad's book is one of the first of these exciting efforts to reach the public domain. Haddad's research makes a strong case for his contention that the advance of neoliberal doctrine and capital interests among Palestinian elites and their international donor backers has resulted in a "Palestine Ltd." model incapable of pursuing, and intrinsically opposed to, national liberation. As the scholarly debate unfolds as to exactly which social, economic and political dynamics underlay this process, and under what conditions it may be reversible, Haddad's contribution constitutes a sophisticated platform for further research and efforts on the ground in the coming years to achieve liberation, both social and national.'

Raja Khalidi, Former Senior Economist,
UN Conference on Trade and Development (UNCTAD)

SOAS PALESTINE STUDIES

This book series aims at promoting innovative research in the study of Palestine, Palestinians and the Israel–Palestine conflict as a crucial component of Middle Eastern and world politics. The first ever Western academic series entirely dedicated to this topic, *SOAS Palestine Studies* draws from a variety of disciplinary fields, including history, politics, media, visual arts, social anthropology, and development studies. The series is published under the academic direction of the Centre for Palestine Studies (CPS) at the London Middle East Institute (LMEI) of SOAS, University of London.

Series Editor:

Gilbert Achcar, Professor of Development Studies and International Relations at SOAS, Chair of the Centre for Palestine Studies

Board Advisor:

Hassan Hakimian, Director of the London Middle East Institute at SOAS

Current and Forthcoming Titles:

Palestine Ltd.: Neoliberalism and Nationalism in the Occupied Territory, by Toufic Haddad

Politics and Palestinian Literature in Exile: Gender, Aesthetics and Resistance in the Short Story, by Joseph R. Farag

Palestinian Citizens of Israel: Power, Resistance and the Struggle for Space, by Sharri Plonski

PALESTINE LTD.

Neoliberalism and Nationalism in the
Occupied Territory

TOUFIC HADDAD

Centre for Palestine Studies

Published in association with the Centre for Palestine Studies,
London Middle East Institute

To my parents, for their steadfastness and sacrifice.

Published in 2016 by
I.B.Tauris & Co. Ltd
London • New York
www.ibtauris.com

Copyright © 2016 Toufic Haddad

References to websites were correct at the time of writing.

SOAS Series on Palestine Studies 1

ISBN: 978 1 78453 657 2
eISBN: 978 1 78672 097 9
ePDF: 978 1 78673 097 8

A full CIP record for this book is available from the British Library
A full CIP record is available from the Library of Congress

Library of Congress Catalog Card Number: available

Typeset in Garamond Three by OKS Prepress Services, Chennai, India
Printed and bound by CPI Group (UK) Ltd, Croydon, CR0 4YY

CONTENTS

LIST OF ILLUSTRATIONS

Graphs

Tables

SERIES FOREWORD

The question of Palestine – with its corollaries, the Israel–Palestine and Arab–Israeli conflicts – has been a key issue of world politics and a major source of world tension since the 1917 Balfour Declaration. Few global issues have attracted so much attention over such a long period of time.

As a result, despite its small territorial size, Palestine has become a key component of Middle East studies in the academic community as well as a field of study in its own right, in the same way that France or Germany are each the subject of individual study while being part of European Studies. This 'disproportionate' status of the Palestine topic is due to several factors.

First is the strategic location of Palestine at the Mediterranean door of the Middle East and the 'East of Suez' world. This strategic position – the source of British interest in Palestine at the beginning of the twentieth century – has been enhanced by the greater importance of the broader Middle East in global affairs as manifested by the high frequency of wars and conflicts in the region since World War II, and even more since the end of the Cold War.

Secondly is the very particular fact of what has been described as a 'settler-colonial' project in Palestine that was boosted by the huge human tragedy of the Nazi genocide of European Jews in 1941–5. The result has been a complex mingling of the Holocaust, which the Zionist movement claims as legitimizing its actions, with what Palestinians call the *Nakba*, or 'catastrophe', which describes the 'ethnic cleansing' of Arab Palestinians from great swathes of Palestine in 1948 by the Zionist drive towards the creation of Israel.

Thirdly is the sheer complexity of the Palestine question engendered by the *Nakba* and the subsequent occupation by the state of Israel of the West Bank and Gaza following the Six-Day War in 1967. As a result of these, the Palestinian people today are living under very different conditions and legal regimes: they encompass those who remained in Israel after the state's establishment in 1948; those, including refugees, under direct Israeli occupation or indirect Israeli control in the West Bank and Gaza; those displaced by the wars of 1948 and 1967 to the eastern bank of the Jordan River, some of them still living in camps, and most of whom became Jordanian citizens; those living in the refugee camps of Lebanon and Syria; those of the diaspora living in other Arab countries; and those of the global diaspora.

Finally, the question of Palestine plays such a major role in Arab politics in general and represents such a major trauma in collective Arab memory that it has been the focus of prolific artistic and literary energy, a drive that goes beyond Palestinians to include creative minds and talents from all Arabic-speaking countries.

This complexity and the unparalleled diversity of contemporary Palestinian locations and situations help to explain Palestine's 'disproportionate' status and account for the abundance of publications on Palestine and its people. And yet, surprisingly, there has until now been no university-based English-language book series specifically dedicated to Palestine Studies. The SOAS Palestine Studies series, published by I.B.Tauris in collaboration with the SOAS Centre for Palestine Studies (CPS) at the London Middle East Institute (LMEI), seeks to fill this gap. This series is dedicated to the contemporary history, politics, economy, society and culture of Palestine and the historiographic quarrels associated with its past.

The subject of Palestine has aroused intense passions over several decades. On such a topic it is very difficult to exclude passion, and the pretension to be 'neutral' is often disqualified by both sides. But we will make sure that none of our books stray beyond the realms of intellectual integrity and scholarly rigour. With the Palestine Studies series we hope to make an important contribution towards a better understanding of this most complex topic.

Professor Gilbert Achcar, Editor
Chair of the Centre of Palestine Studies,
SOAS, University of London

ACKNOWLEDGEMENTS

This book is based on research conducted for my doctoral dissertation at the School for Oriental and African Studies, completed in January 2015. Invisible to the readers of the final product are material, social and spiritual factors which facilitated my work, and without which I could not have even begun working on this project, let alone persisted on to its completion. In that regard, a wide range of people made this work possible to whom I owe immeasurable thanks.

First and foremost are my parents and siblings who supported me materially and personally throughout this process. My father Charles and my mother Anne have not had an easy time managing the complications of what life dealt them. Their selflessness to protect and provide for our family despite this, and despite their own peace of mind, created the basis for me to undertake this endeavour. This work is dedicated to their steadfastness and sacrifice, for which I will forever be grateful.

My uncle William Haddad, aunt Aida, and three cousins, were also always welcoming hosts throughout my stays in London. The security of a roof above one's head and food to eat cannot be taken for granted, and I gratefully benefitted from their generosity and hospitality.

Professor Gilbert Achcar was a tireless intellectual guide, political comrade and caring friend. He was first to encourage me to do a PhD and I learned greatly from his keen eye and wisdom. I immeasurably appreciated his patience and understanding as I stumbled along my path and/or engaged in tangential matters outside my PhD that were nonetheless important to me. My second advisor, Dr Adam Hanieh, was always a welcoming and supportive confidant and friend, to whom I am equally grateful.

The home of Ala Al Azzeh, Rania Jawad and Nala-Hind was a warm and essential base of operations during field research. The latter was made possible thanks to institutional and personal support of different orders: Dr Linda Tabar and Dr Samia Botmeh opened up the resources of the Center for Development Studies (CDS) at Birzeit University. Their friendship and loyalty are not forgotten. The Council for British Research in the Levant (CBRL), and the Palestinian American Research Center (PARC) also both awarded me grants for field research. Dr Mandy Turner, director of the CBRL-affiliated Kenyon Institute, was particularly generous with her time and the resources at her disposal. In addition to reading and commenting on a near-final draft, and hosting me at the Kenyon Institute, she also was a caring friend. Dr Amnon Raz Krakotzkin also went out of his way to help facilitate my ability to do extended research in the field for which I am truly thankful.

Early chapters were drafted in the beautiful rural home of Dr Majdi and Anneliese Shahin in Jordan, facilitated by my friend and colleague Mariam Shahin. Aunt Anneliese, Mariam, George and the steadfast care of Shasikala Mary were inseparable parts of this bucolic setting, keeping me mentally and physically fit for the challenges of writing my final year. Although I would rather forget the latter, a few people played important roles in maintaining my sanity throughout. Whether this was from near or far; is known by them or not; occurred in my last year or otherwise – a deep well of appreciation exists in my heart for the love and friendship shown to me by Julia Joerin, Lichi Damelio, Samane Salimi, Anan Quzmar, Hazem Jamjoum, Izzat Shamroukh, Sami Lutz, Sai Englert, May Jayyousi, Sara Stevano, Mohammed Ayyad, Jack Footitt, Elizabeth Grech, Sanaa Alimia, Khaled Ziadeh, Lamis Deek, Pascale Nader, Aly Guindy, Annabel Turner Saade, Nidal Hatim, Atef Al Shaer, Anthony Arnove, Dalia Taha, Meriem Aissaoui, Hocine Zobiri, Riya Al Sanah, the Al Azzeh family and camp, Fractionals for Fair Play, Teddy's Cafe and Sri K. Pattabhi Jois. As anxiety and despondency attempted to seize upon me, at least one of you was there, shattering the myth of my isolation and individualism. Though it is true that no one will write for you or discipline you to do your work, it is equally an illusion to assume that you are anything but the accumulation and product (previous and on-going) of a great many decisions, sacrifices, dedications and loves – recognized or otherwise, your own and of others. I regret not understanding or appreciating this earlier and finding ways to balance and harmonize these in cosmic felicity.

In addition to those already mentioned, a few key discussants helped lead me in the right direction in the field or challenged me to sharpen my arguments: Raja Khalidi, Nu'man Kanafani, Khalil Nakhleh, Zuheir Sabbagh, Mounir Kleibo, Jamil Hilal and Basem Makhoul. I would also like to recognize the role of teachers who helped me take the path that led me here, specifically Vijay Prashad, Christopher Brown and Hugh Ogden. The mentorship and camaraderie of Tikva Honig-Parnass deserves special note and will always be a part of my intellectual and personal formation.

This text takes special inspiration from the people of Gaza who steadfastly resisted yet another round of Zionist aggression in the late summer of 2014 as I underwent the final stretch of writing. It also draws inspiration from the democratic struggles for social justice which erupted across the Middle East and North Africa, and were ongoing throughout the course of writing. Hopefully this work can contribute to these struggles in Palestine, the Middle East and beyond. Finally, I would like to thank my kind, intelligent and supportive examiners – Professor Ray Bush and Dr Maha Abdel Rahman – first for their appreciation of my work, and second for their wonderful, wise feedback. All errors herein nonetheless remain my own.

INTRODUCTION

Perhaps one of the most iconic images of the second half of the twentieth century is that of the handshake between Israeli Prime Minister Yitzhak Rabin and Palestine Liberation Organization (PLO) Chairman Yasser Arafat during the signing ceremony of the Declaration of Principles (DOP) in September 1993 (hereafter referred to as the Oslo Accords). To many, the image harbingered a hopeful future in so far as it symbolized a moment when one of the world's most intransigent political conflicts was seen as resolvable on the basis of mutual recognition and peaceful negotiations. While the reality to unfold between Palestinians and Israelis as a consequence of the Oslo Accords and subsequent agreements failed to realize these expectations, ultimately leading to a situation where unprecedented levels of political violence became an all too familiar norm, the Israeli–Palestinian 'peace process' nonetheless remains a resilient discursive and political framework in which the conflict is discussed in world media, and between the political leaderships of both sides. Moreover, the transformations this process has ushered in on the ground have assumed a seemingly irreversible character, changing the manner in which Israelis and Palestinians interact with one another, and how Palestinians themselves are governed.

The Oslo Accords have always had their defenders and detractors from both camps, as well as from invested persons, groups and governments internationally. This book is less interested in engaging on the polemical level with these older debates, and is more interested in investigating the incontrovertible economic, political and social realities to emerge in the Occupied Palestinian Territory as a consequence of the explicit agreements and policies devised and implemented by the main actors empowered to formulate and realize these, namely: the Western donor community (led by the United States (US) and European Union (EU)); the main International Financial Institutions (IFIs) – the World Bank and International Monetary Fund (IMF); Israel; and the Palestinian National Authority (PNA).

Reading OPT history through this lens is particularly challenging in light of the need to keep in perspective the complex asymmetric power relations between these powers on the one hand, and the relational manner in which these interactions constitute one another on the other. Here Zachary Lockman's term 'relational history' is helpful for underscoring how the histories of Arabs and Jews in modern Palestine 'can only be grasped by studying the ways in which both these communities were to a significant extent constituted and shaped within a complex matrix of economic, political, social, and cultural interactions' (Lockman, 1996, p. 9). This book will suggest that Western development practitioners should be added to the mix of constitutive players shaping the reality that emerged in the OPT since 1993. Despite their frequent depiction as tangential actors observing an ancient irrational power play they are helpless to stem despite their noble efforts, the Western donor community has played an important role in devising a series of self-described 'peacebuilding' and 'statebuilding' policies which are heavily implicated in the reality to have emerged as a consequence of the DOP's signing, in all its unseemly manifestations. Their interventions have also been justified upon a wider set of ideological and epistemological understandings that reflect an evolving yet normative consensus around what constitutes 'development', how peacebuilding can be activated, and what statebuilding should entail, all within a conflict resolution framework. These policies ultimately rest on theoretical and ideological understandings that intellectually irrigate the development/peacebuilding/statebuilding tactics and strategies adopted. Despite variations in particular tactics, priorities and agendas, these policies can broadly be described as 'neoliberal' in orientation in so far as they reflect the mind-set and increasing pervasiveness of a neoliberal worldview amongst these actors vis-à-vis domestic and international development agendas overall.

The term 'neoliberalism' traces back to German economist Alexander Rüstow, who in 1938 was part of a small group of European and

American intellectuals beginning to organize aroun(
reinterpret liberal values after their questioning in th
economic crises of the 1930s. Though they emerged
intellectual traditions, the early neoliberals found con
resisting the ascendance of a collectivist mindset that had taken root
across the political landscape within various political traditions.
Socialists, fascists and significant numbers of liberals themselves, had
embraced principles of community, rational planning and institutional
design, which the neoliberals felt could only lead to 'totalitarianism' and
'serfdom' (Turner, R., 2007).

Instead these intellectuals sought to push back against these historical
intellectual/policy tides, advocating an individualistic worldview that
fiercely embraced core liberal values of free trade and enterprise.
Neoliberalism's patron saint Friedrich von Hayek stressed:

> We must kindle an interest in – an understanding of – the great
> principles of social organization of the conditions of individual
> liberty as we have not known it in our life-time [...] We must
> raise and train an army of fighters for freedom.
>
> (von Hayek, in Cockett, 1995, p. 104)

The neoliberals adamantly believed that neoclassical economics – the
economic basis of neoliberalism itself – held the key to solving not only
questions of development and growth, but also explicitly political and
social questions as well. This belief has remained salient in the policy
interventions of the Western donor community in the OPT since 1993,
in so far as these actors have refrained from intervening on explicitly
political questions and instead claimed to be engaged only in economic
and technical undertakings. Implicit to their interventions was the
notion that the market's invisible hand would guide Israelis and
Palestinians to peace, provided the international community financially
and politically backed this arrangement and facilitated the creation of an
adequate incentives arrangement. The arrival of these political winds to
the conflict–ridden shores of the Palestinian setting through Western
donor peacebuilding and statebuilding policies thus set the stage for
what happened when 'an army of fighters for freedom' faced off against a
former army of Palestinian nationalist 'freedom fighters', embodied in
the PLO.

Explaining this encounter is complicated by the fact that Western neoliberal peacebuilding/statebuilding represented only one of several strains of neoliberal thought operational across the OPT. Israel's own neoliberal transitioning would equally subject the OPT theatre to this process' downstream effects given the former's continued effective control over these areas even after the DOP's signing. Elements of the Palestinian leadership and society have also come to embrace a neoliberal worldview, integrating it into their vision for national liberation and statecraft.

These overlapping and divergent neoliberal framings and the tensions and synergies they generate thus become important to understand in a wider context where only a limited number of studies address these dimensions at all (see Turner, M. 2012; 2011; 2009; Hanieh, 2013; 2011; Khalidi and Samour, 2011; Samara, 2000; Nakhleh, 2012). This has ultimately led to a particular isolation of the Palestinian question within critical studies of development, peacebuilding, statebuilding and neoliberalism itself, despite the fact that the legacy of these policies has been so large and destructive in regards to Palestinian economic wellbeing, political freedoms, democratic norms and the overall claim to self-determination and national liberation. In fact their legacy has already transcended OPT borders by way of the fact that the World Bank readily acknowledges that its 'best practice' in post-conflict peacebuilding and reconstruction was significantly developed from its experiences in the OPT during the 1990s (see World Bank, 1998).

Without pre-empting discussion of how this encounter unfolded, an explanation of the two rationales of 'peacebuilding' and 'statebuilding' is in order.

UN Secretary General Boutrus Boutrus-Ghali's defined peacebuilding in his 1992 *Agenda for Peace* as 'action to identify and support structures which will tend to strengthen and solidify peace in order to avoid a relapse into conflict' (UN, 1995). Along these lines, 'peacebuilding' justified Western donor interventions in the OPT from 1993–2000, with these states and institutions largely focusing their efforts on establishing the governance structures of the PNA in the delimited areas of its jurisdiction across the OPT. Peace-building activity was subsequently integrated as a parallel track to negotiations during the 'Interim period' and included a series of major local and regional development programs intended to be activated within a self-described 'Marshall plan' understanding of the peace process.[1] These included Israeli–Palestinian cooperation in finance 'for the encouragement of international investment'; cooperation to 'encourage local, regional and inter-regional trade'; and feasibility studies for 'creating free trade zones in the Gaza Strip and in Israel', with 'mutual access to these zones, and cooperation in other areas related to trade and commerce.' They also called for the establishment of a Middle East Development Fund; the development of a joint Israeli–Palestinian–Jordanian Plan for co-ordinated exploitation of the Dead Sea area; construction of a Mediterranean Sea (Gaza) – Dead Sea canal; regional desalination projects and; the interconnection of electricity grids. These projects were understood to create rent allotment opportunities for the Palestinian government to attract and distribute to Palestinian capitalists, within a logic of trickle-down economics. It is worth pointing out nonetheless that donors refrained from describing their actions during this period as intending to establish a Palestinian state – justifying this choice on a supposed fear that this would compromise their neutrality and prejudice negotiations.

A second rationale to donor intervention would emerge in the wake of the collapse of negotiations in July 2000 and the start of the Al-Aqsa Intifada less than three months later. By 2002, 'statebuilding' began to emerge as the new formal operational framework to donor-led development activity, especially after US president George W. Bush and Israeli Prime Minister Ariel Sharon both provided conditional endorsement of a Palestinian state.[2] This formalistic acknowledgement cleared the way for donors to explicitly engage in statebuilding, even though political negotiations between the Palestinian leadership and Israel since the summer of 2000 had functionally collapsed, remaining so as of the writing of these lines (spring, 2016). Statebuilding entailed more concerted efforts to improve the institutional functioning of the PNA, building off from the basic accomplishments of peace-building within a more integrated and exclusively Palestinian government focus.

Both 'peacebuilding' and 'statebuilding' appear self-evident practices insofar as opposition to them can be framed as opposing peace or the right to statehood and self-determination. The problem with such framings is that both peace and statebuilding are highly charged political undertakings that do not derive from a platonic template. The OPT has a deep and complex history to its national actors and political institutions. Western governments and IFIs that work to advance peacebuilding and statebuilding are also implicated in ideological, political and economic projects of their own on a global scale, which they are not disembodied from as they intervene in the OPT. They also have independent and complicated relations with Israel, which harbors interests and agendas of its own towards the OPT, irrespective of PNA or donor interests.

Despite this complexity, certain consistencies in approach can be detected in these interventions since 1993, as captured in the 2006 public remarks of Nigel Roberts, former World Bank Country Director to the OPT from 2001–5:

> A strong Palestinian economy delivering growth, and above all jobs, is a vital part of any beneficial political process [...] Whereas I think that one cannot say that economic growth and economic vitality are of themselves enough to produce a benign political process, one can, however, I think say the opposite, which is that economic desperation, high unemployment, high poverty levels, and a lack of economic dynamism are certainly a fairly good guarantee for social instability and a lack of resolution to these deep-set political issues. In other words, Palestinian economic vitality is a vital component of any peace process.
>
> (Roberts, 2006)

Throughout their engagement in the OPT, Western governments and IFIs have consistently upheld and embraced Roberts' basic contentions, pouring financial and technical resources towards this end. These agents have refrained from engaging in the prickly terrain of political peacemaking, opting instead to focus on improving Palestinian economic wellbeing deemed 'vital' and complimentary to a successful peace process. In what ways is this economic vitality 'vital', and to what effect – Roberts and the broader agenda he represents are less forthcoming. But the appeal of their logic rests in its seemingly common sense reasoning that economic development acts as a form of conflict prevention. As the World Bank writes, 'war retards development, but conversely, development retards war' (Collier and World Bank, 2003, p. 1). Economic prosperity is believed to reduce the willingness of people to fight, helps mitigate the prospect for conflicts arising, perpetuating or worsening, and can actively contribute to conflicting parties resolving differences peacefully.

From this rhetorical commonplace and panglossian worldview, a series of conclusions and policy recommendations necessarily flows: donor interventions should enhance the possibility for economic development, facilitate private sector-led growth and employment generation, and work to raise GDP, thereby unleashing a peaceful impetus and goodwill that can be absorbed and channeled into the Middle East peace process. If these dynamics can be harnessed as part of a wider regional push to liberalize markets and trade, reduce state involvement in economies and attract foreign investment, a 'virtuous circle scenario' could emerge between the Arab states and Israel, with Palestinian–Israeli peace at its heart (Fischer, 1993, p. 4).

An ideological thread within this rhetorical commonplace is thus revealed. Donors appeared to be advocating the implementation of some of the core neoliberal policy tenets as tools to defuse violent conflict. 'Free-market' economics was deemed instrumental to lubricating Israeli–Palestinian peace, with vital Western geopolitical and geostrategic interests also served, considering how this conflict acts as such an extreme source of political tension radiating across the entire region so vital to US hegemony.

This book will interrogate these claims theoretically and empirically, attempting to see whether there is a basis to them. What are the contours of neoliberal conflict resolution and statebuilding in the OPT as it emerged in the development policies of Western donor governments and IFIs from 1993 to 2013? How did Palestinian society – its political and economic elites, and various social classes – negotiate these neoliberal interventions as they unfolded across the OPT? To what extent has neoliberal conflict resolution and statebuilding been successful in inducing the forms of political, economic and social transformation that its designers intend amongst targeted Palestinian constituencies? Can peaceful outcomes amongst Palestinian political and economic elites and social classes be generated through economic incentives and the promise or realization of economic prosperity? What is the extent of these transformations if any? How can they be characterized? What can be said about factors that induce or impede their ability to exhibit forms of traction and resilience, and why?

Answering these questions is long overdue, as the core approaches of neoliberal peacebuilding and statebuilding continue to frame and reproduce donor intervention across the OPT and beyond – with devastating effect, and without accountability for their actions.

Ultimately this research argues that the confluence of divergent and overlapping neoliberal approaches within the political and economic agendas of the main actors resulted – by design or by default – in a scenario that can be described as 'Palestine Limited' or simply 'Palestine Ltd.').

The term Palestine Ltd. has dual signification:

The first connotes how a delimited version of a Palestinian state, located on only parts of the OPT and with highly restricted political and economic powers, came to be understood as 'Palestine' – a de facto state nominally entitled to the benefits of this classification within the logic of international intrastate norms. This new 'Palestine' redefines the historical boundaries of mandatory Palestine, and even the borders of the OPT. Its inchoate formation through the accumulated confluence of donor interventions, ironically functions in a manner that significantly deprives the Palestinian national liberation movement from having a say in the character of the entity being created supposedly on their behalf and where this entity will govern. It is almost as though the generations of sacrifice of the national liberation movement which struggled to realize 'Palestine' – 'from the river to the sea' as a homeland for the dispersed Palestinian people – has now been realized but in a transmogrified form. Palestine Ltd. becomes neoliberalism's Janus-faced version of the former Palestine, emptied of any emancipatory liberationist content, and replaced with the economic and political strictures which enforce and deepen the state of oppression and fragmentation which Palestinians sought to overcome in the first place through their national liberation movement.

The second connotation of Palestine Ltd. relates to the institutional composition of this delimited version of Palestine, as imagined by those who embrace and propagate it. Palestine Ltd. can loosely be described as the operational endgame of Western donor development/peacebuilding/statebuilding interventions, with this entity functioning as a variant of a limited shareholding company (Ltd.) with international, regional and local investors of one type or another. While the dividend to this investment includes direct and indirect financial gains for many of its shareholders, the primary motivation of this arrangement derives from the need to reap particular political, administrative and security returns for its 'investors'. This reality emerged as a consequence of the larger political logic of these players in so far as how they prioritized achieving their ideological, political and economic agendas, within existent restrains and power asymmetries.

From the onset it is important to clarify that Palestine Ltd. is admittedly an oversimplified metaphor that fails to capture the full nuance of the actors, their motivations and how this reality came about. This study will attempt to flesh these aspects out in due course, so as to better understand the wider set of historical and political economic characteristics that permitted the birth of Palestine Ltd. in the first place – rhetorically, institutionally, politically, economically and socially. Readers will then be free to determine if the term deserves relevance and currency.

A Word on Sources

This study relies upon three sets of resources to draw its conclusions.

First are primary source materials produced by Western state development practitioners and their Palestinian counterparts in PNA bodies. Donors have generated an enormous body of knowledge regarding their practices, which assess in detail the state of developmental conditions, and provide recommendations for their improvement. The OPT is densely populated with donor agencies and their appendages, NGOs, INGOs, UN bodies, IFIs, and consultants. To give an indication of the extent of this knowledge production, I refer briefly to the Development Assistance and Reform Platform (DARP) hosted by the PNA Ministry of Planning and Administrative Development (MOPAD) – a non-comprehensive database of proposed, on-going, completed or suspended donor projects in the OPT. DARP registers an astonishing 1132 projects by more than 93 donor agencies from when the database was established in 2010 (no month available) to August 2014.[3] (The population of the entire OPT is estimated at 4.68 million persons at the end of 2015). The UN, which maintains its own database of projects (the UN Project Information System (UNPRIS)) for the 22 UN bodies active in the OPT, lists 412 projects as 'underway' or 'planned' as of May 2012.[4] The World Bank, counts 753 project documents, 186 research publications and 99 projects on its OPT website.[5]

Considering that every funder, development practitioner and project incorporates reams of material that nominally justify their work, one quickly realizes that the potential to get lost in this sea of material is real, requiring forms of vigilance and methodologies of approach to prevent such a scenario.

I tackled this problem by focusing on the works and policies of the mainstream development practice taking place through the formal, organized, multilateral channel of the Ad Hoc Liaison Committee (AHLC) – the overarching donor coordination structure. Here the activities of the World Bank have been central to donor coordination efforts, setting the intellectual compass for donor activity. As Anne Le More has noted 'the US decides, the World Bank leads, the EU pays, the UN feeds' (Le More, 2005). I also refer to publications and projects of the United States Agency for International Development (USAID), the UK's Department for International Development (DFID), and the International Monetary Fund (IMF) as some of the development policy world's central actors in the OPT.

This allowed me to address the donor mainstream, attempting to construct an analysis of the contours of its broad interventions and shifts over time. Although I recognize and occasionally address the diversity of various currents existent within donor interventions – namely, between two broad currents within the donor community – a 'politics first' wing led by the US, and a 'development first' wing led by some EU states – these intra-donor dynamics would need another research to fully flesh out. Despite these divergences, there is still wide overlap between both wings in their development agendas, with these captured through the mainstream multilateral approach of the World Bank and IMF.

On the Palestinian side, a parallel set of literature exists produced by Palestinian ministries and official government bodies. This is supplemented by material from local NGOs and think tanks; the various associations and federations of the Palestinian private sector, and; private corporations and public-private partnerships engaged in the development and statebuilding game.

Overall, a fairly substantial set of secondary source material exists in English and Arabic on Palestinian development during this period, though admittedly, there is greater material focused on the earlier 'Oslo years' as opposed to the later 'statebuilding.' Not enough has been done to take into account important more recent developments in the spheres of the Al-Aqsa

Intifada, statebuilding, and the political division between the West Bank and Gaza (see Brynen, 2000; Wright and Drake, 2000; Bouillon, 2004; Samara, 2001 and; Roy, 1995; 1999). At least thanks to these contributions, we do have a fairly good assessment of the Oslo years (1993–2000) and their implications on the OPT's development trajectory and political economy. The main element lacking in these accounts is the added value of what I believe heterodox approaches uniquely contribute: how class and capital dynamics can be integrated into an understanding of OPT development dynamics.

The second set of resources used to compose this research were interviews with 90 key informants conducted during fieldwork between September 2011 and December 2012, primarily in Ramallah, though with some conducted in Nablus, Bethlehem, Jerusalem and Amman, Jordan. Field research also afforded the opportunity to immerse myself in the rich intellectual and political setting of the OPT, replete with a steady stream of conferences and seminars, hosted by international and local organizations, invariably connected to themes of Palestinian development. Local newspapers, radio, and television all helped add to the marinating mix.

The third and final category of literature this study utilizes is classified documents. It was my good fortune that the Wikileaks 'Cablegate' scandal unfolded during the course of my research, exposing 3194 US embassy (from Tel Aviv)[6] and 2217 US consulate cables (from Jerusalem).[7] It was my double good fortune that the 'Palestine Papers' were also leaked in January 2011 – a body of 1684 internal memos and transcripts from the PNA's Negotiations Support Unit (NSU) that revealed the internal dealings of this unit (see Swisher, 2011). These bodies of classified knowledge proved to be a lucrative trove of material for helping piece together a picture of what was happening in the back rooms of many key powerbrokers and how they interacted with one another.

Additional internal documents to some development agencies have also become available throughout my research. The World Bank implemented an 'open access policy' in July 2010 for its 'research outputs' and 'knowledge products.' Some formerly classified documents from USAID also became available online, apparently because they were declassified, or their publishing embargoes expired. That said, the bulk of my conclusions have been gleaned from a careful examination and cross referencing of the public record, though declassified documents certainly helped me make more confident claims.

Book Structure

This book is divided into three parts, each of which are then subdivided into various chapters that help organize and illustrate their subject matter.

Part I is designed to lay the theoretical, historical and political background providing the reader with the necessary conceptual understandings of neoliberalism, peacebuilding and statebuilding in general, as well as relevant historical economic and political information on the main actors and their motivations.

Part II explores the era of neoliberal peacebuilding (1993–2000) and outlines how the theoretical concepts and modeling outlined in Part I take form and are activated within the lived setting of the OPT.

Part III examines the period of neoliberal statebuilding, and how these policies redesigned and upgraded the previous modeling operational under peacebuilding.

Both Parts II and III also give voice to how the Palestinian leadership and political actors attempted to negotiate the donor–Israeli triangulation game, thus shedding light on dimensions that in my assessment remain poorly understood within the academic literature and political circles alike.

Inevitably, the largeness, complexity and unruliness of this attempted scholarly endeavor necessarily brings with it limitations. That said, without attempting to critically determine the circumstances and factors that led to the rise of Palestine Ltd. in a manner that is neither deterministic, nor naïve, all efforts aimed at formulating a more equitable and just alternative to this reality are likely to be left hamstrung, as the continued sociocide and fragmentation of Palestinian life in the OPT continues through endemic structural violence and pervasive waves of direct violence.

PART I

BACKGROUND

CHAPTER 1

NEOLIBERAL APPROACHES TO CONFLICT RESOLUTION AND STATEBUILDING

Palestine Ltd. does not emerge as the product of a linear teleological path that a cabal of evil politicians devised in a smoky back room in the early 1990s. Although there is a basis to impart premeditation and intentionality regarding specific realities to emerge in the OPT as a result of the DOP, and which have yet to be acknowledged by scholars and commentators alike, it is fanciful to imagine that this is the entire story. Instead, complex dialectical processes rooted in theoretical understandings, normative policy prescriptions, and a host of international, regional and local political economic factors, among others, all contributed to shaping the context in which human agency was exercised and political choices made. Moreover, to propagate the notion that the less-than-ideal and politically unresolved scenario to emerge between Israelis and Palestinian as a consequence of the DOP (to put it mildly) was concocted in secrecy, is also ahistorical and intellectually dubious. It demonstrates ignorance of a good deal of the public record evidenced in negotiated agreements, donor reports and the theoretical and political bases which intellectually ground them. The latter have been fairly explicit in elaborating how development, peacebuilding and statebuilding should function and the ends they should serve, both in general and in relation to the OPT. What is thus needed is a firm grounding of these sources, ideas and histories to understand how the local OPT reality was configured within these, and how they served to shape the policies and choices Palestinian elites and social classes needed to make.

This chapter will introduce some of the main theoretical aspects to neoliberalism's utopian transcript and how these have been translated into organizational form and policy formulations in regards to conflict resolution and statebuilding.

Though not a comprehensive review of far larger bodies of knowledge, the analysis included herein derives from a need to establish the most relevant theoretical and practical elements related to the field before applying them to the OPT case study in subsequent chapters.

Neoliberalism

From Theory ...

The neoclassical economics tradition upon which neoliberal economic prescriptions are grounded, embodies a series of utopian assumptions about human beings, what motivates them, how they make their choices, and how markets and societies function. While its microfoundational subcomponents and broader policy prescriptions and biases have been well studied and critiqued (see Stein, 2008, pp. 55–110), it is the extension of these policies to explicitly political and social realms that distinguish the neoliberal canon. Milton Friedman's *Capitalism and Freedom* refashioned the dry neoclassical economic theory giving it an emancipatory political clothing (Friedman, 1962). According to Friedman, capitalism is not just a theory of individual wealth creation, but an instrumental part of political freedom. He constructs a two-part argument: first, that economic freedom is a dimension of freedom more broadly understood, and hence self-evidently justifying; secondly, that capitalism is an 'indispensable means toward the achievement of political freedom' (ibid., p. 8). Free markets are believed to have a deleterious effect on 'concentration of power,' which to (neo)liberals represents the potential power of 'coercion' (ibid., p. 15). Through free markets, a kind of democratic simulation takes place: by 'removing the organization of economic activity from the control of political authority, the market eliminates this source of coercive power' enabling 'economic strength to be a check to political power, rather than a reinforcement' (ibid., p. 15).

Friedman's ideas disembed and unmoor political praxis from its traditional basis within democratic governance norms, functionally rejecting the consensual democratic notion that political movements or groups that gain the right to govern through an electoral process maintain the right to wield the economic resources and political institutions of the state to implement or further the social, political and economic agendas for which they were elected. Instead, free markets and market incentives are seen as best meeting popular needs and hence should lead development. Markets thus inherently de-politicize and should be instrumentalized to this end:

> The widespread use of the market reduces the strain on the social fabric by rendering conformity unnecessary with respect to any activities it encompasses. The wider the range of activities covered by the market, the fewer are the issues on which explicitly political decisions are required and hence on which it is necessary to achieve agreement. (Friedman, 1962, p. 24)

In 'rendering conformity unnecessary,' Friedman and the broader neoliberal tradition are incapable of imagining forms of 'conformity' that are non-coercive. Any form of cross-identification, interdependence, or social solidarity – including presumably national liberation movements – are coercive by nature and deserve to be melted on the fires of individual choice through markets. If markets instead of governments meet the full spectrum of human need, the requisite for most political practise and decision making dissolves. Political issues and social needs are thus disaggregated into micro-issues that can be commodified and technically addressed through market allocation. Freedom becomes the ability to make an individual choice exercised in the market through the ability to buy or sell, rather than a concept linked to forms of structural oppression and individual or collective rights.

In this modeling, government retains a strictly delimited role providing a means to impose and modify rules, mediate differences and enforce compliance of the 'game' – but should be prevented from engaging in the game itself. In Friedman's words, it is strictly an 'umpire' (ibid., p. 25).

Needless to say, such an arrangement advantages those with capital and access to forms of power and information that can leverage them over other individuals and groups. This blindness to such asymmetries is particularly utopian in so far as it also assumes that the system tends toward equilibrium and that all agents operating within this game have interests in securing perfectly operating market conditions. It also ignores the basic reality whereby market interactions are socially realized – between bosses and workers, and between members of different social classes, and various racial, national, ethnic, gendered individuals and groupings. Because of historical legacies, some individuals and groups enjoy certain economic and political privileges and rights over others, and may use this power to preserve them. Whether this takes place through formal rules, informal norms, or both, a hypocritical dimension of the neoclassical world view should be noted.

This aside, the economic bases of neoliberalism has evolved over time, giving rise to the New Institutional Economics (NIE) of the early 1990s. The latter reinterpreted and developed many of the core tenets of the neoclassical tradition emphasizing the centrality of institutional design and capacity. This was seen as a way to 'incorporate realism into economic analysis, including such factors as economies of scale, imperfect information or even the lack of markets' – issues ignored in neoclassical economics but deemed necessary to ensure that the core neoliberal tenets that emphasized macroeconomic structural adjustment, could finally lead to capitalist 'take-off' (Fine and Van Waeyenberge, 2006).

NIE theoretician Douglass North (1995) understood institutions as 'humanly devised constraints that structure human interaction,' and 'reduce uncertainty in human exchange' (p. 23). They established codes of predictable conduct between agents, with economic performance determined by the interaction between formal rules, informal norms and the enforcement mechanisms of both. Strong institutions that lowered transaction costs, protected property rights and enhanced market efficiency were seen as central to development. Predictability – economic but also political – could thus be generated.

Enforcement of this arrangement ultimately falls upon 'polities' which 'define and enforce the economic rules of the game' (ibid, p. 25). In a key sentence that captures the political nub of his argument, North writes that the heart of development policy 'must be the creation of polities that will create and enforce efficient property rights' (ibid).

This call for creating 'polities' to enforce institutional arrangements has profound implications on fundamental questions of sovereignty, democracy and class relations. It can be read as a call to actively engage in social and political manipulation or engineering with deeper implications when read in light of historical Western development interventions in the 'Third World', and its *mission civilisatrice* (see Paris, 2002). North goes a step further though:

- Political institutions will be stable only if they are supported by organizations with an interest in their perpetuation. Therefore an essential part of political/economic reform is the creation of such organizations.
- It is essential to change both the institutions and the belief systems for successful reform since it is the mental models of the actors that will shape choices.

(North, 1995, p. 25)

This wide-ranging call to engineer a society conforming to neoliberal market imperatives would occupy a central place in the policies and practices of IFIs, including in the OPT.

Finally, it is worth noting that all neoliberal prescriptions were seen as having the best chance of succeeding only after the alternatives were seen to have failed. 'Only a crisis – actual or perceived – produces real change,' Friedman once noted (Friedman, 1962, p. xiv). 'When that crisis occurs, the actions that are taken depend on the ideas that are lying around. That, I believe, is our basic function: to develop alternatives to existing policies, to keep them alive and available until the politically impossible becomes the politically inevitable.' Indeed Freidman's ideas would make headway internationally only after the discrediting of post-war Keynesianism and Third World developmentalism. What is novel to the OPT setting is to see how 'crisis' could arise or be induced through violent conflict, in addition to market failure.

... *to Practice*

This concise overview of neoliberal development's theoretical bases found an institutional home in IFIs whose workings and policies have been well studied and documented (see Stein, 2008). Basic neoclassical precepts were captured in the World Bank and IMF's ten key policy instruments known as the 'Washington Consensus' as implemented through Structural Adjustment Programs (SAPs) (see Williamson, J., 1990). When the empirical data from the experience of SAPs affirmed their failures (leaving aside pre-existent Marxist and Keynesian-inspired critiques), the IFIs amended their prescriptions to incorporate the insights of New Institutional Economics, thus giving birth to a post-Washington Consensus (PWC) (see Saad-Filho, 2005, pp. 116–17; Jomo and Fine, 2006).

During his tenure as World Bank chief economist (1997–2000), Joseph Stiglitz elaborated a more sophisticated comprehensive approach to development that saw the entire process aiming towards 'society wide transformation' (Stiglitz, 1998, p. 72). Following in North's conceptual footsteps, where development policy seeks to influence the 'mental models' of agents, Stiglitz's ideas demonstrate a yearning for development to reach 'deep down into society' such that transformation encompasses 'the way individuals think and behave' (Stiglitz, 1998). Johnson and Wasty (1993) had already shown that externally imposed development models had grave limitations to their prescribed loyalty among donor recipients, and hence to their efficacy overall. Stiglitz thus emphasized the need for the subjects of development to participate in and 'own' their developmental processes, such that markets can work better, and a new society can be brought into being through market selectivity. He envisioned a world where the acceptance of IFI policies was not the product of the arm-twisting conditionalities of previous eras, but of the conscious embracing of donor recipient governments and society, because those who agree to these policies actually see their interests tied with these kinds of linkages (see Lloyd, 1996). By thickening the ownership and participation of recipient communities at least amongst a stable strata of the recipient society, a state's 'social capital' was also seen as strengthened, with development seen as being more sustainable.

The construction of institutional arrangements with built-in incentive structures then becomes decisive for 'operationalization.' The private sector, the state, the community, the family and even the individual, all become the target of development policy incentives with their concomitant reliance upon market selectivity. Primacy is given to the private sector as the main agent of change, with the state seen as a complementary, 'light touch', regulatory force to facilitate lowered transaction costs.

Finally, Stiglitz stresses the integration of all strata of development, while the whole system is integrated within global capital. 'At each level, the strategy must be consistent with the environment within which it is embedded, at levels above and below. And all of the strategies are embedded within an ever-changing global environment' (Stiglitz, 1998).

Although Stiglitz's ideas evolved over time and have been extensively debated (Fine and Jomo, 2006; Lapavitsas, 2006; Van Waeyenberge, 2010; Cammack, 2004; Fine & Van Waeyenberge, 2006; Chang, 2001), his development strategy while at the World Bank irrigates the thoughts and policies that ultimately unfold in the OPT, given he was economist of choice to World Bank president James Wolfensohn during much of the latter's tenure (1995–2005). Wolfensohn would also assume the role of Special Envoy to the Quartet for the Middle East Peace Process during the Israeli redeployment from Gaza (2005), immediately after leaving the Bank.

The evolving neoliberal agenda has long since spread beyond its expected IFI bastions to include the UN system as well.

In 1992, UN Secretary General Boutros-Ghali's *Agenda for Peace* asserted that the organization needed to go beyond its traditional peacekeeping role and focus on issues of state failures, democratic deficiencies and questions of economic self-sufficiency (UN, 1992). *Agenda for Peace* proposed 'nation building' as the solution to redressing underlying grievances that propel civil conflict, which increasingly characterized the types of conflicts that emerged after the demise of the Soviet bloc and while neoliberalism was ascendant.

Appeals to 'nation building' emerged around similar calls for 'sustainable development' circulating in various developmental forums including the UNDP. These emphasized 'development that meets the needs of the present without compromising the ability of future generations to meet their own needs' (UN, 1987). The influence of neoliberalism can be found in the way 'sustainable development' embraced an approach that 'prioritized the development of people ahead of states' while 'decoupl[ing] human development from any direct or mechanical connection with economic growth' (Duffield and Waddell, 2006).

Discourse on 'human security' developed in the 1994 *Human Development Report* equally echoed and advanced this sense of disaggregating the role of the state. 'Human security' emphasized the security of individuals over that of the state, concentrating on a variety of social and developmental issues (poverty, population displacement, HIV/AIDS, environmental breakdown and social exclusion) (UNDP, 1994). While these issues had typically been considered under the state's purvey whose fate was enmeshed in the broader question of its overall economic development and social service/welfare provision, their framing in isolation from one another, decoupled from economic development, permitted their individual targeting by various networks of developmental actors. A discursive framing seemingly concerned with various progressive humanitarian values and human rights conventions helped to facilitate the undermining of the state-led approach to development.

With former state functions disaggregated, the 'good governance' agenda would emerge as a natural complement to 'sustainable development.' The UNDP defined good governance as 'the exercise of economic, political and administrative authority' in ways that are 'participatory, transparent and accountable' (UNDP, 1997). Between 1997 and 2000, 46 per cent of the UNDP budget was allocated to governance programs, while recognizing that the organization was also the world's largest multilateral grant-making agency. Good governance was seen as a means to stamp out rent-seeking activity, and ensure that former state functions were managed and operated according to free-market principles.

As the ascendance of neoliberal ideas on the world stage throughout the 1990s incorporated widening spheres, traditionally distant developmental actors converged around common policy agendas. The UN, which had primarily concerned itself with the politics of peace enforcement up until the end of the Cold War, saw the need to more actively address economic dimensions in its mandate, incorporating 'economic recovery' as part of its conflict resolution and prevention mandate (Gerson, 2001). Alternatively, the World Bank, which had focused on macroeconomic adjustment, began looking to political and governance issues, as part of making its agenda succeed. According to Allan Gerson, former counsel to the US delegation to the UN, 'there is new agreement about one basic point: the scourge of intrastate war will not be contained unless the vicious cycle of poverty, economic injury, and political grievance is broken' (Gerson, 2001, p.102). This convergence ultimately took operational form in the UN Millennium Declaration whereby the role of 'post-conflict peacebuilding and reconstruction' was endorsed as part of the UN's agenda (UN, 2000).

The declaration also pledged to work toward 'greater policy coherence and better cooperation between the UN, its agencies, the Bretton Woods Institutions and the World Trade Organization, as well as other multilateral bodies, with a view to achieving a fully coordinated approach to the problems of peace and development.'

Neoliberal Conflict Resolution and Peacebuilding

From Theory ...

It is important to bear in mind that the absorption and incorporation of neoliberal ideas by institutions engaged in conflict resolution, peacebuilding and statebuilding took place on a changing historical and political landscape after the collapse of the Eastern bloc and the end of its bilateral aid provision. The conflicts which emerged in the wake of this decline informed how Western governments and IFIs molded their ensuing aid/interventions. Wallensteen and Sollenberg (2001) documented 111 cases of armed conflicts in the world between 1989 and 2000, of which 104 were said to be 'intrastate.' In many of these cases the UN was called to play a role in 'peacebuilding' missions, the aim of which was 'to create the conditions necessary for a sustainable peace in war-torn societies' (Annan, 1999a). The World Bank also established a 'Post-Conflict Unit' in 1995 under Wolfensohn, assigned to coordinate interventions in war-to-peace transitions.

The intrastate narrative of wars led to debates around what caused conflict (see Beath *et al.*, 2012). Here the work of Paul Collier, director of the Development Research Group of the World Bank from 1998 to 2003 would come to prominence, using quantitative analytic and comparative statistical approaches to explain conflict through econometrics (Collier and Hoeffler, 1998; 2004; Collier, 1999; 2004; Collier and World Bank, 2003). His research attempted to extract general unifying rules about conflict based on comparative statistical analysis, including explanations for what caused and perpetuated conflicts, and concomitantly, what might contain or resolve them. These approaches tended to enforce a sharp division between political and economic motivations, even though these interventions necessarily needed to pass through political actors and movements on the ground.

Collier claimed two particularly relevant conclusions: first, he purported to have statistically proven that '[c]onflicts are far more likely to be caused by economic opportunities than by grievance,' (Collier, 1999, p. 1) as certain groups are said to benefit materially from conflict in terms of status, power and wealth, thus engendering an interest in initiating and sustaining it ('greed over grievance', the 'greed' theory of conflict); Secondly, he argued that 'civil war powerfully retards development' while 'failures in development substantially increase proneness to civil war' (Collier, 2004). If left unaddressed, poor countries are likely to be stuck in a 'conflict trap' whereby the costs of wars are borne by non-combatants within the country, future inhabitants and neighbors (war as 'development in reverse') (Collier, 2003a).

Collier broadly suggested remedies to both issues, formulating some of the core notions of international conflict resolution and peacebuilding praxis. 'Greed over grievance' could be addressed by initiating policies that effectively 'change the economic incentives for conflict,' while 'reduc[ing] ... the economic power of the groups which tend to gain from the continuation of social disorder' (Collier, 1999). The 'conflict trap' could be redressed 'by intelligent and vigorous deployment of economic, military and political assistance,' because '[c]ivil war is not the inexorable result of historic grievances or ethnic hatreds' (Collier, 2004). In this light, 'governance templates, trade preferences, strategies which squeeze the finances of rebel groups, and military interventions', in addition to increased aid, act as the main instruments of defusing conflict. These policies are justified based upon a humanist rationale whereby '[s]omeone needs to represent the interests of all these people who lose from civil war' (ibid).

In its more specific neoliberal interpretation, peacebuilding attempts to realign these 'market distortions' caused by conflict and incentivize investment conditions and opportunities. 'Maximalists' argue that aid should be used as an instrument of peacebuilding to stimulate economic activity and consciously re-circuit its rent recipient networks. This is begrudgingly acknowledged to take place for political motives, understanding that aid affects 'not only the size of the economic pie and how it is sliced but also the balance of power among the competing actors and the rules of the game by which they compete' (Goodhand, 2002). Donors thus carve out a powerful vertical positioning vis-à-vis their recipients and the rent allotment opportunities provided, in an effort to coagulate a self-enforcing peace and all this entails on the governance level.

The Liberal Peace

Within these general understandings, a 'liberal peace' model emerged among Western donor governments, the UN and IFIs, positing that conflicts could be defused by encouraging the liberalization of the political and economic structures of post-conflict societies.

Political liberalization implied democratization, or 'the promotion of periodic and genuine elections, constitutional limitations on the exercise of governmental power, and respect for basic civil liberties, including freedom of speech, assembly, and conscience' (Paris, 2004, p. 5). Democratic values were argued to be responsive to the will of their peoples, capable of engendering peaceful conduct towards their neighbors, and could be relied upon to form the foundation of stable international order (Barnett, 2006). Economic liberalization implied marketization, or 'movement toward a market-oriented economic model, including measures aimed at minimizing government intrusion in the economy, and maximizing the freedom for private investors, producers, and consumers to pursue their respective economic interests' (Paris, 2004, p. 5).

The 'liberal peace' model is based on the belief that it establishes the political, organizational and economic foundations for addressing, if not the roots of conflict, then at least its externalities. Given the greed-based assessment to conflict, generating and distributing a 'peace dividend' is deemed central to its success. By irrigating political and economic dynamics around a new political economy of 'peace', international peacebuilders believe they create conditions whereby persistent conflicts can be ended on a more permanent basis, providing these actors an 'exit strategy.' In this way, maintaining peace is said to go beyond military and security priorities 'to address issues of governance, democratic legitimacy, social inclusion, and economic equity' (Cousens et al., 2001, p. 1).

The particular neoliberal variant of the liberal peace model comes to identify and emphasize the elements most associated with the neoliberal worldview regarding the role of the state (non-interventionist 'umpiring'), the assumed economic and social organization within this state (market allocation), and the nature of human behavior activating this order (homo economicus, rational deductive thought processes, whereby agents respond individually to market signals, for utility maximization etc.). The liberal peace is expected to establish the foundations of the neoliberal state, and should focus on setting in motion the institutions of a neoliberal political, economic and social order. In practice this has come to mean an emphasis on security, law and order, and functional institutions, all within a market economy that secures property rights.

Given the centrality of markets to neoliberal approaches to peacebuilding, it is market allocation that leads to peace, through increased transactions involving a 'peace dividend'.

This prioritization of a market/economic peace over a social or civil peace also distinguishes neoliberal peacebuilding, and ultimately neoliberal statebuilding overall. Rather than peace deriving from consensual political practices that accommodate questions of political and social justice, rights, and a mediated 'contract' between societal groups, market economics is believed sufficient to drive the process forward resulting eventually in a 'self-enforcing peace'. 'If war is the continuation of politics by other means, peacebuilding can be seen as an opportunity to channel "war" into manageable forms of competition' (Cousens *et al.*, 2001, pp. 11–12).

... *to Practice*

International peacebuilding efforts have reflected the same shifts in neoliberal thought from Washington Consensus models to those of the PWC. Whereas peacebuilding was initially construed in more deductive terms by the international community, and which assumed an approach that attempted to 'map the full range of post-war needs and identify those international resources available to help meet them,' later approaches assumed more inductive approaches that based policy on a more succinct problem diagnosis, thus making it possible to provide 'a more nuanced assessment of what a particular society most needs in order to solidify a fragile peace' (Cousens *et al.*, 2001, pp. 5–9). The former vision was linear in its treatment of conflict and amounted to an inventory of needs that could be filled by international actors, with the larger purpose of peacebuilding remaining vague. Later (inductive) approaches identified specific causal factors to conflict, and proposed solutions. This shift in focus opened the door for international peacebuilding practitioners to disaggregate the larger political issues of contention into manageable tranches or sub-issues, and which could be given a particular humanistic framing ('poverty'; 'unemployment', 'women's empowerment' etc.) decoupled from broader political questions.

Ball *et al.* (1997) outline the particular role IFIs play in conflict prevention and resolution, particularly in establishing conducive social and economic conditions. When teaming up with donor governments, traditional diplomatic instruments become means for bearing influence as part of the peacebuilding process. Among these, 'incentives' or 'positive sanctions' become key tools of leverage. An incentive is defined as the 'granting of a political or economic benefit in exchange for a specified policy adjustment by the recipient nation' (Cortright, 1997, pp. 6–7). These might include foreign aid, guarantees on investments, encouraging capital imports or exports; favorable taxation; granting access to advanced technology; offering diplomatic and political support; military cooperation; environmental and social cooperation; cultural exchanges; debt relief; security assurances; granting membership in international organizations or security alliances; and lifting negative sanctions (Baldwin, 1985, p. 42). Alternatively incentives can be taken away, or sanctions imposed ('negative incentives') when IFIs and donor governments are displeased with peacebuilding performance.

The use of incentives and sanctions designed to induce particular political or economic behavior in general is premised upon behavioral psychology and rational choice theory, whereby political judgements are said to result from individual cost-benefit calculations (Nachtwey and Tessler, 2002). Striking the right balance of 'carrots and sticks' hence forms the basis for influencing policy. Moreover, donors have the potential to greatly synergize their efforts with recipient governments 'clustering' their various roles and demands. Collectively the incentives used to induce peacebuilding have been termed 'peace conditionalities' (see Goodhand and Sedra, 2006; Boyce, 2002). James Boyce describes peace conditionality as using '"aid as a carrot" to encourage specific steps by the recipient' for the purpose of implementing peace accords and the long-term consolidation of peace (Boyce, 2002, p. 8).

Boyce adds that the practice of peace conditionality has the instrumental effect of 'translating the 'grand bargain' of the peace accord into 'mini-bargains' in which specific types and quantities of aid are tied to specific measures that are crucial to moving beyond conflict' (p. 15). This enables donors to 'disaggregate the acceptance and enforcement problems {of peace accords} into smaller and more tractable pieces' (p. 19). Aid becomes a powerful tool within the hands of donors to micromanage the behavior of the recipient leadership and society over time, selectively rewarding or penalizing. The insertion here of a temporal dimension is also worth noting as the selective provision of aid creates various scenarios regarding the ability of governments to deliver jobs and services to their base. In a context where other political competitors exist (as frequently is the case), this temporal aspect can have particularly significant repercussions on the political resilience and 'holding power' of aid recipients.

Equally relevant to the success of peace conditionality as a donor strategy is the elimination of alternative 'options' recipients have, particularly in terms of alternative financial support bases. As Collier put it in his justification of these policies, global efforts should 'focus on reducing the viability – rather than just the rationale – of rebellion' (Collier, 2009). Here the good governance agenda emphasizing transparency and accountability contributes to narrowing the margin of maneuver of donor recipients by taking away or eroding potential 'fall back' positions and resources. Boyce suggests a four-pronged strategy regarding enforcement, which includes 'monitoring compliance'; 'slicing the carrot'; 'combating corruption' and 'inter-donor coordination' (Boyce, 2002, pp. 21–3).

Neoliberal peacebuilding ultimately strives to leave in place the human and institutional capacity for these policies to be sustainable and outlive their interventions. Organizations should be established that will be 'perpetually lived' whereby their existence is independent of the lives of their members (North et al., 2009). This manifests itself in the expressed desire to withdraw financial aid and to have the mechanisms and institutions established by these interventions financed domestically. This begins spilling over into the financial policies of statebuilding processes and the establishment of functional taxation regimes and revenue generation schemes (see Boyce and O'Donnell, 2007).

Consistent with the neoliberal vision for development and its central focus on markets, the private sector is seen as the primary dynamo for promoting peace. Economic liberalization is said to promote peace through regional cooperation and stability, by addressing poverty, and by inducing new styles of politics and identity as a function of the globalization process.

Ultimately the neoliberal development and peacebuilding scholarship aims to make the intellectual case that a momentum of positive incentives towards peace can emerge from such neoliberal conceptions and can reap economic rewards, mitigating incentives to return to conflict. It derives from a functionalist understanding of regional cooperation, whereby relatively insignificant 'low political' issues can create patterns of mutual interest and trust which will eventually 'spill over' into the 'high political' arena, nurturing both bilateral peace settlements and regional economic and political integration (Selby, 2008, p.17).

Acting on these ideas, international peacebuilding practitioners have attempted to deliver on the peace dividend by combining and coordinating their efforts in practice. UN Secretary-General Kofi Annan's *Millennium Report* calls specifically for 'partnering' between the UN, development agencies and IFIs, noting that '[c]onflict prevention, post-conflict peacebuilding, humanitarian assistance and development policies need to become more effectively integrated' (Annan, 2000). Employment and economic opportunities have come to be seen as pivotal to peacemaking, with both the UN and the World Bank actively courting the private sector to engage in post-conflict societies. In a speech capturing the extent to which neoliberal ideas and a pro-business approach has influenced the UN peacebuilding agenda, Secretary-General Kofi Annan once noted:

> A fundamental shift has occurred in the UN-business relationship [...] The UN has developed a profound appreciation for the role of the private sector, its expertise, its motivated spirit, its unparalleled ability to create jobs and wealth [...] In a world of common challenges and common vulnerabilities, the UN and business are finding common ground.
>
> (Annan, 1999b)

By 2009, then-World Bank president Robert Zoellick called for a particular sequencing of processes said to actively reverse 'development in reverse' by 'bringing security and development together first to smooth the transition from conflict to peace and then to embed stability so that development can take hold over a decade and beyond' (Zoellick, 2009). He outlines ten instructive priorities for how this vision of peacebuilding can come about, and which can be seen as guiding principles to the World Bank's international peacebuilding agenda: building the legitimacy of the state; providing security; building rule of law and legal order; bolstering local and national ownership; ensuring economic stability; 'paying attention to political economy'; 'crowding in' the private sector; coordinating across institutions and actors; 'considering the regional context', and; recognizing the long term commitment of peacebuilding activities.

This succinct vision of neoliberal peacebuilding combining economic, political, governance, geostrategic and security related matters on both the local, national and international levels ultimately aims towards what Roland Paris has described as bringing 'war shattered states into conformity with the international system's prevailing forms of governance' (Paris, 2002). Moreover, it equally conveys a hubristic notion that the complex issues of conflict and development can be commandeered through integrated economic, political, governance and security technologies of international development practitioners.

These policies should also be read upon the backdrop of a post-Cold War reality that saw the rise of a unipolar global hegemon in the United States, with a far wider scope to intervene in emerging or ongoing conflicts. In this respect the peacebuilding interventions of Western donors and IFIs in the OPT should be seen as part of a wider set of invasive (in fact military) interventions taking place concomitantly in the former Yugoslavia, Afghanistan, Iraq and elsewhere. The creeping need to justify imperial endeavors in a post-Cold War, post-9/11 world, led to various Western intellectuals defending the emergence of 'empire lite' given the obligation to '[uphold] democracy and stability', because the US has 'inherited a world scarred not just by the failures of empires past but also by the failure of nationalist movements to create and secure free states' (Ignatieff, 2003). Robert Cooper describes how the EU also suffers from a 'post-modern' condition, where the 'modern and pre-modern zones' still pose threats that necessitate 'a defensive imperialism' – one 'acceptable to a world of human rights and cosmopolitan values' (Cooper, 2002). According to Cooper, a 'post-modern imperialism' has already emerged whereby a 'voluntary imperialism of the global economy' operated by IFIs provide help to states 'wishing to find their way back into the global economy and into the virtuous circle of investment and prosperity' (ibid). These overall should be seen as giving the intellectual and political justification to deeply interventionist foreign policy and development practices with obvious affront to the principles of self-determination and Westphalian sovereignty.

Neoliberal Statebuilding

From Theory ...

Peacebuilding and statebuilding practices are closely intertwined and mutually reinforcing processes that seek 'to develop conditions, values, and behaviors that foster peaceful, stable, and sustainable socioeconomic development' (World Bank, 2011a). The World Bank relies upon a definition of peacebuilding that includes 'reconstruction and institution-building; efforts to help countries recover from conflict, and; integrated strategies to lay the foundation for sustainable development.' 'Statebuilding' is the more specialized activity that seeks to 'strengthen, build, or rebuild institutions of governance that can provide the population with transparent and accountable management of public finances and state assets; investment in human capital and social development; the rule of law, basic services and infrastructure, and; an enabling environment for market formation, among other functions' (ibid).

Contemporary statebuilding theory builds off the neoliberal intellectual and policy edifice outlined above and attempts to establish conventions and practices that are governed by stable and predictable rules and relationships within the institutional makeup of the governing order.

Francis Fukuyama's (2004) writings on statebuilding succinctly illustrate the institutionalist yearning for predictability while avoiding the seemingly unpredictable morass of 'politics.' For Fukuyama, the problem is not that states are too strong, but that they are too weak, lacking crucial 'dimensions of stateness' to adequately serve their people or bring about development (p. 1). State performance is assessed according to the institutional capacity of governments to enforce 'order, security, law and property rights' seen as 'the critical institutions for economic development' (ibid, p. 31). A complicated balance of interventions in the legal, economic, political and social spheres, administered through a 'good governance' agenda upholding accountability, transparency, efficiency and participation is seen as the most effective way to establish these institutions.

IFIs and Western governments must hence strive to embed institutional practices through the economic instruments of aid and technical expertise, and the political instruments of diplomacy. Technical expertise is viewed as introducing neutral or scientific elements to the process of government policy formulation and assessment (Critchlow, 1985; Haskell, 1984 in Williams, 2008, p. 40). Scope and depth of institutional embedding is dependent upon local contexts, with IFIs encouraged to focus at the very least on 'core' supposedly 'nonpolitical' fiscal and administrative functions while avoiding raising 'overtly political' final status issues (Fearon and Laitin, 2004; Krasner, 2004; Boyce, 2002).

Ideally, the motivation for this embedding should be the product of domestic demand. However, as Fukuyama recognizes, if this is not the case, outsiders may be compelled to facilitate this process through conditionalities attached to external aid, or 'the direct exercise of political power by outside authorities that have claimed the mantle of sovereignty in failed, collapsed or occupied states' (Fukuyama, 2004, p. 48). The goal of all scenarios must be to have the statebuilding process itself strengthen these institutions, while fostering a local constituency that equally sees this need as tied to its own interests, thereby ensuring long-term sustainability.

Rondinelli and Cheema (2003) summarize the role that governments need to perform in the context of the state's 'changing role in a globalizing society': initiating and sustaining macroeconomic reforms; strengthening legal institutions for economic transactions; enacting and implementing policies that support private enterprise development; improving government efficiency, accountability and responsiveness; providing infrastructure and overhead capital; protecting the economically vulnerable, and; strengthening and supporting civil society organizations (Rondinelli & Cheema, 2003, pp. 36–7).

Not all international statebuilding emphasizes strictly orthodox neoliberal interpretations. Roland Paris for instance has cautioned that in order for both political and economic liberalization to take root in a stable and productive manner, institutions need to be in place before liberalization takes place ('Institutionalization before liberalization') (Paris, 2002; 2004). Early economic and political liberalization is discouraged out of fear that it can re-ignite conflict because both democracy and marketization 'encourage conflict and competition – indeed they thrive on it' (Paris, 2004, p. 156). Debates over the sequencing and prioritization of policies hence becomes relevant even if the general liberal peace model remains intact.

... to Practice

Neoliberal statebuilding in practice has similarly evolved over time in parallel to changing notions of the state under neoliberalism. Earlier models emphasizing macroeconomic fundamentals would evolve beneath institutionalist rationales that called for an expanded state role following the World Bank's partial re-discovery of this need in its 1997 *World Development Report* (World Bank, 1997a). The latter's call for 'improving state effectiveness' would morph a decade later into statebuilding policies calling for 'action to develop the capacity, institutions and legitimacy of the state in relation to an effective political process for negotiating the mutual demands between state and societal groups' (OECD/DAC, 2008, p. 14). The stress on 'legitimacy', 'effective political process' and 'mutual demands' implies that later statebuilding efforts shifted focus from institutional embedding and concern over capacity building, to securing the legitimacy of these endeavors overall. The Organization for Economic Cooperation and Development's (OECD) Development Assistance Committee's guidance on statebuilding, captures the shifting trajectory, synthesizing a position that posits statebuilding as the practice of both building state capacity and institutions in service delivery, while also explicitly highlighting how donors need to be attuned to the 'political settlement' process underlying the emergence of the state, and the legitimacy of the new government and its actions as perceived by society (OECD/DAC, 2010). OECD defines the political settlement as 'an agreement, principally between elites, on the balance and distribution of power and wealth, on the rules of political engagement and on the nature of the political processes that connect state and society' (OECD, 2011, p. 3).

The World Bank, UNDP, USAID and DFID all produced similarly themed statebuilding guidelines (see USAID, 2011; WB-UNDP, 2010; DFID, 2009). This newer 'political' as opposed to 'technical' approach to statebuilding stressed the need for assistance focusing on 'negotiating the mutual demands between state and societal groups', with 'government legitimacy' and 'resilience' instead of 'capacity' seen as the desired principal outcome (OECD, 2008). This approach entailed delicate attentiveness to the expectations of the state and its citizens based on political economic analysis, given that fragility is believed to arise 'from weaknesses in the dynamic political process through which citizens' expectations of the state and state expectations of citizens are reconciled and brought into equilibrium with the state's capacity to deliver services' (OECD, 2008, p. 7). In this way, international statebuilders gain a say in determining what constitutes legitimacy and who is entitled to engage in it. Rent-allotment opportunities created as a part of the peace dividend becomes the reward of the process overall, with statebuilders effectively managing the local political settlement through these means.

Emphasis on the inclusivity of the political settlement inevitably arises given the potential problem of 'spoilers' arising. Initially political settlements were negotiated between elites, as part of 'elite pacts' or 'bargains'. These were seen as formal or informal agreements by the holders of political, military or economic power, and were typically personalized and enforced through coercion and patronage (World Bank, 2011b, p. xv). By 2011 however, the *World Development Report* loosened its criteria of inclusivity emphasizing 'inclusive-enough coalitions' as distinct from 'elite pacts.' (World Bank, 2011b, p. xvi). Elite pacts were seen as motivated by the desire to contain violence and secure the property and economic interests and opportunities of pact members. Inclusive-enough settlements on the other hand, were to involve broader segments of society – 'local governments, business, labor, civil society movements, in some cases opposition parties' (ibid., p. xvii). But the World Bank equally stresses that 'groups may legitimately be excluded where there is an evolving belief among the population that they have sacrificed their right to participate due to past abuses' (p. 124). The 2011 *World Development Report* succinctly notes that there always exists a trade-off 'between wide inclusiveness and the efficiency of subsequent state decision making', and that 'inclusion strategies can change over time as it becomes possible to marginalize consistently abusive groups' (p. 124). This less idealistic approach to implementing neoliberal statebuilding is equally seen in how the UK's DFID devised the parallel notion of 'good enough governance,' reflecting a sense of ennui around the complexity of statebuilding and its challenges, and an overall sense of lowered expectations about its potential outputs, mainly after Western experiences in Iraq and Afghanistan (Kahler, 2009; Grindle, 2004).

Irrespective of these lowered expectations, the identification and formation of inclusive-enough coalitions sets the stage for identifying the correct 'signals and commitment mechanisms' to help consolidate the ruling coalition's hold on power. This process entails domestic statebuilders demonstrating their intentions to break with previous policies usually through public announcements or appointment (signaling) followed up by creating ways to 'persuade stakeholders that intentions to break with past policies will not be reversed, including creating independent functions for implementing or monitoring agreements' (commitment mechanisms). The whole process remains premised and deeply informed by rational choice notions of methodological individualism and axiomatic logic, whereby agents respond to such signaling and commitment mechanism once they arise, thereby generating confidence, trust and legitimacy.

In a context where neoliberal statebuilding gives pre-eminence to private sector-led growth, the private sector itself becomes the principal 'societal group' that must have its demands upon the state listened to and met. This ensures that a profit motive – not an ulterior 'political' motive – animates the arrangements.

Needless to say, these evolving theoretical and policy orientations to peacebuilding and statebuilding remain a far cry from the romanticized, emancipatory notions of self-determination that many post-colonial societies – and currently colonial territories like the OPT – imagined on their roads to independence and national liberation. While the task of seeing how these ideas apply to the OPT shall be taken up in subsequent chapters, most readers with a rudimentary knowledge of international peacebuilding and statebuilding practices in the OPT can already begin to identify how these ideas have already found their place there. Before fleshing out these dynamics in detail however, and elaborating on how they facilitated the rise of Palestine Ltd., a firmer grasp of the historical material realities of the OPT and the political economic and geostrategic logic of the actors engaged in reshaping these realities, is in order.

CHAPTER 2

GETTING TO 'PEACE': SURVEY OF HISTORICAL, POLITICAL AND ECONOMIC FACTORS LEADING TO THE OSLO PEACE PROCESS

This chapter will attempt to provide relevant historical, political and economic information and analysis of the main actors, establishing the context in which neoliberal peacebuilders and statebuilders intervened, and the reality they sought to shape. It is divided into four sections deriving from the hierarchical manner in which neoliberal policies tend to flow in the OPT: the main Western players (led by the US) are addressed in section one, followed by Israeli interests in section two. Relevant political economic dimensions to the Palestinian political theatre are then addressed, starting with the PLO (section three) followed by a closer look at the OPT (section four). As previously noted, discussion of EU and non-Western donors is largely excluded as these donors do not set the peace process agenda and are a subject of research unto their own.

The United States

The signing of the Oslo Accords was a product of a particular historical moment in which the confluence of various ideological, political, and economic factors converged between the key players: the US, Israel, the PLO and the local Palestinian setting. Understanding this convergence is critical to understanding the unfolding sets of opportunities and expectations this process created – as well as restricted – given the existent asymmetrical power relations between them.

The Oslo Accords were signed at the apex of US power, with the early 1990s experiencing resounding achievements in the three wars of position the US fought throughout the twentieth century: the containment/defeat of communist states; primacy over other leading capitalist states, and; the defeat of 'Third World' nationalism (Ahmad, 2004). This created space for the US to pursue, in the words of Aijaz Ahmad, a 'role for itself as the sole architect of the global capitalist system.' New geostrategic and economic opportunities had opened to the US in the wake of the decline of the Soviet bloc, and the defeat of Iraq in the 1990–1 Gulf War, with an ascendant neoliberal zeitgeist now animating its international political economic maneuverings.

Stephen Gill characterizes this push as a form of 'new constitutionalism' whereby a global reconfiguration of political and juridical regimes in each specific territorial unit was underway within the global order, to meet the exigencies of 'disciplinary neoliberalism' (Gill 1995; 2002). This included efforts to 'redefine the terrain of normal politics to "lock in" the power gains of capital and "lock out" or depoliticize forces challenging these gains' (Gill, 2002). The latter could be achieved through 'co-optation, domestication, neutralization and depoliticization.'

Within this broad policy impetus came implications on the Middle East and the Israeli–Palestinian conflict more specifically. As Emma Murphy notes, 'the global phenomenon of economic growth through liberalization of production and distribution (both national and international) required the resolution of regional disputes and the establishment of regional political security if it were to take effect' (Murphy, 2000, p. 49). Geostrategic interests dominated US policy toward the region seen as critical to securing its broader international political economic interests.[1] The consolidating of US military bases in the wake of the Gulf War subsequently gave the US enormous economic and military leverage over the global economy and its economic rivals. 'What better way for the US to ward off that competition and secure its own hegemonic condition than to control the price, conditions, and distribution for the key economic resource upon which its competitors [including Europe] rely?' Harvey notes (Harvey, 2003, p. 25). Protecting its network of pro-US 'moderate Arab states' in the Gulf also played an important role in subsidizing and stabilizing Western economies, given the recycling of Gulf petro-dollars back into Western coffers through military purchases, construction projects, bank deposits, investments in treasury, and securities as had taken place since the early 1970s (Chomsky, 1999, pp. 17–22).

This arrangement nonetheless represented the 'soft underbelly' of the capitalist system because the undemocratic basis of these regimes and the existence of various competing 'radical' traditions in the region (Leftist, Pan-Arabist, and Pan-Islamist), always meant the system was perpetually unstable and could quickly change (Amin, 2003). It is within this context that the US came to recognize Israel as 'a strategic trump card' to this agenda after the latter's 1967 defeat of pan-Arabist leader Jamal Abdel Nasser, and the creeping Soviet influence in the region this accelerated (Achcar, 2004, p. 17). As Achcar notes, Israel was able to play 'a military role as watchdog of imperialist interests in the region', while 'Washington derived political benefits in Arab countries' eyes by showing that it had a grip on the watchdog's leash' (Achcar, 2004, pp. 18–19).

In this context, the question of managing, controlling, and possibly liquidating the aspirations of Palestinian national self-determination acquired significant strategic value for the US, as it was tied to both wings of its imperial strategy: the political, national, geographic, cultural, historical and moral bonds between the Palestinian people and the Arab periphery continually re-raised the various forms of Western imperial subjugation of the region. Equally so, Palestinian resistance to Israel's settler colonial presence never ceased despite the ethnic cleansing of most Palestinians from their homeland in 1948, and the successive waves of their displacement.

While the US had historically rejected the PLO associating it with the 'radical' camp in the Arab world, US policy circles gradually acclimatized to dealing with the Fateh leadership after a series of historical events and processes: the containment or defeat of 'radical Arab nationalism' by external interventions (1967 War, 1982 Israeli invasion of Lebanon, the 1990–1 Gulf War); internal Arab repression (1970 'Black September' in Jordan, the 1976 Syrian intervention in Lebanon); and external cooptation (the 1979 Camp David Accords). Moreover, from the mid-1970s onwards, the PLO began to insinuate that it was willing to accept a two-state solution and generally adhere to the international consensus embodied in United Nations Security Council Resolutions 242 and 338 (see Gresh, 1988).

The outbreak of the 1987 Intifada also signaled a key turning point in US regional designs. For years the US had supported Israeli and Jordanian attempts to drive a wedge between the Palestinians of the OPT and the PLO leadership, by exiling pro-PLO nationalist mayors and forging contacts with 'Palestinian moderates' in an attempt to support an alternative leadership forming while the PLO leadership was exiled in Tunis. But the Intifada signaled the failure of these plans, pushing the US towards dialogue with the PLO as the only realistic option, especially considering the emergent rise of more 'radical' options, notably the Islamic Resistance Movement – Hamas in the late 1980s.

In this context, the results of the 1990/91 Gulf War created strategic and historical opportunities that the US State Department anticipated capitalizing upon. As US historian and former US National Security Council member William Quandt summarizes:

> The defeat of Iraq would convince even the most die-hard Arab militants that a military solution to the Arab-Israeli conflict was impossible. The fact that the Soviet Union had cooperated with the US during the crisis would further demonstrate that the old Cold War rules of the game were being rewritten, and that the US, more than ever, occupied the key diplomatic position. Palestinians and Jordanians, who had allowed their emotions to draw them to Saddam's side, would now realize that they had lost support among Arab regimes and that time was working against their interests. Out of weakness, therefore, the Palestinians might be expected to respond positively to any serious diplomatic overture.
>
> (Quandt, 2005, p. 303)

Quandt's emphasis on the 'weakness' of the PLO is affirmed by a confidential US Central Intelligence Agency (CIA) report issued soon after the Gulf War, uncovered through Benoit Faucon's research (Faucon, 2010). For the CIA, the issue was not that PLO Chairman Yasser Arafat would be unwilling to respond to a 'serious diplomatic overture', but that he would be too weak to keep the PLO together as a coalition of various Palestinian factions in the meantime. 'Arafat's ability to restrain hard-line PLO elements from conducting terrorism is likely to weaken in the months ahead as his financial situation worsens and challenges to his leadership develop,' the agency warned in its 4 April 1991 report (ibid., p. 92, n.18).

While there were those within the US camp who relished the demise of Arafat, the realists understood that the Palestinian issue would not go away in his absence, but actually had the potential to become more unmanageable. 'We've just seen an earthquake,' noted Dennis Ross, then head of US Secretary of State James Baker's policy planning staff (Haley, 2006, p. 37). 'We have to move before the earth resettles, because it will and it never takes long.' According to P. Edward Haley, 'Baker found the analogy "particularly compelling."'

The impetus towards managing, containing and leveraging a form of self-administration over the 'radicalness' of Palestinian national aspirations would be a consistently cultivated theme to US policies towards the Palestinians, beginning in the early 1990s and carrying on into the statebuilding era.

This was seen at the 1991 Madrid Conference whereby the US insisted on a joint Jordanian–Palestinian delegation composed of Palestinian representatives from the OPT. The latter were known by the US to 'all be selected by the PLO, whose role would only barely be disguised,' though this arrangement was necessary so as to allow for the possibility of cutting a deal with the 'moderate' wing of the OPT political leadership (Quandt, 2005, p. 308). As Quandt explains:

> The so-called moderates in the West Bank and Gaza [selected as representatives for the Madrid Conference] had very little mass following. Insofar as they could claim to speak for the Palestinians, it was because they were seen as representing the PLO. The grassroots leaders, by contrast, were often more radical than the PLO, sometimes on the left, sometimes as part of the growing Islamic movement. So to get the moderate Palestinians into the game, and to give them political cover, the PLO was still necessary.
> (Ibid., p. 308)

While the Madrid Conference did not amount to much in terms of agreements reached, its formal stiff-arming of the PLO was intended to maintain pressure on the PLO leadership, impressing upon it that time was not on its side. The cutting of PLO funding from Gulf states – both governmental and remittances of roughly half a million Palestinians working in the Gulf – was hitting the organization hard. Since the mid-1980s, the PLO had run a fairly well-developed 'state in exile' that included an army, schools, orphanages, healthcare centers and embassies with annual spending reaching $220 million (Sayigh, Y., 1997, p. 640). Yet by 1993, more than 70 per cent of its budget had been cut. According to top PLO financial administrator Ahmed Qurei, by the time the DOP was signed, PLO coffers only held two months' worth of functioning budget. 'We didn't have a penny left. We couldn't continue anymore', he later explained (Faucon, 2010, p. 90).

It is important to keep in mind that the US was convinced that the Arab-Israeli conflict was not yet 'ripe' for resolution, as determined by an influential pamphlet entitled *Building for Peace*, produced by the Presidential Study Group and primarily formulated by Dennis Ross and Richard Haass (see Quandt, 2005, pp. 293–5). Internally dubbed the 'the gardening metaphor', the approach outlined that the US, like 'an attentive gardner', must approach this reality cautiously to 'help the ripening process by watering the plants and weeding and fertilizing, but that was pretty much the proper extent of Washington's involvement until the fruit was ripe and ready to harvest' (ibid., p. 294).

The combined political and financial squeeze placed on the PLO after the Gulf War was thus part of a strategy to seize the opportunity created by the historical circumstances to leverage the internalization of the PLO's own weak positioning, forcing it to compromise on key political and strategic questions. Chief among these was the organization's historical rejection of engaging in an autonomy arrangement in the OPT, or negotiating with Israel in the context of continued settlement expansion. Even the 'moderate' PLO-affiliated leaders at the Madrid Conference were fiercely opposed to the latter, seeing it as a recipe for negotiations providing cover for continued colonization and the erasure of Palestinian strategic positioning. The Oslo channel was thus a coordinated US plan through third-party players to create a back channel framework in which the enfeebled PLO leadership could internalize its shift in position, necessarily undemocratically and behind closed doors.

Israel

The evolution of the Israeli state as a by-product of the settler colonial experimentations of the Zionist movement, forged within the womb of

British imperialism, has resulted in several distinct features to its internal and external composition and orientation.

The Zionist character to the state entailed amongst other things, the need for constant attentiveness to its demographic composition ('a Jewish majority'), and the political manner in which its Jewish constituents decided upon collective action while mediating their internal differences (democratic processes) (Shafir, 1989). The latter was the necessary modus operandi its majority 'pragmatist' elements adhered to as a function of the need to get as many Jews as possible to support the Zionist project in Palestine, while also gaining wider Western liberal sympathy before and after the establishment of the state.

Israel's character as a product of an imperial legacy entailed attentiveness to particular services it could offer its imperial masters, and materially entailed an economic orientation that undergirded this. As economist George Abed explains:

> A key feature of the Jewish economy in Palestine was its predominantly external orientation. Its links with the European colonial powers, and especially Great Britain, were far stronger than those it maintained with the indigenous Arab community in Palestine. The metropolitan countries of Europe and North America constituted not only the source of high-level manpower, ideology, and worldview but also, at the strictly economic level, generated the primary source of interaction in goods, services, and capital.
>
> (Abed, 1986, p. 39)

The retention of an external Western orientation to the Israeli state and economy deepened in the context of Israel's political and economic dependency upon imperial tutelage, which ensured continued diplomatic and financial cover for the daily Zionist colonial endeavors of Jewish settlement and military supremacy over the Arab periphery. As Israeli economist Ephraim Kleiman (1997) notes 'the Zionist agenda was obstructed by a set of market failures' whereby 'economic externalities alone were far, far too great to be internalized by private enterprises or private philanthropy.' Israel was thus sponsored as a geostrategic and political investment by Western powers whose services were not that easy to replicate given the strong anti-colonial and national sentiment that pervaded the region as a consequence of earlier periods of repression beneath the Ottomans, European colonialism, and the indigenous resistance this generated. As emphasized by Beit-Hallahmi, 'US Major General George Keegan, a former air-force intelligence officer, has been quoted as saying that it would cost US taxpayers $125 billion to maintain an armed force equal to Israel's in the Middle East, and that the US-Israel military relationship was worth "five CIAs." There can be no doubt that from the US point of view, the investment in Israel is a bargain, and the money well spent' (Beit-Hallahmi, 1987, pp. 196–8). This constant pro-military footing has historically created different pressures for Israeli capital including the disincentivation of foreign direct and portfolio investment inflows, the failure to fully exploit the potential of production and services such as tourism, high risk premiums limiting the ability to borrow from external sources, restrictions on mobility, welfare losses in terms of inefficient regional trade and financial arrangements, and slow development of joint infrastructure projects (El-Naggar and El-Erian, 1993).

These dimensions combine to give Israel a unique political determination – one which gives primacy to ideological and strategic factors over economic considerations domestically. In order to successfully manage this Zionist arrangement, it needed to resolve structural complications as a result of its 1967 conquests and the continued presence of a large Palestinian (non-Jewish) population there (roughly one million strong in 1967, 4.68 million by the end of 2015).

Gilbert Achcar's exploration of the Israeli 'solution' to this dilemma is highly revealing as it provides important clues to Israel's future actions, backed by its Western allies (see Achcar, 2004, pp. 205–22). He recounts how soon after the 1967 Occupation, senior Israeli military and political figure Yigal Allon devised a plan that permitted Israeli control over the OPT, seemingly preserving its 'Jewish nature' and democratic reputation. Provision of Israeli citizenship to Palestinians beneath Israeli occupation would have eroded the former, while, denial of citizenship, the latter. Allon's answer was to annex around 35–40 per cent of the land and to redeploy from areas of highest Palestinian population density, which subsequently would be administered by Jordan. The arrangement would allow Israel to absolve itself of the administrative and security burden of the Palestinians of the OPT, while nominally removing demographic and democratic concerns from its agenda. A key dimension to the plan thus revolved around finding or creating a surrogate governance authority to perform this role, even though Israel rejected the establishment of another state in these areas. As Achcar describes in regards to the Plan's endgame:

> Since the creation of a Palestinian state, that is, an entity enjoying the attributes of political and military sovereignty, had always been categorically rejected by the entire Zionist establishment, the three possibilities envisaged for the enclaves were to reunite them with King Hussein's Jordan, or to federate them with Jordan, or again to constitute them as an 'autonomous entity'.
>
> (Achcar, 2004, p. 213)

Over time, fuller dimensions of this plan were fleshed out in principle as well as on the ground. Allon would later endorse a version of his plan that also envisioned Palestinian self-rule via the PLO leadership, enclaved within new Israeli frontiers. 'Certainly, if the PLO ceased to be the PLO, we could cease to consider it as such,' opined Allon in 1977. 'Or if the tiger transformed itself into a horse, we could mount it. At that moment, we would deserve some headlines in our favor' (Achcar, 2004, p. 14).

Geographically, the OPT was to be fragmented with Israel controlling a frontier strip stretching roughly fifteen kilometers in width west of the Jordan River. Jerusalem would be annexed with the eastern boundaries of Jerusalem extending to the Jordan River, functionally splitting the West Bank in two. The Gaza Strip was to be connected to the West Bank enclaves, 'with rights of circulation, but without creating a corridor,' while keeping Israel's control over the Egyptian border and access to Sinai. Overall, the Allon Plan was meant to service the incremental colonization and annexation of lands and resources via settlement construction so as to physically occupy territory that Israel sought to control directly in the case of any final agreement, or otherwise.[2]

It is within these broad ideological and geostrategic determinants that the specific political economy of the Israeli state in the run-up to the Oslo process takes meaning.

Precisely because of its fundamental political determination, the Israeli economy 'could not but adhere to certain étatiste policies if it wished to see its program carried out' and hence 'has always been [. . .] highly controlled and regulated' (Kleiman, 1997). A 'military Keynesianism' developed in Israel, which tended to service what Nitzan and Bichler describe as a 'Weapondollar-Petrodollar Coalition' of oil companies, armament contractors and OPEC who accumulated capital based on perpetual cycles of Middle East 'energy conflicts' and 'oil crises' (Nitzan and Bichler, 1996; 2002a; 2002b). However Israeli military spending faced sharp cuts at the end of the Cold War, as did weapons exports, and pressures to liberalize the domestic economy mounted. According to Bichler and Nitzan, Israeli capital was also interested in the rising 'Technodollar-Mergerdollar Alliance,' based on a form of accumulation where profits derived from open markets in both goods and people instead of war and conflict. The latter alliance was based on civilian high-tech, privatization, corporate mergers and acquisitions, and entering new markets in the global South. This induced the major Israeli capital formations that had been coddled by the Zionist movement and the state since before its establishment, to seek to break from their nurtured cocoon, and integrate within dominant capital. They were however prevented from doing so because of restrictions of the Arab primary and secondary boycotts, as well as the continued existence of Israel's capital controls (Hanieh, 2003a; 2003b).

Moreover the persistence of the 1987 Intifada posed important political and moral questions for the Israeli state and its control of the OPT, while beginning to reverse what had previously been a net profit for Israeli manufacturers who treated it as a captive market (Hever, 2010, pp. 51–7). With oil prices collapsing, the decrease in Palestinian remittances from the Gulf, and declining economic conditions overall, the OPT was turning into 'a net burden' (Tuma, 1989). The accruing of these factors had already led to influential and powerful organizations like the Manufacturers' Association of Israel, representing local industrialists, and linked to the Labor Party, calling for a settlement with the Palestinians in the early 1990s, which did not exclude the possibility of establishing a Palestinian state (Honig-Parnass and Haddad, 2007, p. 34). Additionally, a group of young Israeli politicians began emerging from Zionist Left political movements demanding forms of liberalization to end the corrupt étatiste economic arrangements that had led to the Israeli economic crisis of the mid-1980s (see Razin and Sadka, 1993, pp. 26–38). According to Joel Beinin, this new economic-political tendency 'advocated jettisoning the ideological and institutional encumbrances of Labor Zionism in favor of an export-led, profit-driven economy, privatization of public sector enterprises, free-markets, and an orientation toward integration with Europe' (Beinin, 1998, pp. 23–4). This program appealed to many upper-middle-class and elite Ashkenazim who envisioned a 'modern, secular, European Israel' and yearned 'to live in a market culture of profit, pleasure, and individualism liberated from the ideological constraints of traditional Zionism and the vexing task of suppressing Palestinian national aspirations' (ibid).

The PLO

The PLO's international notoriety commonly derives from its historical association with the armed guerilla groups which compose it and their actions and links to various 'Third World' liberation movements. This image however tends to obscure a more sober assessment of how armed struggle actually fit in to the PLO's program. In fact, one of the main conclusions of Palestinian historian Yezid Sayigh's monumental study of Palestinian armed struggle is that contrary to its romanticized image as one of the preeminent guerilla movements of the 1960s and 1970s, 'the movement as a whole lacked the single-minded determination to take the practice of armed struggle to the elevated position it occupied in formal doctrine' (Sayigh, Y., 1997, p. 664). Instead, armed struggle practically served an alternative agenda, providing 'the central theme and practice around which Palestinian nation-building took place, and laid the basis for statebuilding by driving elite formation and militarization and allowing political legitimation.'

This important conclusion should not be seen in isolation from the fact that this process of elite formation was greatly influenced by Arab patron states that feared the Palestinian movement, or otherwise wished to control or influence it. Fateh was the organization of choice sponsored by the Arab states in the wake of the eruption of the Palestinian revolution, precisely because it was the most conservative, rooted in petit bourgeois nationalist politics mixed with Islamism (Achcar, 2004, pp. 129–53). Soon after the 1968 takeover of the PLO by the inchoate Palestinian guerilla factions, Egypt and Saudi Arabia rushed to support Fateh to contain Palestinian revolutionary organizing and its infectious appeal upon other Arabs, as both states found reassurance in its distinctly anti-ideological political line, and its equal rejection of class as a category of differentiation within the movement's thinking and practice. That is to say, Fateh embraced 'an explicit rejection of any inter-Palestinian class struggle perspective or political struggle against the Arab regimes' (p. 133). The fundamental unwillingness of Fateh to challenge either regional or internal alignments of power and class, masking these conflicts beneath maximalistic slogans, would inform and delimit the movement's ability to devise alternatives to its unenviable predicament.

The diasporic nature of the Palestinian leadership, which made it dependent upon host states that were at best cautious and at worst oppressive and meddling in Palestinian organizational affairs; Israel's never shy use of military tactics which exploited these contradictions, striking Arab host countries to shake their resolve toward the Palestinian cause; together with the PLO's own expressed political commitments to ingratiate the movement within the regional order at the expense of domestic reform or revolutionary movements – all created powerful inducements towards a 'stageist' approach to achieving Palestinian rights. Especially after the territorial loss of Jordan and Lebanon as bases for organizing, and after the exile in Tunis, a survivalist, pragmatist position emphasizing the need for a Palestinian state 'even on a square inch of Palestine' strengthened, quoting Fateh co-founder Salah Khalaf (Cobban, 1984, pp. 60–1). Behind this existed a 'double degeneration' of Fateh – bureaucratic and bourgeois – whereby it was so integrated into the PLO that it 'became hard to tell the two apparatuses apart' (Achcar, 2004, p. 135). The Fateh/PLO had thus become a 'state apparatus without a state looking for a state at the least cost.' The elimination of many of Fateh's top-tier political and military cadre through assassination weighed the remaining institutional leadership in favor of those with managerial and financial roles inside the movement. Mahmoud Abbas (Abu Mazen) and Ahmed Qurei (Abu Ala) – two key figures during the Oslo years – held the positions of Treasurer, and Head of Fateh investments portfolio (*Samed*), respectively.

Faucon's (2010) intriguing account of the financial history of the PLO provides insight into the degree to which Arafat exploited his dominance over finances to leverage personal control at the expense of political or ideological conviction, or a modicum of institutional democratic practice. According to one story recounted by Freih Abu Middein, a former PNA justice minister, Arafat would point to the pen he kept in his pocket before his PLO comrades saying 'This is my secret' – an anecdote referring to the cheques only he was authorized to sign (Faucon, 2010, p. 4). Although this control indeed buoyed him, it was not always enough to buy him out of the political dead ends the movement encountered. After the exile from Lebanon, Arafat was forced to increasingly rely upon the influence and power of wealthy Palestinian businessmen who could help widen his margin of maneuver.

The affluent offered Arafat forms of respectability and influence that afforded him access to wider regional and international power structures. Indeed it was these contacts that helped save the PLO in previous crises, most notably, the mediation conducted between the Nablus business-man and prominent member of notable family, Munib al-Masri, and the Jordanian regime in the wake of the 1970 Black September incidents. The same strategy was employed by Arafat to establish contact with the Reagan administration in the 1980s, via Palestinian billionaires and contracting magnates Said Khoury and Hasib Sabbagh, who had forged connections to Stephen Bechtel Sr., the son of the founder of US engineering and construction giant Bechtel, considered a 'pillar of the US Republican establishment' (Faucon, 2010, p. 71). George Shultz had been a Bechtel executive who ran the company's Saudi Arabian projects before being appointed Secretary of State by Reagan in 1982. It was this channel that was credited with facilitating the 'green lighting' of US–PLO dialogue after Arafat explicitly accepted US conditionalities regarding the 'recognition of Israel' and 'renouncing of terrorism' in 1988.

Such business connections however deepened the PLO's ties and dependency upon the existent regional order – particularly its more conservative elements in Jordan and the Gulf. The Palestinian elite had largely made their wealth providing different forms of services to these states and the Western companies they dealt with (Hanieh, 2011). Khoury and Sabbagh, founders of Consolidated Contractors Company (CCC) subcontracted for Bechtel in the Middle East, building housing and catering services for the US military after the 1990–1 Gulf War in Qatar (Faucon, 2010, pp. 71–2). The duo also formed a partnership with prince Talal bin Abdel Aziz, father of Saudi investor Walid bin Talal, and brother of King Abdullah. Munib al-Masri established the Engineering and Development Group (EDGO) that did exploratory work for Philips

Petroleum and secured lucrative contracts with Mobil Corp. in Chad, Total SA in Libya and Royal Dutch Shell PLC in Saudi Arabia. Sabih al-Masri established ASTRA which made its start providing food to the Saudi military and eventually the US army there (see Hanieh, 2011; Nakhleh, 2012).

While it is impossible to fully weigh the influence of this factor upon PLO decision making, it remains an important question to pose considering both the diminished policy space available to the PLO in the run-up to the signing of Oslo, as well as the prominence and wealth these actors enjoyed in years to follow as a consequence of their proximity to power.

The partial tethering of PLO interests to these networks would inevitably inform the course of PLO approaches to the Oslo arrangement given how neoliberal conflict resolution and statebuilding modalities generated rent allotment opportunities within a private sector-led growth model. These groupings were to form important 'investors' in Palestine Ltd., providing a national capitalist façade that seemingly enabled the management of the Palestinian question along predictable, profit-rearing lines, as opposed to 'political'/national ones.

Palestinians in the OPT

The debilitating nature of Israeli policies vis-à-vis the Palestinian economy pre-Oslo is well established in the scholarly literature with the need to highlight only a few characteristics here that have been particularly salient for the Oslo years (Abed, 1988; Arnon, 2007; Naqib, 2003, Kubursi and Naqib, 2008; Hamed, 2008; Roy, 1995). Most pertinent to recall is the OPT's overall developmental character which esteemed Palestinian economist Yousif Sayigh first described as suffering from 'heavy, far-reaching, and debilitating dependence on the Israeli economy' that was 'so special and atypical', that it 'went beyond the bounds of the dependency paradigm' (Sayigh, Y. A., 1986). Here it was not the 'invisible hand' of market forces but the 'visible hand of the occupying power' which 'twisted, distorted, and stunted' the Palestinian economy. Building off of Sayigh's insights, Sara Roy characterized the OPT developmental condition as 'de-developed' – a key term that would later gain adoption within development scholarship beyond the Palestinian setting. De-development highlighted the political and ideological determination of the OPT's economic failures under Zionist settler colonialism, as opposed to those generated from market or governance failures. It implied:

> The negation of rational structural transformation, integration and synthesis, where economic relations and linkage systems become, and then remain, unassembled (as opposed to disassembled as occurs in underdevelopment) and disparate, thereby obviating any organic congruous, and logical arrangement of the economy or of its constituent parts. Unlike underdevelopment, some of whose features it possesses, de-development precludes, over the long term, the possibility of dependent development and its two primary features – the development of productive capacity, which would allow for capital accumulation (particularly in the modern industrial sector); and the formation of vital and sustainable political and economic alliances between the dependent and dominant economies and the dependent economy and the international financial system generally.
>
> (Roy, 1995, pp. 129–30)

These features need to be constantly borne in mind in light of the neoliberal orientation of peacebuilding/statebuilding interventions and the exuberance they tended to generate internationally and even partially locally. Roy's work emphasized why Israel could not accept even the most anodyne articulation of Palestinian nationalism:

> The imperative of expanding Israeli sovereignty produced an economic policy that prioritizes integration over separation, and dispossession over exploitation. Moreover, the expansion of Israeli sovereignty also demanded the rejection of Palestinian nationalism and the weakening or suppression of those forces, largely institutional, that could promote that nationalism.
>
> (Roy, 1995, p. 117)

When it came to managing conditions on the ground, Israel's occupation entailed the imposition of a one-sided customs union arrangement over the OPT from 1967 to 1993, operationally functioning as an 'asymmetric trade scheme' (Naqib, 2003). The Palestinian economy was cut off from its Arab periphery and natural trade partners, while the cost of Palestinian capital and intermediate goods rose as a function of the four-fold increase in Israeli-imposed tariffs and convergence tendencies between the Israeli and Palestinian economies. According to Arie Arnon (2007), Israel's policies were framed by the joint yet contradictory need to prevent the division of the land into two states, and two economic (and political) sovereign entities, while also negating the possibility of creating the establishment of a single political and economic entity – 'neither two, nor one.'

Israel predictably protected its markets from competitive Palestinian goods (mainly agriculture) while dumping its excess uncompetitive export products on the captive OPT market. It also resold older generation technology to Palestinian proto-industrialists, ensuring a permanent technological and skills lag, while deepening uncompetitiveness overall.

Restrictions on Palestinian use of natural resources (particularly land and water), as well as productive sectors (agriculture and industry), while equally discouraging investment, collectively contributed to a weak private sector and the proliferation of small enterprises that were often family run. In the small industrial sector that was able to plant roots, about 40 per cent of workers were engaged in subcontracting to Israeli companies, mainly in textiles (Fischer, 1993–4). Palestinian labor was reliably plentiful and exploitable, especially amongst refugee camp dwellers, while Israel's land confiscation policies and pressures on agriculture disincentivized farming. Nonetheless, the export of mainly 'low skill' labor to Israel, together with the remittances received from 'higher-skilled' workers in the Gulf, was the main source of OPT growth until the 1987 Intifada (Boullion, 2004, p. 43).

The native OPT bourgeoisie tended to emerge from urban, semifeudal roots, with powers and legitimacy rooted in pre-capitalist modes of production (see Doumani, 1995; Manna', 1986). It responded in different ways to occupation with sections abandoning the OPT's deadend status, moving onto lucrative positions as intermediaries between Gulf and Western capital, and others staying put trying to make ends meet, be it as patrons of Jordanian influence, or as independent capitalists (with admittedly limited means).

Less privileged Palestinian social classes tended to sell their labor to Israel (usually agriculture or construction) or establish/work for small family-owned shops and businesses. Both dynamics skewed their proletarianization and prevented the crystallization or stabilization of distinct classes and class consciousness (Sourani, 2009, p. 34). Those who were 'non-Jewish' laborers in Israel or Jewish settlements fell within the hierarchy of Israeli capital-labor relations, but were excluded from Israeli political struggles, and those of its organized labor federation, the Histradrut. Those in family businesses were forced into relations of production that enforced the internalization of exploitation within the workshop/family, thereby strengthening the values and social structures that tended to reproduce and sustain these – patriarchal gender norms and tribal/clanism.

Ironically it was Israel's policies of de-development in the OPT which served to catalyze new forms of resistance to both the occupation and Palestinian notables and the class stratification they oversaw.

By the late 1980s a new political elite began to emerge from more marginalized social classes, be they villagers, refugees or members of the professional educated classes. Glenn Robinson's research is particularly instructive for documenting the social transformation and political mobilization these classes would initiate during the 1987 Intifada (Robinson, 1993; 1997a; 1997b; also see Hiltermann, 1991). He credits the political mobilization of these new classes to three structural changes Palestinian society was undergoing: the 'dramatic rise' of wage labor after 1967, which 'transfigured a basically peasant society'; extensive Israeli land confiscations; and the wide-spread availability of university education after 1972 (Robinson, 1993). All three factors 'helped to break traditional patron-client relations that had been the social base of the old elite and paved the way for the rise of a more extensive, better educated, more rural, and non-landed elite which had gained cohesion in the Palestinian universities' (ibid).

The combination of these factors prepared the ground for the mass recruitment of Palestinians into political factions engaged in social and political mobilization. Student groups, labor unions, women's commit-tees, and professional relief organizations affiliated with PLO groups as well as Islamist bodies, mushroomed by the mid-1980s. These provided organizational institutional frameworks for new identity formation, further making possible sustained collective action that would become the driving basis of the 1987 Intifada. They also became sites where cross-factional, cross-class and cross-regional constituencies could interact and influence one another while filling service-related gaps that Palestinian society suffered from as a consequence of Israel's complete neglect and the hardships created by the Intifada (Hiltermann, 1991a; 1991b).

Two major solidarity networks of European NGOs[3] working in the OPT held a major conference in Brussels with representatives from their Palestinian partner organizations, over the course of September/October 1992, entitled 'Development for Peace.' There, all facets of the OPT's 'de-development' were raised in panels and addressed by the emergent Palestinian social service provision elites. Khaled Abdel Shafi (1992), son of Gaza notable and Red Crescent Founder Heidar Abdel Shafi, then described the situation:

> The urgent need for social services in the OPT does not need detailed explanation: it is basically due to the occupation's creation of economic constraints and a heavy social burden [...]. The number of martyrs has risen to over 1,200 leaving families without anyone to support them. Moreover the number of wounded and disabled has reached more than 12,000 persons, most of whom need rehabilitation. The number of prisoners and detainees exceeds 10,000. According to the estimates of international, local and Israeli institutions, economic conditions have deteriorated considerably; income levels have decreased while unemployment has increased. In short the number in direct need of social services has increased enormously [...]
>
> (Abdel Shafi, 1992)

Abdel Shafi's words bring a sense of the palpable crisis Palestinian society was undergoing in the context of the Intifada and the inexistence of adequate support structures to meet these needs:

> In view of these factors, socio-economic conditions require the presence of a wide network of social services to provide at least minimum requirements. Scientific and accurate monitoring of needs, specifying the number of people in need of social services, where they live and the sort and amount of services they need, is a complicated task requiring detailed statistical studies. *A central institution must carry out this task.*
>
> (Emphasis added, ibid)

Indeed, Abdel Shafi would go on to chide the fact that several institutions and popular committees working in social services 'tended to follow political guidelines of political organizations', which in his view 'contradicts the social objectives of these institutions and their commitment to humanitarian services.' Scholars like Hiltermann (1991a; 1991b) and Peteet (1991) have also noted how the popular movements engaged in workers and women's organizing had strong 'nationalist' goals they wished to serve, which sometimes appeared to relegate the worker or gender rights they were purportedly organizing on behalf of. While distinguishing precisely where 'nationalist' versus 'gender' or 'worker' rights begins and ends is a political distinction equally related to tactics and strategy, these debates illustrate how the impetus to organize and 'professionalize' the service delivery functions of national political actors foreshadowed conditions that would allow for the disaggregation of these services, and the hiving-off of their technical/ service functions from a national/political agenda.

PART II

PEACEBUILDING? 1993–2000

CHAPTER 3

MODELING A RESOLUTION

A great deal of commentary on the years 1993–2000 tends to heavily weigh the importance of individuals (Rabin, Arafat, Netanyahu), how they acted, and the unpredictability of events themselves (the Rabin assassination, the eruption of the 1996 Tunnel Uprising or the wave of Islamist suicide bombings of the mid-1990s), citing these as important causes for the failure of the Oslo Accords. While these personalities and events certainly left their marks on the history of the peace process, they must be read as part of a larger historical context and tend to take attention away from far more consistent dynamics established as a consequence of the entire process' structural design and modeling. Invisible to the public spectacle of the peace process itself, a blueprint mentality heavily characterized donor approaches to the OPT. Even before the DOP was signed, donors actively worked to restructure the OPT's political economic conditions, formulating plans and justifications that permitted advancement of their consensual political agenda for the OPT.

The planning and modeling undertaken before the DOP was signed and implemented was undertaken in an effort to shape how future negotiations would take place, and how a neoliberal peacebuilding agenda could be operationalized as part of this. These plans all embodied a hubristic belief in an ability to engender and harness a political will to solve the 'Israeli–Palestinian' conflict, but one which almost exclusively focused on the Palestinian side, moving it closer to accepting the undisclosed parameters donors set for the peace process overall. In this respect, the political will donors sought to engender was not to be induced by addressing the questions of political justice inherent to the conflict itself, but instead focused on addressing its externalities, in the belief that resolutions of these questions eroded the political content and potency of the conflict from within. Moreover, the models selected began to formally institutionalize, manage and enforce the pre-existent asymmetrical power arrangement between Palestinians and Israelis, marketing this as peacebuilding. Inspired by various elements of the neoliberal development and peacebuilding mindset, the US and the World Bank used economic modeling and game theory, consciously attempting to mold and shape a Palestinian economic, political and institutional order, and the choices Palestinian political and social forces needed to make. These models were skewed to privilege certain outcomes over others and went so far as to attempt to predetermine particular winners and losers, despite these powers feigning neutrality and claiming to be engaged in a purely technical mission. Needless to say, through these models, a framework and modus operandi was established by donors vis-à-vis the Palestinians that worked to subvert rather than undergird implementation of the various international resolutions pertaining to the conflict.

Negotiations

The opening of the secret Oslo channel (organized out of a side gathering to the London round of the Madrid track in December 1992) by the Norwegian government, created the 'safe space' in which the PLO was encouraged to come forward and reveal its true positions. The PLO was penned in on three sides – the US, the Israeli and the Arab – with only one perceived direction left open for its survival. PLO negotiator Ahmed Qurei [Abu Ala] writes 'under these circumstances, we had no alternative but to go to Oslo when the idea presented itself, however unlikely or unpromising it might seem. Such a meeting seemed a last hope to keep our cause alive' (Qurei, 2006, p. 36).

Both Assistant US Secretary of State Daniel Kurtzer and Israeli negotiator Uri Savir independently confirm some of the key 'breakthroughs' in the discussions which showed strong colorations of a neoliberal peacebuilding worldview:

[Norwegian Deputy Foreign Minister Jan] Egeland called Kurtzer March 23 [1993] [. . .] to say there had been a 'major leap forward' at the recent [third] round of Israel-PLO talks. The two sides had agreed that the interim self-governing authority would have 'jurisdiction' over the West Bank and Gaza, that final status negotiations would begin in the third year of interim self-government, that Jerusalem would be excluded in the first stage of jurisdiction, and that elections under international supervision would be held within three months of a full agreement on principles.

(Kurtzer et al., 2013, p. 39)

Savir, the first standing Israeli governmental representative to personally engage on a face-to-face basis with PLO representatives in the Oslo channel, also recounts in his memoirs:

Later, in Oslo, Abu Ala would emphasize two key elements for our secret talks that impressed us: a pragmatic progression from easier to more difficult issues, which would allow for the development of trust between the parties; and Palestinian-Israeli cooperation, mainly in the economic field.

(Savir, 1998, p. 4)

One additional crucial conditionality appears to have sealed the deal, at least in the minds of the US and Israel: the agreement's arbitration mechanisms. Savir's memoires recount this direct stipulation made to Qurei:

As to outside arbitration, you [the PLO] must decide whether we are to act as partners, and solve all our differences through dialogue, or request Security Council-like arbitration and end up with a pile of resolutions that will remain no more than numbers.

(Ibid., p. 13)

Herein lies the key ingredients of what would become the DOP and which preserved US and Israeli strategic interests while reflecting a distinctly neoliberal conflict resolution modeling:

- the acceptance of a negotiations framework that separated 'political' issues from 'economic';

- the disaggregation of the conflict into 'mini-conflicts' addressed over time, and with the most divisive/fundamental of these issues, saved for later;
- the creation of an 'interim self-governing authority' to be created as an intermediary between the occupied population and the Israeli occupation, affirming an autonomy arrangement as opposed to real sovereignty, and;
- the arbitration of disputes based on negotiations between the parties, rather than through recognized international legal frameworks.

The first two elements stem directly from the core neoclassical worldview that it is indeed possible to neatly divide political and economic issues. They are linked in so far as this separation allows for the disaggregation of issues over time based on the assumption that this division allows for the resolution of distinctly 'economic' issues deemed easier to resolve, and which are believed to unblock and lubricate the political.

Element three – the creation of an 'interim self-governing authority' – specifically allowed for the devolution of tasks from the occupying powers to the new authority. As long as genuine sovereignty was not devolved however, such devolution resembled an outsourcing/ subcontracting of the Occupation's responsibilities, within an autonomy arrangement consistent with the Allon Plan – a scenario the PLO had always rejected after its initial suggestion as part of the 1979 Camp David talks.

Four, regarding arbitration: neoliberal worldviews tend to emphasize the centrality of law and judicial systems in the mediation of disputes, based upon the supposed impartiality of this system, as well as the disdain for extra-judicial means (political or social, let alone military struggle). In this case however, 'the law' was interpreted to mean not the legal framework of international humanitarian law as applicable to an area under military occupation or relevant UN resolutions,[1] but the 'law' as interpreted by and brokered through the US as the process' only external arbiter.

On Modeling

As negotiators worked out the particular structure and content of the future Accords, initiatives were being set in motion in Western states led by the US to formulate means through which the specific economic dimensions to the accord-in-making could be instrumentalized to advance the latter's overall political 'ripening' intentions. Best known amongst these was MIT and Harvard's Kennedy School June 1993 initiative, where roughly thirty Israeli, Jordanian and Palestinian economists were brought together with senior economists from the two prestigious US universities. The group attempted to theorize how an orderly economic transition to an Israeli–Palestinian accord could come about, and resulted in *Securing Peace in the Middle East: Project on Economic Transition* issued by the Institute for Social and Economic Policy in the Middle East (ISEPME and Fischer, 1994). One of the report's steering committee co-chairs was Stanley Fischer, a former vice president and chief economist of the World Bank and later head of Bank of Israel.

The report strongly reflected the neoliberal worldview of the period expressed in its working assumptions and larger policy prescriptions. The latter were based on the assumption that 'a Palestinian entity with economic sovereignty' can be established with a market economy, dominated by the private sector, that could eventually form the basis for a free-trade area between the Palestinian entity, Jordan, and Israel (see Fischer, 1994; Fischer *et al.*, 2001). It also recommended establishing a Middle East policy research institute, and a 'Middle Eastern Bank for Cooperation and Development' (MEBCD) whose goal was to develop joint Palestinian, Jordanian, and Israeli projects. Donors were to be majority shareholders (at least initially) eventually transferring this control to regional member states/'entities', 'once the bank was operating successfully' and once 'the peoples of the area learn to work together' (Fischer, 1993/94).

The Harvard-MIT proposal avoided the politically sensitive issue of Palestinian statehood though the specific Palestinian economic contributions to such a regional arrangement were nonetheless fully examined. When Stanley Fischer was later asked what the dubious term 'economic sovereignty' meant, as though such a thing could exist independent of a political framing, he answered 'we had to find a formula that would enable the Israelis to take part without a big argument about political sovereignty and that would allow the Palestinians to get involved without denying that there was more in this for them than merely the right to "run a business better" [. . .] The term "economic sovereignty" seemed a good way of dealing with the political problem we faced in getting the two sides to talk to each other about something that was clearly far more than the Palestinian autonomy that was being discussed at the time' (Fischer, 1994, pp. 53–4). Fischer's comment is instructive for revealing how such brainstorming venues were not really designed to create the space for a genuine free exchange of ideas, but were rather designed to preserve less apparent, invisible criteria defined by the political sensitivities of the US and Israel. Despite the 'peace' orientation of the exercise, mention of a Palestinian state by intellectuals was considered political leprosy by the organizers; ambitious and profitable regional engagement with or via Palestinians was however considered fair.

Moreover, the work of the Harvard/ MIT economists resonated with an incipient US vision to transform the Middle East into a free trade area akin to that established between Canada, Mexico and US in the 1994 North American Free Trade Agreement. In this arrangement Israeli and Western capital interests would be preserved and privileged through subcontracting and free trade. These ideas were also in circulation at the time thanks to Shimon Peres' vision of a 'New Middle East' (Peres, 1993). The latter had written a popular book that advocated political stability, economic development, national security and democratization forming the mutually reinforcing pillars of a regional order. Within this vision, neoliberalism could induce regional economic peace across Israel, Jordan, the OPT and Egypt, potentially forming the basis of a political peace, though without necessarily being dependent on this outcome. 'We are not seeking a peace of flags; we are interested in a peace of markets,' Peres is reported to have said (Davidi, 2000).

Modeling the Economic and Social: The World Bank

The task of how to model the OPT's institutional and economic arrangements fell predominantly on the World Bank, which would play a central role in formulating the technical solutions required of this arrangement, while respecting the invisible political agendas of its most important backers. The Bank's role (aspired and occasionally realized) was to be so involved in policy formulation, finance, technical assistance and donor coordination that it claimed knowledge superiority over the OPT and attempted to operate as a kind of shadow government to the PNA (see Kanafani and Cobham, 2007).

World Bank involvement began when it was initially asked to provide support to the Madrid Conference chair regarding 'analyses of the key economic issues and developmental challenges facing the Middle East region', upon the request of the talk's co-sponsors, the US and then USSR, in October 1991. Its role would expand in the second (Paris) meeting (October 1992) of the Multilateral Working Group on Economic Development where it was called upon to assess 'the development needs and prospects of the economies of the West Bank and Gaza Strip' – a mission it was tapped to perform by the US State Department, who described the Bank's contribution as 'critical to the success of the overall peace process' (Shihata et al., 1992/94, p. 20). The origins of World Bank involvement in the OPT together with the manner in which its work therein was legitimized,[2] and later carried out, all point to an exceptional, unique mandate that can only be described as politically determined par excellence.

The Bank sent a field mission to the OPT in early 1993 in preparation for what would later turn into its first major study on the area – the six volume *Developing the Occupied Territories: An Investment in Peace* study, published only two weeks after the signing of the DOP (World Bank, 1993, V.I–VI).[3] The Report outlines a path to reforming, reorganizing and stabilizing the OPT's economic and social balance, shaken by the Intifada, and preparing its economic integration into the broader set of regional neoliberal interests. In this way, the Report lays the parameters for Bank operations in the OPT for years to come as the US-designated lead development agency, and representative of the donor community consensus at large.

Perhaps the first thing noticed when one reads this report is how World Bank economists very obviously ignored reference to the exaggerated political determination of the OPT under a protracted settler colonial arrangement characterized by massive social and political upheaval and structural deformities and inefficiencies of all kinds. Instead the Report maintains a dry, technicist tone to its analysis and suggestions, even though its very suggestions necessarily imply resolution of political questions over the powers of the entity being created, and the areas of its jurisdiction.

The consistent yet feigned political blindness of the Bank's approach is demonstrated by the way in which it saw an economy 'in turmoil,' with four main 'structural imbalances and distortions': 'heavy dependence on outside sources of employment for the OT[4] labor force; an unusually low degree of industrialization; a trade structure heavily dominated by trading links with Israel and with a large trade deficit; and inadequacies in the provision of public infrastructure and services.' While each of these 'structural imbalances' was deliberately engineered or a de facto consequence of de-development, this is not mentioned by the Report, as the Bank was engaged in '*a technical mission*' (emphasis in original, Vol. I, p. 1). The Bank was not there to pick sides or connect any dots, given that Israelis and Palestinians already tended to 'disagree, and disagree often passionately' (ibid., p. 1). Nonetheless, the parties shared a supposed 'urgent need for stimulating economic development in the OT,' with the Bank's report aiming to build on this 'shared objective' (ibid., p. 1).

Within this vein, while the Bank acknowledges the importance of a political settlement between Israel and the Palestinian leadership, its real concern appears to lie elsewhere:

> Political settlement and peace is a necessary, but not a sufficient, condition for economic development in the [Occupied Territories]. Much will also depend upon the quality of economic management in the post-peace period and the strategic choices made in managing the OT economy. Choices on two issues will be particularly critical: the balance between the roles of the public and the private sectors in the OT; and the nature of OT economic links to the rest of the world, particularly neighboring countries.
>
> (Ibid., p. 13)

The Bank's preference was for private sector-led growth across the OPT, because 'economies that have prospered in the past have relied primarily on the private sector, working in undistorted markets, as the primary engine of economic growth' (ibid., p. 13). As for its economic links, the Bank takes as an unquestioned article of faith that 'given the close economic relations with Israel that have evolved over the past 25 years, the economies of the OT and Israel are bound to be inextricably interwoven for the foreseeable future.' The option of 'turning inwards' is hence rejected, with the West Bank and Gaza needing to 'open up opportunities elsewhere, especially with Jordan, Egypt and the Gulf countries while maintain[ing] open trade relations with Israel' as the strategy that 'would make sense' (ibid., p. 14). The Bank even goes so far as to raise the idea of a free trade area with Israel, 'linked with a significant opening of trade to Jordan and Egypt', but ends up noncommittal on this prescription.

Despite these clear neoliberal earmarks and prescriptions however, and which would maintain Palestinian economic subservience to Israel, while likely also transforming it into a conduit for markets further afield, the Bank nonetheless calls for the public sector to 'clearly have an important role to play in economic development, particularly during the transition period' (ibid., p. 13). This rather uncharacteristic prescription is befuddling, especially for the year it is written (1993), when the Washington Consensus was still in full swing.

Note carefully the wording used by the Bank:

> The upgrading of physical and social infrastructure, a key priority for improving living standards of the population and for stimulating private sector development, would have to be undertaken mostly by the public sector as private sector interest in financing such investments is likely to be limited, at least for some time. Even where private sector initiatives may be forthcoming (e.g., in some segments of health services), a sound sectoral policy framework to safeguard the interests of both the providers and users of such services needs to be established.
>
> (Ibid., p. 13)

The report provides a list of functions the public sector should undertake to enable 'a supportive business environment within which the private sector could flourish,' and which are predictably in line with the general neoliberal tendency (ibid., p. 13).

Two rationales are provided to justify Bank advocacy of some form of strong(er) public sector: first, the non-interest of the private sector in engaging in the OPT in the absence of basic upgraded physical and social infrastructure; and second, the need to ensure that a 'sound sectoral policy framework' exists, to safeguard 'interests of both the providers and users.'

The first part of the rationale is self-evident: on what basis would the private sector sufficiently move in a setting like the OPT without a Palestinian public sector ever formerly really existing,[5] and without a sufficient track record, risking its capital under enormous uncertainty and without any real guarantees? In a nutshell, the Bank rationale argues for the need to first create a framework within which an incentive structure could be 'hung' if the expectation that a private sector could be activated within it were to take place.

The second rationale – the need for a sound sectoral policy framework – is less self-evident however, and appears to directly contravene the fundamental neoclassical vision that markets themselves are best at allocating resources and services without governmental intervention.

The answer can be found in the Report itself.

The above excerpts providing the rationale for a prominent public sector role are taken from the Report's *Volume One – Overview*, which like most Bank executive summaries, generalizes the deeper discussions upon which its conclusions are based. It unsurprisingly becomes the part of the report most often read and cited (certainly when the report is six volumes). However, the rationale for this second justification is based on a discussion buried deep within *Volume Six*, having to do with the role of the public sector in relation to 'human resources and social policy.' Here the Bank is forced to engage with the reality that the Occupation's policies engendered mobilized social formations that have already engaged in service provision.

Volume Six specifically focuses on the health, education and social welfare sectors, and concludes that 'the development of a coherent policy framework and the creation of effective public sector institutions are *prerequisites* for improvements in the contributions of these sectors' (emphasis added, Vol. VI, p. x).

What accounts for this quasi-étatist bias in an era of 'less is more'?

The World Bank rationalized its position based on its field mission to the OPT, which exposed that expenditures on health, education and social welfare programs were disparate and controlled by five clusters of institutions, 'none of which' it claimed 'is either responsive, or accountable, to the entire community' (World Bank, 1993, VI, p. x). For example in the health sector, services were being provided by institutions operated by the Civil Administration, the United Nations Relief and

Works Agency (UNRWA), private voluntary organizations and private, for-profit providers. It particularly noticed that, 'people living in poorly served areas have begun to receive basic health and social services from networks of grassroots voluntary organizations that have expanded very rapidly since 1987' (ibid., p. xi). Although right after the 1967 occupation, over 85 per cent of all health services delivered in the OPT were provided by the public sector, by 1991 that figure had dropped to 37 per cent managed by the Israeli Civil Administration, and 10 per cent provided by the UNRWA. Thus, voluntary and for-profit sectors together controlled more than half of all healthcare spending. Moreover the services that the voluntary and for-profit sectors were providing were more sophisticated at times and occupied certain specialty niches. For example, roughly half of primary health care facilities were owned and managed by private, voluntary organizations. Thirty per cent of acute-care hospital beds and half of all hospitals were operated by the NGO sector. The West Bank had five privately owned CT scanners.

Although the general tendency was to act mum on the nature of these services, the Bank was aware that the grassroots organizations amongst them 'were formed in order to provide an institutional framework for securing greater Palestinian independence in meeting the need for basic health services' with each organization having 'a close tie to one of the leading Palestinian political factions' (VI, p. 24).

Here the Bank found an 'inefficiency' problem as well as one to do with 'accountability':

The institutions that supply health care, education and social welfare services have been accountable not to the community but rather to segments of the population. These institutions have obtained funds from conventional domestic sources, including general revenues, special taxes and user charges, but they have also relied extensively on foreign grants and private donations. This pattern of funding has led to uncoordinated efforts; overspending on capital equipment in some sectors and underspending in others.

(VI, p. 51)

The Bank's sudden concern with 'uncoordinated efforts' is noteworthy when considering how its overall approach advocates for market allocation, whose essence is fundamentally uncoordinated.

Moreover, the concern for 'the lack of a broad sense of accountability to the public' is also worth highlighting considering what was then a 25-year military occupation. It lumps together the health service provision of the Israeli Civil Administration – which failed to add even one hospitable bed since 1967; those of UNRWA – whose basic health care provision to more than 940,000 registered refugees operated on a $20 million budget for 1991 – roughly twenty dollars a head; and the work of voluntary NGOs, who at least made efforts – and succeeded – to more than double the number of primary health care facilities serving in the OPT over the six years since the beginning of the Intifada – with all these statistics gleaned from the Report itself.

The Bank's answer to the 'inefficiency' and 'unaccountability' problems however lies in 'the development of a sound policy environment' and the creation of 'a responsible body [...] to develop a coherent health policy and to coordinate activities in the sector' (VI, p. xv). The role of this body was to 'not seek to control sector activities directly but rather should seek to achieve greater coordination.'

The second basis for a Palestinian public sector is hence laid. A 'responsible body' was needed to coordinate policy and give it coherence. But around what basis or set of policies? Here the Bank is not entirely clear. It does however recommend:

> The creation of institutions that are more accountable to their clients, governed and operated under transparent rules, and equitable in their treatment of all residents of the area. These changes will have to be erected around institutions that provide for participation by the affected public and that are *seriously accountable, either through the market or through a political mechanism.*
> (Emphasis added, VI, p. 51)

No evidence of a precise agenda is provided, however a disciplinary element to the equation has been inserted in the form of the need for 'serious accountability', either via markets or a political mechanism. 'Markets' would appear to be a way of saying that social service provisions must be reformed to meet the need for efficiency and accountability. If sufficiently developed they could presumably create entirely new institutions, or force existing ones to operate more 'accountably', via being forced to provide better services. A 'political mechanism' can be introduced to either impose forms of legal conformity/coordination over recalcitrant, inefficient, or 'political' organizations, or by providing the services itself. In either case however, the need to hold in check service provision through a combination of policy tools appears to be the main motivation.

What is not self-evident from the manner in which these recommendations are presented however, is that neither technique to enforce 'serious accountability' has the ability to arise organically from the existing political context of the OPT. Both marketization and developing the tools of an enforceable political mechanism required explicit forms of external intervention — financial stimulation, political consent and technical provision — which collectively were believed to induce the 'accountability' so desired.

'Markets' for health care provision could hardly be created without substantial external inducement embodied in generous financial provision to existent or competing/potential providers. A proficient institutional and legal edifice to ground and regulate either new players or reform the old would equally be needed. Likewise, the use of a political mechanism ('a responsible body') would clearly require Israeli and international approval.

Collectively such an arrangement would thus give those with the power to facilitate, regulate and control the creation of 'markets' or 'a political mechanism' an invisible power of leverage, should they choose to use it. It is precisely this power to operate on the meta-framework of the Palestinian context that would give Israel and Western donor states the most powerful and determinative of hands in the narrowing or widening of all Palestinian developmental sectors. While the technicist language in conformity with neoclassical economic arrangements assumed perfect market conditions, in fact it was international donors and Israel that maintained the ability to doubly filter the forms of power and subsequent margins of policy space Palestinian enjoyed.

While traces of a political agenda to these policies are already inferred through these 'technical' prescriptions, the Bank cannot avoid but making recommendations that reveal a more explicit political agenda. This is seen for example, in the Bank's final prescriptions regarding the role of the responsible bodies and the end game of the coordination process. Assumptions about the jurisdictional and political parameters of politically sensitive topics such as the Palestinian refugee issue are revealed in the Bank's description of the role of the 'responsible [public sector] body' as serving, among other functions to 'seek to interrupt the link between refugee [. . .] and entitlement to subsidized health care' (VI, p. xv):

> Access to free or highly subsidized services (including health care, subsidized housing services and assistance in the education of children), now available only to registered refugees, should be extended to others on the basis of relevant criteria, rather than refugee status. At present large numbers of people maintain their refugee status simply in order to remain qualified for these programs in the event of a personal economic crisis.
>
> (VI, p. xx)

Here, the Bank's prescriptions advocate the creation of a public sector to play a role in facilitating a process that could lead to a reduction in the number of registered, self-identifying refugees by blurring the entitlements associated with such a status vis-à-vis other social groups. As the Bank's logic goes, many refugees only maintain their own refugee status because of a *quid pro quo* of subsidies and entitlements. The Bank thus ignores rights-based concerns to do with the fact that these communities fled or were forcibly transferred during wartime, and have since been denied their right to return to their homes because of the exclusionary basis of Zionism and Israel. Rather than call for the return of refugees as required by international law and UN resolutions however, or for the liquidation of this entitlement overall – something that would further destabilize the conditions in the OPT – the Bank calls for a more general depoliticization of the entitlement regime by making these services available to all 'on the basis of relevant criteria.' The Bank infers that the equalization of entitlement provision could lead to lessening the amount of those who update their refugee status, thereby disempowering this issue's numerical potency. The implicit assumption here is that improved living conditions can abrogate political rights.

To clarify and sum up these recommendations: the Bank called for the creation of a public sector to act as a direct service provider and coordinator of other providers to regulate unregulated, unaccountable, political grassroots organizations. It also foresaw this public sector playing an inhibitor-like role to one of the fundamental issues of the

Palestinian-Israeli conflict – the issue of Palestinian refugees. Both recommendations equally require time to realize their ends – to align and make accountable the former (service provision actors), and to lessen numerically the latter (the refugees). And all this while feigning non-intervention in political matters.

In this way, the Bank attempted to reduce social pressures on a Palestinian leadership negotiating delicate political questions like the right of return of Palestinian refugees. In so doing, aspects of the conflict's fundamental issues of contention up for negotiations – borders, settlements, water, Jerusalem – were being gerrymandered across time, before being tabled. That the World Bank would presage such a strategy before it even established offices on the ground, or the PNA was even created, hints at a heretofore unacknowledged role of Western donors and IFIs in the conflict. Under the guise of peacebuilding, conflict resolution and development, IFIs and other donors intended to influence political outcomes through their intervening in the socio-economic dimensions of Palestinians in the OPT, while Israel worked to strengthen its geostrategic and settler colonial agendas.

Here we also see buds of what would later be a consistent hallmark of World Bank practice across the OPT over the years: identifying issues based or related to the conflict – in this case, refugee protection, social provision and entitlement; attempting to isolate its economic dimensions (in this case, in health, housing, education) from its political ones (the right of return, the right to housing, protection etc.); followed by efforts to mollify the former (in this case, through generalizing entitlement via 'markets' or 'political mechanism'), while disregarding the latter (leaving it to the asymmetry of power in the negotiations process).

Such tactics would be consistently used by the Bank and many donor agencies, throughout the course of their work in the OPT, mirroring the neoliberal vision that political issues could be disappeared through market mechanisms. This is ultimately expressed by the Bank as it articulates its preferred blend of 'markets' versus 'political mechanism', in the third to last paragraph of the entire study:

> In view of the political complexity of the area, many political mechanisms are not likely to be workable; hence, markets and competition should be given greater attention than is customary.
>
> (VI, p. 51)

With the tone of parting words of advice, the Bank recommends that Palestinians not raise their expectations too high regarding the extent of the powers of their future political regime. It is unclear what criteria the Bank considers certain political mechanisms 'workable' or not, nor why it feels the need to make such a remark in the context of its 'technical mission.' Nonetheless, the Bank's role, as far as its paymasters are concerned, would appear to have been accomplished. A combination of 'markets and competition' and a 'political mechanism' (with weight to the former) can be effectively relied upon to bring about forms of economic stability, raised standards of living and integration into regional neoliberal visions. Between the two, the disciplining and aligning of social movements takes place, while the inhibiting of potentially thorny political questions is strengthened. To do this, a form of artificial external inducement is necessary to initiate and enable these processes, with the Bank positioning itself to undertake this role as primary coordinator of PNA start-up funding, and eventually recurrent budget costs.

Modeling the Political – USAID

The above example illustrates how the international consensus of the donor community activated through the World Bank couched political ends in an obtuse economic discourse.

Donor interventions foresaw exploiting their advantageous financial positioning to manipulate or realize certain economic and governance outcomes. While teasing out these motives and outcomes entails delicately reading between the lines of the Bank's reports, more explicit evidence of manipulative donor intention can be found in a series of USAID documents that expose efforts to model the OPT's political arena and how to structurally advantage or disadvantage its various actors (USAID, 1993a; 1993b; 1993c; 1996).

Modeling OPT political outcomes could not be publically disclosed because it violated donor neutrality and was formally argued to be something left to the contending parties to determine. The Israeli and Palestinian leaderships were supposed to work out the extent and scope of Palestinian political powers and where and when they would be exercised – a main reason why the DOP left the question of statehood and borders to final status negotiations. Spelling out any particular political scenario in advance would destroy the 'deliberate ambiguity' built into the accords (Benvenisti, 1993), and only too obviously reveal questions of power and political imperatives. This nonetheless did not stop the US government from privately exploring what scenarios best preserved its interests, and in which way. An 'investment in peace' of this scope was not going to be left to chance or even 'markets', especially in an era of US unipolar hegemony and in a geographical area of such strategic significance.

One of the ways it did this was through the USAID Democratic Institutions Support Project (DIS) of its Near East Bureau, a subproject of its Governance and Democracy Program (GDP). The latter's nominal purpose was to 'strengthen the political and legal institutions which underlie democratic governance' (Miskin, 1992, pp. 33–4). However it specifically articulated a concern for 'the relationship between political and economic liberalization, and the challenge of supporting processes of democratic institutional reform that will further economic liberalization objectives' (ibid).

DIS contracted Chemonics International to analyze the political economy of specific Middle Eastern countries, 'developing country action plans/strategies and ultimately, designing country activities' (USAID, 1993c, p. 1). Individual academics were then hired to write up these analyses. Little scholarship and few primary source materials are available discussing the GDP program or DIS' work in the OPT in particular (see Miskin, 1992; 1994; USAID, 1993a; 1993b; 1993c; 1996). After reading those that are, it is not surprising to understand this dearth in primary sources, considering their politically sensitive nature. Concerns over how to identify 'winners and losers' from reforms, or 'how interest groups could act collectively' or 'form coalitions with each other' illustrate a serious attempt to understand what makes political and social formations 'tick', both amongst supporters and opponents to the US agenda (USAID, 1993c, p. 6). DIS' 'Political Economy Reviews' were intended to provide the starting analytical basis for GDP programming given 'that the risks of making a mistake in this sensitive technical area were particularly high in the Arab world, and that the costs of such mistakes to USAID programs and to US interests more generally could be serious' (ibid., p. 7).

DIS commissioned two 'institutional assessments' (USAID, 1993a; 1993b) for the OPT designed 'to give USAID background on the political affiliations of the many NGOs with which the Agency works in the Occupied Territories, to analyze their institutional capacity, and to present potential institutional outcomes of several different scenarios for autonomy' (USAID, 1993c, p. 9).

Both reports were written by Glenn Robinson[6] of the Naval Postgraduate School, and were acknowledged in a Chemonics annual report to have 'provided helpful background information to those officials whose responsibilities greatly increased in the wake of the Rabin-Arafat handshake' (USAID, 1993c, p. 10).

The more interesting of the two reports for our purposes is 'Palestinian institutional configurations in the West Bank and Gaza under four autonomy scenarios', dated May 1993 (USAID, 1993a).[7] Despite the perspicacity of its analysis, the report appears not to have aroused any previous scholarly attention. The study, 'not for distribution' and 'not to be quoted', for 'discussion within USAID' and 'not necessarily representing the views or interpretations of USAID or the US government,' is nonetheless a remarkable look into how the US government attempted to conceive of fundamental power dynamics in the OPT, exploring how different scenarios neutralized or empowered existent social constellations. Unlike the previous World Bank report whose public nature, 'technical' mandate and 'economic' orientation results in a cautious yet couched language, the internal nature of this document leads to more explicit political analysis and conclusions.

Robinson quickly identifies the major Palestinian institutional clusters in the OPT and their alleged factional associations (including Fateh, the Popular Front for the Liberation of Palestine (PFLP), the Palestine People's Party (PPP), two wings of the Democratic Front for the Liberation of Palestine (DFLP), and Islamists), together with those of Jordan and Israel (see USAID, 1993a, p. 8, Table I).[8] This overt identification of the factional affiliation of Palestinian organizations is no small matter considering that Israeli military orders made such affiliations illegal and subject to the closure of these organizations and the imprisonment of their staff.

He then assesses that the 'autonomy period will be highly political' given that 'virtually all meaningful institutions in the West Bank and Gaza are clustered around particular political interests which seek to influence or control Palestinian society' (ibid., p. 6). The real struggle of the period will hence be fought amongst existent politically organized and tied institutions, rather than with foreign NGOs, UN institutions, and non-partisan charitable associations.

Based on an implicit Gramscian-like understanding of political organizations engaged in wars of position and movement in their efforts to seize state power, Robinson then applies a form of game theory, exploring what would happen in the OPT if two variables were manipulated under the autonomy scenario-to-be: the speed of its implementation (slow versus rapid) and the extent of autonomy implemented (full versus limited). He then constructs a matrix charting the possible scenarios and characterizing them, elaborating on their implications and pay-offs, given that 'each of the four autonomy scenarios would create a different pattern of institutional "winners" and "losers" because each would create a different set of political winners and losers' (USAID, 1993a, p. 24, Table II).[9]

Robinson defines 'full autonomy' as 'an arrangement which gives Palestinians authority over virtually all spheres of administration, including land and water use; in other words, a nearly sovereign state in all but name' (USAID, 1993a, p. 22). Its alternative was to limit autonomy powers 'to certain municipal functions, devoid of a national authority, and applied exclusively to people, not land.'

The speed of autonomy devolution would also have significance for an institution's strength given that 'certain institutional clusters will be rewarded and others hurt by the type of autonomy actually agreed upon.' The report reckons that because institutions differed in the levels of their centralization and grassroots connections, 'as a general rule, the more slowly an agreement is implemented, the more likely would be the centralization of institutional power by a national authority undermining local institutional power' (USAID, 1993a, p. 23). Within this basic framework, Robinson draws up his assessment for the winners and losers of all possible scenarios (ibid., pp. 25–33). His conclusions are remarkable in light of what would eventually play out between Israel and the Palestinians throughout the course of the Oslo Accords.

Robinson's analysis makes clear to US administration officials that the US and Israel were in a powerful position to pick the winners or losers of any political agreement struck, by manipulating its speed of implementation and the extent of autonomy devolved.

For instance, these powers had the ability to encourage an arrangement that would foster institutional pluralism had they selected the devolution of 'full autonomy, rapidly implemented.' Such an arrangement would have 'inhibit[ed] the consolidation of institutional power by denying Fateh the necessary time to starve its competitors of resources' (ibid., p. 27). The existent 'institutional vibrancy outside of Fateh would, in effect, be politically "locked in" by a quick transition.' Such a scenario would seemingly have been the most democratic and reflective of existing power balances.

Alternatively, Robinson assesses that the US had the power to fully empower Fateh by providing 'full autonomy, slowly implemented.' Such a scenario would have allowed Fateh to strengthen its position vis-à-vis other political factions because it would have the 'space and power necessary to consolidate its own position through vastly enhanced patronage resources which are sure to follow any agreement' (ibid., p. 25). Prolonged transfer of authority would 'give Fateh the necessary time to bring grassroots institutions under centralized (i.e. Fateh) control', while 'more locally-based, decentralized institutions would be gradually starved of resources, and thereby made increasingly marginal.'

However the Oslo Accords and the manner in which matters played themselves out between 1993 and 2000 – whether by design, or circumstance – were closer to Robinson's other two models: the 'institutional paralysis' and 'Millet' models.

'Limited autonomy, rapidly implemented' would result in Palestinian 'institutional paralysis', because it would freeze existent institutional arrangements. Unable to 'break the back of the decentralized grassroots organizations' because of the rapidity of the agreement's implementation, Fateh's 'dominant – if beleaguered' positioning would result in the organization 'immediately seek[ing] to consolidate its position through a program of institutional centralization' (ibid., p. 30). The result would see it seeking 'to bring Jordan on deck as a junior coalition partner in order to enhance its political position.' Robinson recognizes this to be a development 'viewed positively in Washington, Tel Aviv and Amman,' and hence 'must be considered the most likely one.'

Despite this external approval however, Fateh was equally likely to 'be harshly criticized by other factions', and could 'split its own ranks for accepting such a deal' (ibid., p. 30). 'Institutional gridlock', 'political infighting' and even 'civil war' are all seen as the arrangement's likely fallout (ibid., p. 2).

The final scenario imagines an arrangement based on 'limited autonomy, slowly implemented', which was believed to produce a scenario akin to what Robinson describes as the Ottoman-era 'Millet system.' The latter 'provided religious minorities administrative autonomy over many of their own religious and civil affairs, but denied these groups any independent political power or sovereignty' (ibid., p. 32). If Palestinians were only gradually granted restricted authority over municipal functions, 'overall authority would clearly rest with Israel and, to a lesser degree, Jordan.' Robinson predicts that this scenario would elicit 'near total' opposition, and 'one would expect a continuation of the Intifada if it were implemented.' He even notes that 'Israel would be less constrained in its handling of the Intifada because of the implied acquiescence of the Arab states and the US in the arrangement' (ibid., p. 32).

While there is no question that what Israel devolved to Palestinians under the DOP and other subsequent agreements was a 'limited autonomy' arrangement, given Palestinian restricted access to land and water, what complicates the application of Robinson's model to the reality eventually created during the Oslo years is the issue of the arrangement's speed.

In the case of the Gaza Strip, the speed of implementation must be considered 'rapid.' The PNA was allowed into the Gaza Strip first in 1994, and the scope of its jurisdiction there (even if restricted) was left virtually unchanged thereafter.[10] Gaza hence was closest to Robinson's 'institutional paralysis' model, which saw that 'civil war is possible.'

In the West Bank however, the speed of implementation was more protracted. The various agreements struck between 1993 and 2000 made the devolution of autonomy there 'slowly implemented'[11] and hence closest to the Millet system expected to lead to 'continuation of the Intifada.'

Robinson's models however never anticipated that these institutional arrangements could be applied *in different ways to different territories*, further enhancing the US and Israel's powers to select winners and losers locally under different institutional arrangements.

The fact that US policy makers were well aware that the very structure of the accord they supported and helped engineer would likely lead to a hybrid situation akin to the institutional paralysis and revised Millet system models Robinson describes – with Israel and Jordan as its institutional winners; and with the knowledge that these policies had a good chance of leading to civil war and/or an intifada – all before one accord was even signed, one suicide bomber was detonated, or Rabin's assassination took place – begs the critical re-examination of US policies, intentions and historical narrative during this era.

There are other remarkable insights this document acknowledges that have significance for what later transpired. The institutional composition of the OPT was marked by disparities in basic organizational competencies. While for instance, the Palestine People's Party (PPP) is characterized as having 'the oldest and best developed institutional structure in the West Bank' (p. 25), and the institutions of the PFLP are characterized as being 'potent' and having a 'capable, decentralized grassroots presence' (p. 14), Fateh is seen as having 'a relatively weak set of institutions' (p. 9) as a function of its 'emphasis on patronage and personality-driven politics.'

The eventual channeling of aid through Fateh by donors thus affirms that Western states led by the US, consciously selected the *least* institutionally competent and accountable organizations to support, while excluding those considered more competent. Moreover, their enabling of the institutional networks most reliant on 'patronage and personality-driven' agendas – Fateh and Jordan – can be described as facilitating an overall policy turn that encouraged political atavism. In this manner, international support to Fateh and the upgrading of its institutional power and capacities should be seen as a step backwards from the advances made during the 1987 Intifada, which, as previously noted, had led to the rise of social and political formations that strongly rebelled against the traditional patron–client relations that characterized the social base of the old elite, and which Fateh would inevitably reach out to so as to consolidate its base. In this respect, international donors can be credited with encouraging a form of reverse-development, in the sense that they consciously sponsored forces whose power was based on re-establishing and deepening patronage networks previously shed or broken.

Moreover, Fateh could be relied upon to attempt to marginalize the gains of the more progressive, institutionally-based social formations (as opposed to those that were personality-based), while equally drawing upon patronage networks linked to Jordan.

Robinson:

There is a close relationship between Jordan and the conservative wing of Fateh. Fateh may well seek to use Jordan as a balance to both leftist factions of the PLO and Hamas, and Jordan would seek to use Fateh as a tool to politically 're-enter' the West Bank.
(USAID, 1993a, p. 18)

While the 1987 Intifada greatly eroded the vestiges of Jordanian designs on the West Bank, resulting in King Hussein's 1988 'disengagement' renouncing political claims to the territory, Jordan nonetheless retained important influence across the OPT. In addition to control over select Islamic institutions, particularly in Jerusalem (the Waqf), Jordan was also the seat of one of the West Bank's main banks (the Cairo-Amman Bank), controlled by Sabih al-Masri from the notable al-Masri family in Nablus, and operational in the West Bank under a 1986 *pre*-DOP Jordanian-Israeli agreement. It was also the institutional base for a clique of elite Palestinian families termed the 'King's Palestinians' whose rise was attributed to the generosity of contracts in the quasi-private sector, thanks to their loyalty to the regime (see Bouillion, 2004, pp. 38–40).

Thus, via tri-prong penetration in the West Bank – Fateh's right-wing orbit; Islamic institutions; and powerful historical families tied to commercial enterprises on both banks of the Jordan River – Jordanian influence was positioned for strengthening. Needless to say, the Allon Plan had always envisioned a form of Jordanian tutelage.

Finally, it is worth noting that Robinson's report assesses the OPT's Islamic movements as maintaining a 'far weaker institutional presence in the West Bank and Gaza than any of the major PLO factions' and with their organizations 'generally not well-suited for development' (USAID, 1993a, p. 17). After describing Hamas' 'modest institutional network in the areas of health care and education', it equally notes the absence of an organizational presence in agriculture, industry and finance. He thus concludes 'the Islamic movement does not have an institutional framework for the promotion of economic development, and thus could not efficiently use development aid during autonomy' (ibid., pp. 17–18). Hamas is thus not seen as a serious competitor to Fateh, though its popular support could nonetheless 'certainly inhibit the transfer of power to Fateh during autonomy.' Robinson's accurate assessment of

Hamas' institutional strength at the time illustrates how the explosive conditions generated by the Oslo framework subsequently led to a tremendous growth in its institutional network, political relevance, and social penetration.

To sum up these findings more generally, the above examples from the World Bank and USAID disclose critical insights regarding the nature of Western donor interventions in the OPT before the DOP was even signed. They illustrate the decidedly political biases of these actors in an attempt to control and steer the process that was about to unfold, while suggesting that the DOP framework and implementation was the product of well-researched plans that articulated broad goals and how to achieve these institutionally. While a considerable amount of critical scholarly attention of the Oslo process has focused on Israel's actions – and international inactivity – this chapter has attempted to highlight how the policy formulations of the international donor community complimented and informed Israeli tactics and strategies, while also bearing substantial responsibility for the reality that unfolded.

Donors were wedded to a distinct neoliberal worldview to conflict and conflict resolution and saw the integration of the Israel/Palestine reality into global capitalism and its geopolitical exigencies as determined by the US. Assembling the necessary information, plans and socio-political dynamics was thus seen as necessary to achieving these ends, requiring clear interventions and framings of the OPTs political economy. The ideas and plans formulated and circulated, equally reflected the contradictory theoretical and practical elements characteristic of neoliberalism more generally. Palestinian governance structures promoted by donors were to be shaped by both centrifugal and centripetal forces: the creation of aspects of a strong public sector which could centralize, coordinate, align, discipline and coerce; and a decentralized, weak, non-state, dominated by regionally integrated markets, foreign powers, and institutional paralysis locally. Moreover the conscious effort to reverse-develop the OPT's socio-political culture and behavior, without addressing the fundamental political determination of de-development, must also be noted as a prominent characteristic of the planning/modeling impetus overall.

CHAPTER 4

THE VOYAGE:
NEOLIBERAL PEACEBUILDING
IN PRACTICE 1993–2000

The government is committed to an interim solution, because, let's face it: if we shall decide today to cut a permanent solution, we shall have to turn to the maps. And under the present climate, I do not see a possible agreement on a map. So we have suggested, instead of having a permanent map, we have a transitional voyage from the present planet to a new planet, and that the voyage has a calendar and it shouldn't last more than five years.

Shimon Peres (MFA web, 1993)

Shimon Peres' frank acknowledgement that Palestinians and Israelis did not see eye to eye on many of the issues in the peace process sounds honest, while his suggestion for a staged transition to peace negotiations, reasonable. Impressions of the Israeli–Palestinian conflict as deeply rooted historical and religious struggles reinforce liberal Western sentiments to approach conflict resolution there cautiously and sensitively. However a more critical look at Peres' quotation suggests the existence of nagging questions lurking behind seemingly commonsensical framings: the 'transitional voyage from the present planet to a new planet' he describes – how was such a journey actually to come about? Who was to navigate and according to which roadmap? Who pays, and where does the voyage end? How are the decisions around these questions to be determined?

Previous chapters have suggested that Israel had longstanding ideological motivations and political objectives vis-à-vis the OPT and its population, and that these were already operationalized in a worked out plan. They have also suggested that Western donors embraced their own ideological and political affinities, and attempted to advance these agendas by embedding them in policy design and modeling. This chapter will explore how these models took shape on the ground and to what effect.

The 'transitional voyage from the present planet to a new planet' was to rely on the roadmap of neoliberal peacebuilding to do the navigating. Israel was also the power determining which pathways this voyage was permitted to travel down.

In principle, this was an experimental journey into the neoliberal imagination and its utopian assumptions about the presumed mechanistic workings of market forces and their ability to solve political questions – in this case, questions rooted in deep-seated political grievances stemming from settler colonialism, ethnic cleansing and the continued denial of national self-determination.

In practice it was a journey into Israel's world of elucidating the boundaries of its own economic, political and ideological contradictions, and the neocolonial dimensions to this process. It was also a journey into the contradictions of the theoretical and practical divisions of neoliberalism itself, as manifest in the gaps exposed between the international commitment to the values it claimed to uphold, and the exclusivist, violent and repressive reality it helped deepen.

Overview of the Structure, Character and Practice of Neoliberal Peacebuilding 1993–2000

Before delving into the specific policy context of the OPT, it is worth first clarifying that any notion of a singular 'neoliberal conflict resolution' or 'peacebuilding' paradigm should be abandoned to avoid speculating that there is a robust intellectual or political cohesion and teleology to the project of neoliberal conflict resolution overall. Even though neoliberal ideas inspired the overall impetus of the peace process and informed the architecture of its conflict resolution/peacebuilding modalities, it was ultimately the dominion of donors and governments to interpret and enforce these ideas according to their interests, while doing so under specific political and power arrangements and hierarchies. Although there was considerable overlap between Israel and the donor community regarding how the peace process would operationally function and towards what end, important discrepancies existed between and within them, and would prove significant as matters progressed.

Here, note should be made that no mention of a Palestinian state was explicitly endorsed by the international donor community as the end game of the arrangement during this period. The donor community lacked consensus on this issue, and shied away from adopting a formal position on this matter beneath the justification that it was beyond their jurisdictional purview, would pre-empt political negotiations and anger Israel.

International policies during the Oslo years (1993–2000) thus cannot be described as 'statebuilding', but should more appropriately be classified as (neoliberal) peacebuilding. The distinction is important because it meant that rather than donors focusing on what they disagreed on, they poured their resources and energies into what they were agreed upon: establishing a Palestinian authority and assisting with its design, training and funding. A total of $3.622 billion would be disbursed by all donors during these years (1994–9)[1] towards this end, of which $2.775 billion was disbursed in development aid (Fischer *et al.*, 2001). The US was the single largest donor (about 15 per cent), followed by the European Union as the largest bloc of donors (combined, about 42 per cent). Japan would contribute an additional $369 million, evening out the US, Western Europe and Japanese contributions at more than 70 per cent of all aid received. The remaining 30 per cent came from Arab countries (roughly 8.5 per cent) and funds including the UN system, and other donor countries (ibid. Also see Brynen, 2000, pp. 113–60; Taghdisi-Rad, 2011, pp. 11; 67–87; Le More, 2008, pp. 84–110).

The unanimity of political will amongst donors to establish a 'Palestinian Interim Self-Government Authority' for the Palestinian people in the West Bank and Gaza Strip, as the DOP put it, was no easy task considering the state of the OPT after the 1987 Intifada and the 1990/91 Gulf War. As the World Bank would later note, attempting to defend itself against internal critics:

It needs to be borne in mind that at the time of Oslo, there was no Government: no Ministry of Finance, no Ministry of Education, no

Ministry of Health. Virtually everything had to be started from scratch [...]. There were thus huge gaps [...] that our Palestinian counterparts and the donor community sought the Bank to fill.

(World Bank, 2002a, p. 65)

Of course it is not entirely accurate that the World Bank was 'starting from scratch,' considering the existence of the Israeli Civil Administration, the work of UNRWA, the existence of the PLO bureaucracy, and the work of the popular committees which had formed during the Intifada, organizing Palestinian communities particularly in health and education sectors. The exaggeration should be seen as an attempt in part to justify the World Bank's aspired role as the preeminent international development institution of the Oslo years.

As recounted previously, Western donor governments and IFIs under US leadership essentially instructed the World Bank to assume control over economic planning, laying down the broad policy guidelines of Palestinian development. As Nabil Sha'ath, the PNA's first Minister of Planning would note in an interview, 'Palestine in the peace process, was economically somehow given to the World Bank. When I first came in, I found that there was a World Bank mission that was working with PECDAR [the Palestinian Economic Council for Reconstruction and Development – the World Bank-established entity to coordinate donor aid (*see below*)], and that the mission had a total plan for Palestine that excluded Jerusalem, that excluded any terrestrial infrastructure [...] We could not build roads, we could not build any connectivity' (Sha'ath Interview).

While this role would meet significant opposition from the Palestinian side in the early years, the World Bank remained a key institution to the overall donor arrangement. A 2003 World Bank publication would look back at its then-ten-year involvement in the OPT and describe it as 'a role more central [...] than in any other major post-conflict situation before or since' (Schiavo-Campo, 2003, p. 9). As the first Secretariat to the Ad Hoc Liaison Committee[2] – the complex aid coordination structure of the peace process – it would engage in everything from research, design, oversight, evaluation, finance, coordination and mobilization of resources to the OPT, primarily to the PNA, though also to the private sector and to international and local NGOs. As one World Bank report put it, assessing its own work, 'donors constantly relied on the Bank for intellectual leadership' (World Bank, 2002a, p. 65).

Aside from this leading intellectual role, the World Bank Group[3] administered $270 million on behalf of other donors through the Holst Fund, financing recurrent and start-up costs of the PNA; established a Trust Fund for Gaza and the West Bank (TFGWB) financing 22 projects totaling $326 million, and mobilized considerable additional donor financing (ibid., p. 1). By 2005 it had spent 6 per cent of all funds dispensed in the West Bank and Gaza (WBG)[4] since 1993, and administered an additional 14 per cent on behalf of other donors (World Bank, 2005a, p. 5).

The World Bank's experience in the OPT would also be internally credited for laying the groundwork for the formulation of the Bank's own post-conflict reconstruction policy (World Bank, 1998).

Given this complex role and positioning within the international donor aid practices of the Oslo years, it is fitting that a good portion of the examples used herein derive from its policies and practices.

Instrumentalizing the Liberal Peace

The backroom hatching of the DOP and the political compromises it entailed, invited harsh criticism from prominent Palestinian nationalist figures who understood the significance of its implications. 'Let us call the agreement by its real name: an instrument of Palestinian surrender, a Palestinian Versailles,' quipped Palestinian intellectual Edward Said (Said, 1993). Countering this image of surrender became important for the Western donor community, given what must have been their own understanding of and appreciation for the fact that the deal was won under extremely asymmetrical conditions that were almost existential for the PLO, and indeed did incorporate significant political and strategic compromises on the latter's behalf. Creating a guise of the genuine conflict resolution and peacebuilding nature of the process unfolding was thus important for generating support from Palestinians, Israelis and the international community. Towards this end, the most significant counter to this critique invoked by the international community and the parties themselves (Israel and the PLO) thus came from promoting the fact that the DOP embodied a 'liberal peace' paradigm. These powers argued that the establishing of a functional central governance entity, which respected democratic practice and liberal economic approaches represented the exercising of the full spectrum of liberal values, and was the best opportunity for peace and security.

Liberal political praxis was enshrined in the September 1995 Interim Agreements which called for 'direct, free and general political elections' for a legislative council such that 'the Palestinian people in the West Bank and Gaza Strip may govern themselves according to democratic principles' (Chapter 1, Article II, Elections, also see Annex II). Once formed, the Palestinian Legislative Council (PLC) held regular sessions between its two headquarters in Ramallah and Gaza City, where parliamentarians (with salaries paid for by the EU) drafted legislation, including laws that·attempted to safeguard various human and civil rights.[5]

International promotion and financing of liberal and democratic political values was not restricted to support of this nominally democratic entity, but extended to aid given to a wide array of civil society organizations, and those that directly engaged in democracy promotion in their political or service agendas. Total aid to the 'civil society' sector throughout Oslo totaled roughly 15 per cent of total aid given to the OPT (IMF, 1999).

The World Bank would also partner directly with Palestinian civil society organizations. Its Palestinian NGO Project (PNGO) gave grants to smaller NGOs providing social services and was the 'first such arrangement of its kind for the Bank.'[6] The project distributed $42 million to the Palestinian NGO sector over two phases, and claimed the project to have been so successful in fulfilling its goals ('reaching more than 213,000 beneficiaries, compared to the projected 50,000') that it subsequently ran two more phases. Although the issue of Palestinian NGOs and the elites these organizations generated, tangentially relates to this study, it cannot be addressed in any serious depth here, while already the subject of some recent research (see Challand, 2009; Da'na, 2014).

Such activities in any case certainly bolstered the image that the Oslo process and its international support intended to facilitate liberal political praxis, decentralization and political pluralism.

Equally so, the development and policy literature of international donors was rich with the promotion and facilitation of principles and projects of free market capitalism and private sector development.

Consistent with the neoliberal globalization narrative of the era and its 'New Middle East' zeitgeist, Annex III and IV of the DOP outline a series of major local and regional economic and development programs intended to be activated within the 'Marshall plan' understanding of the peace process.[7] These included Israeli–Palestinian cooperation in finance 'for the encouragement of international investment'; cooperation to 'encourage local, regional and inter-regional trade'; and feasibility studies for 'creating free trade zones in the Gaza Strip and in Israel', with 'mutual access to these zones, and cooperation in other areas related to trade and commerce.'

Several of the World Bank's programs would also explicitly focus on promoting the private sector, whether in terms of the Gaza Industrial Estate, major tourism development projects, or an investment guarantee scheme to provide guarantees against political risks (see Part III). An important 1997 legal development program would spend $10 million to set up 'a legal framework adequate to support a modern market economy and encourage the growth of the private sector' while 'increasing the efficiency, predictability and transparency of the judicial process' (World Bank, 1997c). According to the project's justification, 'the existing legal frameworks in the West Bank and the Gaza Strip are generally recognized as not fully adequate to support a market economy, let alone a modern one.' As such 'many of the laws in the WBG are in need of modernization and would constrain the ability of domestic firms to achieve regional, let alone international, competitiveness.'

During the Oslo years, the World Bank was especially caught up in the neoliberal euphoria of the 1990s, with a particular excitement regarding the presumed *tabula rasa* nature of the PNA. A 1997 publication captures this uncritical atmosphere:

It is no longer just a theory that the private sector is the key to prosperity. It is a fact, demonstrated during the past few decades by the ability of the private sector to achieve miracles in adapting to the demands of a globalizing world economy. However, success hinges on the ability of the state to define appropriately its role and actions within the process of development, allowing the private sector to realize its potential.

For most countries, achieving this is not straightforward. Governments spend years and considerable resources disentangling themselves from the legacies of the past. The Palestinians, though facing many hurdles, are fortunate in not having to deal with the legacy of a command economy, a welfare state, or an inflated public sector.

By providing the right enabling environment, the public sector will pave the way for the private sector to lead the Palestinian economy into a better 21st century.

(World Bank, 1997f)

Encouraged by the world's development institutions, PLO Chairman Yasser Arafat would make his own euphoric statements, declaring how 'with continuous effort we will work to make Palestine economically the Singapore of the Middle East, and proud home of investment and successful businesses' (quoted in USAID, 2002b).[8]

Hidden Agendas

While the liberal peace model may have served as a powerful image to win international and domestic support, especially in the early Oslo years, identifying static indicators like elections or the existence of certain financial and commercial codes as evidence of a liberal political and economic praxis is superficial. It overlooks crucial questions regarding how these policies fit together within the larger peacebuilding model under activation, which strongly conflicted with liberal political and economic values and practice.

The DOP and subsequent accords however would not promote a liberal peace and this was largely known in advance by Israel, the main donors, and the PLO leadership. Rather, the neoliberal peacebuilding model in operation distinctly sponsored and fostered illiberal tendencies by the PNA in the social, political and economic spheres, which were consciously supported for political ends by Israel and donor governments.

Parts of this story are well known already. The Interim Agreement's call for a 'strong police force' (Article XII) or Rabin's call for the Palestinians to 'rule by their own methods' were all early indications of the suppressive nature of the authority envisioned, which was identified early on by the critical scholarship (see Achcar, 1994; Said, 1995; and Usher, 1996, p. 74). In this regard, this research shall deal only passingly with the illiberal military/security aspects of the Oslo arrangement.

Equally well disclosed are aspects of fiscal corruption, off-budget accounts, monopolies and cronyism that the Arafat regime engaged in, which the international community was quick to draw attention to after the outbreak of the Al-Aqsa Intifada, demanding institutional reform and good governance. In truth, Western donors and IFIs began actively pressuring the PNA to reform in the late 1990s, perhaps most formally through the publication of the Council on Foreign Relations' (CFR) European Commission-financed 'Rocard Report' whose executive summary notes:

> The Palestinian Authority must make extensive changes to ensure good governance – including a participatory political system, a pluralist civil society, sustainable development, and a free market economy – during transition to a permanent settlement and beyond. Among other measures, the report urges that the Palestinian Authority adopt a constitution, establish accountability for the executive branch to the legislature, centralize all public revenues and expenditures in the Ministry of Finance, encourage devolution of programs and projects not related directly to the conduct of the presidency to appropriate ministries and municipalities, and ensure the independence of the judiciary.
>
> (CFR, 1999, p. 3)

What is less known is that the PNA's 'corrupt' ways were first seen as a necessary asset by the international community. As former US ambassador to Israel Martin Indyk would later put it, '[t]he Israelis came to us and said basically, 'Arafat's job is to clean up Gaza. It's going to be a difficult job. He needs walking-around money,' because the assumption was he would use it to get control of all of these terrorists who'd been operating in these areas for decades' (CBS News, 2003). Employment in the PNA, kickbacks, and payoffs were some of the means of the patronage system Arafat built, which only he had the legitimacy to construct under such political conditions (continued occupation and settlement construction, autonomy etc.).

Israel facilitated this arrangement by collecting and then depositing PNA fuel revenues in a Tel Aviv bank account only accessible to Arafat and his trusted financial investor, Mohammed Rashid (aka. Khalid Islam) (see IMF, 2000). Internationals played their part in this arrangement by facilitating start-up costs overall.

Thus the Rocard Report's call for PNA reforms was in fact an early attempt by the international donor community to contain and process rising domestic concerns for these practices, which also began to be publicly revealed as a consequence of the 1997 PNA Comptroller General report and a PLC report of 1998 (JMCC, 1998). In this respect, it was an attempt to constructively 'improve the efficiency and credibility of the emerging Palestinian self-governing institutions',[9] and should be read as such, rather than a full-blown excoriation of PNA practices, which would come later. Indeed as Raja Khalidi insightfully notes, '[p]rior to the year 2000, the international community was careful not to rock the PNA governance boat too hard so as not to compromise the much trumpeted "economic dividends of peace" widely seen as central to the success of the Oslo process' (Khalidi, 2005). Despite the knowledge (and partial facilitation) of financial mismanagement and corruption, this did not prevent donors from pledging $3.3 billion to the PNA at the Washington conference of donors in November 1998 for the coming five years (IMF, 1999, p. 39).

Scholarship has failed to examine Western donor contributions to these practices, through their peacebuilding activities. However even what appeared to be bonafide peacebuilding projects are revealed to be heavily steeped in intricate political calculations designed to service particular agendas that were generally left unwritten. In truth, a good deal actually appears to *have* been written, although this was understandably not fully disclosed at the time, or requires a sensitive reading of the material released. Additionally, recent years have seen the release of further material from these years, that has henceforth escaped sufficient academic exploration. The point here is to stress that the modeling and implementing of a working political, social and economic arrangement, embodied in an intra-Palestinian political settlement and elite bargain, was not something left to chance by these forces, but was equally something that could not be fully publicized. In this regard, international efforts would attempt to reproduce previous Israeli and Jordanian efforts at elite creation/manipulation, albeit this time through the Palestinian political and economic leadership and aid/occupation structure. Evidence of this can be deduced by critical examination of the coded writings of the donor community itself and a forensic excavation and cross-referencing of its policies, programs and realities.

Here it is helpful to begin at the end of this period (the year 2000) where donors contemplated what would then amount to be their collective failures. The Palestinian economy had drastically under-performed compared with the World Bank's initial hopes, impoverishing Palestinians and making the notion of a 'peace dividend' ring hollow. Of the six scenarios elaborated upon in the World Bank's 1993 *Investment in Peace* report, the results were invariably worse than the worst-case scenario.[10] Six years after the DOP's signature, the OPT's GDP per capita had declined by almost 8 per cent, with senior IMF economists describing OPT growth performance as 'disappointing' (Fischer *et al.*, 2001).

Critical scholars were more blunt. Writing in 1999, Sara Roy commented:

> The years since the Oslo agreement have seen a marked deterioration in Palestinian economic life and an accelerated de-development process. The key features of this process have been heightened by the effects of closure, the defining economic feature of the post-Oslo period. Among its results are enclavization, seen in the physical separation of the West Bank and Gaza; the weakening of economic relations between the Palestinian and Israeli economies; and growing divisions within the Palestinian labor market, with the related, emerging pattern of economic autarky. In the circumstances described, the prospects for sustained economic development are nonexistent and will remain so as long as closure continues.
>
> (Roy, 1999, p. 64)

Whatever its characterization, Western donors needed to assess the causes of the OPT's dysfunctional economic state during the Oslo years and what to do about it. To this end, the World Bank and the government of Japan jointly produced an important aid effectiveness study to assess the donor community's collective work after the interim period came to an end, and on the eve of Camp David negotiations (World Bank and Japan, 2000). Its conclusions are insightful as the report is forced to reveal the criteria by which donors measured the effectiveness of their aid. Here it quotes the Organization for Economic Cooperation and Development's (OECD) Development Assistance Committee's (DAC) 1997 *Guidelines on Conflict, Peace and Development Cooperation* (OECD/DAC, 1997), which emphasized the centrality of donor assistance in supporting 'political progress towards peace' in areas undergoing war-to-peace transitions:

> On the one hand [donor aid] is intended (as in other contexts) to foster sustainable social and economic development. On the other it is also intended to support political progress towards peace [...] While it may sometimes be difficult to articulate and analyze, this 'peacebuilding' objective must form the cornerstone of all development co-operation strategies and programs.
>
> (World Bank and Japan, 2000, p. xi)

Remaining in the realm of the conceptual, the report emphasizes the 'particular (often country- and time-specific) requirements of promoting peace':

> The peace and conflict impact assessment of development projects differs from 'evaluation' in the conventional sense because its scope extends far beyond the stated output, outcomes, goals, and objectives of conventional development projects or programs. Rather, it attempts to discern a project's impact on the peace and conflict environment – an area it may not have been designed explicitly to affect. Thus it is quite possible that a project might fail according to limited developmental criteria [...] but succeed according to broader peacebuilding criteria.
>
> (World Bank and Japan, 2000, pp. 5–6; citing
> Bush, K., 1998, p. 2)

Inching towards disclosure of the political intentions of its aid, the World Bank quotes yet another OECD/DAC report underlining 'the need to recognize the highly political aspects of developmental assistance in such contexts':

> Aid managers need to face up to the political nature of all aid. This involves recognizing that perceptions matter as much as facts in aid impacts; that who gets which piece of the cake is usually as important as the total size of the cake; that efficiency may sometimes need to be traded for stability and peace; that the development discourse can be used for many political purposes; and broadly, that process is as important as product.
>
> (World Bank and Japan, 2000, p. 6; citing Uvin, 1999, para 8)

In this rare deviation from an 'apolitical', 'technical' posturing, the report finally outlines in minimalist form, the peacebuilding objectives the donor community accomplished, which the Bank evaluates as 'positive':

> slow[ing] the overall economic decline, contribut[ing] to economic growth, and strengthen[ing] key institutions and local capacities. In doing so, donors have contributed to political stability, thus helping to sustain continued Israeli–Palestinian negotiations.
>
> (Ibid., p. xx)

At first glance, the aims of political stability and sustaining negotiations may seem reasonable peacebuilding agendas, even when recognized as more 'political' than 'developmental.' But as Nu'man Kanafani and David Cobham point out, this actually represented a *shift* of the specific criteria/indicator of evaluation of the Bank's *initial* objectives:

> The international community feared that the economic crisis (which resulted from the political failure) would lead to the eventual collapse of the peace process. Therefore, avoiding a human tragedy and preserving the structure of the PNA were the top priorities. This means in reality that the overall aim of foreign assistance to the WBG has actually shifted over time, from the provision of a peace dividend to the avoidance of collapse.
>
> (Kanafani and Cobham, 2007)

This shift exposed the logic and rationale behind Western donor intentions who led the peace process. Without a viable PNA, there could be no negotiations, no peace settlement, no stability, no dividend. It thus was the essential cornerstone uniting all donor policy, including Israel, which was included within the donor structure because it collected and released Palestinian custom revenues. Israel drew the 'red lines' to the PNA's economic, geostrategic and civil powers. The internationals, accepting of these limits, and accepting of Israel's ability to define them, were to catalyze neoliberal peacebuilding by providing direct support to the PNA, attempting along the way to mold its character, inclinations and performance.

CHAPTER 5

THE ENFORCER:
STRUCTURAL DETERMINANTS
OF PALESTINIAN POLITICAL
ECONOMY: THE ISRAELI
CONTRIBUTION

It has already been suggested that the atmosphere of congeniality, hope and historical compromise between former enemies depicted in the famous image captured soon after the signing of the DOP on the White House lawn on 13 September 1993, was contrived and ahistorical, masking a more duplicitous and even Machiavellian arrangement. Though it might appear especially harsh to describe Israeli and donor approaches to the conflict with such incrimination, it is difficult to escape such assessment when a critical reading of this period is undertaken, with the added insight of historical perspective and the declassification of formerly confidential material.

Even the image itself fails to disclose the serious gaps in trust that existed between the parties until the very last moment the DOP was signed. According to Mahmoud Abbas' personal memoir of events, up until the very last *half hour* before the signing ceremony took place, the US and Israel apparently tried to trick the Palestinian delegation into signing an agreement that did not mention the PLO in the document's preamble, instead replacing it with the 'Palestinian team in the Jordanian Palestinian delegation' (see Abbas, 1995, pp. 205–16).

In the memoir's second to last chapter entitled 'The Surprise', Abbas recounts the 'final hours before the signing ceremony' as written-up by Hayel al-Fahoum, a member of the Palestinian delegation in Washington and director of the West European Section at the PLO Political Department. Quoting al-Fahoum, the copy of the DOP to be used for signing on the morning of the signing ceremony, had the words 'Palestinian team in the Jordanian Palestinian delegation' as the Palestinian party mentioned in the accord's preamble. The Palestinians refused to sign and even refused to leave their hotel rooms until it was changed to read 'Palestine Liberation Organization.' After early morning consultations, Shimon Peres agreed to substitute the former wording for 'The Palestine Liberation Organization.' The Palestinian team then left the hotel for the White House. When Abbas went to check the final draft half an hour before the planned signing ceremony to begin at 11 a.m., the revised draft *again* did not mention the PLO, but only 'The Palestinian delegation.' Only after a second round of arguments was the 'Palestinian Liberation Organization' added to the document, first as a handwritten amendment co-signed by both sides, and then, in a revised printed copy (see ibid., p. 236).

Given that recognition of the PLO was one of the main reasons why the organization signed the DOP in the first place – representing one of Israel's few political concessions mentioned in the document itself, vis-a-vis the Palestinians and their leadership – this last minute maneuver sharply contrasts with the photogenic appeal of the signing's media portrayal. It should also be seen as Israel holding on to its long-held vision to impose Jordanian influence over Palestinian politics and governance, and is consistent with Robinson's previous forecasting.

The above anecdote may in fact be more broadly consistent with other aspects of how the DOP and later agreements were negotiated and implemented.

Israel was a tenacious negotiator that enjoyed crucial advantages over its adversary in virtually all respects, ensuring the agreements it signed upheld these powers without recourse to external forms of arbitration or counter-leverage.

For 26 years prior to the DOP, Israel controlled the OPT's land, water, economy, geostrategic positions, resources and people. It gathered extensive (and exclusive) intelligence on all of these and used it in various settler colonial endeavors ranging from material exploitation of natural resources to political subjugation of the indigenous population. Thus when it came time to delineate its priorities and devolve specific civil, economic, administrative and security responsibilities to an emergent Palestinian authority, it clearly had the upper hand over the PLO, and leveraged its power and knowledge asymmetry at the negotiations table.

Negotiations were not simply a diktat. Indeed the DOP did embody an exchange of needs between the parties. What Israel possessed militarily, geo-strategically and economically, it lacked politically – an air of legitimacy to its settler colonialism, and the consent of the occupied population and great parts of the world community that saw it as usurper and colonizer. Alternatively, what the PLO had politically – a hard fought legitimacy of representation – it lacked in power, geographical positioning on the ground and financial backing.

The accords thus assumed the character of a delicate exchange whereby Israel selectively relinquished direct (and costly) military and civilian administration of Palestinian concentrations, for the purpose of erecting a controlled, limited self-governance autonomy model. In doing so Israel intended to win a proxy administrative and 'security' enforcer, paid for by the international community, and time to initiate new waves of settlement expansion. Israel's control over Palestinian lives would no longer be reliant upon 'old-fashioned' techniques of direct colonial oppression, with its complications of 'shooting and crying' (see Beinin, 2005), but were undergoing a significant but delicate restructuring, outsourcing considerable portions of its responsibilities to the Palestinian authority-to-be.

It is this exchange which lay at the heart of the DOP and satisfied the minimal needs of both sides: the preservation and ability to expand Israel's Allon Plan and settlement impetus, and the PLO's survival and reconstitution in the OPT after years of displacement, with the belief in the open-ended possibility that the fate of Palestinian rights was yet to be determined.

Negotiations and their architecture were an uneven playing field that the international community uncritically tolerated and never fundamentally questioned. Formal negotiation procedures ensured Israel's final veto rights in all disputes, albeit couched in a series of procedures that reproduced the same characters, parties, interests and positions. The DOP determined that all dispute resolution was to be resolved by negotiations through a 'Joint Liaison Committee' composed of equal numbers of Palestinians and Israelis. Their decisions were to be reached by agreement. Disputes that could not be settled through negotiations could be resolved, 'by a mechanism of conciliation to be agreed upon by the parties' (DOP, Article XV). The DOP added that the parties could agree to submit to arbitration for matters 'which cannot be settled through conciliation' but in this case as well, the Arbitration committee, will be to the agreement of both parties.' As the Israeli government and the PLO came to agreement on security, economic matters and civilian affairs, the same structure of dispute resolution was essentially replicated under different names – the Joint Civil Affairs Coordination and Cooperation Committee, the Joint Coordination and Cooperation Committee for Mutual Security Purposes, the Joint Water Committee, and the Joint Liaison Bureau (at 'border' terminals).

Thus, a hierarchy of self-referential and clearly deterministic fora were created that enabled Israel to be its own decider and enforcer, with little the PLO could do about it without leaving the arrangement in toto.

Azmi Shu'aibi, former mayor of El Bireh, Legislative Council member and important reform figure, used the following metaphor to describe the arrangement in an interview:

> Oslo was like going to the Turkish bath. First you take off your clothes in the first chamber and give them to the man at the desk. Then you go into the next chamber, to wash, and the next to steam, and then massage etc. But if for some reason you feel like you don't like the process and want to leave, it's not like you can decide to do it, just like that. The attendant still holds your clothes.

Precisely because the process of attempting to reconstitute and mold the PLO into an administrative/security proxy could only take place in the context of Israel devolving specific administrative and 'security' duties on particular geographic locations, the process assumed the character of Israel negotiating *with itself*, with the Palestinian presence in negotiations and even ultimately on the ground, functioning in many cases as merely symbolic. In fact this is precisely how Shimon Peres described the negotiations of the Paris Economic Protocol (PER) which delineated economic relations between Israel and the OPT: 'In some ways we are negotiating with ourselves' (Ha'aretz, 14 February 1994, cited in Murphy, 1995, p. 36).

This pattern was replicated in dozens of different sites bureau-cratically and on the ground and would inform how Palestinian social classes, particularly its private sector, would adapt to the Oslo years. Though the PNA had some means of governing, it was Israel that was understood to be the real power that Palestinian society needed to mediate.

Consider, for example, the issue of how Palestinians were to exit to Egypt or Jordan – a fundamental test for building (or breaking) the Palestinian sense of the right to travel in freedom and dignity as a consequence of the peace accords.

The 1995 Interim Agreements (Annex 1, Article IX) dictated that Palestinians wishing to travel to Egypt or Jordan via land were to pass through a Palestinian counter at the crossing terminal for the purpose of having their documents and identity checked by a Palestinian official, 'according to a procedure promulgated by the Manager of the Palestinian wing' (Interim accord, Section I, 2). The Palestinian official would then pass the documents to an Israeli official 'via a drawer installed for that purpose.' The passenger would then 'wait in front of the Palestinian counter' until 'the documents shall be checked by an Israeli official without unjustified delay,' and would include the Israeli official 'also check[ing] the passenger's identity indirectly' – a task conducted previously by the Palestinian official. The Israeli official would then return the documents to the Palestinian official who would then return them to the passenger, including a white card denoting whether the passenger had the right to pass. The passenger would then be directed to the exit of the Palestinian wing 'where he will then hand over the white card to a Palestinian official,' who will then 'pass the white card to the Israeli official,' who in turn 'will allow the passenger to pass if the card is valid.'

When seen in this light, it is not difficult to understand how many of the bureaucratic and institutional structures created by the Oslo process added a second layer to what most Palestinians already perceived as an over-bureaucratized, illegitimate system, ultimately based on Israeli prerogatives and brute force. Moreover, the creation of this second layer was seen by many Palestinians – certainly in circumstances like the one described – as in the best case, redundant, and in the worst, embodying the potential for predation by particular interest groups linked with the networks that ran it. The Oslo process after all created clear distinctions regarding the 'lock-in' and 'lock-out' taking place – politically between those who supported the accords and those opposed; and economically between those who would benefit and those disenfranchised, based on their proximity to power and political decision making. It even created distinctions within those locked in, through the creation of a 'VIP status,' and further created distinctions within the VIPs, creating three separate categories (Interim Agreement, Section I, 4).

The creation of a profusion of sites where a process of preferential differentiation could take place, first by Israel and then by the Palestinians, should be seen as a major feature of the peace process regime. Beneath the banner of Palestinian national representation and administration lurked the creation of a hierarchical intermediary, bureaucratic body that represented an infrastructure or apparatus in which interests of various forms could be hung and leveraged through various formal and informal institutions and networks. The history of the peace process would hereafter become a history of the struggle of contending forces over the character and alignment of the political, economic and power interests embedded within this apparatus, which of these were dominant, and what ends they would serve.

Israel's role in shaping the character of the PNA must be understood as emerging from the extent of military, geographic, political and social control it was able to create and leverage over the Palestinians through the various accords. Here it is beneficial to quickly mention Jeff Halper's analysis, which neatly compliments our description of the constrictive regime that the peace process established, reminding us how Palestinians lacked the means to mediate or mitigate this leverage from external forces (Halper, 2000). For Halper, Israel was establishing a 'matrix of control' that immobilized Palestinian life into an elaborate three-tier set of interlocking mechanisms. These included active, forcible measures of control (arrest, trial and torture, administrative detention, extensive use of collaborators and undercover army units); more subtle control mechanisms deriving from 'facts on the ground' (land expropriation, settlements, by-pass roads and the concomitant bureaucratic/territorial divisions of Areas A, B, C in the West Bank, areas H-1 and H-2 in Hebron, Yellow, Green, Blue and White Areas in Gaza, closed military areas, Israeli controlled industrial parks, aquifers, religious sites, army bases and 'open green spaces'); and yet even more subtle bureaucratic or 'legal' mechanisms (including 'closure', 'master plans' around settlements, and the permit system, preventing freedom of movement, family reunification, work, travel, local or international study, and building permits.) This list illustrates the comprehensive nature of the physical, social, economic, and institutional leverage Israel held over the Palestinians, achieved and tweaked by the reality created by the interim arrangement (also see UNOCHA, 2010a).

Halper sums up the matrix of control as akin to the Japanese game of 'Go':

> Instead of defeating your opponent as in chess, in Go you win by immobilizing your opponent, by gaining control of key points of a matrix so that every time s/he moves s/he encounters an obstacle of some kind [...] The matrix imposed by Israel in the West Bank, Gaza and East Jerusalem, similar in appearance to a Go board, has virtually paralyzed the Palestinian population without 'defeating' it or even conquering much territory.
>
> (Halper, 2000, p. 15)

The Economic Enforcer

The formal military, geographic and bureaucratic dimensions of the regime established by the Oslo Accords were essential compliments to the regime's economic aspects, which are particularly revealing for our study.

Large amounts of literature have been generated on the Paris Protocol on Economic Relations (PER), though those of the United Nations Conference on Trade and Development (UNCTAD) stand out for their consistency and perspicacity (UNCTAD, 1994; 1996; 1998; 2004; 2006). It is also quite remarkable to read a UN institution describing the PER as having never been 'the right framework for underpinning a sovereign economy' and constituting 'a hostile basis for rebuilding a war-torn Palestinian economy' – quite a strong position for a body of its kind, and indicative of the fact that economists at UNCTAD were only too aware of the PER's limitations, and from early on (UNCTAD, 2009).[1]

The PER allowed Israel to formalize the one-sided customs union that it had imposed over the OPT since 1967. It did this by ensuring that Palestinian tax collection and customs duties on Palestinian imports would be aligned with Israel's regime. In doing so, it entrenched and codified a lopsided arrangement advantageous to Israeli economic interests in the context of Israel's own liberalization, ignoring the structural differences and levels of development between the two economies. The Palestinian economy effectively became linked to Israel's rights and obligations under the World Trade Organization 'without enjoying any of the benefits of these agreements' (UNCTAD, 2009). OPT markets would soon be flooded with cheap commercial goods, further inhibiting productive sectors, entrenching trade as the largest economic sector, and dependency on Israel overall.

The PER also functionally put a series of key macroeconomic policy tools out of Palestinian reach, which could have been used to protect, direct and stimulate their own economy. As UNCTAD would note, 'fiscal, monetary, exchange-rate, trade and labor policy instruments necessary to design and implement effective, coherent and integrated policies to achieve sustainable and equitable economic development,' were denied to the Palestinians (UNCTAD, 2011b). This, on top of the fact that Palestinians were prevented from accessing their human and natural resources freely.

These, and a host of other disadvantages, flaws and fiscal leakages,[2] have led scholars like Adel Zagha and Husam Zumlot to describe the arrangement as allowing 'Israel to develop aspects of both integration and containment,' facilitating what Khan describes as a regime of 'asymmetrical containment' (Zagha and Zumlot, 2004, p. 120; Khan, 2004, p. 49). Israeli control over Palestinian tax collection and trade ensured that the Palestinian trade regime would be aligned with the Israeli trade regime (integration) while Israel still retained control over the power levers over the OPT's physical movement and a good part of its fiscal streams (containment). 'By ensuring that the Palestinian economy could be hurt in an asymmetric way by Israeli decisions, the Israeli state ensured that the Palestinian economy remained in a state of sustained vulnerability' (Khan, 2004, p. 49).

In this context a reasonable question emerges regarding Israeli motivations for these policies and the accords more generally, beyond the security/administrative proxy role of the PNA. Was it all just a ruse? To what extent did Israel seriously envision the possibility of a Palestinian state, or at least Palestinian–Israeli or Arab–Israeli economic projects that were not just about domination, but encompassed aspects of sharing and cooperation within a neoliberal framework?

Framing Israel's role strictly as an 'enforcer' indeed overlooks and flattens significant political and economic behavior that was not just about rejecting Palestinian development. Clearly under the Rabin government, significant and major joint development projects were proposed and considered by both sides with active support and participation of the international donor community and the Arab states. These early (pre-Netanyahu) projects expressed a vision of the neoliberal globalizing Israeli classes who pushed them on and were instrumental in creating the forward moving momentum that helped win over significant sections of Israelis and the international community to support the peace process.

The problem was however that Israel was able to fulfill significant aspects of these interests without negotiations at all. Moreover, after various domestic 'blowback' (both Israeli and Palestinian) surfaced as a consequence of the accords and their implementation, the incentive to realize a broader peace with the Palestinians eroded both socially and even amongst the elite which had supported it.

Although a deeper study of Israeli intentions during the Oslo years lies beyond the scope of this study,[3] a revealing interview carried out with top Palestinian negotiator Dr. Nabil Sha'ath was able to shed light on some historically ignored dimensions.

As a top figure in the PLO and Fateh, and as then Minister of Planning and International Cooperation (MOPIC) from 1994 until 2003, Sha'ath was party to the highest level discussions with Israeli counterparts at a moment when the Rabin administration and the political and economic forces behind it were heavily vested in the globalization rhetoric and Shimon Peres' 'New Middle East'. Sha'ath described an early 1990s meeting with then Minister of Energy Moshe Shahal that captures important yet marginalized aspects to Israel's motivations during this earlier stage of the peace process:

> [Shahal] tried his best to create a relationship with me when I first came in. He came with a Rabin proposal: 'Let's share the energy trade, the energy industry and energy transportation.' 'What do you mean?' I said. 'There is going to be peace,' he said. 'You are not going to be happy if we simply use that peace to get

back the pipelines through Haifa from Saudi Arabia and from Iraq [which were built by the British and stopped operating after the establishment of Israel in 1948]. So I'm suggesting that we go together to the Arabs to share fifty-fifty, the export of gas through pipelines that come to Gaza and to Ashdod. They are closer in Gaza and Ashdod than Haifa, and Haifa is already a very busy port. So we get pipelines from Saudi Arabia. You get 50 per cent exported out of Gaza [and] 50 per cent of [what's] exported out of Ashdod. We are now negotiating with the Egyptians, setting up a major refinery in Alexandria. We'll split our share and you take 50 per cent of it. If you want any petrochemical industries, it will be developed through Arab-Israeli cooperation. We share the ratio you want. And we set up a joint energy board that would devise energy policies [...]

Israel up till this moment – 1994 – was still fuelling all of its power stations with coal, coke, imported from Australia. And therefore, replacing coal with gas became very important. Where would you get the gas from fairly economically? There isn't, except in the Arab world. [...] Despite all the promises [former Egyptian president Anwar] Sadat made, he could not deliver one drop of the Nile's water to the Israelis. But the Israelis thought that with energy they could develop cheaper desalination. Therefore, water and energy were linked through energy, and that's why they thought of these mega projects like the Red-Dead sea and Dead-Med[4] – all of these were basically to bring about water through energy [...] To Rabin it looked like the Palestinian Authority was a very necessary component for seeking water and energy from the Arabs.

(Sha'ath Interview)

Israel's energy and water concerns tend to be sidelined or forgotten as part of the scholarly mix of factors lying behind Israel's intentions and behavior during the peace process. But they deserve to be centrally re-inserted in light of Sha'ath's quotation, considering later Israeli moves in energy and water-related spheres.

Israel and Egypt would sign an agreement to lay a gas pipeline only two months after the DOP was signed (November 1993), dubbed the 'peace pipeline' between El-Arish and Ashkelon, and which eventually became operational in 2008 after much delay.

Israel would also sign a preliminary contract with Qatar for the supply of $2 billion worth of natural gas in 1995, a week before the assassination of Rabin (November), though this would never materialize (Miller, 1995).

James Stocker's research on the politics of oil and gas in the eastern Mediterranean is instructive for laying out additional major developments in this sphere, which have emerged since the 1990s when the dynamics of Oslo were in full swing (Stocker, 2012). According to Stocker, the discoveries of the 1990s made the region stand 'to become one of the world's most important sources of natural gas over the next half century,' with at least 122 trillion standard cubic feet (tscf) of natural gas (US Geological Survey, 2010). The reserves are conceived of as not only serving as a source of energy to regional residents, 'but potentially for those of Europe and other areas' (Stocker, 2012).

Natural gas was discovered off the Gaza coast in 1999 after British Gas (BG) was awarded a 25-year exploration license from the PNA. Two wells, Gaza Marine 1 and 2, were drilled yielding an estimated 1.4 tscf (see Abualkhair, 2007, p.2210). Part of the deal with BG entailed Israel receiving the surplus for its power stations, once Palestinian demand was met. Israel however refused to pay market price, deadlocking matters between the developers and Israel, resulting in BG eventually walking away from negotiations in 2007 (see Kattan, 2012). The amount of gas discovered off of Gaza was seen as able to cover Palestinian needs for 15 years, and was expected to supply 10 per cent of the energy requirement of Israel (Offshore Technology web).

Things changed when Israel discovered gas of its 'own' in the Tamar gas field (January 2009) and the Leviathan field (December 2010), with 8.4 and 16 tscf of reserves respectively – quantities considered good enough 'to solve Israel's energy problems for the next several decades,' according to Yossi Langotsky, an instrumental figure in Israel's search for gas (Sasson, 2010). The Tamar field began producing gas in 2013, while the Leviathan (with larger quantities) remains to be developed, with the operation likely to be complex and expensive (Kattan, 2012).

Since June 2012, Israel has also been extracting natural gas from the Noa field located in an area that may be subject to claims by Palestinians and which could be exhausted before an agreement is reached (Stocker, 2012). The US Sixth Fleet regularly patrols the areas of exploration, with the US company Noble Gas heavily involved in works. The Noble Consortium – a US–Israeli consortium (led by Noble Gas) developing Tamar – is considered the 'biggest winner' of Israel's gas finds so far (Sasson, 2012).[5]

Attention to advances in Israel's water supply are also significant to note in light of the gas discoveries. The Israeli National Water Strategy of 2004 would foresee expanding water supply by 25 per cent through desalination over a decade (Dreizen, 2004). With rising assurance in energy supplies, Israel proposed establishing five major desalination plants along the Mediterranean coast intending to provide 505 million cubic meters of water a year in 2013 (a goal met) and 750 million cubic meters a year by 2020 (Tal, 2008; Israeli Water Authority, 2012). This decision was made in part thanks to technological advances that have 'radically altered the water situation in Israel' dramatically lowering costs of desalination from one dollar per cubic meter to around forty cents – savings that 'will grow further thanks to the use of Israeli natural gas instead of electricity to power the plants' (Elizur, 2014).

As water specialist Mark Zeitoun noted, 'the desalination of seawater is today poised to significantly alter the hydropolitics of the region' (Zeitoun, 2008, p. 61). These advances have essentially meant that 'there is now a surplus of water in Israel, thanks largely to the opening of several new desalination plants – and the development of natural-gas fields that can power them cheaply' (Elizur, 2014). Interestingly, according to Elizur, Israel has avoided publicizing this major improvement in its water security, 'for political and economic reasons' (ibid).

In light of Israeli proposals around energy, Sha'ath's interview also highlights what some political economists on the Middle East have already noted – the economic *non*-complementarity between Israel and the Arab world (see Tuma, 2000, pp. 87–91).

Israel is not really after the consumer goods industry [as was assumed (and feared) by many Arabs to be one of the reason why

Israel sought peace – to enforce regional economic hegemony].
Israel cannot compete with Japan, China, Thailand and Turkey on
[production of] consumer goods [. . .] Israel has, because of years of
boycott by the Arabs, changed its economic trade direction. And
so, it is not interested in the Arab market.

(Sha'ath Interview)

'Not interested' may be an exaggeration, as we shall see in the following
chapters: with roughly five million Israeli consumers to 240 million
Arabs as of the early 1990s, the opening of regional trade would be to
Israel's advantage in terms of consumer markets. However, Sha'ath is
correct in so far as this overlooks a series of significant impediments to
the implicit functionalist assumption that a 'peace dividend' would
emerge and be shared through regional trade.

Elias Tuma shows how even if free trade were established between
Israel, Jordan, Egypt and the OPT, the only evident complementarity
between their economies would be in energy supply, labor and
technology (Tuma, 2000). Egypt however, is already selling surplus
energy to Israel; labor supply – abundant across Egypt, the OPT and
Jordan – is governed by military and political factors rather than
economic, with peace failing to yield open labor markets (quite the
opposite in fact); as for technology, it is Israel which produces advanced
technology and technologically-intensive commodities in demand in
other Middle Eastern states, with this indeed being to Israel's
advantage. Nonetheless, trade in these commodities has been precluded
so far as a result of the conflict, resulting in alternative suppliers, or when
it does happen, occurs through third parties at a low volume. Socio-
psychological hurdles remain deeply ingrained, while low technology
levels in Jordan, Egypt and the OPT limit exports to less capital- and
technology-intensive products, limiting foreign exchange earnings and
the value of imports that can be financed domestically.

A second key point Tuma makes is that Jordan, Egypt and the OPT
are 'competing rather than complimentary economies,' with each having
surplus labor, being dependent on agriculture and service sectors,
importing their manufactured goods and technology, and being short of
capital (ibid., p. 95). The competitive nature of Jordanian and
Palestinian economies is important to keep in mind considering
developments to emerge as a consequence of future neoliberal

statebuilding practices and the 'winners' it generated. In any case, Israel was less interested in trade with Arab states and more interested in accessing markets further afield – Japan, India, China – but which had largely been closed off because of the Arab boycott. After the DOP, Israeli exports to Asian countries increased by a third in the first nine months of 1994, accounting for 12.4 per cent of total Israeli exports compared to only 8.1 per cent in 1992 (Murphy, 2000, p. 56). Bilateral trade between Israel and South Korea in 1993 also increased by 50 per cent, while China became a welcoming market for Israeli defense exports, industrial technology and agricultural products by 1995. This stated, it shouldn't be forgotten that the heavy orientation of Israel's economy around military expenditure and 'permanent war' was also a major disincentive to transitioning to 'peace' (Nitzan and Bichler, 2002c).

The Closure Technology

One final aspect to Israel's behavior during the Oslo years needs to be mentioned given Roy's (1999) earlier allusion to it as 'the defining economic feature of the post-Oslo period' – Israel's closure policies.

While the Paris Economic Protocol acknowledged that both sides would 'attempt to maintain the normality of movement of labor between them, subject to each side's right to determine from time to time the extent and conditions of the labor movement into its area' (PER, Article VII – Labor, Section 1) the reality to emerge during the Oslo years was more reflective of the broader tendency under neoliberal globalization for the commodification and hyper-regulation of labor power (see Farsakh, 2002).

Capitalist constituencies in Israel differed in their approach to closure and Palestinian labor and trade flows. Those in the agriculture and construction sectors, reliant on Palestinian labor, were said to have become the biggest lobby for the Palestinian permit system during the 1990s, despite Israel's mixed experience with importing Eastern European and East Asian labor. Industrialists, fearful of being set awash in cheap Palestinian products, were more skeptical to free trade. Israeli industrialist Muzy Wertheim, chairman of Coca-Cola Israel, warned that unrestricted Palestinian penetration of Israel's market could throw tens of thousands of Israelis out of work, and called on the powerful Israeli

Industrialists' Association 'not to succumb to euphoric predictions, but to suggest to Israeli decision-makers practical arrangements that will permit the Palestinians to administer their own economy, but will control the flow of goods between Israel and the territories to ensure fair conditions of competition' (Gavron, 1994).

The closure system should thus be seen as a key institutional/technological innovation of the neoliberal regime created by the peace process to balance these general economic concerns, together with the demographic and political.

During the Oslo years, Israel would develop and implement the closure and permit system over Palestinians building off the geostrategic map resulting from the Interim agreements. Although these were not permanent borders, they delineated sufficient boundaries of separation that well suited Israel's 'neither two nor one' political and economic contradictions (Arnon, 2007).

Although the nominal excuse for the closure policy was the exigency of security, as Amira Hass (2002) describes in her research on this policy's history, the Palestinian right to freedom of movement had been respected by the Israeli authorities since 1967, even when there were fierce Palestinian attacks against Israeli civilians in Israel, with 'no one demand[ing] that entrances to Israel be sealed off.' In the context of the 1987 Intifada however and the 1990–1 Gulf War; with the more pronounced rise of Israel's demographic concerns as a consequence; and with Israel's own neoliberal globalization impetus in full swing, the norm of freedom of Palestinian movement was reversed to one of blanket denial, with exceptions made for particular categories including workers, merchants, people in need of medical treatment, collaborators and VIPs. She also highlights how this great inversion of policy, and the ability to control Palestinian internal movement, had been planned *before* the Madrid Conference and was greatly heightened through the Interim agreements themselves, which established the bureaucratic-military machinery of the 'pass' system with significant input from Israel's internal intelligence arm, the Shin Bet. Closure was hence a policy formulated and implemented before any Palestinian suicide bombings took place, and was used as a tool by the Israeli army and political class to begin formalizing the contours of its settlement map and the economic arrangement with the OPT. It fragmented Palestinian space while attempting to induce and extract collective and individual behavioral changes from the Palestinian leadership and society. As Hass notes:

> Closure also had very clear immediate advantages in the negotiating process underway. Particularly under Rabin and Peres, the use of closure as an instrument of economic leverage over the PA was blatant. 'You arrest this one or that one, and we'll give you 500 more work permits' and 'If you behave yourselves and agree to our (slow) implementation timetables, we'll allow you to export more vegetables and release from Israeli customs the heavy machinery you imported' were the unexpressed but widely understood premises underlying negotiations.
>
> (Hass, 2002)

The effect of closure on Palestinian labor and economy was dramatic (see Farsakh, 2002). Before the 1994 Interim arrangements, around 115,000 Palestinians – roughly 30 per cent of the labor force in the West Bank and more than 40 per cent in Gaza- legally worked in Israel (Beinin, 1998). But with the heavy full closures imposed in 1996–7, these figures dropped to 18 and 6 per cent respectively, spiking Palestinian unemployment to around 20 and 30 per cent (Arnon, 2007).

Two hundred and thirty days of full closure were imposed in 1996 and 1997 (PECDAR, 2003, p. 42), with nearly 50 per cent more internal closures in 1997 (Beinin, 2002). Closure became a technology to fragment the internationally sanctioned unity of the OPT and to leverage various Palestinian social classes, given that it forced each Palestinian to engage with it on an individual basis. It also effectively became a 'switch' that when turned off, could eliminate one third of work force jobs, with the giving of an order.

Israel's closure effectively allowed for what Arnon describes as 'a growing, unilaterally imposed, separation,' (Arnon, 2007) which had key political and economic dimensions lurking behind the impression of its ad hoc security nature. In the absence of the ability to hermetically seal the West Bank during this period – something Israel wasn't actually attempting, and still fails to have in place even with its physical construction of the 'separation fence', with this only preventing physical movement of people and goods (not rockets, for example) – security could hardly be assured through a permit system. But it became a perfect excuse for domination, while camouflaging the process of selective separation and integration that Israel was engaging in. As Farsakh (2002) notes, '[i]ndeed, closure was the most effective means of restricting the mobility of workers and demarcating boundaries between Palestinian and Israeli areas.'

The subject of closure is repeatedly raised in documents of the 'Economic Negotiating Group' revealed in the 'Palestine Papers.' Maher el Masri [MM], head of the Palestinian delegation in the (economic) talks, pleads with his Israel counterparts Avi Ben Bassat [AB] and B. Bar Zion [BB] to show reason, but to no avail:

> MM: One of the loopholes of the Paris agreement is that it was drafted in a vacuum. When facts on the ground changed, the whole Paris Protocol fell apart. Why? Because of the security factor. The general concept that should be acceptable to the security people is that only those involved in a security problem should be harmed. Others who are cleared by Israeli security – should be immune. There should not be collective punishment. That should be addressed in the economics chapter of the agreement.
>
> AB: We're against collective punishment. Closures were not punishment. They were a reaction – maybe a big reaction – to an extreme problem of bombs and hundreds of Israelis dying. I cannot bind the security people in the economics section.
>
> BB: I'm afraid that if we go to the security people and ask them to define, the definitions will be more restrictive than what we have in normal life.
>
> AB: We will leave it for the security teams. But as Avi Ben-Bassat, citizen of Jerusalem – not Director General – if my security team gives you what you want, I will start worrying. I don't think they should be sharing this information or revealing their criteria.
>
> (Palestine Papers, August 21, 2000)

Not quite two hundred (177) Israelis were indeed killed by Palestinians within the Green Line from the signing of the DOP to the outbreak of the Al-Aqsa Intifada. 47 of these (26 per cent) were Israeli military force members (see Tables 5.1 & 5.2).

Four hundred and ninety-nine Palestinians would be killed in the same timeframe, 66 of these by Israeli civilians.

Table 5.1   Israelis killed within the Green Line.

Year	Israeli civilians killed by Palestinians	Israeli security force personnel killed by Palestinians
1993–13.9.93	6	5
14.9.93–31.12.93	3	2
1994	47	4
1995	9	21
1996	38	15
1997	25	0
1998	1	0
1999	1	0
2000 until 28.9	0	0
Total	130	47

Israel's 'security' prerogatives needed to be kept secret because ultimately they were protecting and attempting to realize specific political and economic considerations.

One crucial related dimension to this arrangement cannot be allowed to go unnoticed for its enduring effect on Palestinian political economy. The heavy closures imposed by Israel on the OPT in the mid-1990s were so damaging to the Palestinians economically that the international donor community feared the sudden rise in unemployment would destabilize the peace process overall. They thus shifted the focus of their aid interventions from an initial focus on infrastructure and long-term development spending to emergency support for employment creation in the hopes of securing the financial viability of the Palestinian administration.

International donor aid and Western taxpayers effectively – and ironically – became the Palestinian job protection plan and economic safety net. While neoliberal policies internationally were advocating cutting down the role of the state and the size of the public sector, in the OPT, donors oversaw and facilitated a momentum that would see the dramatic rise of this sector – one that would hit 103,000 by 2000 and an estimated 180,000 employees by 2012 – 22.7 per cent of the total labor force (PCBS, 2012, p. 109). The need to create public sector jobs was part of a broader logic of donors to buoy the PNA and served to hide

Table 5.2 Palestinians killed in the OPT (including East Jerusalem).

Year	Palestinians killed by Israeli security forces	Palestinians killed by Israeli civilians
1993–13.9.93	124	5
14.9.93–31.12.93	30	8
1994	106	38
1995	42	2
1996	69	3
1997	18	4
1998	21	6
1999	8	0
2000 until 28.9	12	0
Total	430	66

Source (both 5.1 & 5.2): B'tselem http://www.btselem.org/statistics/first_intifada_ tables [Accessed 12 April 2014] On 13 September 1993, Israel and the PLO signed the Declaration of Principles which began the Oslo Process. The Al-Aqsa Intifada began on 29 September 2000.

unemployment and strengthen its position, often through the purchase of patronage.

It is significant to note how the political narrative of the 'peace process' emphasizing peace through 'negotiations' and 'security', facilitated this Israeli maneuver. Israel was able to use the security pretext to get international donors – primarily the EU, heavily invested in funding social sectors and budgets – to bankroll the implementation of its particular form of unilateral and selective disengagement from the OPT. This should be seen as embodying a cunning form of manipulating historical conditions, discursive frameworks and inter-donor rivalries to achieve strategic aims.

Thus, with the task of establishing a Palestinian governance structure largely realized during the Oslo years, nominally resolving aspects of its demographic concerns; with hope that its energy and water security needs were independently resolvable; with its neoliberal classes able to expand globally; and with Israeli producers keen on maintaining the captivity of the Palestinian market and labor – all without opening up the 'final status' issues for negotiations – the disincentive for making political concessions that would lead to the loss of any Israeli privileges over Palestinians thickened.

Ultimately with rising internal Israeli opposition to the harshness of Israeli liberalization measures and the inequalities and resentment this fostered; and with the assent of national-religious and ethnicity-based politics exacerbated by this neoliberalization, a more holistic picture of relevant factors emerges, widening existing explanations of Israel's behavior and how it sought to preserve and expand its interests (see Shafir and Peled, 2002). Add to this the Israeli political and military establishment's decision (under Rabin and Peres) to engage in provocative military operations[6] and reasonable questions emerge surrounding what led to the mid-1990s shift in Israeli policies that seemed to signal an abandonment of the 'New Middle East' vision of the peace process. Whether the abortion of the peace process was ultimately a strategic decision cultivated by a version of the Israeli deep state, or was instead the consequence of a less linear historical trajectory is inconsequential to the reality that the DOP created: Israel was able to lock-in certain institutional, political economic, military and class gains through the accords during the interim period, while Palestinian concerns and interests remained perpetually delayed in final status negotiations, with virtually no external counterweight to this political determination or internal means of arbitration within negotiations which could be relied upon to counter it. Israel's insidious contributions to the explosive reality to emerge by the time the July 2000 Camp David II negotiation are thus revealed, over and above the more visible oppressive reality characterized by the continuation of occupation and continued settlement construction.

CHAPTER 6

THE GUESSTIMATE: STRUCTURAL DETERMINANTS OF PALESTINIAN POLITICAL ECONOMY: INTERNATIONAL AID CONTRIBUTIONS

Reflecting on his time as Director of the World Bank's West Bank and Gaza assistance program between 2001 and 2006, Nigel Roberts[1] would acknowledge the very unscientific manner in which Western donor aid levels given to the PNA were actually determined:

> The history of donor assistance to the Palestinians, indeed, is notable for its lack of performance conditionality, with aid levels determined to a large extent by guesstimates of what is needed to 'maintain political momentum' or, in recent years, to 'permit the survival of the PA'.
>
> (Roberts, 2005, p. 24)

Two elements are of note to Roberts' assertion.

First, Robert's claim that donor assistance lacked conditionality is not entirely accurate, although how one determines this really depends upon the framing of terms. Formal conditionality measures do emerge after the start of the Al-Aqsa Intifada. It also should be borne in mind that the entire aid framework was conditional on accepting basic restrictions to Palestinian activity. But classical conditionality policy tools were not used during the Oslo years because they were seen as less functional to the political objective being sought – the creation of the PNA to begin with. The 'walk-around money' nature of some fiscal streams had a built-in element to them whereby internationals implicitly sought the PNA to perform beyond official forms of accountability. Moreover, to apply conditions to a non-state entity with extremely limited means of independent fiscal generation meant that to condition aid on various reforms was antithetical to the entire project being constructed. Conditionality ultimately made little sense: it would be self-defeating to withhold finances to a project the donors were determined to establish. In the absence of these finances, efforts to establish the Authority would fail making things worse for donors. In this respect, the establishment of the PNA was very much seen as a project of the international donor community itself – a necessary bureaucracy and institution capable of capturing the political, geostrategic, demographic and economic expectations of it backers.

Second, given that the former head of one of the most powerful development institutions during the peace process acknowledges that a 'guesstimate' actually determined donor aid levels for the purpose of 'maintain[ing] political momentum' and 'permit[ting] the survival of the PA', it would seem appropriate to read back upon the international donor community's interventions in the OPT based on this admission in retrospect.

Consistent with the neoliberal peacebuilding mindset, the initial aim of Western donor aid was to produce and distribute a coveted 'peace dividend,' deemed central to the accord's success. This was explicitly admitted by Jean Louis Sarbib, World Bank's Vice President for the Middle East and North Africa Region, in an internal World Bank evaluation report:

> It was well understood that the best chance of success for a peace which would benefit not only the Palestinian and Israeli people, but the region as a whole, was the quick and tangible delivery of a 'peace dividend'.
>
> (World Bank, 2002a, p. 66)

Instead of placing in Palestinian hands the tools of their own development, under conditions in which they could exercise these powers, the international community and Israel placed select powers and resources in select hands, and under select conditions that were intended to reap political and institutional results. The dividend was supposed to 'provide tangible benefits to the Palestinian population' with the intention to forge a lasting internal political settlement amongst Palestinian social classes and actors (World Bank, 1994, V.I, p. 7).

The provision of a peace dividend however was to take place in the context of the phased nature of the Accord's implementation – dividing negotiations between an 'Interim period' and 'Final status' issues, and the Interim period into further tranches. Moreover, it soon became obvious that the restrictive nature of Israel's economic and geopolitical regime over the Palestinians was so encompassing that it acted as a major obstacle to the free-market principles and economic development that the international community was publicly encouraging for the Palestinian economy.

Nu'man Kanafani and David Cobham (2007) illustrate the way in which the core policy recommendations of the Washington Consensus (Williamson's ten point plan), and some of the most typical strategies applied in Poverty Reduction Strategy Papers of the World Bank were rendered inapplicable or useless in the context of Israel's broader policies (See Kanafani and Cobham, 2007, p. 82, Table 3a). For instance, five of the ten key policies making up the Washington Consensus – tax reform, financial liberalization, the exchange rate, tariffs and quotas, and foreign direct investment – 'could not be applied to the WBG because the PNA did not have control of the relevant instruments and/or because the key problems lay elsewhere.' Three others – privatization, competition and property rights – were seen to be similarly inhibited, although to a lesser extent; while those policies that could be applied – fiscal control and public expenditure redirection, were indeed called for by the IFIs.

How are we to understand the seeming contradiction between the overarching neoliberal imperative for free markets, Israel's closure policies, and donor agendas?

While Israel's restrictions would appear to set donor and Israeli policies on a collision course, the response of the donor community is particularly revealing. Donors would split along lines of their larger political and geostrategic interests, ultimately reflecting their competing national/imperial ambitions:

- The US, and those in the EU who tended to side with more 'pro-Israel' policies (Britain, Germany, the Czech Republic, the Netherlands and Italy) – saw free market economics as subordinate to vital political imperatives. This functionally meant that the US gave the green light to Israel to interpret its prerogatives and act according to its interests, free from donor scrutiny, while Palestinian economic concerns needed to be submissive and responsive to these demands. Though this wing would also consistently support forms of capitalist development of the PNA, this support was always subordinated to Zionist criteria, enforced by Israel, with the US invariably backing up its ally and 'security' criteria. We will call this the 'politics first' wing of the donor community;
- The second wing – 'development first' – was composed of the remaining EU donor community (Belgium, France, Greece, Ireland, Malta, Portugal, Spain and Sweden). It supported Palestinian economic assertiveness outright, and didn't feel that the US or Israeli political imperatives had the right to seriously impede this process beyond realistic 'security' criteria. This wing consistently supported the PNA and its pro-market agenda as well, believing that sheer capitalist interests should dominate the political. While it might be argued that 'development firsters' were 'market purists', this depiction hides the way in which EU aid became a way to expand political influence, potentially weakening that of the US, in pursuit of individual national interests of each state, and regional neoliberal ambitions of the EU overall. In this respect, denying Palestinian economic freedom essentially meant not only weakening the EU's institutional recipient/client, but also rebutting the attempt to expand EU imperial and individual state influence.

The division between donors should not however be seen as strategic. Both wings were committed to the peace process and its *modus operandi* overall, though they may have had secondary tactical differences over priorities and sequencing. All nonetheless shared the basic 'peace dividends' logic of peacebuilding and behind that, the erecting of the PNA as its main facilitator. This consensual arrangement made Yasser Arafat the main conduit of strategic rents, with the apparatus and bureaucracy of the PNA seen as the framework through which their allocation was largely realized.

Public Sector Peacebuilding: Empowering the Authority

Facilitating Arafat's neo-patrimonial regime entailed working on various levels. Perhaps most important was the international community's commitment to fund PNA recurrent costs, financing rising levels of employees in the civil and security sectors. The establishment of the Holst Fund and its successors,[2] assumed this cost, financing 23,000 Palestinian employee of the Israeli Civil Administration who 'moved' to the PNA in February 1994. By April 1996, the number of employees jumped to 65,000 – a figure seen within the World Bank as the cut-off limit for justifiable employment numbers, considering the need to 'transfer administrative and security responsibilities from Israel to the PNA' (World Bank, 2002a, p. 27). Donor financing of PNA employment would however continue to rise, reaching 103,000 by the end of 1999.

The World Bank would later face criticism for allowing the wage bill to swell to such proportions – levels deemed 'unsustainable' in the neoliberal worldview. Rebutting these accusations, the Bank argued that 'the unique political pressures that existed in this post-conflict context' justified this (ibid., p. 28). 'Guesstimates' of the resources needed to 'maintain political momentum' and 'permit the survival of the PNA', clearly differed between donors and the recipient PNA. So too did the risks for each party. The World Bank nonetheless acknowledged that 'there is evidence that these increases are not related to increasing responsibilities of the PA' – a backhanded way to say that it was Arafat who took his liberties in this domain, though this was not donor intention that he was taking it this far (ibid., p. 27).

The Palestinian Economic Council for Development and Reconstruction (PECDAR)

While donors turned a blind eye to Israel's use of off-budget accounts to help Arafat 'clean up Gaza', they expected their own funds to be used with more discretion and beneath their control. They did this by creating the Palestinian Economic Council for Development and Reconstruction (PECDAR), designed to serve as an implementing agency for donor funds, and rationalized as a means 'to channel funds and provide accountability and transparency' (USAID, 1996a, p. 12).

PECDAR is what is known within the World Bank as a 'Project Implementation Unit', usually consisting of autonomous or semiauto-nomous 'units' that aim 'to fill in the technical skills gap in the administration of development assistance programs in the Bank's borrower countries' (IEG web). PIUs act as intermediary conduits through which 'appropriate technical experts [. . .] provide advice on critical policy issues, [enhance] the efficiency of project implementation and management, and [strengthen] quality control' (IEG, 2000). They are also seen as a 'useful tool to establish professional linkages.'

The World Bank's Independent Evaluation Group (IEG) acknowledges that PECDAR was specifically modeled on the Lebanese PIU, the Council for Development and Reconstruction (CDR), which played a major role in post-Civil war reconstruction (IEG web. See also Leenders, 2012). It may be helpful noting that the World Bank's Operations Evaluation Department (OED), which conducts impact assessment, found that CDR 'became so powerful that it became a "super-ministry" with far-reaching powers that some of its authorizations had to be divested from it and returned back to the normal ministries' (IEG, 2000).

PECDAR's scope of operations in the OPT was clearly more circumscribed than that of CDR. But the World Bank certainly envisioned the agency as having a powerful mandate in theory and practice. In fact, it is not an exaggeration to describe PECDAR's imagined role as substituting or filtering a great deal of the potential role of the inchoate Palestinian ministries coming into existence, thanks to its structure and heavy reliance on 'technical expertise.'

A diagram of PECDAR's structure published by the World Bank in its Emergency Assistance Program (EAP) clearly shows how in order for the PNA ministries to implement policies, they had to go through the 'PECDAR Group' – a body with a double decision making structure within it, which gave international donors front line positions in determining projects, through embedded international consultants (see Appendix 1).

The EAP describes PECDAR's functioning as intending to manage aid and undertake 'investment implementation functions'; 'provide the nucleus for economic policy formulation, overall expenditure programming, training policies and other functions of economic self-governance,' for 'a transitional period of time' (World Bank, 1994, p. 111).

The wide potential interpretation of these functions, their open ended nature, and the important political and economic functions they straddled, appear all the more dubious when the EAP describes how these ends were to be structurally realized.

'Overall policymaking' and 'program guidance' would lie with PECDAR's all-Palestinian Board of Governors. However behind this formal 'local ownership' structure, program and project implementation and monitoring would all lie with the Director of the Project Management and Monitoring Office (PMO), which was designed to be heavily reliant on in-house contracted consultants. Despite structurally appearing as though the PMO was submissive to the Board's demands, the role of consultants in virtually all aspects of project design and implementation would in fact render their role far more significant:

> To the extent practicable, the PMO will rely on the services of competent consultants (including for management and procurement) [. . .] to assist agencies in the implementation of investment projects. The use of consultants would help ensure that PMO remains lean and agile, capable of responding to the challenges of managing a complex program in a changing environment.
>
> (Ibid., p. 112)

'Reputable, competent, and internationally recruited' consultants serving as 'sector specialists' in education, health, power and telecoms, water and sanitation, roads and transport, solid waste and environment, would staff the PMO, advising its director on 'best practice.' Additionally, managing and procurement consultants would assist with 'overall programming and budgeting'; 'payment certification and the design and maintenance of project accounts'; 'development of effective operating procedures and systems'; 'project screening and evaluation'; 'contract evaluation and award'; and contract, project and program monitoring (p. 113). In all cases, 'projects and programs of implementing agencies, including even those where PECDAR itself is the implementing agency, would have to be screened and reviewed by the Managing Consultants prior to final approval and financing' (pp. 113–14).

Given its expansive mandate, it is not surprising that PECDAR engendered understandable suspicion within the PNA's incipient ministries. According to the World Bank, technical assistance to the PNA totaled $450 million between 1993 and mid-1999, sucking up almost one fifth of total donor aid (World Bank and Japan, 2000, p. 107). And although initially envisaged as a transitional body 'until the PNA could establish technical ministries capable of taking over,' (World Bank, 2002a, p. 22) the organization would remain as a parallel structure to the PNA and its ministries up to the present.

PECDAR would be the subject of controversy amongst ministries given its overlapping agenda with those of economy, finance and particularly planning and international cooperation (MOPIC, later MOPAD). Notably this initial competitive and resentment-engendering dynamic created by the World Bank's use of PIUs is a recurrent phenomenon in many theatres given the fact that these units are paid on higher salary scales than governmental civil servants, enjoy better facilities (offices, cars) and can often attract higher specialized skill sets.

The Community Development Project

PECDAR's performance was highly rated by the World Bank as 'a competent and reliable agency' that was 'efficient', 'transparent' and 'critical to project implementation' (World Bank, 2002a, p. 22).

Although a more detailed analysis of PECDAR's activity is beyond the scope of this research, one of the things the agency did engage in was patronage fostering. As previously noted, the comprehensive closures of 1995–7 propelled the World Bank to shift focus to address emergency short-term employment relief. One such project was the Community Development Project (CDP), initiated from March 1997 to December 1998, which aimed to 'rehabilitate and restore basic economic and social infrastructure in towns and villages in the West Bank and Gaza, and increase temporary job opportunities for unskilled and semi-skilled laborers' (World Bank, 2000a, p. 2).

The CDP was a typical project reflective of donor responses to the economic hardships created by closure and the political impasse the peace process was undergoing. The French Government, the European Investment Bank (EIB) and the OPEC Fund would also fund similar programs through PECDAR. CDP utilized a seemingly straightforward rationale: 'under-investment in public infrastructure over the years, especially in the small municipalities and village councils in West Bank and Gaza have contributed significantly to deterioration and to inadequate levels of infrastructure services' (World Bank, 1997d, p. 1). To add to this, 'severe unemployment (at times as high as 50 per cent) has, in addition to eroding the capacity of the municipalities and villages to maintain their infrastructure, depressed living standards and increased economic and social hardship.' CDP thus sought to rehabilitate or restore basic economic and social infrastructure using the number of microprojects implemented as the key performance indicator. 500 small infrastructure projects costing between $20,000 and $100,000, were initially targeted (ibid., p. 2). The project secondarily intended to give a boost to local suppliers and contractors, while creating 750,000 labor days, or roughly 30,000 temporary jobs for a minimum of one month.

Initially, CDP was supposed to be administered by PECDAR and implemented by local government units. The project description specifically warns against 'interference by line ministries in daily operations' claiming this 'would compromise PECDAR's effectiveness and ability to approve projects in an unbiased and rapid manner' (World Bank, 1997d, p. 3). However once the project began, the lack of input from the Ministry of Local Government (MoLG) led to a behind-the-scenes struggle over who would control and select subprojects. The World Bank was forced to retreat on its initial insistence that PECDAR select subprojects, rationalizing this shift in an implementation completion report three years later as the consequence of a 'lack of coordination' that 'caused some confusion within the communities on who was in charge,' instead of as a deliberate attempt to side-step central government (World Bank, 2000, p. 17). MoLG would subsequently win rights to select subprojects submitted by communities, leaving PECDAR for their implementation.

Although we do not know much about the back room struggle to control the project, the World Bank's initial desire to bypass the PNA governmental body responsible for such projects on the local level is significant. The World Bank's initial suspicion of 'line ministries' should indeed be read as an attempt to circumvent the political channels that Arafat controlled. However the eventual reversal of this policy also tells us that Arafat was powerful enough on the ground to resist the creation or fostering of potential alternative patronage networks. In both cases patronage was being fostered: the difference was, who controlled the process – Arafat, or PECDAR under World Bank influence.

Although we shall return to this issue further down, it is worth noting that we see here evidence of the PNA demonstrating independent agency and decision making that was able to resist in one way or another the comprehensive domination of the international donor agenda and its priorities for project implementation. It would be this sense of agency, repeatedly demonstrated, that would ultimately convince both 'politics firsters', and 'development firsters' that a fundamental shift in donor strategy was needed. Arafat demonstrated unforgivable independence for attempting to preserve a margin of policy space that he felt he was entitled to, and which he felt he had been promised by the international community when agreeing to the 'job conditions' of establishing and running the PNA.

The significance of the CDP however does not end there. Despite these back room rivalries, CDP publically relayed pride in its upgrading of 125 village access roads; its improvement of 19 water and sanitation networks, and its establishment of 32 community centers and public buildings, 12 health centers, 52 educational facilities, and 8 social centers (World Bank, 2000, p. 2). The World Bank would also trumpet its ability to penetrate the Palestinian periphery claiming it as 'one of the first projects in West Bank and Gaza to address the needs of smaller municipalities and villages which had for the most part been neglected by post-Oslo donor assistance' (ibid., p. 5). CDP's final 'Implementation Completion Report' would claim the highly specific '374,765 beneficiaries' in 248 communities, created over 280,000 person days of employment, and built capacity within PECDAR, MoLG, and the participating municipalities and village councils,' with all this for the revised project value of $20.2 million (ibid., pp. 5–9).

These accomplishments were nonetheless, sharp revisions from the project's initial targets. The number of projects implemented was less than half the original target, and the number of person days of employment created was only 37 per cent. Donor enthusiasm for funding unemployment and dilapidated local infrastructure projects had clearly cooled in the context of the political struggle over the project's control, while the long start-up time to get the project running and the fact that by 1998, the Netanyahu government began loosening the comprehensive closure policy, also likely influenced donor decision making. Of course the exact cause of donors' temperamental approach towards these projects can never be fully ascertained, despite the initial portrayal of these projects as developmentally and politically exigent. In this respect, the entire CDP experience gives an indication of how international donors instrumentalize developmental needs to serve political ends, while demonstrating behavioral capriciousness.

Buried in the back pages of the implementation completion report (which initially had restricted distribution, but was released with the change in the World Bank's 2010 access to information policy) is discussion of how the results were arrived at. As CDP neared an end, the World Bank sent teams to undertake several Beneficiary Impact Assessments (BIA) sampling 30 per cent of projects, and interviewing beneficiaries in focus group discussions and one-on-one interviews.

One of the criteria the BIA was concerned with was assessing the project's impact on political stability:

> The CDP has been one of the first interventions to target rural and peri-urban areas of West Bank and Gaza and the resulting support for these projects has contributed positively to the people's confidence in their government. This support could translate to greater support to the government policies such as the on-going peace process.
>
> (Ibid., p. 11)

The BIA reveals that recipients were very happy with the program and credited PECDAR and the PNA for the good work. Project implementation was also seen as professional and above table:

> The local communities and their representatives made repeated mention of PECDAR's accuracy and transparency with financial transactions and dealing with contractors. Their regulations such as mandatory presentation of invoices, receipts and approvals from line ministries for the undertaken subprojects are highly acceptable within the communities.
>
> (Ibid., p. 36)

This clean bill of health earned CDP a performance rating of 'highly satisfactory' for project outcomes. But this narrative begins to come under suspicion when elements of BIA's own findings are cross-referenced. For example, BIA's interrogation of the project's sustainability noted:

> The subprojects have potential for sustainability as they meet the needs of the communities. But, sustainability is questionable on the grounds that the beneficiaries are not directly Community members are represented through the local government (municipalities, village councils and local committees) [sic]. However, the representatives are not elected. In addition, the meetings between the local government and the beneficiaries are also limited. [...] Beneficiaries believe that Ministry of Local Government, line Ministries are responsible for the sustainability and maintenance of these subprojects.
>
> (Ibid., p. 38)

Although BIA's shorthand and garbled, grammatically incorrect writing style is difficult to fully comprehend, it alludes to something that reveals a great deal. Arafat established MoLG in an attempt to control local government by ruling through appointed persons in the periphery. Its political importance would increase in the context of Israel's closure policies as it became the main avenue through which Arafat aligned with select rural and urban elites, marginalizing the forms of self-governance that emerged during the 1987 Intifada and which had pushed aside the role of traditional elites and families. But this maneuver may also have staved off the potential entrenching of alternative elite networks.

Local representation had always been a sensitive subject in the West Bank, including for Israeli and Jordanian authorities. Israel only allowed for elections to be held three times during the 27 years of its 'direct' occupation, notably cancelling them after the victory of pro-PLO mayors in 1976. Jordan chose to rule West Bank towns through appointed municipal councilmen. With the establishment of the PNA in 1994, local elections were supposed to be held in 1996, the same year as those of the PNA presidency and legislative council. Arafat however cancelled these, preferring instead to establish alliances through patronage networks based on party affiliation, or powerful families.

His choice was not by chance. Opposition parties that had boycotted the PLC elections indicated their intentions to participate in local elections, which could have created substantial hurdles for implementing both PNA and international donor plans had they succeeded. This meant that Fateh supremacy was by no means assured on the local level, as had been the case in the January 1996 PLC elections, which the opposition factions boycotted. Local elections would also have favored local representatives from the OPT, over those from the PLO returnees. Local elections were thus likely to have been a more genuine representative contest between all Palestinian political factions, as well as the family clans and traditional notables powerful on the local level.

Arafat was not about to leave results to chance. His decision to cancel local elections facilitated the key reversion of power dynamics between ascendant elites of the 1987 Intifada and traditional family elites that had been pushed aside by the former, and would be a defining characteristic of the PNA regime and powerbase during this period. As Palestinian economist Nidal Sabri (2003) notes, municipal representatives were appointed via MoLG based on presidential appointments and a political (Fateh dominant) and clan quota (Sabri, 2003, pp. 157–67). The central government also made sure it controlled all municipal and town expenditures, engineering and plans, with most projects and expenditures requiring ministerial approval. This arrangement was Arafat's way to enforce centralization and control over the local, ensuring his people ran the show and were kept on a short rope. In this way, he could stave off other political networks forming or formed in the periphery, be they oppositional factions, or alternative powerful families, who could also have Jordanian alignment, or even be associated with the former Israeli collaborator network, the 'village leagues.' All in all, the PNA established 76 municipal councils, quadrupling the previous amount under the Civil Administration. Most important of these were 14 municipalities, run by 1046 municipal members and presidents of local councils. 51 village assemblies were also set up for villages with populations under 1000 persons; and a further 268 project councils were established in urban settings led by 1642 members – all of whom were appointed. No laws existed during the Oslo years to regulate or organize this sector's work and only 13 women were represented on municipal boards.

Given the social composition of the CDP's benefactors, the positive feedback the project received in the BIA should hardly be seen as surprising. The very people who were appointed by the central authority to run local government were the very persons empowered through the CDP to strengthen their positions locally, with all of this deemed fully transparent and highly successful.

Reading between the lines, the BIA report's acknowledgement that it funded the local appendages of Arafat's patronage network subsequently leads its authors to recommend that in future projects, the selection of subprojects should be 'based not only on the demand from communities, but also on the basis of the type of beneficiaries making the demand' (World Bank, 2000, p. 39). The report recommends prioritizing 'proposals coming from poor and vulnerable groups', using 'increased number of public consultations to facilitate better participation of beneficiaries in subproject selection and finally screening the proposals at the project unit level to understand who from the community is making the demand.' All these were seen as 'mandatory to create an impact on the desired beneficiaries, and to deter possible complaints of bias and subjectivity' (ibid., p. 39). Clearly donors resented their inability to fully set Palestinian developmental agendas and determine the networks sustaining them.

The Politics of Democracy and Governance

The case of CDP and the invisible power struggle between the PNA and international donors over who controlled development projects is a fitting illustration of donor-recipient dynamics during the Oslo years.

On the one hand, donors facilitated rent-allocation means to build the nascent power of the apparatus and polity under formation. On the other, they were cautious not to empower too much, and consistently sought ways to deepen their influence within the PNA and create alternative networks outside it, flanking it via NGOs and the private sector.

Evidence of this donor dynamic can be repeatedly demonstrated across different sectors of the arrangement being erected throughout the OPT between the public, private and civil society spheres, and how they interacted with international donor aid. Indeed it is important to illustrate these efforts, because they demonstrate the direct ways in which donors sought to impose their own political rationale to Palestinian governance and development within the Oslo arrangement and the specific filter of their 'politics first'/'development first' agendas.

This dynamic is consistently apparent in USAID's 'Democracy and Governance' (DG) subproject of the 'Democratic Institutions Support Project' (DIS) – the same DIS referred to in Chapter 3, which provided the revealing insights of Glenn Robinson's research on how to map and assess institutional winners of the interim arrangement.

Similar to the latter documents, the 1996 'Democracy and Governance Strategy' paper produced by DIS was also 'for discussion within USAID', 'not for general distribution', 'not to be quoted', and does 'not necessarily represent the views or interpretations of USAID or the US government' (USAID, 1996a, p. 1). But likewise, the desire of the contractor (Chemonics) to boast of its accomplishment in the project's 'Final Report' reveals that the draft DG strategy produced for DIS was indeed 'used in preparing a mission strategy' by both the USAID mission and USAID/Washington, and that 'DIS provided analytical input to USAID that helped render the mission DG strategy more reflective of its dynamic environment' (USAID, 1996b, pp. II–3). Irrespective of the specific contributions of the DG strategy paper to USAID's eventual strategy (which can never truly be determined without full disclosure of archival material), it is the lines of analytic approach that most interests us.

The report's authors express concern that the PNA's 'state building' activities were 'likely to contribute to a tendency to centralize power in the executive branch' (USAID, 1996a, p. 20). They then revealingly caution:

> If this tendency is not tempered, there is a strong risk that such centralization will undermine even well-intentioned democratic initiatives.[3] [...] Finding the proper balance between concentrated and dispersed power will be a major challenge for the Palestinians. Indeed, the potential exists for imbalance in either direction.
>
> (Ibid., p. 21)

Evidently, USAID would seek to embrace this challenge just as much as the Palestinians. The report advocates a complex governance structure to temper the empowerment of a centralizing PNA, once the 1996 PLC elections had given Fateh an outright majority in parliament. Indeed, Fateh took 50 seats in the PLC and a further 16 others through Fateh members who ran as independents, with the remainder split between secular independents (16), independent Islamists (4), and two members affiliated with other political parties.

Fateh's victory in the PLC elections however was no surprise (as previously noted), given the boycott of elections by the main PLO opposition parties (the PFLP and DFLP) as well as by the Islamists (Hamas and Islamic Jihad), who protested the Accords themselves, and the undemocratic way in which the entire Oslo process had been conceived, agreed and implemented – something the US had intended from the start (see Chapters 2 and 3). Now, with Fateh empowered through parliamentary elections to lead its developmental program through the structures created for it by donor funding, USAID would begin 'bending the stick' in the other direction, instrumentalizing democracy and the development discourse overall towards a new political end:

> Donor funding in the DG sector is currently being concentrated at the national level, primarily on the establishment of the executive and legislative branches, which obviously are essential components of any democratic system of government. This increases the risk that authority will become concentrated at the top-away from civil society and local government. In order to prevent that, assistance needs to be provided to civil society, local government, and to the judicial system, as well as to those processes, such as elections and information dissemination that mediate relations between and within government and civil society.
>
> (Ibid., p. 21)

Donor power to operate on this level of Palestinian politics, determining the degree and scale of centralization of Palestinian governance institutions, while claiming to be doing so for the sake of democracy, remains a key feature of the architecture of Oslo arrangement. In fact the USAID document felt entitled to intervene still deeper regarding the very composition and political character of Palestinian governance institutions.

First the composition of the governance institutions being erected:

> The distinction between local and national government risks being accentuated by the 'insider-outsider' division of the body politic. If authority becomes concentrated at a given level, it is likely to correspondingly favor insiders or outsiders, thereby inhibiting the rapid and beneficial merger of the two groups, a precondition for effective, democratic self-governance in the West Bank and Gaza. The mix should be more like a marble cake than a layer cake, with a complex pattern of concentrations of authority.
>
> (Ibid., p. 23)

USAID clearly saw itself as an equal 'cook in the kitchen', and was aware of its preference in 'cake.' Emphasis on a 'marble cake' over a 'layered cake' was motivated by concern over the social composition of the governing body being created. This stemmed however not from concern over democratic inclusivity (which was a priori rejected by the US) but rather from the need to forge inseparable common interests among the diverse constituents involved in the PLO's return to the OPT and their intermixing with 'local' Palestinians. More specifically, the US understood early on that the 'winners' of the Oslo arrangement needed to be from diverse social constituencies, such that 'inclusivity' melded local and expatriate elites. It thus was calling for a strategy of 'inclusivity of elites', rather than political inclusivity.

The USAID document would almost go so far as to explicitly say what the parameters of legitimate political policy were to be:

> The ideologies espoused by many of the [Palestinian political] parties need adjustment to meet present circumstances. The ideology of national liberation is no longer relevant if an agreement has been made that implicitly or explicitly renounces claims formerly made to Palestine. The ideology of radical socialism, espoused by the PFLP and DFLP, is in crisis globally and no more suitable to conditions in the West Bank and Gaza than it has been deemed to be in Eastern Europe, Latin America, or elsewhere. The ideology of Islamism in its radical variants is inconsistent with much of what has been agreed in negotiations

between Israel and the Palestinians and is, therefore, unlikely to serve as the basis for legitimate political action. Political parties will need to change their nature and function to adjust to the new reality.

(Ibid., p. 17)

Private Sector Peacebuilding

Donor aid to the private sector equally embodied undisclosed political goals as illustrated in attempts to establish industrial estates and free zones.

Industrial estates appealed to donors because they bundled together a package of neoliberal economic and political targets deemed capable of helping to overcome a range of 'obstacles to economic growth' (USAID, 1995, p. 5). According to USAID, these included 'security concerns regarding the transit of Palestinian workers into Israel'; 'problems in the timely movement of goods between the Palestinian Territories and Israel'; 'high rates of unemployment'; and the 'lack of a cohesive legal and regulatory framework for private sector development in general, and investment regulation in particular' (ibid., p. 5). They were also seen as a means to help 'mobilize capital from overseas Palestinians' (ibid., p. 8).

Israeli economic and political circles also saw industrial estates as mechanisms to 'restructure the relations of [Palestinian] dependency,' according to Palestinian economist Sami Abdel Shafi (Usher, 1999, p. 44). 'Daily migration of mass Palestinian labor into Israel' was to be replaced by 'a system of sub-contracting between Palestinian capital and sectors of Israeli capital.' Israeli economist Ezra Sadan, described by the *Jerusalem Post* as 'a champion of Greater Israel in his politics, but a neoliberal when it comes to economics', is seen as the godfather of this economic strategy, after a series of reports he wrote on the Gazan economy in the early 1990s (*Jerusalem Post*, 14 May 1993 in Usher, p. 44). Sadan proposed industrial estates as a subcontracting solution that would explicitly take advantage of deep pools of refugee labor Gaza had to offer (Sadan, 1991; 1993).

The World Bank would conduct initial pre-feasibility assessments analysing existing legal incentive and institutional frameworks and surveying potential investors. Nine zones were planned (three in Gaza and six in the West Bank) catering to large, export-oriented, and small-and medium-sized investors. By mid-1995, the World Bank called for supporting the Gaza Industrial Estate (GIE) as the pilot project on a site located on the Israeli 'border' at Karni.

USAID contractor The Services Group, Inc. would develop a detailed 'Investor Targeting Strategy (ITS) Study' assessing OPT competitiveness vis-à-vis potential regional competitors (USAID, 1999). Detailed sectoral proposals were developed in light manufacturing (apparel, electronics, food processing, plastic packaging, and furniture), professional services (information technology related sectors, such as software development, call center and help desk services, and data conversion) and location based services (logistics handling for products that can be transported via air and warehousing). Israeli, US, European and East Asian investors were targeted.

In its stead, the World Bank would identify the principal issues constraining private sector development, and worked to amend these through the knowledge, resources and technical fixes at its disposal. 'High levels of political uncertainty' were to be addressed by a 'Political Risk Insurance Fund', to 'provide cover to international investors' (World Bank, 1997e, p. 4). 'Lack of adequate infrastructure' was to be addressed by donor support to developing off-site infrastructure, 'linking the sites to the regional grids' (USAID, 1995, p. 10). The World Bank would invest $20 million in legal development with clear objectives to 'assist the PA in [...] putting in place a legal framework adequate to support a modern market economy and encourage the growth of the private sector' (World Bank, 1997c, p. 2).

To further give weight to these initiatives, US president Bill Clinton would extend the 1985 Israeli–US free trade agreement to the West Bank and Gaza in October 1996. The EU would follow suit in 1997, with its own Euro-Mediterranean Interim Association Agreement on Trade and Cooperation. USAID would go so far as to organize a study tour to the Dominican Republic, Thailand, and the Philippines in late 1996 for senior staff of the Ministry of Industry and the Palestinian developer, 'to gain a deeper understanding of issues regarding policy for, and operation of, industrial and free zones' (World Bank, 1997e, p. 9).

Clearly, industrial estates and free zones were seen as central to the neoliberal economic development model of the OPT during the Oslo years. But this issue needs to be explored more closely in terms of how the project's implementation attempted to service a specific neoliberal peacebuilding agenda that will have important repercussions for the evolution of Palestine Ltd. conceptually and practically.

Industrial estates fit into neoliberal peacebuilding in two main ways:

First, these estates offered the possibility for the nascent PNA to provide rent-seeking opportunities to bring on board wealthy diasporic Palestinians and get them to invest in the OPT and the peace process overall. By promising profits, generating foreign direct investment, trade and employment (50,000 jobs estimated for GIE alone – 20,000 of these direct), a win-win-win situation was envisioned between government, investors and labor. Preferred Palestinian capital formations could lock-in strategic sectors of Palestinian economic development at an early stage of the PNA experiment, thanks to donor support for training, technical assistance, and infrastructure investment. Israeli and international capital would also benefit through subcontracting arrangements and the unique legal specifications of the zone.

Second, industrial estates were part of a wider dynamic whereby donor aid facilitated the enrichment and organization of the private sector and its interests, and helped to create mediums through which it could begin to raise and leverage its concerns vis-à-vis government. These sites of private sector 'self'-organization and public-private interfaces would later become conduits through which donor aid could channel and pass on particular policies and plans that served their (donor) neoliberal peacebuilding agenda.

Donor Aid, Rent-seeking and Buy-ins

The economic rent of industrial estate development was, in this case, allotted to the Palestine Industrial Estate Development and Management Company (PIEDCO, sometimes referred to as PIECO in early policy drafts). PIEDCO is a subsidiary of the OPT's dominant private sector holding company PADICO, controlled by a branch of the elite al-Masri family of Nablus, and dominated by diasporic Palestinian investors mainly centered in Jordan and the Gulf region. PADICO obtained preliminary concessions to own, develop and operate the GIE in 1995, but only made moves on the project after gaining assurances that donors would cover the cost of off-site infrastructure. The latter was to include roads, electric power supply, storm water management, wastewater treatment facilities, water supply facilities, solid waste disposal facilities and telecommunications facilities – many of which were actually outside the GIE property.

PIEDCO was formed with an initial share capital of $15 million, and invested $13.9 million in the project on the ground. The World Bank's International Finance Corporation (IFC) would add $1 million in equity participation; USAID came up with an $8 million 'A' Loan, later offering a $7 million 'B' Loan'; and finally, the European Investment Bank (EIB) matched these commitments with its own $1.1 million equity investment and an $15 million loan (World Bank, 1997e, p. 19).

The generous support PIEDCO received as the project's developer would be supplemented by the PNA's favorable '49-year nominal ($1) lease agreement' for the estate's 48-hectare plot of land, valued at $23.5 million (ibid., p. 19).

The project also promised the opportunity to offer additional opportunities of 'buy in.' USAID's 1996 environmental assessment report of the GIE reveals some of the back room ideas under discussion for the project's development, including the construction of a power plant in Gaza that would feed it and other estates (USAID, 1996c, p. 25). Indeed this scenario seemed headed towards fruition with a June 1998, 20-year power purchasing agreement (PPA) signed between the PNA (via the Palestinian Energy Authority (PEA)), and the Palestine Electricity Company (PEC) – a newly found company co-owned by a consortium[4] of investors led by Palestinian billionaire Said Khoury (co-founder of Consolidated Contractors Co (CCC), one of the world's largest contracting companies) and Enron International, a branch of what would become the disgraced energy titan Enron Corporation. At the time, co-development of the Gaza Power Plant's (GPP) 136 megawatt, $140 million facility was the largest foreign direct investment in the OPT. But it only became possible after the United States Overseas Private Investment Corporation (OPIC) agreed to provide Enron with up to $50 million in political risk insurance, and the subsequent fast-tracking of the deal by the Clinton administration. Although linking the GIE to the GPP would never take place (leaving the plant reliant upon Israeli power), disclosure of the GPP's establishment is revealing in terms of illustrating the cynical and speculative logic of neoliberal peacebuilding and development.

The US Treasury Department officially redacts substantial portions of the 9 March 2000 OPIC 'Loan Guaranty' proposal for Enron International, and its 'Discussion and Recommendations', citing the existence of 'privileged business information.'[5] However thanks to the bankruptcy of Enron in 2001,[6] the US Justice Department released documents from an Enron Board of Directors meeting in which internal discussion and approval of the deal took place (US Dept. of Justice, Enron, web).[7] The document describes Enron's risk assessment in the deal in which the company took 50 per cent of the common equity in PEC, seen by Enron as PEC having 'an exclusive right for 20 years to all future Gaza power generation.' The small technical detail that the power plant's turbines would run on distillate fuel, but 'provide the flexibility to switch to natural gas, if it becomes available,' should also be noted.

Enron would carefully assess the various political and financial risks involved in the deal but evidently found the assurances to move ahead. The PNA provided guarantees not to interfere in the PEC 'in any way.' The risk that the PNA 'may be replaced by another sovereign entity or that Palestine may fall under the sovereignty of another country' was assuaged by the fact that 'PEC has sophisticated local and international Palestinian investors who have local influence, including indirect participation by the PNA and public ownership (expected to be 33 per cent) following PEC's initial public offering.' The existence of the US government as 'a strong supporter of the project', and 'positive assurances from the Israelis relating to the project' equally made the investment appear more stable and lucrative. While noting the fact that 'Israel will cease to receive revenues from power sales', the Enron document conveys that the PNA's Energy Authority (PEA) would import and purchase its distillate from an Israeli refinery, thus making sure that Israel's economy benefitted as well.

Here a revealing element arises. Enron was concerned with the possibility of fuel supply interruptions and increased fuel costs. This risk is rebutted in an explanation about the nature of the power purchasing agreement (PPA) that PEC signed with the PNA:

> The PPA is equivalent to an energy conversion agreement, whereby PEA is responsible for the procurement, purchase, and delivery of the distillate fuel to the plant. PEC has no obligation to arrange for the fuel supply. Non-delivery of fuel is a force

majeure event under the PPA. In this event, PEC can terminate
the PPA, and PEA would be obligated to make a termination
payment in an amount equivalent to the sum of PEC's
outstanding debt, third party liabilities, PEC's equity, and the
present value of projected shareholder distributions discounted
at 10 per cent.

(Enron, web)

What this effectively meant was that it was the PNA that bore the risk
and financial costs of the deal. If the PNA wasn't able to procure,
purchase and deliver fuel, it would be legally liable in a court of law,
and be forced to pay back investors the sum of their investments.

The PEA's responsibility to procure fuel to PEC also needed to take
place *irrespective* of whether or not the power plant was functional at full
capacity which it was being paid for, or even at all. Only in 2007 would
the World Bank reveal the explicit details of this arrangement, buried
in a highly technical 'Energy Review' for the West Bank and Gaza (see
World Bank, 2007, pp. 65–7). Only if the PNA requested a test to
ensure energy production (which it had plenty of time to prepare for),
and the GPP failed an availability test, and then failed to restore the
plant to operation within 90 days, could a default situation arise.
Needless to say, these were highly favorable conditions for the PEC and
its electricity sales arm, the Gaza Power Generation Company (GPGC).
Moreover the PNA was bound to this arrangement for 20 years, once
the plant became operational (2004) – a sum that in 2006 amounted to
roughly $30 million annually. Two of the six transformers were also
being paid for by the Swedish government as aid to the PNA, making
the Swedish taxpayer one of the main funders of this rent arrangement
(ibid., p. 60). In a further twist, one of the PNA's main private sector
investment arms – the Palestinian Commercial Services Company
(PCSC), run by Arafat's trusted financial man, Mohammed Rashid, had
a 6 per cent share in the deal as well (see PEC Annual Report, 2004,
p. 9; Enron web). The World Bank (2007) would estimate the PEC's
ex-ante rate of return to equity (ROE) at 28 per cent, a level that 'lies in
the range of ROEs sought by Independent Power Producers [IPPs] for
investments in high-risk business environments.' In a word, this
lucrative investment was fair game. Needless to say, if we look at the
electricity quantity produced by the PEC, the cost of producing one

kilowatt of energy can be up to four times the cost of the original fuel that is bought from Israel (Shaban, 2013).

Although we shall return and contextualize these practices below, it suffices to note that deals like the GIE and the GPP facilitated by international donors, clearly provided or had the capacity to provide a lucrative 'peace dividend.' But they were also highly extractive, distortionary, and cynical.

US speculative capital benefitting from favored capital group status in the US itself, and operating under the wings of US government agencies, also profited, as long as it could survive its own reckless investment practices. Ultimately, Enron's collapse would lead to Morganti Development, an affiliate of the CCC group, buying out Enron's 33 per cent stake.

The process of buying-in Palestinian elites through such peace-building-development measures functionally created a consortium of Palestinian economic elites as the benefactors of this arrangement, tying them to the PNA, and the PNA to them, often in a manner that leveraged their risk on to the PNA and indirectly onto donors themselves.

Indeed it was a peace dividend of a peculiar kind. As the case of the GPP attests, the dividend would even be paid if peace prevailed or not. In fact, in 2006 when the plant was bombed by Israel and ceased producing electricity entirely (not speaking of its regular low production output, estimated by some at 30MW instead of 140MW),[8] the company still realized $7.4 million in profits (PEC Annual Report, 2006, p. 4).

Industrial Estate Regulation, Governance and Leverage

The significance of industrial estate development to neoliberal peacebuilding agendas does not end here. Key to understanding their significance lies in analysing their regulatory and governance arrangements and how the institutions and dynamics initiated during the Oslo years would have increasing significance for the internal balance of forces between Palestinian social classes in the long run.

Industrial estate development and regulation had initially fallen under the Palestinian Investment Act of 30 April 1995, which foresaw the creation of the 'Palestinian Higher Agency for the Promotion of Investment' (PHAPI). This initial investment governance agency was overseen by a 15-member board, in a 10:5 ratio of government to private sector. This functionally meant that the central government – the PNA – had a permanent board majority. USAID saw this as 'a departure for current best practice worldwide' given that 'experience has shown that a lean organization with heavy private-sector involvement will be more effective in meeting its objectives' (USAID, 1995, p. 12).

USAID's power to mobilize and actualize the industrial estates project gave it strong leverage to improve the project's conditions overall. In a document detailing 'next steps and possible roles for USAID support' prepared by contractors Coopers and Lybrand in September 1995, USAID was made aware of Palestinian draft legislation underway in the PLC to create a Palestinian industrial estates authority to govern and provide incentives to investors in the estates. 'Given the concerns already raised regarding the Investment Act, it would be prudent to provide assistance to the PNA in finalizing the industrial estates law as soon as possible,' it noted (ibid., p. 13). USAID carefully monitored the legislative process that was formulating a revised law on industrial zone governance, and provided nine pages of detailed comments 'of required final changes [...] taking into consideration international best practice and [the consultant's][9] experience with free zone laws in over 30 countries' (USAID, 1998, p. 111, Annex C1 and C2). It would also develop a detailed business plan, with month-by-month milestones for the future governing authority, including the authority's financial model and even a 'Draft Agenda & Preparation Plan' for the body's first Board Meeting. Perhaps most importantly, the senior USAID consultant on the project would write a 35-page draft regulation of the Palestinian Industrial Estate and Free Zone Authority (PIEFZA) Law, articulating how the Authority would actually implement the regulations defined in the law (ibid., pp. 74–109).

The PIEFZA Law would eventually be passed in October 1998, and articulated that PIEFZA governance would be overseen by an eleven-member board, chaired by the Minister of Industry, with a 7:4 ratio of government to private sector.

USAID lobbying should certainly be seen as influential in narrowing the government to private sector ratio from 10:5 under PHAPI to 7:4 in PIEFZA. However clearly USAID influence should not be over-exaggerated. PIEFZA would still be a government-dominated body. Indeed a majority of the USAID consultant's 'required final changes' do not in fact make it into the final law – a fact which would appear to demonstrate a preserved sense of autonomy on behalf of the PNA, yet again. USAID nonetheless appears to have been successful in lobbying for and winning the dividing of investment regulation functions from investment promotion – a division it saw as necessary in its first evaluation of the 1995 Investment Act. This functionally came about through the USAID-sponsored creation of the Palestinian Investment Promotion Agency (PIPA), formed after passage of the 'Law on the Encouragement of Investment in Palestine' no (1), also in 1998. This agency would be composed of an 8:5 ratio of government to private sector on its governance board, narrowing the ratio between the two yet further.

At first, the hiving-off of 'investment promotion' from 'investment regulation' may seem cosmetic or managerialist. But the logic of this cleavage can only really be understood in a broader historical and political context. The actual role that PIPA was intended to play by the US did not derive from it acting externally as an agency capable of conducting outreach towards potential international investors, but instead revolved around an *internal* orientation vis-à-vis the PNA, and how the latter would approach development, regulation and even the larger political negotiations process.

PIPA was/is a body solely dedicated to raising Palestinian competitive advantage in potential foreign investment opportunities in the OPT. The Encouragement of Investment Law which saw it come into being, would, among other regulations, specify that 'no investor will be discriminated against on any basis whatsoever'; that the PNA may not nationalize any investment; and that investors could freely transfer all financial resources out of Palestine, in a convertible currency of their choosing. PIPA aimed to establish a 'one-stop-shop' to facilitate investor concerns over permit issuance and 'reduction of routine administrative procedures at various official offices.' Generous tax-free incentives were also provided for different categories of investors, with the top bracket enjoying a five-year income tax exemption, followed by a 10 per cent nominal rate for the following 20 years.

The success of establishing PIPA and PIEFZA should be seen in a wider context however. That is to say, emphasis on the particular ratio of government to private sector representation on the governing bodies of such key regulatory institutions should not obfuscate what was a much more central achievement to the neoliberal peacebuilding agenda – that being, the creation of these institutions to begin with.

PIPA and PIEFZA were exemplary of the international donor community's facilitation of the creation of sites within the PNA apparatus that would act as interfaces between the government and the private sector. Semi-state institutions like PIPA and PIEFZA, but also the Palestine Standards Institute (est. 1996), the Palestine Monetary Authority (est. 1994), and much later, the Palestinian Capital Markets Authority (CMA) (est. 2004), were all established with generous international support from both wings of the international donor community.

The very creation of these bodies facilitated and formalized an arena in which dialogue, lobbying and power-broking could take effect. They constituted a foothold in an apparatus that the private sector previously did not formally have, and within an apparatus (the PNA) that formerly did not exist – an apparatus that was beginning to dominate the OPT economy. General government inflows to the Palestinian economy in 2000 would total $243.5 million out of $761.4 million, or 32 per cent.[10] $233.6 of this (96 per cent) was provided by donors.

It is significant to report here that USAID clearly envisioned a possible political role for the institutions it helped set up, in addition to an aggressive neoliberal economic agenda. In the case of PIEFZA for example, USAID envisioned an entity that could 'modify investment laws and incentives and provide services that are equal to or better than those offered by competing locations in the region,' making the industrial estates and free zone program a 'world-class investment location in the eyes of investors worldwide' (USAID, 2000, pp. 11–12):

> Over the next three years, PIEFZA should evolve much more toward a customer-oriented, facilitating and promotional body, and become less of a traditional government regulatory authority. This evolution is mandated by both international best practices, and the highly competitive environment in which Palestinian Industrial Estates/Free Zone [IE/FZ] program is operating. PIEFZA has endorsed this role in its 1999 Business Plan by committing itself to be a 'streamlined, responsive, private-sector oriented organization.'
>
> (Ibid., p. 13)

PIEFZA was also seen as being 'in a unique position to identify key policy issues that negatively affect the quality of the Palestinian investment climate' (ibid., p. 16). This would evidently mean, in the eyes of USAID, that PIEFZA needed to assume a political role to fulfill its economic mission, both internally vis-à-vis the PNA, but also vis-à-vis Israel:

> Much of the land that is most suitable for development in WBG is located in Category C or B areas according to current Israeli definitions. In order to ensure that land access does not pose a constraint to the development of the IF/FZ program, *PIEFZA will have an important advocacy role to play with the Israeli authorities during the period prior to the final status solution to get this designated for industrial use.*
>
> (Emphasis added, ibid., p. 17)

Here we see USAID calling upon PIEFZA to assume an explicitly political role in regard to lobbying for land rezoning. Ironically, it is a backhanded admission that the economic problems of the OPT could not be solved without political solutions, though USAID was being clearly circumspect and selective in its choice of encouraging the mobilization of private sector actors to lobby an occupying army to rezone its own occupation regime.

It is worth pointing out that this lobbying role may indeed have eventually been practiced, in regards to the Jenin industrial zone. Thanks to leaked documents about this estate, Israel appears to have indeed rezoned land from Area C transferring it to Area B, to facilitate both the construction of the industrial estate, as well as the legal expropriation of that land by the PNA, for that purpose (Silver, 2012). In this case, the zone was to be developed and run by a Turkish company, which, like PIEDCO, equally benefitted from a lucrative 49-year lease agreement (renewable for an additional 49 years). The PNA even went to the extent of expropriating the estate's 918 dunums of land, paying out $9.73 million to land owners, many of whom did not wish to sell (see MoU document via Silver, 2012).

Private Sector 'Self'-Organizing
International donors would also work directly to encourage the 'self'-organization of the Palestinian private sector.

Some bodies which received support were older institutions like the Federation of Palestinian Chambers of Commerce, Industry and Agriculture (FPCCIA), though this was a largely a post-2000 development. Others were entirely new creations encouraged to organize through international development aid, such as the Palestine Trade Centre – Paltrade, the Palestinian Information Technology Association (PITA), and the Palestinian Banking Association (PBA).

Perhaps the most important coalition to emerge from such assistance was the Private Sector Coordination Council (PSCC), established in early 2000 representing nine Palestinian organizations from the private sector. PSCC would emerge from Paltrade's National Trade Dialogue (NTD) Project, which was funded under the World Bank Technical Assistance Trust Fund (TATF). The concept underlying NTD came from a USAID-funded Market Access Project (MAP) that was contracted out to US consultants Development Alternatives Incorporated (DAI). Both PSCC and Paltrade would act as forums through which recurrent dialogue sessions with the government would take place, and where different sets of private sector recommendations could be formulated and raised.

In 2008, PSCC would put forward draft legislation for the creation of a private pension system. Its draft was based on a study composed by Levant Studies and Consultancy Services (LSCS) as commissioned by the Portland Trust.[11] LSCS was a short-lived Ramallah-based consultancy firm whose website (acting as its only public façade), listed no clear governance board or personalities. Investigation into LSCS revealed its website domain was registered by Bassil Jabir, former Director General of the Reform Support and Coordination Unit under the PNA Minister of Councils – the main body devising Palestinian reform, starting in 2002. One informant also disclosed it to be the operating headquarters of Salam Fayyad and showed this researcher a copy of an email signed by the latter from that email address. Since 2013, LSCS ceased to exist.

Thus a private sector interest group (PSCC) set up by international donor aid (the World Bank and USAID) advanced a lucrative pension privatization scheme, based on a consultancy report, commissioned by an international NGO engaged in venture capitalism (the Portland Trust), and written-up by a shadowy local consultancy firm, with links to senior PNA government officials. Clearly donors felt comfortable using aid in a grey zone, encouraging both private sector and government bureaucrats to take advantage of the PNA's own rent-allotment opportunities for personal enrichment in a context that lacked democratic regulatory oversight.

To sum up, by working on both sides of the private sector/ government regulation divide, as well as the civil society/government divide, Western donor states and IFIs created individual networks of influence within the OPT's political economy, and gained positioning along both sides of its social and economic cleavages. This was the civilian corollary to what donors were already doing in the security sector, 'bypass[ing] PNA and international mechanisms that had been established to coordinate security assistance, [and] instead dealing directly with their preferred organizations', according to a 2010 US Congressional Research Service document (Zanotti, 2010, p. 6). The report even recognizes that donors fostered 'a fiefdom mentality among competing security chiefs to address short-term objectives,' which 'might have undermined their own calls for a more consolidated PNA security sector answerable to civilian control and the rule of law' (ibid., p. 6).

A pattern can thus be detected: donors functionally and consistently demonstrated a manipulative tendency of shifting influence, finances, and legitimacy towards ends that fundamentally ensured another layer of control and influence enveloped Palestinian national developmental aspirations. This layer privileged private sector interests over national/ public ones, even though it equally needed a functional public sector body to administer service provision and enforce 'security.' While the public sector needed to be built, it also needed to be flanked by powerful interest groups external to it (within the private sector and the NGO community) and networks of allies internal to it as well (security sector personnel and select alliances with select individuals in ministries, PECDAR etc.) The gridlock and tension generated by this arrangement in the context of stalled negotiations, and under conditions of sustained de-development, prepared the explosive conditions that would eventually erupt once the July 2000 Camp David summit failed. In this way, the Oslo years demonstrate international institutional support for a basic governance infrastructure that could absorb and manage the contradictions of its enforcers – Israel and the Western donor community. Israel's contradictions were embodied in its consistent 'neither two nor one' approach which framed its political and economic approach vis-à-vis Palestinians, together with policies of de-development; Western donor contradictions were embodied in the tension between their support of free market capitalism in the OPT, and their respect for Israel's final say in economic and political matters beneath the cover of 'security.' It is these dual tensions which the Palestinian leadership and social sectors needed to negotiate in a context of the PLO's own contradictory national narrative regarding the realization of national rights on the one hand, and the agreements it signed on the other, which gravely constrained its margin of maneuver.

CHAPTER 7

PALESTINIAN POLITICAL ACTORS NEGOTIATE NEOLIBERAL PEACEBUILDING

The previous two chapters outlining Israeli and international donor contributions to structuring Palestinian political economy have already gone a distance in explaining the context in which Palestinian political actors were operating, and the degree of policy space they realistically acted within. It is nonetheless helpful to summarize this context to set the stage for understanding how Palestinian actors negotiated this arrangement, formalizing some of the understandings implied in the above illustrations.

One way of assessing international donor practice in the OPT is to stress, as Sahar Taghdisi-Rad (2011) does, that these actors sought 'to work around the conflict' (p. 11) and were 'unable and unwilling to exert any pressure on the Israeli side' (p. 197). Both wings of the international donor community indeed washed their hands of applying any tangible coercive leverage against Israel to get it to resolve any aspects of the conflict on the basis of international law or even basic principles of equality within the negotiations framework.

On the other hand, international donors were really undertaking a different objective entirely. They were not engaged in direct and substantive resolution of conflictual issues, but in molding the larger framework in which Palestinians experienced the conflict. In attempting to create a 'peace dividend' they sought to establish and stabilize a Palestinian authority capable of being molded in certain ways that would allow it to absorb and internalize the various political and economic contradictions of Israel and the international donor community.

The main tool of leverage in this process was donor aid provision disbursed with varying degrees of calculation over time, across the governance sector (civil and security), private sector and 'civil society', creating forms of hierarchical dependency and accountability that restricted Palestinian political maneuverability.

Palestinian development was to remain fundamentally determined by its vertical linkages with Israel and the international donor community, rather than by any horizontal linkages that its disparate, fragmented parts could forge with themselves. The public and private sectors, the security forces and substantial parts of Palestinian civil society (which included much of the Palestinian left political factions) would all begin to become enfolded in this politics of vertical aid dependency and the liberal political machinations it entailed. In the process, the PNA would come to functionally act as a subcontractor to the devolved responsibilities that Israel sought to shed – direct security functions, and certain civil functions – all of which were politically, ideologically and economically costly to Israel and Zionism more broadly, and none of which were enough to fulfill Palestinian rights or expectations.

Donors allowed for the PNA to create and distribute rents from within this delimited hierarchical arrangement, ultimately enforced by Israel, in the hopes that a workable social, political and economic order could be forged across the OPT. This fundamentally meant that far from acting as passive observers, international donors, like Israel, were actively intervening in the constitutive balances of the OPT's social relations, along lines of their particular collective and individual interests.

Political rent generation and allocation however needed to be carefully calibrated. On the one hand, too much centralization of the executive could strengthen the national and economic basis of the PNA, 'threatening' Israel with a reconstituted national movement far closer to Israel than Tunisia. Too weak of an entity would fail to be able to perform sufficiently to extricate Israel from the political, economic and demographic contradictions it was straddling, and which largely motivated the Oslo arrangement overall. A failed PNA would mean the failure of this entity to credibly perform in terms of service provision and security, thus eroding its power, and possibly even resulting in internal attempts to dismantle, reform or capture the apparatus from within.

The conflict resolution model consciously empowered Fateh to take 'local ownership' of a state-like apparatus that was tasked with buying-in different elements of Palestinian social and political classes, to tie them to the emergent political economy of the peace process regime itself, dominated by Israel and the donor community as the ultimate guarantors of its capital flows. The PLO chairman was envisioned as the primary forger of the first intra-Palestinian elite bargain of the OPT that could consolidate a political settlement capable of stabilizing the OPT socioeconomic and political order. International donors were to facilitate and enable the establishment of the PNA because Arafat was the only figure who could stitch together this consensus and give the apparatus and arrangement overall, an air of credibility needed for it to 'work.' He was thus perceived as providing the necessary legitimacy to the arrangement by the donor community and Israel, capable of setting in motion an institutional arrangement and related political economic order that would otherwise not have been able to operate had it lacked the forms of political legitimacy or charisma that Arafat brought it.

The early years of this arrangement demonstrate wide international and Israeli backing of Arafat and his ways, including of the PNA's repressive qualities, notably, the events of 'Black Friday', where 14 Palestinians were gunned down by PNA police in a protest in Gaza City on 18 November 1994. Aside from the repressive security function which the PNA needed to prove to both assert its power locally and its trustworthy 'partner'-like status vis-à-vis Israel and the internationals, aid actively facilitated Arafat's powers of buy-in by financing PNA start-up costs and providing lucrative contracts for state infrastructure and economic investments to favored capital groups. Israel's deposits in presidential bank accounts on monopoly rents paid for off-budget expenses that could not be declared to international donors, but were a necessary part of local rule – such as financially sponsoring Palestinian prisoner families, the families of martyrs, and providing employment to former prisoners and Fateh activists in the security services.

These buy-ins would also result in the Palestinian economy becoming characterized by a widening split between the primary benefactors of the new political economy (composed of public sector elites and a primitive state-like bourgeoisie of a deformed non-state), and those excluded from this arrangement.

The latter were to include the marginalized political forces of the PLO who were displaced from their former leading position in the national movement during the 1987 Intifada, emergent Islamist groups, and even sections of Fateh itself. Moreover, the arrangement would economically disenfranchise the great majority of private sector economic actors who were employed in small and medium size enterprises, with less than ten employees, often family owned. Those cut-out from access to the channels of rent allotment would play a part in forming the basis of rising internal opposition, whether in the form of increased support for the Islamic opposition, or through demands for a more inclusive political settlement amongst Palestinian economic and political actors through the PNA arrangement itself. The inchoate opposition would emerge from different social classes and included among other demands both political dimensions (calls for increased democratic accountability, holding firm to national principles, rejecting negotiations under continued conditions of occupation and settlement expansion) and economic reforms (against corruption, government competition in the economy, calls for widening the benefactors/or eliminating the unfair privileges certain sectors of the economic and political elite enjoyed as a consequences of the Oslo arrangement).

By the end of the Oslo years, international donors would become increasingly skeptical of Arafat's methods and questioned his ability or desire to deliver the political dividend of a final peace deal amenable to US and Israeli interests. Though it is difficult to precisely gauge and target the origins, motivations and triggers of increased donor skepticism around Arafat, it is clear that the international community was ready to retire the 'Arafat model' by the second Camp David negotiations in July 2000, and would make efforts to do precisely that when the Al-Aqsa Intifada broke out.

We will now look closer at the arc of Palestinian approaches and responses to the unfolding Oslo arrangement, attempting to shed light on its practices, discursive justifications, and their tensions.

National Narratives

Jeffery Paige's *Coffee and Power* provides a useful analytical tool for our study when it comes to interpreting the responses of various Palestinian social classes to the Oslo arrangement (Paige, 1998).

Paige's research is concerned with understanding how coffee elites came to support three radically different governance systems in central America (conservative authoritarianism in El Salvador, revolutionary socialism in Nicaragua, and social democracy in Costa Rica), but with all three eventually converging in the 1980s upon parliamentary democracy and the espousal of neoliberalism.

He finds part of his answer in an analysis of the elite narratives of the coffee elites themselves. For Paige, elite narratives are evidential trails that disclose how elites justify their actions and elide or mystify the implicit contradictions of their power. He adopts a Marxist under-standing of ideology, which he takes to mean an inherently 'distorted or mystified view of the social reality.' In this reading, the generation of ideology as a set of beliefs:

> is a product of a particular social process of inversion, first in the realm of reality, and second in the realm of ideas. The production of ideology is an attempt to resolve in the realm of ideas contradictions that are unresolvable in the realm of social reality.
>
> (Paige, 1998, p. 340)

Ideology's inversion and concealing of fundamental contradictions structures the creation of elite 'narratives', which Paige defines as 'stories that have a beginning, middle and end, a cast of characters, a set of events, and a sequence of action leading to a resolution of the problem with which the narrative began' (ibid., p. 341). He quotes John Thompson's observation that 'stories are told which justify the exercise of power by those who possess it – situating them within tales that recount the past and anticipate the future' (Thompson, 1984, p. 11).

Here we turn to Nabil Sha'ath again as one of Fateh's most influential intellectual/political figures. Sha'ath is internally credited for drafting Fateh's ten-point plan, which pioneered the staged approach to Palestinian liberation. It is seen as a pivotal plan in PLO history as it signified the end of a maximalist liberationist discourse and a transition into its 'pragmatist' phase that was exclusively Palestinian nationalist, politically conservative and ultimately focused on establishing an independent state in the OPT, rationalized as a base from which wider Palestinian rights could be realized.

Previous chapters have disclosed how Sha'ath was frustrated to return to the OPT to find PECDAR and the World Bank attempting to dominate economic and development planning. Now we explore his own vision for economic development as the PNA's first and long-running Minister of Planning (1994–2003), to understand the sources of that frustration.

For Sha'ath, there is teleology to Palestinian praxis, framed through the 'ideology' of 'statebuilding.' The Palestinians signed Oslo because it preserved the main national issues as negotiable, while allowing for the creation of an interim government:

> The Israelis avoided completely saying that [the Interim period] is preparatory for a state. They never accepted that in Oslo. We saw nothing but that. We saw this Interim period as a preparatory period for setting up a fully sovereign independent Palestinian state on the West Bank and Gaza, and our economic policy was designed to reflect that.
>
> (Sha'ath Interview)

Within this mindset, Sha'ath outlines what he saw as his 'first and most important goal', recounted in the following lengthy excerpt. It establishes the basic ideological framework rationalizing PNA behavior, but which also created a discursive space for alternative interpretation:

> From the very first day the Authority was set up, my role as Minister of Planning and International Cooperation was 'where do we separate from Israel' and 'where do we reconnect with Israel.' I wanted as much independence in the infrastructure, in pursuing international economic policy and in pursuing a strategy for *our own* economic growth that is linked *the minimum* with Israel.
>
> I'll tell you physically what I mean. Electricity came in to Gaza from Israel via 16 entry points [. . .] Every sector all the way down [the strip] to Rafah [in the south], got its electricity directly from

the closest Israeli kibbutz. There was absolutely no network. So we decided to build an electricity network that would enable us to build a power station that would start giving power to all of Gaza, and eventually with the safe passage [connecting Gaza to the West Bank, we] would be able to export power.

Telephones? If you call Khan Younis from Gaza [both located within the Gaza Strip], you are re-routed through Israel. There is no direct connection. And so we worked very hard to set up a ground telephone company that would connect Gaza totally separated from the Israeli system, but with a connection through Israel with the West Bank. We started buying a satellite station in order to uplink all our international telephone connections [...] We fought to separate the postal authority, the Palestinian internet nomenclature ('.ps'), the Palestinian telephone code (970). I fought battles in every international organization to separate Palestine. I always had to go back to the UN in order to set up a separate statistical nomination for Palestine. Whenever we were able to change 'OPT' we went to 'Palestine.' This was really symbolic but the essence of it was to *separate* Palestine from Israel [...] The essence was how to connect Palestine and disconnect as much as possible from Israel.

(Sha'ath Interview)

Perhaps Sha'ath's narrative of statebuilding and separation is overly informed by its contemporary contextual setting[1] and its marked *lack* of sovereignty or separateness from Israel. That said, it is not an inaccurate depiction of what the PNA attempted in these years, going to extensive lengths to create 'Palestine' discursively, statistically, logistically, and ideationally, linking this concept to a governance structure (the PNA), a security apparatus and a group of privileged capital formations meant to anchor and seed the OPT economy.

Emphasizing 'statebuilding' as the motivating ideology of the PNA during the Oslo years was also a way for Sha'ath's narrative (and the PNA overall) to try and fashion their policies within the existent political consensus of the time. This held that accepting Palestinian self-rule while still under conditions of occupation, approximated political treason. The PLO had explicitly opposed the variants of these plans in the past. Thus, Sha'ath's emphasis on PNA statebuilding ideology and praxis during the Oslo years, attempts to justify the PLO's decision to take power over the PNA under these circumstances, emphasizing that a genuine interim government as a predecessor for a sovereign state, could be analytically distinct from an entity that was institutionally and juridically no more than a limited self-governing autonomy arrangement along Allon Plan lines. In this way Sha'ath deviates attention from the determinative issue as to whether the actual terms of the deal that was signed contained assurances or even the likelihood that the PNA's real statehood ambitions were practically and institutionally realizable.

Carrying on with the narrative organized around the principle of 'separating from Israel' and 'connecting Palestine', Sha'ath describes his efforts to assert and define an economic and developmental line independent of the heavy role envisioned by the IFIs:

> Economically, for the strategy of development, my first job was to destroy the World Bank. To totally separate the World Bank from Palestine – so that it will just be a donor. And I succeeded. By 1997, the World Bank was just a donor, and it was listed in all our activities as 'one of the donors' – exactly like UNDP. But the role of the World Bank in deciding our economic strategy; the role of the World Bank in setting up our priorities; the role of the World Bank in coordinating the donor efforts [whereby the PNA had to go through the World Bank in order to even invite donors] – we completely destroyed that. We created a donor coordination mechanism – the Ad Hoc Liaison Committee (AHLC) and the Local Aid Coordination Committee) – with all of these mechanisms created to get the World Bank *out*, so it would become just a donor. [...] Within 3 years, I was able to totally change donor relations into a bilateral situation with a multilateral coordinating mechanism just used to put pressure to bring about higher bids for the bilateral. And in the end, all aid became bilateral.

> (Sha'ath Interview)

Here again, the heavy contemporary embrace of the World Bank and IMF over the OPT's economic reality may color Sha'ath's recollection of these historical events. But his explanation is nonetheless revealing in other respects. Despite an expressed mutual desire to engage in the neoliberal economic developmental plans of the Oslo Accords as part of the peace process, relations between the international donor community and the PNA were inevitably strained and contentious.

Figures like Sha'ath had well-formulated ideas regarding Palestinian development and how statehood could economically arise. The PLO had been running a state-like apparatus in diaspora for decades providing services in health, education, embassies, military training, and social welfare provision for widows, orphans and prisoner families in several Arab countries and unofficially in the OPT. It also had extensive investment portfolios around the world. Many of the PLO's leading figures were seasoned professionals with years of statebuilding-like experience in the Arab world, particularly the Gulf region. The PLO also had well-developed research institutions, which were engaged in monitoring, translating and analysing contemporary political and economic transformations and debates.

Given this background, it is not surprising to hear figures like Sha'ath, with a PhD in public administration from the University of Pennsylvania's Wharton School, extensively elaborating his vision of the OPT. He saw the materialization of 'Palestine's' potential in various economic sectors, including hi-tech, tourism and regional location-based services. He imagined Palestine becoming 'India on the Mediterranean' in terms of software development, inspired by a previous trip to India and his former relations with Rajiv Gandhi. He imagined a lucrative tourism sector that could capitalize on its 'Holy Land' status, bringing 20 million tourist per year. His vision was large:

> We can be the home of transit trade, transit industry, transiting oil pipelines, a hub for communications, providing high-level services to the community around us such as research organizations, consulting companies, banks, insurance companies, schools, universities. This was my vision of an independent state of Palestine and I of course sought to translate that into infrastructure requirements in terms of water, electricity, roads etc.
>
> (Sha'ath Interview)

Despite the sharp contrast between the grandness of this vision and the poverty of its realization, the very existence of the plan says a lot about how the Palestinian leadership approached economic development even within the restrictive domains of the Oslo process. The PNA was more than willing to engage with the neoliberal logic of the mid-1990s. Yet it nonetheless did so from within a framework that asserted this project *as flowing from a national economic and statebuilding process and logic.*

Sha'ath's vision should also be put in context as it was not the only economic vision under consideration. In July 1993, the PLO issued its own 'Program for Development of the Palestinian National Economy for the Years 1994–2000,' (PDP) prepared by top Palestinian economist Yusif Sayigh for the PLO's Department of Economic Affairs and Planning (PDP, 1993). Although the PDP envisaged 'the promotion and flowering of a market economy,' it balanced this tendency with a call for 'suggestive or indicative programming.' The plan ambitiously called for $11.6 billion in public investments over seven years, including 13 per cent for both agriculture and industry; 6 per cent for services (incl. public); 6 per cent for energy; 50 per cent for public housing and construction and 25 per cent for infrastructure.

The PDP was a national vision that should be read as the inverse of the World Bank's *Investment in Peace* report described in Chapter 3 (see Khalidi, 2014). It attempted to reverse the 'distortions' of the Occupation by promoting self-reliance. It was socially sensitive, calling for massive investments in affordable housing, as well as social welfare provision and equity. A balance was to be struck between export promotion and protection of domestic industry, through import substitution (IS), while agriculture was to anchor the OPT's economic recovery. Perhaps most importantly, it asserted the Palestinian right to economic decision-making, but emphatically cautioned:

> It must be obvious by now that the political factor is the *sine qua non* for success in the deployment of substantial efforts and financial and technical assistance to meet some of the more pressing social and economic needs of the Palestinian people [. . .] Whatever may and can be achieved under occupation, it will remain no more than a palliative: no comprehensive and integrated social and economic development can be undertaken under occupation while the Palestinians cannot exercise their inalienable economic rights as a minimum.   (PDP, 1993)

The PDP's vision of economic development was admittedly composed in July 1993, before Oslo was even signed. It nonetheless remained an important political document that asserted to all those willing to listen, that well-developed Palestinian plans existed that attempted to seriously grapple with the years of politically determined de-development.

Despite the existence of these plans, the opportunity for their implementation would be far-fetched under the Oslo arrangement. Although the PDP was distributed by the Palestinian delegation at the 30 October 1994 Casablanca donors conference, it was actually PECDAR's 'Invest in Palestine' Annex which was the accompanying fundraising document, representing the interests of the World Bank's Emergency Assistance Program (see EIR, 1995; World Bank, 1994). In a wider context, the PDP was anachronistic to its times with the winds of economic policy blowing in far more neoliberal directions. For instance, the mentioned Casablanca conference where it was distributed represented the flagship event where the regional neoliberal vision was launched (see Casablanca Declaration, 1994). The Summit's declaration outlined a vision for 'a comprehensive peace and a new partnership of business and government dedicated to furthering peace between Arabs and Israelis.' Sixty states and more than a thousand businessmen attended. The Arab boycott of Israel was functionally rescinded and regional economic cooperation initiatives were proposed including the establishment of a Middle East and North Africa Development Bank, a regional tourism board, and a regional chamber of commerce and business council to facilitate intra-regional trade relations. Attendees furthermore 'pledged to show that business can do business and contribute to peace as well; indeed, to prove that profitability contributes mightily to the economic scaffolding for a durable peace.'

When set in this light, the orientation of Palestinian development policy begins to be seen within a spectrum of possible developmental visions. Sha'ath's developmental vision was far more neoliberally integrationist and conservative than that of Sayigh's. Yet despite this, even Sha'ath's vision, which represents a center/right-national neoliberal developmental vision, would eventually prove politically and economically unpalatable to the donors.

In any case, Israeli policy would make sure that *no* national development policy had the chance to take root. Not long after the launching of these developmental approaches (end 1994), the reality on the ground would change only too quickly. Israel's closure policies would evaporate the potential for the OPT to be a reliable economic hub in the neoliberal regional order, while the PNA and donors scurried to prevent economic collapse. No Palestinian developmental vision could be realized during the Oslo years (or thereafter) because it was structurally delimited by the Oslo framework and because political and historical circumstances witnessed decisive strategic and economic moves by Israel (closure) that changed economic and political relations with the OPT, and the perception of the OPT as a potential investment locale.

Finally, it is worth contextualizing Sha'ath's claims of modest victories in achieving certain expressions of independent national economic statebuilding – victories such as statistical recognition of 'Palestine', the creation/recognition of an independent nomenclature, and forms of infrastructural connectivity. He also claims the rebuffing of IFI development plans and the emergence of bilateralism.

The PNA *was* able to resist donor domination of their agenda, demonstrating occasional agency and pluck, albeit recognizing that this was only a margin of maneuver within a structurally delimited setting. On the other hand, we also know that the fight over policy direction and decision-making did not end with the partial stiff-arming of the World Bank. While the creation of the Ad Hoc Liaison Committee and the Local Aid Coordination Committee may have been a means 'to get the World Bank *out*,' they nonetheless preserved a donor aid structure whereby these new structures of donor coordination, as described above, simply reproduced self-referential dispute resolution mechanisms, which gave Israel full veto rights, and which formalized and reflected Israel's existent 'practical' veto rights, through its overseeing of the institutions of closure. The Oslo arrangement thus facilitated the ability of Israel and the internationals to quickly change scale and scope of operations to filter and flank Palestinian development policy space and practice.

Finally, the achievement of bilateralism behind the Oslo year's aid arrangement would also mean that the PNA was able to obtain and negotiate forms of bargaining power vis-à-vis donor countries, as opposed to being confronted with a fully coordinated multilateral developmental agenda. Here too, the degree of maneuver the PNA actually obtained should not be exaggerated.

The combination of Israel's restrictive and coercive geopolitical policies and military map, organized around Israeli settler colonial ambitions, their 'security,' and Palestinian de-development on the one hand, and donor state adherence to and abidance by this general framework in their work on the other, meant that Israel and international donors held crucial strategic cards in determining the shape and character of Palestinian development. The peacebuilding paradigm in effect was structured to asymmetrically determine the basic parameters and framework of Palestinian national and developmental activity. This included in various strengths of influence: establishing the boundaries of acceptable political discourse and activity; the jurisdictional and qualitative nature of economic and governance activity; the extent, balance and allocation of capital and information flows and rent allocation; and even regarding the design and emphasis of legal frameworks. In all these regards, a great deal of Palestinian policy space regarding crucial issues to their national movement were considerably narrowed by this regime *a priori*. The degree of policy space Palestinian elite classes could thus enjoy as a result of bilateralism was only the product of the extent of contrast and contradiction between the various interests and priorities of the donors themselves as filtered by Israel, but was not a space that was the product of circumventing the structural limitations of the arrangement overall.

While the PNA indeed found ways to exploit internal competition between donors to its advantage resulting in marginal boons to its agenda, this should not be confused with (or elide, as Sha'ath implies,) erasure of the structural impediments to Palestinian development itself and the formal institutional means through which this was enforced — military occupation and closure on the one hand, donor funding protocols on the other.

CHAPTER 8

RENTS, RENT-SEEKING AND THE POLITICAL SETTLEMENT OF THE OSLO YEARS

So far our discussion has approached our subject matter by providing detailed illustrative historical, political and economic evidence of the character of the Oslo arrangement, and the way elements of Palestinian society, notably the PNA and favored capital formations, acted within this context.

While previous sections have already extensively discussed the issue of rent provision and buy-in, we have not gone to the extent of specifically determining and analysing the nature of Palestinian rents or their outcomes. Moreover we also must come to understand how rent provision fit together as part of a larger political and economic framework, both vis-à-vis Israel and the donor community, as well as vis-à-vis the balance and distribution of rights and powers across Palestinian social sectors. In a word, we must attempt to account for how the structure of rent provision informed the political settlement.

Here the theoretical and context- (OPT) specific contributions of Mushtaq Khan emphasize several enduring points worth reiterating before adding our analysis (Khan, 2000a; 2000b; 2004).

For Khan, the neoclassical and neoliberal fixation upon rents, rent-seeking activity, and their effects on political and economic outcomes, has obscured the analytical relevance of rent analysis overall. This is because mainstream economic and development analysis concentrates almost exclusively on the input costs of rent-seeking, seeing these as

socially undesirable and growth/efficiency retarding, while concomitantly avoiding considering rent outcomes.

But like other elements of the neoclassical worldview, this approach is
utopian and fails to be substantiated by the empirical record. Khan
instead stresses the need to differentiate between different rents and their
outcomes as the 'efficiency and growth implications of different rents can
be very different' (Khan, 2000a, p. 21). Over-fixation on rent-seeking
costs fails to consider the efficiency and growth implications of rents
created and maintained through rent-seeking (ibid., p. 13). That is to
say, 'rents can sometimes be efficient and in other cases essential, for
promoting growth and development' (ibid., p. 23). The challenge thus
becomes how to 'identify the conditions which determine whether value-
enhancing and value-reducing rents are created and the magnitude of the
rent-seeking cost' (ibid., p. 7).

To undertake this challenge, Khan analyses particular forms of rent
and rent-seeking activity: monopoly rents, natural resource rents, rents
based on transfers organized through the political mechanism,
Schumpeterian rents, rents for learning, and monitoring and management rents. He also emphasizes that the particular character of one rent
should not be extrapolated to other types in regards to their efficiency
and growth implications, and concludes by summarizing:

> No simple efficiency or growth implications can be read off from
> the observation that rents exist. The presence of rents can
> sometimes signal a dynamic and efficient economy, just as the
> absence of rents can sometimes signal inefficiency and stagnation.
> [...] The efficiency associated with a rent is assessed by looking at
> the immediate, or static, net social benefit (NSB) associated with
> the rent and comparing it with the net social benefit achieved in its
> absence. The growth implications are assessed by looking at the
> growth of output (or net social benefits) in the presence of the rent,
> compared with the growth achieved in its absence.
>
> (Khan, 2000a, p. 67)

Finally it is not enough to know the types of rents and the rent-seeking
costs but also to know who engages in rent-seeking and how it is
organized. Khan emphasizes that considerable amounts of rent-seeking
costs in developing countries are spent in patron-client networks with

the rents produced as a result also often distributed within these networks:

> Thus there is likely to be a 'circular flow' whereby part of the income from rents created for patrons as rent outcomes in one period provides the resources for inputs of rent-seeking expenditures on clients in the next period. This sustains their organizational power and allows further rounds of rent-seeking.
>
> (Khan, 2000b, p. 91)

Set aside for the moment these fundamental understandings of rent and rent-seeking as we turn to Khan's application to the Palestinian context.

Khan's argument is heavily informed by its historical context written around the height of the Al-Aqsa Intifada when international donors adopted calls demanding the democratization of the PNA and the imposition of a good governance agenda. This was deemed necessary because Arafat was being criticized for being a neopatrimonial autocrat whose economic dealings had emerged as obstacles to economic growth and development. Substantial evidence of monopolies, corruption, clientelism, and government competition in the private sector was on hand to back up these claims and was now being publicized so as to create pressure to push through institutional reforms. Khan's analysis thus attempts to integrate his analysis on rents and rent-seeking to the OPT in an effort to cut against and expose the hypocrisy of the good governance and neopatrimonal framework as applied to the OPT and adopted by the international donor community. In this context, Khan *et al.*'s (2004) work articulates an important scholastic and political rejoinder to the mainstream developmental approach that confronted the PNA, though the critique failed to dent the continuation of this approach, then or since.

Khan's (2004) contributions concentrate on describing the types of rents and rent-seeking that emerged under the PNA, which 'were directly the result of the specific arrangements set up by the Oslo agreement' (p. 36). He focuses on Palestinian rents with an interest to contextualize the particular experience of Palestinian rent and rent-seeking within a broader international context, likening its rent management issues to those of other developing countries and their rent outcomes. He identifies three main types of rent and rent-seeking in the areas administered by the PNA during the Oslo years: monopolies, redistributive transfer rents and corruption. While he is careful not to sound in any way apologetic, he notes that in each case, there was a logic to the emergence of the rent/rent-seeking activity and that these rents had the potential to rear net-positive social benefits if construed as part of a larger program of social transformation and capitalist development within a national statebuilding process.

The small nature of the Palestinian economy for instance induced the likelihood of 'natural' monopolies, particularly in regards to utilities. The nature of trade relations as a result of the PER also meant that it was to the advantage of the PNA to control key commodities like cement and petrol. The PNA could protect its market and centralize and capture revenue that might otherwise have gone to Israel through these rents. Temporary monopolies were also attractive incentives for potential diasporic investors.

As for redistributive (transfer) rents through the political mechanism, Khan sees these too as having been politically necessary to stabilize the PNA polity as is the case in societies undergoing developmental social transformation. While he acknowledges that the system of rent allocation was held by the executive, he emphasizes that this was what the internationals and Israel wanted and expected in the first place, when they created off-budget accounts, in addition to budget support to the PNA. Moreover, he importantly emphasizes that the executive 'retained the ability to determine the type and allocation of redistributive rent' (ibid., p. 39) – with Arafat maintaining his ability to discipline his underlings. Khan also argues that redistributive transfers were part of a strategy to 'make resources available to emerging capitalists to accelerate the emergence of capitalism' (ibid., p. 39).

As to corruption, Khan has no issues with acknowledging that evidence of predatory extortion or bribery existed. However he rightly balances this acknowledgement by pointing out that there is no evidence that such rent-seeking was comparable to the corruption of Israeli border officials, or the looting of Israeli soldiers during military operations. More importantly he stresses, 'the rent-seeking and corruption associated with these kinds of rents were the result of specific rents that were created and managed as a necessary part of the Oslo Agreements' (ibid., p. 42).

In sum, Khan's assessment is a delicate reading of a complex arrangement but one that argues in a nuanced manner that the rents observed in the Palestinian theaters were 'compatible with aspects of a predatory state, others with a fragmented clientelist state, and others with a developmental state' (ibid., p. 45). Ultimately he concludes that because Israel was only really offering Palestinians a fragmented client state based on asymmetric containment, it was the Palestinian leadership's rejection of this fate and its attempts to break out of these developmental strategies that ultimately induced the international community to invoke the good governance agenda and its accompanying critique of neopatrimonialism (ibid., p. 50).

Alternatively, Khan stresses that the Palestinian developmental strategy could have worked despite its leakages (which were regulatory issues, not fundamentally at variances with aspects of a developmental state and capitalist praxis), and demonstrated a rationality given the overall rent structure and political framework.

While Khan is helpful in describing the basic features of Palestinian rent-seeking activity and contextualizing them within a broader context of development, his analysis is problematic on various levels. In part, the problems stem from the fact that his critique is too informed by the prevalent political discourse and pressures of its time (2004) and are designed to argue against the liberal assumptions emerging from the donor community that saw democracy and good governance as the answer to Palestinian economic ills. This was, as Khan correctly notes, a deliberate and false conflation between domestic critiques of the PNA's performance in regards to economic and nationalist statebuilding goals as determined by its Palestinian constituency, and international donor critiques that Palestinian rent-seeking explained why economic growth did not sufficiently occur.

Some discussion of Khan's analysis is thus required to be able to realign and reassess this period. This is possible and necessary given the passage of time and the fact that current circumstances allow us to more critically assess Palestinian development policies without the need to politically and scholastically rebut and expose international donor hypocrisy, as Khan's analysis did at the time.

First, it cannot be stressed enough that the entire Oslo arrangement was politically determined. That meaning, the financial streams international donors and Israel controlled and allocated to the PNA were strategic rents – political transfers that could not and would not be transferred to another polity, thus pronouncing their rent-like characteristics. The rent-seeking that took place via the PNA was thus for *derivative* rents that emerged as a consequence of the larger strategic rent from donors. The derivative nature of Palestinian rents and hence rent-seeking activity underscores how any analysis of this phenomenon must be undertaken from a perspective that considers the net social benefit of the *original* rent and not just its derivative. This is important to note, because Khan's earlier (2000a) theoretical work stresses that the 'efficiency associated with a rent is assessed by looking at the immediate, or static, net social benefit (NSB) associated with the rent and comparing it with the net social benefit achieved *in its absence*' (*emphasis added*, p. 67). It thus becomes incumbent to analyse how the derivative rent fits into the net social benefits *of the original strategic rent*.

Thus, in the absence of this strategic rent and its accruing 'net social benefits', the cost for Israel to carry out civilian and security duties associated with the PNA would be far higher. The marginal cost of the next best competitor to rent-like political transfers of the Oslo arrangement through the Fateh–led PNA was extremely high for Israel – with all of this assuming that costs ('prices') are calculated from an Israeli and international perspective, not a Palestinian one.

In this regard, one wonders whether Khan's assessment of the marginal costs associated with political transfer rents is as 'irrelevant' as his earlier work suggests (see Khan, 2000a, p. 67, Table 1.2). Here Khan had described among other things, whether 'prices' resulting from different kinds of rents are higher than their marginal costs. In monopolies, for instance they are always higher; natural resource rents and Schumpeterian rents, they aren't; and in cases of rents for learning and monitoring, it is possible but not always the case ('maybe') that prices are higher. Yet when it comes to assessing the marginal cost of (political) 'rent-like transfers' – Khan claims this to be 'irrelevant.'

It may be necessary to revisit this contention given that in the case of the OPT at least, the cost of providing the original strategic rents to the Arafat-led PNA for its own rent provision schemes *significantly reduced the cost Israel had to pay to do the job itself.* In this respect the strategic rents that Fateh received were certainly efficiency-enhancing from an Israeli and international donor perspective.

It is equally significant to note that Fateh (and the ring of its associated businessmen), implicitly understood this structural condition of the political and institutional 'market.' It thus believed it could leverage this cost differential to its advantage to perpetuate its capture of political rent transfer arrangements, as long as it could prevent the emergence of potentially cheaper competitors. We must keep this element in mind when considering how future international efforts to reform the PNA indeed *do* attempt to create such an alternative cheaper competitor, by emphasizing technocratic governance and exploring the possibility to transform the particular character of the rent provision from political transfer rents to managerial and monitoring rents (see following Part III).

Second, Khan's evidence for the existence of rents with a developmental character is flawed. To understand why, it is necessary to comprehend his definition of rents with a developmental character, which is largely based on extending his theoretical contributions on developing states undergoing capitalist social transformation to the Palestinian context. The provision of this definition in full herein takes place because it highlights two overlooked factors that will have crucial implications in the future: the character of Palestinian development to emerge during the Oslo years and thereafter, and the nature of international donor policy interventions to the OPT.

First the character of rents within developmental states:

> The conditions and capacities required for a developmental state need to be carefully identified because the range of rents such a state creates can be superficially similar to those created by predatory or fragmented clientelist states. For instance, a developmental state could create temporary monopoly rents, but in this case, it would be to attract investment and encourage risk-taking, and these rents would be managed to achieve these goals. A developmental state could also create transfers and redistributive rents to accelerate the emergence of capitalists and to maintain political stability, but these transfers would be managed so that their efficiency costs were controlled, and the net effect was an acceleration of developmental transformations.
>
> (Khan, 2004, p. 55)

Now their application to the OPT:

> To test if rent-management in the Palestinian context displayed any developmental state characteristics, we should look for evidence of rent allocations that maintained political stability and provided conditional support to emerging capitalists. A developmental state would have to have a much greater degree of sovereignty than was allowed to the PNA under the Oslo Agreements. Nevertheless, although this is not widely recognized, there were elements in the rent-allocation organized by the PNA that were consistent with a nascent developmental state. The scale was inevitably small given the powerful external constraints facing the state, and the short time period before the first normal period of development ended in 2000. But there is evidence that the PNA used rents to attract expatriate Palestinian capitalists who had substantial investment funds and entrepreneurial experience. Many did invest in Palestine under the PNA despite the extreme uncertainty regarding the future of the Palestinian state formation experiment. The PNA also displayed some ability to correct mistakes in the allocation of rents, re-allocating rents to those who might be more efficient (and who could therefore offer bigger benefits to the PNA over time). The ability to override factional interests and to correct misallocations of rents despite factional opposition is a characteristic of developmental states that distinguishes them from fragmented clientelist ones, and enables them to ensure that rents remain growth-promoting.
>
> (Ibid., p. 55−6)

According to Khan, 'evidence of rent allocations that maintained political stability and provided conditional support to emerging capitalists' is thus sufficient 'to test if rent-management in the Palestinian context displayed any developmental state characteristics.'

If we accept this definition, both sets of evidence he pursues (and finds) to justify this developmental state characterization are problematic.

As to the first criteria (transfers to maintain political stability) − admittedly, this is a question that is difficult to judge: whether the rent outcomes of political transfers led to political stability. Clearly one would have to set a time frame and develop highly specific and difficult-to-assess criteria to even attempt to answer if this were the case. It should be equally noted that Khan himself has no problems acknowledging that other rents (predatory and clientelistic ones), which could be confused for developmental rents, indeed did have negative net social benefits. But the nature of the PNA's rent allocation as being *derivative* rent emerging from the broader strategic rent coming to the PNA via Israel and Western donors, should be a clue as to their ability to reap 'stability', while equally raising questions as to their 'net social benefit.'

PNA rent provision was only allowed to take place in the first place because it marginalized significant local political and economic actors, failed to adhere to democratic criteria, and embraced authoritarian practices in a broader context of military occupation and settler colonialism. Political stability within the overall OPT context clearly did not emerge – quite the contrary, an Intifada broke out. Moreover, while political stability of the PNA may have nominally arisen during these years, it was a stability that would increasingly be challenged by those it marginalized and was a *relative* stability forged in relation to the *instability* of relations with the Israeli military which had ruled over the OPT population with an 'iron fist' – literally the name of Israeli PM Rabin's policy to crush the 1987 Intifada.

The shift from direct Israeli military rule to PNA rule, based in part on political rent transfers, resulting in a modicum of stability *vis-à-vis the PNA itself*, should not obfuscate the fact that Palestinians still saw the Israeli occupation as the primary source of their deferred liberty and development. They thus remained a 'destabilizing' force to Israel throughout the Oslo years, as evidenced in continued attacks against Israeli targets and significant popular upsurges during this period.[1] In this context, separating the larger OPT instability vis-à-vis the occupation, from the internal Area A and B 'stability' is illusory, while papering over the repressive and undemocratic methods that gave the appearance of this stability. The PNA's own decision to cancel the 1996 local elections should be read as a sign that both the PNA and donors feared the potential for 'destabilizing' elements to take political expression and 'legitimate' governance powers. That Palestinian society did not erupt against the PNA during the Oslo years, and reserved the bulk of its 'destabilizing energies' for Israel, should be read only as an affirmation that they understood – correctly – that the primary contradiction preventing their wellbeing rested with Israel and not the PNA. Rebelling against a primary contradiction, while largely ignoring a secondary one, in a context of limited resources, demonstrates a rational assessment of the nature of Palestinian oppression, and not the success of political transfers to engender stability.

As to the second criteria evidencing developmental state rent allotment – the provision of 'conditional support to emerging capitalists' – here Khan's analysis is also questionable. His evidence focuses on the fact that 'the PNA used rents to attract expatriate Palestinian capitalists who had substantial investment funds and entrepreneurial experience', resulting in 'many expatriate capitalists investing in Palestine under the PNA.' But this blurs the true nature of these capitalists and the transfers they received. That is to say, these were not 'emerging capitalists' as his criteria demands, but actually *well-established capitalists*, albeit not necessarily located or based out of the OPT.

Here the works of Adam Hanieh (2011) and Khalil Nakhleh (2012) are enlightening to our discussion.

Hanieh (2011) describes how the capital accumulation of expatriate Palestinian elites 'occurred as part of the accumulation processes of other regional capitalist classes.' Hanieh stresses the particular importance of the Gulf area which acted as 'the central zone of activity for displaced Palestinian capital,' resulting in Palestinian expatriate capital largely developing as 'a distinct sub-sector of the Gulf capitalist class.' He further stresses that 'the core of its accumulation is not the West Bank and Gaza Strip, but remains firmly located in the Gulf region,' with the field of accumulation conceived of 'at the regional scale.'

Hanieh's points are important to consider when further exploring the character of the diasporic capitalists specifically targeted for buy-in to the PLO's statebuilding project.

With their numbers too small, and their political visions too diverse to speak in class terms, their patterns of capital accumulation are nonetheless consistent in so far as their wealth derived from their positioning as junior partners to the existing pattern of politically determined accumulation within the Gulf states. This meant that they benefitted from forming alliances and providing services for local elites both within the government and within what Achcar describes as the Arab world's 'state bourgeoisie' – the Arab 'bourgeoisie deriving its economic power from the state, while functioning as private capitalism' (Achcar, 2013, p. 58).

Achcar relies on Max Weber's definition of politically determined capitalism as a function of:

1) 'opportunities for predatory profit from political organizations or persons connected with politics,' 2) 'profit opportunities in continuous business activity which arise by virtue of domination by force or of a position of power guaranteed by the political authority,' and 3) 'profit opportunities in unusual transactions with political bodies.'

(Weber, 1978, vol. 2, pp. 164–65; in Achcar, 2013, p. 63)

As some of the Arab world's best educated and skilled engineers, consultants and businessmen of the 1950s and 1960s, Palestinians were well-positioned to sell their labor and services to the emergent Arab states and state bourgeoisie, often in the capacity of contractors and intermediary service providers for the large US/European energy companies active in the Gulf oil industry. Moreover their non-indigeneity meant these Palestinian capitalists were domestically less complicated to manage, as they were outsiders constantly reliant upon the larger legal/citizenship framework of their host countries to assure continued accumulation. Those Palestinians who made it up the chain of the Arab world's politically determined accumulation, did so based on their explicit non-threatening nature vis-à-vis their hosts and patrons, as well as the combination of valuable skills and influence they could provide in the context of early state formation and the undemocratic nature of these states' political settlements.

Both Hanieh and Nakhleh give detailed insight into the accumulation histories of figures like Sabih al-Masri, Munib al-Masri, Hasib Sabbagh, Said Khoury, Abdel Majid Shoman, Omar el-Akkad and Basel 'Aqel. These histories clearly affirm how their patterns of accumulation fit into the region's politically determined accumulation, to the extent that the former provided various services to both Arab and international militaries, and helped facilitate the opening of markets in similar services to international capital (such as CCC's alliance with US construction giant Bechtel).

Existent notions of comprador capital or the lumpen bourgeoisie thus do not quite capture the complex role these capitalist groups played. These were *non-indigenous* elements within the existing class structure and political economy of their host states. They helped consolidate the particular form of politically-determined accumulation of the Gulf states, thus entrenching patrimonial rentier states. Their intermediary role between international capital and local elites consolidated the latter's local positioning and state formation, while ensuring a healthy cut from the transaction came their way. But these actors had no sway in the local political settlement of their host states. On the contrary, their intermediary non-indigenous positioning within the politically determined accumulation structure of these states, made them the natural conduits through which both Western political powers, and local Arab elites, mediated their relations with the emergent, 'radical' PLO.

Both Hanieh and Nakhleh provide solid evidence of this role as these capitalists proved themselves as reliable back channels facilitating important political turning points, including the PLO's withdrawal from Jordan in 1970 after the events of Black September, the saving of the Jordanian dinar after the mass capital flight of the early 1990s, and the PLO's acceptance of UN Resolution 242 as a precondition to open US-PLO dialogue (see Nakhleh, 2012, pp. 50–5). They thus reinforced the conservative underpinnings of the regional order, with their power and wealth inseparably deriving from their familiarity and penetration of these channels. Moreover, the increasing reliance of the PLO upon such channels after the defeat of 1982 improved their historical leverage vis-à-vis the PLO and the national movement overall.

Seen in this context, Khan's portrayal of these emergent capitalist benefactors of conditional rents within patterns consistent to a developmental state, obscures how these were in fact established capitalists, heavily steeped in the existing regional economic and political order and its accumulation patterns.

It is difficult of course to judge what particular combination of national and economic motivations inspired these capitalists and their decisions to invest in the 'green field' of 'Palestine.' That said, certain objective facts about their investments can still be stated:

Firstly, the OPT setting was clearly only one of several investment fronts within their investment portfolios.

Secondly, like any capitalists, they were highly sensitive to the existent institutional, political, and economic regime and its incentive structure and power balance. They thus sought wherever and whenever possible, forms of guarantees or protections to ensure their investments were safe. Indeed, as we have seen with the Gaza Power Plant, expatriate capitalist formations engaged in this investment only after receiving extremely extractive conditions and political insurance protections. Investment in industrial estates too, only emerged after generous international and PNA subsidies. In fact the most profitable Palestinian holding company exemplary of the supposed 'emergent capitalist' narrative, is PADICO. But far from being a company cut from the tough accumulation context of the OPT setting, PADICO was incorporated in 1993 under the Liberian Off-Shore Business Corporation Act in Monrovia and was only registered in the OPT in 2009 (see PADICO Annual Report, 2010, p. 57). As a foreign company it could enjoy generous tax benefits with this form of registration also beneficial in allowing the company to retain powers of international mediation.

The existing economic order and incentive regime should also be kept in mind as from a capitalist perspective, there were *multiple* regimes of different scope and power that these actors operated within. These included the PNA legal regime to navigate, but also the Israeli, Jordanian, the Egyptian and even those of the Gulf states.

The multiplicity of economic frameworks of varying state (and non-state) orders, highlights a particular quality to the arrangement that these forces operated within and needed to respond to. In order to survive and thrive, Palestinian capitalists needed to retain optimum flexibility in accommodating to the existing regime within which they operated, without ever over-extending themselves to the extent that they potentially violated political and economic arrangements made in other regimes and settings. We shall call this optimum flexibility character to these formations 'chameleon capital', whereby the capitalist changes color to the existing regime he operates within.

Thirdly, there was nothing guaranteeing that these emergent capitalists would not eventually show themselves willing to retreat from the OPT setting to safer theatres, once its vulnerability and risk was exposed. Indeed there is evidence that some did precisely that.

Finally, while the *conditional* nature of these rents is a key factor behind Khan's characterization of them as potentially developmental, one must not lose sight of the fact that the executive's regulatory power was not only restricted by Israel's ultimate control over territory, but the nature of this regulation was embedded largely in informal patron-client relations, as opposed to legalistically, enforceable contractual arrangements. As the arrangement's central neopatrimonial figure, it was Arafat alone who really retained the power to call in the rents and the rent-seekers, and who could potentially allot these rents more 'efficiently.' This as we shall see, would make the system highly vulnerable in the context of his absence. Because the nature of the arrangement centralized power in the personhood of a neopatrimonial leader, the structure of Arafat's power relied upon tiers of various patrons and clients constantly engaged in competitive dynamics for access to the executive above them. No clear criteria to discern efficiency or legitimacy existed amongst them, other than power and Arafat's assessment of what was necessary at a given time. Thus in his absence (ultimately through death) the system effectively witnessed the death of its prime regulator, in a context where Arafat's successor (Mahmoud Abbas) was of a weaker political stature within Fateh and Palestinian society.

Together, these factors raise questions as to the genuine developmental character of these rents.

But there is one additional factor that Khan fails to interrogate in respect to his criteria for evidence of developmental rents – that being, the character of the development conditions overall.

Khan restricts himself to the net social benefits of rents and how they were regulated or not, but he insufficiently integrates this with the overall character of Palestinian development conditions, characterized as *de-development*. This meant that Israel consistently enforced the 'negation of rational structural transformation, integration and synthesis, where economic relations and linkage systems become, and then remain, unassembled [...] and disparate, thereby obviating any organic congruous, and logical arrangement of the economy or of its constituent parts' (Roy, 1995, p. 129).

The rent provision opportunities of the PNA were thus a particularly extreme variant of politically determined capital prevalent throughout the Arab world. Achcar describes this overarching character as one whereby:

> The absence of any real rule of law in virtually all Arab countries [. . .] fetters the development of the type of capitalism led by entrepreneurs willing to take risks of the sort implied by investment in fixed capital with long-term amortization. In contrast, speculative or commercial capitalism motivated by the pursuit of short term profit thrives under such conditions. Such capitalism coexists and, often, combines with the state bourgeoisie's 'politically determined capital'.
>
> (Achcar, 2013, p. 62)

Thus in the context of the OPT's double absence of rule of law (as a function of Israel and Arafatist neopatrimonialism), combined with the de-developed character to the OPT economy (enforced by Israel); and its trebly politically determined nature overall (donors, Israel, the PNA) – a particularly deformed economic transformation emerges. *PNA rent allocation opportunities go toward rent-seeking opportunities that can exist and remain profitable despite de-development and the lack of sovereignty, and with some of these even having the potential to thrive under continued occupation and even conflict.*

One does not need to prove this by alluding to the 'extreme' case of the Palestine Electricity Corporation – which would reap a 7 per cent annual profit in the same year it was bombed by Israel.

The best way to illustrate this is by looking at the investments of the Palestine Commercial Services Company (PCSC) itself – the main private sector investment arm of the PNA during Oslo. In a context of politically determined accumulation, the PCSC's investments can only be read as the PNA's investment in its own rent allotment provision, ensuring it captured some of the revenue it was providing to its preferential capitalist groups. These investments overwhelmingly have a character of being secure and profitable largely irrespective of overarching developmental and political outcomes, and contribute low value added.

Thus we see the preponderance of investments such as hotels (the Jericho Resort Hotel and Casino, Bethlehem Convention Center, the Jacir Palace Intercontinental), cement, telecommunications (Paltel and

Palcell), consumer goods (APIC), food stuffs (flour mill, Coca Cola, vegetable oil, and cigarettes), electricity (the PEC); insurance companies (Ahlia and the Gaza Insurance Company); and elements associated with inputs to real estate development (steel, concrete, aluminum, glass), as well as real estate itself.

By the end of 1999, PCSC assets totaled $345 million, of which $292m was in the form of equity holdings (IMF-PA, 2000). It is telling that its most valuable holdings were a 30 per cent stake in the Jericho Resort Hotel and Casino 100 per cent of the Cement Company; 35 per cent in Palcell (the early operator of Jawwal mobile phone service); and 8 per cent in the Palestinian Telecommunications Company (Paltel). These investments alone accounted for about one-half of PCSC's total assets. PCSC net profits (after provisions) for 1999 totaled $77m, of which approximately $18m came from the sale of cement (EIU, 2000c, p. 45).

We get further indication of the unproductive, low value added and potentially speculative nature of Palestinian capitalist investment by looking at the performance of the Palestine Securities Exchange. The latter was created as an unregulated private sector investment-promoting wing majority owned by PADICO, which attempted to formalize the trade in shares of the main private sector Palestinian capital formations to benefit from the Oslo arrangement. PSE's al-Quds Index would witness impressive 53 per cent gains for 1999, earning the exchange title as 'one of the Arab world's star performers', according to the prestigious Economist Intelligence Unit's subscription-based country reports (EIU, 2000a, p. 32). Trading volume more than quadrupled to $68.9 million, while the US dollar value of shares rose by 219 per cent, to over $150 million. Market capitalization stood at $849 million. The EIU report however carefully notes that investor interest was concentrated on the stocks of two firms – Palestine Telecommunications (Paltel) and the Palestine Development and Investment Company (PADICO) – which together accounted for around 75 per cent of the market's capitalization. The value of Paltel's stock rose by 66 per cent in 1999, while PADICO also had a 25 per cent stake in Paltel (EIU, 2000b).

All this goes to show that the developmental character of these rents was not self-evident or predisposed by any means, with their 'net social benefit' hard to characterize as positive or negative, in a scenario where most of these rents appear capable of being profitable in contexts of both peace and conflict.

It is appropriate to end this section by alluding to how this arrangement would play itself out in the context of the end of the five-year Interim period, and the eventual commencement of the final status negotiations.

As noted earlier, international donor skepticism of the Arafat-led PNA was rising by the end of the Oslo years, while domestic voices of disenchantment with the overall peace process and the PNA's economic and political performance became more pronounced. The post-Washington Consensus was also rising in international donor policy frameworks, with the OPT setting particularly vulnerable to forms of donor experimentation there, given the high dependency on foreign aid and the limited policy space of Palestinian national actors.

In this context, donors would begin to walk back their previous tacit support and facilitation of rent provision within a neopatrimonial framework, and began to instrumentalize the good governance agenda to pressure Arafat on institutional reform. The World Bank-Japan 'Aid Effectiveness' report published on the eve of the Camp David negotiations, would remarkably expunge any direct Israeli responsibility for the political and economic outcomes of the Oslo era. It would go on to argue as 'the central finding of the aid effectiveness study' whose 'fundamental importance cannot be overemphasized' that:

> In the absence of a clear and unequivocal commitment to reform at the highest levels of the PA, there is little prospect for progress [. . .] [W]ithout reform, donor assistance will not be as effective as it otherwise might be. Indeed, without such reform, there is little likelihood of real, sustained economic growth.
>
> (World Bank and Japan, 2000, p. 118)

The report ends on a clear post-Washington Consensus note, claiming that while 'donors have an important role in promoting reform, and hence increasing the effectiveness of their assistance programs [. . .] reform cannot and should not be imposed from outside,' with this process needing to be Palestinian-owned and led (ibid., p. 118). Donors were signaling that they were looking for alternative 'local owners.'

Thus the theoretical foundations and policy basis for rolling back the neopatrimonial system international donors were instrumental in establishing in the OPT under Arafat, was laid. In its place a particular variant of post-Washington Consensus 'statebuilding' would eventually emerge.

As part of the pressure against Arafat, the World Bank and IMF began explicitly pushing for full disclosure of PNA's financial dealings, including its monopolies and involvement in the private sector. In August 1999 the PNA agreed to the establishment of a Higher National Committee for Institutional Development 'to enhance performance of public institutions (World Bank and Japan, 2000, p. 118). Five months later, the PNA would announce the establishment of the Higher Council for Development to oversee revenue administration, investment funds, and borrowing. By May 2000, just before the Camp David negotiations would take place, the PNA disclosed the investments of the PCSC and gave assurances that it would restructure its public investments and privatize some of its assets. Those it retained would be consolidated into the newly formed Palestine Investment Fund (PIF), with its profits overseen by a central account under the Ministry of Finance.

Although it would still take several years before the IFIs and donors would succeed to obtain full disclosure of PNA investments, the policy orientation was clear: donors were attempting to remove the discretionary financial power of the PNA executive, and narrow its policy space. The rent allotment schemes they had initially empowered Arafat to allocate, or which Arafat manipulated to gain increased policy space, were now to be fully audited, attempting to disclose and make accountable the full network of neopatrimonial power which did a great service in anchoring Arafat's rule. Indeed this policy shift would only accelerate in the wake of Arafat's rejection of the July 2000 Camp David offer and the start of the Al-Aqsa Intifada.

This shift would inevitably lead to the increased waning of Arafat's utility in the international peacebuilding/conflict resolution modules embraced by international actors. He had proved himself successful in forging a governance structure capable of providing basic civil and security functions. Moreover, the assent of the post-Washington Consensus was providing theoretical and policy formulations that claimed to be able to reap more predictable political and economic growth-enhancing outcomes. The apparatus only Arafat could have forged, now needed to be extricated from his grip. Full withdrawing of his financial maneuverability was thus crucial to this end, with the incremental institutional reforms of 1999 and 2000 starting a process that would continue apace during the Al-Aqsa Intifada until his death, ultimately aimed at affirming his obsolescence.

PART III

STATEBUILDING?

CHAPTER 9

REFORM AND STATEBUILDING

The international drive for 'statebuilding' in the OPT emerges from the failure of the international community's original neoliberal peace-building model during the Oslo years. The failed negotiations at Camp David in July 2000 and the eruption of the Al-Aqsa Intifada two months later, quickly exposed how the peacebuilding paradigm in operation was inadequate to reap a political accord between Israel and the Palestinians, let alone Israel and the rest of the Arab world. By its own standards it could not deliver a significant or inclusive 'peace dividend'; fostered illiberal political and economic tendencies among the Palestinian leadership; and ignored the clear abuse of power asymmetries both on the ground and in negotiations, which undermined the process' supposed endgame. In this respect, the Western donor community could not avoid being regarded as partially responsible for the explosive reality to emerge in the OPT, which reeked of failed Palestinian expectations.

Western donor responses to this failure however would not entail any serious questioning of the pre-assumptions behind their model and policies, or the self-imposed delimited mandate that contributed to it. On the contrary, the Al-Aqsa Intifada and Israel's response would provide an opportunity to deepen and advance their former positions towards the Palestinians still further, albeit this time in the shadow of Israel's coercive military exploits. Moreover, the crystallization of the post-Washington Consensus (PWC) within development praxis during this period, which promised more efficient and predictable outputs, appealed to OPT donor practitioners reeling from the mercurialism of Arafat's neopatrimonial ways.

The PNA's circumscribed, non-sovereign powers and financial dependency, enforced by Israel, would now reinforce donor confidence in demanding full disclosure of where, how and to what end PNA finances (and not just donor aid) were spent. With the basic apparatus of the PNA bankrolled and erected during the Oslo years, donors worked to actively mold and inscribe its budgetary, legal and institutional order in ways that went far beyond anything that had come previously – a fact that tends to be overlooked because much of this activity took place while world attention was preoccupied with the US' then-ongoing involvement in Afghanistan and Iraq. The post-Washington consensus agenda calling for good governance, democracy and the need to create the institutions for private sector-led growth, found willing allies in reform-minded elements of Palestinian society, coloring (and often camouflaging) a sense of Palestinian ownership to these processes. In truth, the most significant reforms imposed on the Palestinians came beneath the most coercive of leverage: the military pressure of Israel and the conditionality policies of the donor community.

The dovetailing of foreign and domestic reform agendas, albeit deriving from different origins and needs, would nonetheless find common cause beneath the statebuilding rubric. But like its neoliberal peacebuilding predecessor, neoliberal statebuilding would reproduce and deepen similar contradictory tendencies deriving from its utopian, feigned technical mission. In fostering a new discourse, institutional arrangement and 'development' praxis in PNA areas, neoliberal statebuilding would further distort the OPT's political economy and social relations, while ultimately giving rise to the maturation of Palestine Ltd.

Reform of the PLO and later the PNA, have been longstanding Palestinian demands raised by opposition parties, respected independent personalities and even voices within Fateh (Abdel Jawad, 2002). The PNA's own comptroller issued a report in mid-1997 stating that $326 million of its $800 million budget for 1996 (nearly 40 per cent) had been misallocated (JMCC, 1998). Such reports largely fell on deaf ears however, with the PNA executive failing to investigate these claims indirectly encouraged by uninterrupted donor financing. By the end of the Oslo years, international concern around reform was growing, but the donor community still treated the matter delicately and in partnership with the PNA leadership.

The donor impetus for reform would decisively strengthen however after new political circumstances emerged in the wake of failed negotiations at Camp David and the outbreak of the Al-Aqsa Intifada. While the latter tends to be compared to its better organized, less militarized predecessor, the Al-Aqsa Intifada nonetheless demonstrated concerted collective efforts to advance the Palestinian cause through means other than the Oslo framework. Two broad camps emerged: 'oppositionists', comprised of Islamists (Hamas and the Palestinian Islamic Jihad), Leftists (mainly associated with the Popular and Democratic Fronts for the Liberation of Palestine [PFLP and DFLP]), together with sections within Fateh, saw the Intifada as a means to upend the Oslo framework, and concentrated on 'resistance' mainly through militarization, once the large popular demonstrations were violently suppressed by Israel (Haddad, 2001). Alternatively, the 'cautious opportunists', led by Arafat and sections of the PNA leadership, tended to view the Intifada as a means to improve conditions in negotiations, but were careful not to be seen as supporting or orchestrating it. Some elements in the PNA leadership more decisively opposed the Intifada altogether, at least in the way armed activity was being carried out, but tended to maintain a low profile. In this context, the Al-Aqsa Intifada lacked a clear, defined strategy or unifying program, and the accompanying discipline to enforce such a program. Over time, this disunity, tested under Israeli military force, would splinter the Palestinian body politic, resulting in the oppositionists to Oslo and the oppositionist to the Intifada eventually capturing and institutionalizing themselves within distinct territorial boundaries of Gaza and the West Bank, undergirded by their own political economies and trajectories of accumulation strengthened during these years (2000–7). The contradictory politics of neoliberal statebuilding would play a key role in hardening these divisions within the Palestinian body politic, while Israel's use of military violence against the Palestinian leadership and society would catalyze these dynamics.

Understanding this transition without getting tied down in a lengthy historical accounting of the timeline of events and their analysis thus entails focusing on the specific approach of each camp (the Israeli, the Western donor, and the Palestinian) towards these developments and how reform fit into their respective visions.

Israel, the Intifada and Reform

Before elaborating upon the reform process and the transformations it entailed, it is worth first pointing to the events which triggered this series of events, namely the controversial moment of the Al-Aqsa

Intifada's eruption which began with Sharon's visit to the Al-Aqsa mosque compound and the heavy military response of Israeli police and soldiers to ensuing protests. This provocation was a deliberate and successful attempt to enflame the situation on the ground, creating grounds for ending the peace process framework, and severely weakening or defeating the Palestinian nationalist leadership in pursuit of extending Zionist settler colonial aims (see Honig-Parnass and Haddad, 2007, pp. 17–55). This, after the failure of Camp David (2000), where the terms presented to the Palestinian leadership did not come close to Palestinian national claims or international legal principles (Malley and Agha, 2001; Malley, 2001). Barak's 'generous offer' was a 'fraud' which was offered in bad faith to paint Palestinians as rejectionist, thereby legitimating future action against them (see Reinhardt, 2001).

Certainly Anthony Cordesman's disclosure of the existence of the Israeli army's operational 'Field of Thorns' plan – dating back to 1996 – also points to the existence of a well-thought out plan in the event of a Palestinian uprising, which in retrospect appears to have been largely followed through on (see Cordesman, 2000; Elam, 2000). Israeli journalist Akiva Eldar brings evidence that substantiates the suspicion that Israeli Defense Force commanders 'stoked the fires of the Intifada and carried out something of a military coup' (Eldar, 2005). Basing his claims on the evidence of Raviv Druker and Ofer Shelah's book *Boomerang*, Eldar relates that 'high-ranking intelligence officers marketed the "no partner" myth to serve the interests of Barak and Sharon, despite there being no support for this in the assessments of Military Intelligence, the Shin Bet or the Mossad' (see ibid; Druker and Shelah, 2005). Eldar elaborates on:

> a long series of Israeli acts of sabotage on cease-fire initiatives that ended in terror attacks, alongside a long series of foul-ups in the construction of the separation fence, the delay of which continues to exact a human cost. [Druker and Shaleh] accuse ministers Shimon Peres and Ben-Eliezer of criminal negligence by lending a hand to the deterioration in the situation in the territories, and by standing idly by while Sharon, Mofaz, Ya'alon and Dichter undermined every chance for an easing in the hostilities.
>
> (Eldar, 2005)

Irrespective of the possibility of pre-meditated intention in Israel's instigation and perpetuation of the Al Aqsa Intifada, its attempts to pacify the uprising were certainly the product of a centralized command structure that calibrated distinct tactics to conform with strategic political aims. Though these may have changed or shifted at different times given the calculus of local or regional political circumstances, or the particular orientation of the echelon in power at the time and its priorities, violence and its threat, has practically served a host of different Israeli political goals during this period. These include:

- general suppression of popular resistance as practiced by individual Palestinians or national factions, in pursuit of quashing Palestinian power and claims, while engendering 'deterrence';
- killing, injuring or arresting specific Palestinian political and military cadre, weakening Palestinian leadership, organization and social cohesion;
- destruction of basic infrastructure, including PNA and 'civil society' governance functions and service provision capabilities, together with the social devastation this entailed;
- deepened, forcible fragmentation of Palestinian population centers from one another;
- expansion of land grabbing activity including settlement and 'separation barrier' construction, and;
- forced dispossession of specific populations from select areas (notably, the 'buffer zone' in Gaza), amongst others (UNOCHA, 2010b).

Israeli military violence was hence employed with an intention to enforce and defend strategic goals and an implicit political logic that was by no means strictly security oriented. Rather, Israel's use of military violence constituted one component of a much larger set of diplomatic, economic and social policy tools used against Palestinians after the Intifada began, attempting to enforce a new political reality on the ground and equally within international and Palestinian consciousness and relations. While these policies would evolve under different conditions and timescales, they included the wholesale rejection of the PNA as a legitimate negotiating partner ('not a partner to peace'), the de facto freezing of political negotiations and non-acquiesce to Palestinian national claims ('not negotiating with terror'), and the acceleration of what Palestinian historian Saleh Abdel Jawad refers to as a case of 'sociocide' (Abdel Jawad, 2013).

The results of these policies have been well documented by human rights organizations and academic scholars with no need to significantly delve into their human, social or material costs (see Roy, 2004; Ajluni, 2003; reports of Palestinian Center for Human Rights, 2000–5; B'tselem, 2000–5). The main thing to note from this extensive record of human suffering is to point to how Israel's military doctrines often included a significant psychological component intended to 'burn into Palestinian and Arab consciousness' certain 'lessons', in the words of Israeli Chief of Staff Moshe Ya'alon (quoted by Shavit, 2002). When seen in combination with the broader set of political and economic policies Israel adopted after the start of the Intifada, it is clear that Israel intended to induce a powerful shock-like effect within Palestinian society and leadership alike. This was critical to creating sudden conditions of crisis whose reverberations would be experienced on all levels of Palestinian life, leveraged in both active and passive ways.

The trail of Israel's military operations in the OPT since 2000 embody this desire to repeatedly induce a state of shock, crisis and disorientation. From lightning assassination strikes (via drones, death squads dressed as Arabs, and exploding telephones), to full-fledge military assaults, often biblically titled (Operations 'Defensive Shield', 'Days of Penitence', 'Summer Rains', 'Cast Lead'), Israel's military doctrines are widely seen as pioneering within counterinsurgency circles. Yet these military policies, shocking as they are, tend to draw attention from more insidious and long-term consequences of 'passive' forms of coercion Israel employed. Here, Israel's immediate halting of VAT and customs payments to the PNA, and the imposition of an increasingly hermetic closure policy (including the erecting of upwards of 700 checkpoints and obstacles to movement and access, the enforcing of 'borders' through robotic machine guns etc.), functionally weaponized this regime, transforming it into a modern version of the medieval tactic of besiegement.

Former World Bank Country Director to the OPT Nigel Roberts would describe these effects when speaking to an audience at the Jerusalem Fund in 2006 (Roberts, 2006). To Roberts, the Palestinian economy experienced 'two shocks' during the Intifada: the immediate implementation of closure (September 2000) crippled labor flows and trade, resulting in sudden contractions in employment and personal income. Israel's 'reoccupation' of the West Bank 'A' areas (March 2002) would compound these effects, by paralyzing internal movement within the OPT. The results were 'really of historic proportions':

> Our estimate was of something like 40 per cent of personal real incomes were lost in the course of that two year period [2000–2]. This is a contraction in personal incomes that exceeded the worst two years of the Great Depression, where personal incomes contracted by something just over 20 per cent. [...] That doesn't happen. This was really dramatic.
>
> (Roberts, 2006)

The results of these dramatic tactics were documented by an August 2002 survey by Johns Hopkins and Al-Quds Universities, which found that 53 per cent of Palestinian households in the West Bank and Gaza Strip had to borrow money to purchase food (see CARE, 2002a; 2003b; 2003c as cited in Roy 2004, p. 386). Moreover, 22.5 per cent of children below the age of five suffered from chronic (13.2 per cent) and acute (moderate and severe) (9.3 per cent) malnutrition. Levels were worst in Gaza where 13.3 per cent of children under five suffered from acute malnutrition (a condition known as 'wasting'), putting it in the company of Eritrea in 1995, and just below the Congo in 2002 (see Roy, 2004).

All this well before Israel unofficially put 'the Palestinians [in Gaza] on a diet, but not to make them die of hunger,' according to Israeli political insider Dov Weisglass (quoted by Urqhart, 2006).

The consistent psychological dimension to Israel's active and passive military doctrines, which induced far-reaching crises should be read as a variant of Naomi Klein's 'shock doctrine', whose strategic value lies in its ability to induce behavioral changes (Klein, 2007). Referencing a CIA manual on 'coercive interrogation', Klein writes:

> The way to break 'resistant sources' is to create violent ruptures between prisoners and their ability to make sense of the world around them. First, the senses are starved of any input (with hoods, earplugs, shackles, total isolation), then the body is bombarded with overwhelming stimulation (strobe lights, blaring music, beatings, electroshock). The goal of this 'softening-up' stage is to

provoke a kind of hurricane in the mind: prisoners are so regressed and afraid that they can no longer think rationally or protect their own interests. It is in that state of shock that most prisoners give their interrogators whatever they want – information, confessions, a renunciation of former beliefs.

(Klein, 2007, pp. 16–17)

Klein applies her notion of the shock doctrine to different historical-political settings – from the invasion of Iraq to post-Hurricane Katrina humanitarian relief – reading in these efforts attempts by 'disaster capitalism' to 'achieve on a mass scale what torture does one on one in the interrogation cell' (Klein, 2007, p. 16).

In this context, the 'shocks' and crises of Israel's military and economic policies attempted to disorient and traumatize Palestinian society and leadership. The intention was to soften them to concede on various national, political, institutional and organizational levels either directly through force, or by harnessing the potential these policies harbored to induce the internalization of change and its need, which subsequently could be described as 'reform.' Moreover, particularly because the reform agenda consistently demanded governance reforms facilitating improved conditions for private sector interests, it also whetted the appetites of those positioned to enrich themselves on the backs of reform and reconstruction aid, embodied in a particular tranche of Palestinian politicians, capitalists, and consultants. In this way, a variant of 'disaster capitalism' would come to characterize the economic and development activity of both the public and private sectors, spawned in the rush to take advantage of the wave of incentives donors provided when neoliberal statebuilding was given the 'green light' to advance.

Western Donors and Reform

In the earlier years of Israel's use of violence against the uprising, Israel apparently considered the option of simply doing away with the PNA. Writing in 2002, Israeli commentator Akiva Eldar describes how Israel's top military brass considered the 'constructive destruction' option, entailing 'laying waste to the PNA, reinstating full Israeli control of the kind that existed before the first Intifada, and reaching an imposed settlement with obedient canton administrators' (Eldar, 2002).

While Eldar notes that 'the generals quickly wiped the constructive destruction option from their slate', what precisely Israel pushed forward through its maneuvers and doctrine has yet to be sufficiently interpreted.

Understanding its choices however cannot be seen in isolation from the maneuvering and policies of the Western chaperones to the peace process, which provided the parameters of Israel's larger political space of maneuver. While Israel holds many of the material cards determining the quality of Palestinian livelihood, it is Western donors who craft the boundaries and content of 'legitimate' political expression. Here the statebuilding agenda would play the critical role of working on the political, social, economic and technical fronts, attempting to elucidate the character and parameters of the select political and economic activity given space to operate and potentially thrive in the OPT. In this sense, the relational dynamic between Israel's coercive measures on one hand, and the empowering dynamics of international statebuilding policies on the other, must be highlighted. This is not to suggest that they were necessarily coordinated together. It is only to suggest that these dynamics co-existed and were reflected upon and experienced by the Palestinian leadership as such, irrespective of coordination.

It is in this context that donors transitioned onto a more aggressive forward footing on reform.

Previous chapters disclosed World Bank country director Nigel Roberts' claim that the history of donor assistance to the Palestinians indeed was 'notable for its lack of performance conditionality.' But this is disingenuous, as there were in fact at least two official waves of conditionality.

The first began in November 2000 after Israel cut VAT and customs transfers only one month into the Intifada, and was led by the European Commission. Various budget support mechanisms[1] were established that disbursed €235 million against a series of PNA reforms until December 2002. Conditionalities included an April 2001 declaration of understanding reached between the PNA Ministry of Finance (MoF), and the EU and IMF focusing on 'measures designed to support transparency and sound fiscal policy' (World Bank, 2002b, p. 66, n.113). These included consolidating fiscal accounts under a single MoF managed-account; a payroll freeze, to be followed by managed expansion only; the full transfer of payroll responsibilities to the MoF; and the initiation of steps to unify and reform existing public sector pension systems in concert with World Bank technical assistance (ibid., p. 66). They also included promulgation of the Judiciary Independence Law by end-August 2002, the establishment of a ministerial-level body to monitor the implementation of the administrative reform program, and the release of an action plan to unify the different public sector pension schemes by end-September 2002 (ibid., p. 98, n.160). About €10 million of non-targeted budgetary assistance was released monthly subject to IMF issuance of a 'comfort letter' that provided macro-economic monitoring of the PNA budget (EU, 2005).

On paper, these reforms were rationalized as necessary for ensuring budgetary austerity within the context of the PNA's financial crisis. Indeed the targeting of budgetary assistance was seen as strategic by donors insofar as it went to the heart of the PNA's ability to maintain financial solvency, carry out services, pay its base of supporters, and remain in power. By March 2002, the World Bank was describing the PNA as 'effectively bankrupt' (World Bank, 2002b, p. v). Its budget deficit surpassed $825 million in 2001 and was $710 million in 2002, before external financing (World Bank, 2004a, p. 1). Even with about $1 billion in donor aid during this period, the combined residual deficit reached over $500 million. The PNA was also accruing debt to banks totaling $176 million (5.4 per cent of GDP) by the end of 2003, with the total stock of its arrears reaching $384 million (12 per cent of GDP) (ibid., p. 2).

In this respect, the EU's conditional budgetary assistance helped some 75,000 households (half a million Palestinians, or 15 per cent of the population), to receive their salaries in 2002. It also was (self-) credited for having important trickle down effects, considering that civil servant salaries totaled 40 per cent of total consumer demand for goods and services (ibid., p. 2). Together with other job creation and emergency assistance programs, the World Bank congratulated donors for having 'cushioned the Palestinian people, while helping preserve a governance structure for the future' (World Bank, 2002b, p. 64).

But a more honest political reading of these reforms attests to them beginning the process of radically 'structurally adjusting' the PNA to decentralize and disempower its executive, removing its discretionary administrative and financial powers, while exposing the overall structure to much greater oversight. In doing so, Western donors were functionally rolling back the executive powers they had sanctioned within the former neopatrimonial model and began transitioning into a new 'statebuilding' phase, theoretically grounded in the New Institutional Economics of the PWC. In fact a 2012 World Bank document assessing public financial management reforms in MENA during this period would explicitly acknowledge that 'the reform process was highly politicized' with a 'general concern that the reforms were removing some of the earlier discretion of expenditure that supported the patronage based system' (Ahern, 2012, p. 173).

Discussions on reforms between the PNA and donors, as well as among Palestinians, were ongoing throughout this period, but were constantly conducted beneath the shadow of escalating Israeli military activity.

As the Intifada and Israeli military maneuvers crescendoed in early 2002, the World Bank and PNA composed a joint understanding that 'explicitly committed' the PNA to a series of measures that would have far reaching repercussions for Palestinian society when they eventually had the opportunity to take full form in years to come (see World Bank, 2002b, pp. 93–8). These would include commitments to maintain expenditure discipline, including an 'austerity budget'; the devising of transparent reporting mechanisms for all ministries, overseen in monthly meetings; and the 'strengthening' of the PNA's core economic management institutions focusing on MOPIC, MoF and the Ministry of Economy and Trade (MOET). The understanding would also call for instituting medium-term policy measures that began to clearly transpose PWC notions onto the PNA.

Despite the dire circumstance in which it was composed, Western donors were clearly setting their sights on longer-term factors of the Palestinian economy and its governance structure, as opposed to addressing the emergency state of the OPT. It rationalized this prioritization of institutional adjustment as follows:

> Some have argued that it makes little sense to focus at this stage on anything else [besides the day-today conditions created by crisis of the Intifada], but the PNA believes the opposite – that extreme cash shortages, a decaying investment climate and serious impediments to implementation require greater budgetary

efficiency, enhanced internal coordination and a better operating
environment for the private sector [...]

(Ibid., p. 94)

According to the statement, this was to come through policies that
would:

- **promote the transparency and accountability on the public
  sector,** including strengthening the financial control environment;
  the common application of public procurement standards and
  guidelines; and the strengthening of the capacity of a public auditing
  entity;
- **review the organizational structure of the PNA** including the
  roles, mandates and functions of all ministries and agencies;
- **reform the civil service** that would 'at the right time following the
  current crisis', downsize it;
- **promote 'plural service delivery',** including developing the
  capacity of municipalities to deliver services and to develop joint
  programming with NGOs;
- **strengthen social safety net provisions,** and;
- **engage private sector support,** including the 'creation of an
  environment conducive to investment.' This particular dimension
  could be realized by pushing forward a series of laws developed with
  international consultants, including those covering capital markets,
  insurance, securities, companies and competition, and financial leasing.
  The document also set its sights on 'the large unused lending capacity
  of the domestic banking system', where the OPT's loan/deposit ratio
  was seen as too low in comparison to most developing countries – 35
  per cent, compared to 70 per cent. The understanding would also
  target 'ensuring adequate competition' (designed to eliminate
  monopolistic practices) and 'promoting economic legality': 'The
  PNA believes that the predictability of the legal system is vital, since
  investors must have confidence that contracts can be enforced and that
  they can be protected by the law' (ibid., p. 98).

Within days of the PNA signing onto this PWC blueprint in the
context of a crisis, partially manufactured, Israel would launch
the largest and most destructive of its military operations during the

Al-Aqsa Intifada. Operation Defensive Shield began at the end of March 2002, and played a hugely catalytic role in accelerating the reform agenda. Following Arafat's own 33-day besiegement in his *moqata'a* compound (which only ended with the handing over of six 'wanted' individuals there to international jailers, and the promise that he would publicly encourage Palestinians to desist from attacking Israel), a PNA Ministerial Committee for Reform (MCR) was established. The latter would compose what later became known as the '100-Day Reform Plan' of 23 June 2002 – the most comprehensive PNA proposal of reform to date, and which the World Bank would later acknowledge to '[bear] a strong resemblance' to the agenda outlined in the World Bank/PNA joint understanding (World Bank, 2003, p. 40). Significantly it would agree to the establishment of the Palestine Investment Fund (PIF) 'to manage all commercial and investment operations of the PNA', while also directly addressed security and political reforms which international donors saw as no less urgent to the administrative and economic/fiscal (see Appendix 2).

One day after the 100-Day Reform Plan was announced, George W. Bush would deliver his 24 June 2002 White House lawn speech, providing principle backing to a Palestinian state with provisional borders, but clarifying that:

> A Palestinian state will never be created by terror – it will be built through reform. And reform must be more than cosmetic change, or veiled attempt to preserve the status quo. True reform will require entirely new political and economic institutions, based on democracy, market economics and action against terrorism.
>
> (Bush, G. W., 2002)

Bush called on the Palestinian people 'to elect new leaders, leaders not compromised by terror', and 'to build a practicing democracy [. . .]' Only when the Palestinians would have new leaders, institutions and 'security arrangements with their neighbors', would the US support a Palestinian state 'whose borders and certain aspects of its sovereignty will be provisional until resolved as part of a final settlement in the Middle East.'

Bush's speech would officially sanction 'statebuilding' in the OPT, while effectively declaring the end of Arafat's political utility. It would also formalize an era where Palestinian political, economic and security functions were deemed to be in a state of perpetual transition toward donor-defined criteria for how a state under occupied conditions was to function. This is why the US accepted in-principle recognition of a state only after establishing exactly what the parameters of this state would be, and ensuring that all keys to realizing the 'what', 'when', and 'how' of a Palestinian state – 'Palestine' – went through channels it controlled.

While media attention after Bush's speech would largely focus on the political struggle to wrest powers from Arafat through the creation of the post of Prime Minister, Western donors would redouble their efforts on the PWC-inspired governance agenda, establishing an International Task Force on Palestinian Reform (the 'Quartet plus Four' consisting of the EU, Russia, the US and the UN, plus Japan, Norway, the IMF and World Bank). The latter began identifying clear benchmarks by which progress could be measured in each of seven areas: financial accountability, ministerial and civil service reform, market economics, judiciary/rule of law, local government, civil society and elections. Each reform sector would be complimented with 'Reform Support Groups' so as to identify 'appropriate donor instruments for providing necessary technical assistance and financial resources, which would be required both immediately and in the medium term' (World Bank, 2002c, p. 1).

As the wheel of reform turned, Arafat's discretionary powers would be increasingly withdrawn. In February 2003, he agreed to appoint a Prime Minister, and in March signed an amended version of the Palestinian Basic Law that introduced comprehensive changes to PNA governance features. Presidential powers would be greatly reduced in scope, with the newly created post of Prime Minister now empowered to form a government through the Council of Ministers that the latter oversaw.[2] Article 21 of the amended Basic Law explicitly outlined that 'the economic system in Palestine shall be based on the principles of a free market economy.' By May 2003, Mahmoud Abbas would take up the Prime Minister post, the creation of which had been a condition for the US releasing the Road Map. The latter was to be 'performance-based and goal driven,' thus formalizing internationally sanctioned conditionality for resumption of a political process and not just for funding.

One year after the 100-Day Plan was released, the World Bank would write that 'there is now no way back' and that the PNA must deliver a successful reform program or lose both domestic and international legitimacy (World Bank, 2003, p. xv). Great international donor hopes would be placed on Abbas to lead the way, but these would be dashed with his 8 September 2003 resignation. By the end of September, the World Bank would send a team to conduct a 'Country Financial Accountability Assessment' (CFAA), which would conduct the most detailed assessment to date of the 'major improvements' undertaken by the PNA, as well as the 'significant number of actions which still need to be implemented' (World Bank, 2004b, p. 1). The report meticulously details the state of every feature of the PNA's public financial management system including the tracking of all funds, the creation of a central treasury account, budget construction, accountancy, payroll, the PNA's commercial investments and 'state'-owned enterprises, the role of public institutions, external and internal auditing, procurement, fiscal reporting, the role of the PLC in these matters, and the legal basis underpinning this entire arrangement.

When finally published in June 2004, the CFAA reported that all PNA revenues were being paid into the Central Treasury Account (CTA) and that salaries of 56,000 security service members were being paid through direct deposit, as opposed to the former arrangement of receiving cash. It also noted that the 'large discretionary transfer appropriation for the President's Office has been virtually eliminated' (ibid., p. 3) – sums that had equaled almost $50 million in 2003, reduced now to $0.62 million for 2004. Perhaps most significantly, all PNA equity holdings had officially been consolidated into the PIF, together with virtually all PNA-owned enterprises either folded into the PIF, put under direct MoF oversight, or disbanded. CFAA was also able to disclose that PIF's total assets stood at $799 million – considerably higher than the 1999 disclosures of the PCSC, whose assets were then reported at $345million (ibid., p. 34). The additional capital appears to have been formerly undeclared PNA equity in regional mobile telecommunication providers, including Orascom Telecom Algiers (23 per cent – valued at $90 million), Orascom Telecom Tunisia (20 per cent – $50 million) and Fastlink (Jordan – 14 per cent – $66 million). The PNA's regional investments in telecom directly associated it with the politically determined capital of the Arab regional order – Orascom being associated with the billionaire Sawiris family connected to former Egyptian president Husni Mubarak and his son Jamal; and Orascom Tunisia, which was in partnership with Mohamed Sakher el-Materi, son-in-law of former Tunisian dictator Zine el-Abidine Ben Ali (see Wigglesworth, 2010).

Based on the findings of the CFAA, the World Bank would devise its second major wave of conditionality – the Public Financial Management Reform Trust Fund (PFMRTF) – and which may be considered the final institutional coup de grace against Arafat's institutional/financial power (World Bank, 2004a). PFMRTF was aimed at targeting what the CFAA had called 'residual weaknesses in financial accountability' related to the lack of adequate public financial statements, inadequate auditing, and the undeveloped oversight role of the Palestinian Legislative Council (PLC) (World Bank, 2004b, p. 3). It specifically aimed at leveraging donor budgetary support through a single channel against a number of clearly defined financial accountability benchmarks. Two sets of 'time-bound performance benchmarks' were set up, each lasting six months. In each case, the World Bank was charged with 'supervising the implementation of the agreed reform measures, monitoring and certifying compliance with the benchmarks, and making disbursement decisions accordingly' (World Bank, 2004a, p. 7).

The incessant barrage of reform conditionality leveraged over the PNA leadership between 2000 and 2004, and under conditions of existential threat – literally, the barrels of guns – should generally be seen as having been overwhelmingly successful in what they set out to do. The World Bank would later describe them as 'among the most far-reaching of those implemented in the Middle East and North Africa (MENA) region during the last decade' (World Bank, 2012, p. 165). By the time Arafat mysteriously fell ill at the end of October 2004, forcing his departure and eventual death in Paris on 11 November, the most significant financial and institutional elements to his power had been removed, though his political clout clearly remained. While controversy surrounds his death and rumors of his possible assassination continue to circulate, there can be no controversy over the fact that Western donors led the charge to eliminate his institutional and financial reach over Palestinian politics, and were successful in doing so at least on paper. Whether this was sequenced or not with Israeli policies is secondary to the result.

A significant historical footnote to this sequence of events relates to how Arafat's acquiescence to these reforms meant that the 'new' system erected retained his blessing, and preserved its nominal legitimacy once he departed the scene. Arafat had allowed for the new system's activation believing he, as the patriarch, could ensure it performed according to his will. Had he departed the scene leaving intact an 'unreformed' regime, the legitimacy of his successor and the system overall was far more likely to have been challenged by competing heirs. In this respect, the reform process sanctioned Arafat's own obsolescence while creating a road map to preserve the structure of the apparatus he helped establish, but was no longer permitted to lead. He also left behind an apparatus that would no longer be controlled or ballasted by his charismatic presence and regulatory power.

In a candid conversation with an admiring US columnist Thomas Friedman, hosted by the Aspen Institute in July 2009 in the company of prominent US, Israeli, and Arab dignitaries, future Palestinian Prime Minister Salam Fayyad would acknowledge that Arafat deserved the credit for the reforms, not him:

> Many people [...] associate reform with the post-Arafat era; not true in finance. I can tell you for the record for history; it started with earnest, in the summer of 2002. We did a lot of things. By a year later, most of everything that had to be done in terms of the basic elements of reform were completely introduced.
>
> (Aspen Institute, 2009)

Arafat's success in this domain, was thus his own undoing.

Palestinian Reform

International pressure for reform could not have been as effective as it was, had it not been for its ability to capitalize on existent Palestinian divisions and disaffections regarding the way things had been run in the OPT as a consequence of the Oslo Accords and the regime it established.

Reformist tendencies were wide-reaching in Palestinian society, and encompassed a surfeit of internal Palestinian dissensions and gripes of different orders and magnitudes. As described in previous sections, the Oslo Accords and the neopatrimonial regime it helped establish, was negotiated in secret, locked-out significant sections of the OPT's political and economic actors, engaged in illiberal economic and political practices, and marginalized what had been the ascendant political forces of the 1987 Intifada. Western donors were well aware of these practices and were equally informed of its social and economic fallout, in part thanks to many donors also funding NGOs that monitored this set-up.

A spectrum of opposition forces to this arrangement thus pre-existed the Oslo process, to which were added new forces produced by this process, with varying degrees of their reformist character.

Political maximalists saw the Intifada as the opportunity to fundamentally restructure and reorient Palestinian politics, and were largely associated with the opposition political factions, both Islamist (Hamas and Islamic Jihad) and secular (the Popular Front for the Liberation of Palestine – PFLP, and the Democratic Front for the Liberation of Palestine – DFLP). These forces saw in the Intifada a vindication of their initial oppositions to Oslo, and the opportunity to redirect the Palestinian national trajectory, politically and institutionally.

In truth, this maximalist position was not matched by a serious political, institutional or economic potential or commitment on behalf of these groups, with the exception of Hamas.

The secular opposition conceived of reform of the PLO itself (not just the PNA) but had few tools of leverage against Fateh domination of the PLO's organizational structure and finances. These forces had long accepted the quota system within the PLO's hierarchy, which allotted them forms of institutional power within various committees and a proportional allotment of finances. But because this quota system had been established in earlier periods of the PLO (late 1970s and '80s), when the Left's strength vis-à-vis Fateh was greater, their powers within the PLO system were over-represented by the time the Al-Aqsa Intifada transpired. This meant that any truly democratic reform of the PLO of the kind these groups nominally demanded, would have weakened these organizations financially and institutionally, despite perhaps advancing their claimed political interest in democracy itself.

Political and institutional weaknesses also hamstrung these factions in posing an alternative, or deepening their bases of support locally.

Besides their political and ideological disorientation in the post-Soviet world, these factions had largely become absorbed in the phenomenon of NGOization during the Oslo years (see Hammami, 1995; 2000). Their secular, liberal discourse and reputation as efficient grassroots activists during the 1987 Intifada made them candidates for 'professionalizing' their activities during the Oslo years when waves of international donor financing washed over the OPT – be it 'peacebuilding' or 'solidarity' aid. As a consequence, many of the most capable sections of the Left factions became institutionally embedded in various human rights, health, agriculture, women's, children's, and democracy-promotion organizations, with high amounts of cross-membership on these organizations' governing boards amongst their managing directorates. These organizations and the members of the Left factions employed in them, were tied into the political economy of post-Oslo donor aid, despite their opposition to Oslo, thus enforcing their vertical dependency on overwhelmingly Western donor funding, as opposed to being politically and financially accountable to their grassroots bases. Moreover, their remuneration of employment in dollars or euros on salary scales that the private and public sectors could not compete with, enabled NGOs and INGOs to recruit amongst the OPT's ablest talent. This also skewed living costs in the OPT (particularly property rents in Ramallah and Jerusalem), unbalancing the burden of the PNA's tax base (with INGOs not paying taxes at all).

To add to this, it would be inappropriate not to mention Israel's active role in weakening secular and left political streams as well. Israel's August 2001 assassination of PFLP Secretary General Abu Ali Mustapha, the detention of his successor Ahmed Sa'dat soon after, and the arrest or killing of scores of other PFLP activists meant that the organization (at least what was considered to be its more radical wing) was effectively neutralized by early 2002. The DFLP, significantly smaller in size, with a membership largely comprised of urban intellectuals, was closer to adopting a reformist approach with the PNA anyway, and tended to confine itself to such activity through its associated NGOs, in the context of the various waves of reform taking place.

The Islamist opposition on the other hand was better positioned to offer a transformative redirection to Palestinian politics outside the Oslo framework. Islamic Jihad largely eschewed the capture of 'state' power and focused its efforts on military activity. But Hamas, in line with its Muslim Brotherhood roots, saw institutional embeddedness and societal transformation through religious observance, as key to eventually taking power. Its institutional base of charitable associations undergirded by deep independent financial networks unbeholden to the same political accountability criteria of Western funders, gave the movement enviable latitude of maneuver within the circumstances – certainly compared to secular groupings and the PNA itself.

Indeed, Hamas would effectively harness its political, financial and institutional positioning within the OPT when the movement chose to participate in the 2006 Legislative Council and local elections, doing so under the 'Change and Reform' bloc. In doing so, Hamas significantly revised and moderated its stance on participating in elections under occupation, and explicitly sought to capture the institutions of the PNA, seeking to redirect them along lines unbeholden to Oslo's political parameters. Perhaps most distinctive in this regard was the bloc's explicit commitment to all of historic Palestine and the acknowledgement that the Palestinian movement was 'still living a phase of national liberation, and thus [Palestinians] have the right to strive to recover their own rights and end the occupation using all means, including armed struggle' (see Change and Reform political program, pt.4).[3] Only after asserting these as part of the movement's principles, does its electoral platform then extensively elaborate on various themes the movement wished to address, including 'administrative reform and fighting corruption', 'legislative policy and reforming the judiciary', 'public freedoms and citizen's rights', 'economic, financial and fiscal policy' and 'labor issues' (ibid; also see Hroub, 2006).

But this attempted program of reform would only come after the major internationally driven institutional reforms of the 2000–4 period described above. The latter ignored domestic maximalists altogether and instead relied upon what we shall term the 'pragmatic reform wing', composed of a far more circumscribed reform constituency and agenda that derived from political and social forces that had already accepted the political parameters enforced by the Oslo arrangement over the Fateh-controlled PNA. Unlike the maximalists, these forces looked to the PNA and its political mandate within the Oslo parameters as a *fait accompli*, and focused their critiques upon reforming existent governance structures, efficiencies and internal balances of forces. Indeed a key constituency of pragmatist reformers emerged from within the PNA and Fateh itself, particularly members of the PLC, who had long attempted to realign and democratize the PNA – figures like Azmi Shu'aibi, Hanan Ashrawi, Hasan Khreisheh, Jamal Shawbaki, Hasan Abu Libdeh, Nabil Amr, Mohammed Hourani and Marwan El-Barghouti amongst others. In concert with a coalition of more autonomous members of

Fateh, personalities from various NGOs, academics and elements of the domestic private sector – a loose, domestic constituency backing reform existed capable of giving this process pragmatic, national and liberal colorations. This constituency however lacked a cohesive political framework or project that either guided their work, or mediated their own differences.

This constituency and their variegated agendas thus found congruity and resonance within Western donor PWC-inspired reform initiatives, which also stressed the need for 'local ownership' of the reform process. Soon after Bush's speech, the World Bank would write that genuine administrative and financial reform 'cannot be imposed from the outside' and noted that 'public opinion polls have shown near unanimity on the need to uproot corruption, base public sector employment on qualification and merit, achieve a more efficient justice system, and improve the performance of ministries' (World Bank, 2002c, p. 2). Here the World Bank selectively sought to frame the reform agenda as though domestic reformers shared the same objectives of the violent coercion of Israel and international financial conditionality measures. However even with its delimited technical reading of the OPT's 'obstacles to economic growth' which needed reforming, the World Bank was gerrymandering Palestinian priorities for reform. Its own study examining the West Bank and Gaza's governance and business environment during the Oslo years (1996–2000) and conducted a year earlier had shown that Palestinians consistently identified *political* factors related to the Israeli occupation as the primary obstacle to business growth: 'policy instability and uncertainty' was seen as a major or moderate constraint by 77 per cent of Palestinian businesses surveyed, with Israeli security procedures identified as their number one regulatory and administrative burden (see Sewell, 2001, pp. 3–5; Figure 2). While corruption indeed registered as the second greatest constraint, followed by inflation, concern over corruption was on the decline when the results of the same survey were compared to those of 1996 – from 85 per cent to 71 per cent. The World Bank also acknowledged that 'informal payments to officials occurred less often than in other developing countries and regions', and there equally 'did not appear to be a problem of corruption in procurement' (ibid., Summary).

Despite these results which point to an exaggerated and politically opportunistic nature to Western donor corruption accusations, fixation on governance reforms and anti-corruption measures would take priority within Western donor agendas over addressing the political constraints Palestinians faced due to the occupation. Moreover it would form the intellectual and political space that the pragmatist reformers would step into, even though the reformist credentials of most of this constituency predated the Western donors' new-found concern for the PNA's institutional efficiency.

Azmi Shu'aibi was a central figure in the first wave of reforms, and was not associated with any political faction. A former mayor of El-Bireh elected to the PLC in 1996, Shu'aibi participated in the establishment of the PNA, and served as its first Minister of Youth and Sports. Within a year he resigned from the government to focus on drafting some of the most important reform initiatives to take place within the PLC in his capacity as a member of the Legislature's Economic Affairs, Public Budget, and Basic Law drafting committees. He also participated in assessments of the General Auditor, and drafted preliminary notes on judicial and security sector reform. He would later found and direct the umbrella group Aman – the Coalition for Accountability and Integrity (est. 2000), which received the endorsement of Transparency International in 2006.

For Shu'aibi, reform of the PNA was part of a long-standing national commitment to basic democratic and civil principles, which strengthened national cohesion, claims and efficiency. The PLO's transition from a diasporic revolutionary movement operating within suspicious and often hostile Arab environments, to an incipient statebuilding project based in the OPT, had left the institution saddled with undesirable 'mentalities' and practices for the tasks the PNA now needed to perform (Shu'aibi, Interview).

He describes his participation in drafting the Basic Law for example as part of a struggle with the PNA executive over 'those who wanted to imitate the Arab governments where there is hegemony of the executive, limited powers for the judiciary, where the Attorney General belongs to the executive, where the parliament has limited powers, and there is no inspection or oversight.' For Shu'aibi, the PNA's financial system had institutionalized the PLO arrangement in diaspora giving priority to survivalist and flexibility considerations. 'There was an old mentality inherited from the PLO that "we are in a revolution" and "we don't need restrictions – let us be free in our movements." [...] Arafat had a saying "Save your white pennies for a black day." He personally did not wish to benefit from this money, but it would give him flexibility to employ people and foster patronage, as he negotiated with various parties and factions.'

Domestic pragmatist reformers were not blind either to the political intentions behind the reformist agenda of Western donors, but saw the advancement of their cause as something that both predated donor demands, and was something that was desirable within a civil, liberal statebuilding framework. In fact there was no illusion amongst Shu'aibi that it was Israel and the international donors who had both fostered corruption and stymied reforms to begin with: the Israeli Labor party encouraged the neopatrimonial arrangement when 'they gave the monopoly structure! [...] Some [Labor party members] even left the government and became investment partners and advisors to the PNA!' The Likud, politically opposed to Oslo to begin with, 'saw in these [corruption] practices an opportunity to increase pressure and hurt our image, to weaken us politically, inciting against the PNA until the world was convinced it was not a party that could be trusted.' International donors were no less complicit: 'the Americans, the Germans, the English – all of them knew the situation. But in so far as they were happy with Arafat, they closed their eyes to it and in some periods encouraged him.'

This put domestic reformers like Shu'aibi in a near impossible situation, whereby 'we who pushed reforms felt shame, as though we were working for the Netanyahu agenda.'

The 2002–4 international standoff over Arafat's powers was particularly contentious as the Fateh forces within the pragmatist reformist coalition split from their independent cohorts. Shu'aibi quotes West Bank Secretary General and PLC member Marwan Barghouti who told him 'I will walk with you where you wish to go with it [reform.] But if this is to confront Arafat personally I will step aside. If you force me to side between the legal sovereignty and the sovereignty of Arafat, I will choose Arafat's. So please don't put me in this position' (quoted from Shu'aibi, Interview).

Shu'aibi would personally come under verbal attack by Arafat who ordered local Fateh members to issue a public leaflet (*bayan*) deriding him as 'Azmi Chalabi' – playing-off of the last name of the controversial Iraqi figure Ahmed Chalabi, largely seen as having been a political stooge to US war efforts in Iraq around the same timeframe (2003). Shu'aibi would suffer two heart attacks during this period under the intense pressure, and described a visit by his reformist comrades from Fateh to his hospital bed: 'They came to me and were crying. They felt that they had let me down' (Shu'aibi Interview).

Other elements of Fateh apparently were less loyal. According to an extended interview conducted with Mohammed Rashid after the Arafat's death:

> Arafat formed an opinion of the situation even before the formation of the Abu Mazen government. He was convinced that there was a sector from within [Fateh] who had distanced themselves from him. Some of them – nine or ten of them – used to meet in a building that Arafat began to call the 'building of shame' [benayat el 'ar]. There were people who began to speak against him, who saw him as an obstacle, people who were distant and stopped coming to him. A group thus began forming that became accustomed to the notion that Arafat was the obstacle, and it would be better for all that he left.
>
> (Al-Arabiyya, 2012)

Former minister and high-ranking Fateh member Nabil Amr would survive an assassination attempt (but lose a leg) in July 2004. Amr had published an extended letter in the Arabic daily *Al Hayat*, highly critical of Arafat's rule (Amr, 2002).

Awareness of a convergence of interests between domestic and international reform agendas was a constant feature of the reform process overall. Indeed the delicacy of birthing an 'organic' reform process in the context of Israel's ever-present military maneuvers in the OPT is demonstrated by the manner in which the Palestinian reform agenda was being funded by the same Western donors who were imposing conditionalities on the PNA and had adopted the 'security first' line, demanding Arafat crack down on the Intifada.

We see this in the Palestinian Reform Support Groups set up to mirror the work of the seven areas of reform specified by the International Task Force on Reform, established in July 2002 after Bush's speech.

The National Democratic Institute's (NDI) Civic Forum Institute (CFI)[4] was the main body to funnel the domestic reform initiative into practicable form, doing so through the organizing of regional plenums in late 2003 and early 2004, under the 'Reform: A Palestinian Perspective' project, funded by the German government (via the Friedrich Naumann Foundation) (CFI, 2003). The project hosted eight public sessions on each of the seven reform sectors (56 in total), bringing together (in their count) 2000 local specialists, academics, PLC members, representatives of national factions, community leaders and civil society institutions. This Palestinian equivalent of the *Loya Jirga*[5] was designed to 'give more national media attention and public momentum to promote the reform and development process with the widest possible official and social participation' (ibid., p. 9).

The proceedings of these conferences are a transcript of the very real frustrations and crises that had grown in light of the Oslo years' neopatrimonialism, exacerbated by the devastation wrought during Intifada.

A session on judicial reform for example, describes a completely over-burdened and neglected system, with only 39 judges appointed to work for the entire OPT (CFI, 2003, p. 131). The Hebron district had only one employee to issue summons' for some 470,000 persons in the district. According to the Ministry of Justice, 130,000 separate lawsuits had been filed in West Bank courts in 2003. The blossoming of tribal law and mediation services throughout the OPT was in part the natural result of this extreme judicial bottlenecking – a scenario which empowered traditional elites and powerful clans. It had been the revival of traditional elites and the clan system overall which had facilitated the PNA's penetration throughout the OPT setting.

Indeed it was not difficult to look at most features of the PNA's operations and find a system steeped in 'inefficiencies' and 'transaction costs' of every possible kind. 'We cannot blame the occupation,' decried Dr. Raffiq Abu Ayyash, a professor of International Law at Al Quds University in Jerusalem (ibid., p. 35). 'There are many issues that the occupation has nothing to do with,' he said, then pointing to the conspicuous absence of representatives from the Ministry of Justice at the conference.

Undoubtedly Abu Ayyash was correct in many respects, as were dozens of others who voiced their frustrations with the way things had been run. They were also correct in their repeated assertion that 'reform is not only a Palestinian demand, it is an urgent Palestinian need,' (Hassan Abu Libdeh, then Secretary General of the PNA Council of Ministers) (ibid., p. 45), or that 'the reform that we want is that of the civil society organizations,' which is 'totally different than the European and American reform [sic]' (Muhsin Abu Ramadan, chair of a coalition of Gaza-based NGOs) (ibid., p. 76).

What was less obvious was that these efforts to bring about greater transparency and accountability were double-edged: while they did have the potential to improve Palestinian accountability to one another regarding the rights, resources and decision making processes they enjoyed under the PNA arrangement, they did nothing to challenge the fact that accessing these resources, exercising these rights, and having the opportunity to implement decision making processes, remained entirely conditional upon de facto Israeli and Western donor approval, given the former's control over the OPT and the latter's power over funding and the provision of political legitimacy in international political and financial arenas.

This would become abundantly clear after Hamas won the 2006 PLC elections, resulting in a Western-imposed financial blockade over the new government, and the arrest and imprisonment of dozens of its elected parliamentarians and local officials. The Palestinian banking sector's refusal to deal with money transfers to the new government, out of fear that it too would be cut from operating within international capital circuitry, would lead to a situation where the new government had to rely on cash being transferred in suitcases across or beneath the Egyptian border. Eventually, the Hamas government opted to form a national unity coalition which, in any case, was short lived (17 March–14 June 2007), and faced grave uphill battles for funding and implementing its program on the ground.

In this respect, it is worth questioning who enjoyed the majority net benefits from implementing these transparency and accountability reforms, considering that they allowed Israel and Western donors to deepen their knowledge of, influence over and penetration within the institutions of Palestinian governance and the material bases of the movement's resources. Moreover, from the commanding heights of financial powers and their ability to sanction political legitimacy, donors were in an optimum position to observe the existent and emerging reformist streams coalescing before them, ensuring they did not challenge their undisclosed political agendas for how the peace process overall was supposed to operate. The World Bank would acknowledge this strategic positioning in a backhanded manner in describing the role donors played in inducing reform, which it saw as having been 'especially useful in providing strategic guidance and in strengthening the hand of the reformers in internal debates by linking support to the reform agenda' (World Bank, 2012, p. 174).

CHAPTER 10

'FAYYADISM'

Fayyadism is based on the simple but all-too-rare notion that an Arab leader's legitimacy should be based not on slogans or rejectionism or personality cults or security services, but on delivering transparent, accountable administration and services.

(Thomas Friedman, *New York Times*, 4 August 2009)

Key to making the intellectual, political and moral case that institutional reform of the type demanded by the Bretton Woods institutions offered a net gain for the Palestinian movement, was the figure of Salam Fayyad.

Fayyad was a career employee of the IMF (1987–2001), starting his career in the Fund's headquarters in Washington DC, and later (from 1995 on) becoming the first Resident Representative to the West Bank and Gaza, once the IMF opened a local office. Fayyad credits his being tapped for the latter position to his 'good friend' Stanley Fischer, then IMF Deputy Managing Director, who would later assume the position of Governor of the Bank of Israel (2005–13) (Aspen Institute, 2009, p. 9). He also described his work – 'doing what the IMF does, making life a little bit miserable for authorities' – as having been 'highly rewarding' (ibid., p. 10). The IMF offered him the opportunity to have his 'own profession', while 'doing it for a very, very good cause, for people I belong to and I'm one of.' In this respect, Fayyad should be seen as embodying a nationalist, professional *esprit de corps* that was ideologically neoliberal in orientation, with no sense of contradiction between either objective. On the contrary, Fayyad saw in his fealty to neoliberalism a pathway to national liberation (see Khalidi and Samour, 2011).

Throughout his career at the PNA – twice as its Finance Minister, and twice as Prime Minister[1] – he embraced this ethos, intellectually rationalizing this strategy and programmatically pushing it forward on the ground. Operationally this focused on a 'building blocks' approach, attempting to address wherever and whenever possible, core structural aspects to PNA governance features in line with a PWC vision.

In regards to public financial management for example, Fayyad was less concerned with 'looking at the "sexier" aspects of managing the public finance question – corruption, who took what, when and how' and instead focused on, '[stopping] the leakage' structurally and '[making] sure the system functions well here on out' (World Bank, 2012, p. 170). It would be this structural and 'institutional basics' approach that Fayyad would attempt to orient and mobilize the Palestinian national project around during his various tenures in power. Fayyad would articulate the nub of his vision in his Aspen Institute conversation:

> As one of my professors in economics [. . .] was fond of saying, 'you need to have potatoes to make potato chips' [. . .] The potatoes from the Palestinian point of view are the institutions capable of delivering good governance to the Palestinian people. The institutions of the Palestinian state in the making [. . .] Security, law and order, justice, public finance, economic management, welfare, all of the functions that any responsible state should feel obligated to provide.
>
> (Aspen Institute, 2009, pp. 34–5)

Fayyad continues:

> My message all along to people was the world wants us to have a good public finance system, but is that against our interest? What's wrong with that, let's do that. I mean, we need to do it [. . .] With every step that we take in the direction of institution building, that's a step closer to our freedom, to our statehood [. . .] If this is about statehood, then let us build toward that. I do not

need anyone to remind me that we're doing it under occupation, I know that. But we are doing it because we are under occupation, in spite of the occupation, to end it.

(Ibid., p. 36)

Fayyad would have this approach guide his various interventions and programs of action overseen by the various governments he participated in or led. It would culminate in the 'Palestine: Ending the Occupation, Establishing the State,' program of August 2009, which should be seen as the crown jewel of the neoliberally-informed Palestinian statebuilding trajectory (PNA, 2009). If the PWC vision nominally emerged within mainstream development praxis as a means to facilitate economic take-off within the framework of a more responsive, capable state that promoted rule of law and citizen empowerment, while preserving the basic tenets of market hegemony and the privileging of private sector interests, it was now to be harnessed for the purpose of launching the bid for Palestinian statehood and national liberation.

The program emotionally appeals to Palestinians to unite behind the statebuilding agenda over a two-year period:

Together we must confront the whole world with the reality that Palestinians are united and steadfast in their determination to remain on their homeland, end the occupation, and achieve their freedom and independence. The world should hear loudly and clearly, from all corners of our society, that the occupation is the true impediment which has frustrated our efforts to realize the stability, prosperity and progress of our people and our right to freedom, independence and decent life.

(Ibid., p. 4)

Ending the Occupation is a visionary document that attempts to provide a holistic framework and set of solutions to what were, by this point, well-known and wide-reaching concerns amongst Palestinians and Western donors. It first articulates a series of national political goals and from theses elaborates on the institutional development needed to harness Palestinian capacity to achieve these ends. National goals are not restricted to the objectives of 'ending the occupation', 'protecting Jerusalem', or 'release of prisoners', but also include the need to 'achieve economic independence', 'consolidate good governance' and bring 'equality and social justice to all citizens.' An integrated vision of 'priorities, policies and programs' are then articulated for each of the major statebuilding sectors – governance, social, economic and infrastructure – together with how all associated ministries and governmental agencies fit into this plan.

'Good governance' is explicitly 'elevated to the status of a national goal in and of itself' with the basic aim to 'meet the demand of our people for transparent, accountable institutions that deliver services, social development, economic growth, and career opportunities free from favoritism and wastefulness.' The PWC agenda is given complete freedom of expression upon the Palestinian setting, with the government 'committed to building effective institutions', 'consolidating the rule of law', '[reinvigorating] public oversight mechanisms', and '[promoting] integrity, transparency, and accountability.'

Ending the Occupation would be the guiding light of the PNA's political vision, and should be read in concert with the two other comprehensive medium term tri-annual national planning processes undertaken by Fayyad's government during his tenure: the Palestinian Reform and Development Plan (PRDP) for 2008–10, and the National Development Plan 2011–13 (NDP) (PNA, 2008; PNA, 2011). Both plans establish a comprehensive framework of goals, objectives and performance targets, attempting to integrate policy making, planning and budgeting processes, while aligning spending with national policy priorities. They also articulate a government program oriented around private sector-led growth aimed at attracting foreign direct investment, reducing public spending ('fiscal discipline'), and reducing Palestinian dependency on foreign aid.

The PRDP explicitly calls for 'slimming down' the PNA with its sights set on reducing the wage bill. Fiscal reforms are envisioned through hiring freezes, freezes in public salary increases for three years, and retrenching the number of public sector employees. Subsidy provision of utility fees ('net lending') is also targeted, with these subsidies formerly going to cover electricity costs, mainly in refugee camps. 'Utility provision will be based on economic principles and will be provided under a full cost-recovery basis' – a policy enforced by introducing pre-paid utility meters and requiring citizens to present a 'certificate of payment' of utility bills, in order to receive public services. 177,000 prepaid meters would be distributed to municipalities in the West Bank, and 50,000 to Gaza during this time, despite the latter being under a different government and under siege (PNA, 2011, p. 19). While the combination of fiscal discipline and revenue generation/ recovery measures were strengthened on the one hand, the PRDP incorporates a targeted approach to addressing the 'poorest of the poor' who, once identified 'through an objective and transparent process' will be entitled to 'a specific "lifeline" level of electricity.'

The NDP continues in the same tradition, claiming to improve upon the PRDP in its preparation of 23 sector strategies. It sets even more ambitious fiscal discipline measures designed to restrain public sector spending, increase public revenue generation, while further aiming to enhance 'the institutional environment to private sector investment and growth' (p. 23).

Through a combination of 'sound' macroeconomic policies, fiscally 'prudent' revenue and expenditure plans, the promotion of foreign and local investment, and the preparation of the Palestinian economy for ascension to world trade and world customs organizations, financial independence and economic stability are presented as within reach. A reduction of 'bureaucratic red tape' also serve to provide investors and companies with the 'confidence and certainty needed to do business in Palestine.' It promises economic measures to improve the competitive-ness of Palestinian products and services while also attempting to create new strategic sectors oriented around a 'knowledge based economy', the revival of the industrial zones idea, while taking advantage of certain export niches, particularly in agriculture and ICT services.

The NDP furthermore articulates a vision of 'effective and smart regulation by government', which can ensure that 'many services currently provided by the public sector can be run more efficiently and sustainably with a higher degree of private sector involvement.' Overall, a public-private partnership model is envisioned that engages the private sector, '[building] an economy and society that are less reliant on public expenditure as a driver of economic growth.' Fayyad had been pushing the issue of privatization at least since 2006, when he made a speech declaring 'everything can be privatized except security, which is the responsibility of the Authority' (Al-Ayyam, 2006).

For those struggling to make ends meet, the NDP envisions a social protection strategy building-off of the 2009 overhaul of the PNA's cash assistance programs – the Palestinian National Social Safety Net Program (PNBSSP) – as administered by the Ministry of Social

Affairs. This reformed social safety net program aims at 'rationalization of the social safety net to ensure that essential social assistance is delivered to those most in need', and to 'develop and promote economic empowerment programs targeting poor and vulnerable citizens and households to help them lift themselves out of dependency to self-reliance.'

Overall, the NDP aims to eliminate the PNA's dependency on external aid, while 'making measured progress towards ensuring that Palestine has strengthened economic institutions capable of managing rapid economic growth that will ensue once the occupation ends.'

Needless to say, the NDP and PRDP have significant political and national implications embedded in their liberal, 'self-evident' justifications, when viewed in light of the broader historical Israeli and Western imperial agendas described in earlier chapters. The aims of their 'outputs' would appear to correspond with significant elements of an autonomy arrangement: both plans consciously aim to ensure the PNA is run on the most cost-effective budget possible, thus lessening donor and Israeli financial costs; citizen needs are to be addressed in a responsive and efficient manner, thus mollifying various inefficiencies and problems, many of which are likely to be structurally associated with the occupation and de-development; the privileging of private sector interests over those of the public, would seem to weaken common solidarities and collective public interests, in favor of individually-rooted and profit-seeking motives; while larger questions of collective political and social rights are effaced and substituted with targeted interventions for the most needy, and an ethos of self-help entrepreneurialism.

Moreover, the embarking on this path in an explicitly preparatory manner for 'once the occupation ends' is a form of acknowledging that these plans intend to create a kind of 'stand-by' infrastructure for the public and private sectors even though no mechanism for actually ending the occupation is practically articulated. This 'stand-by' nature is important to underscore, as the assumption that these institutions and procedures innocuously remain in place, awaiting liberation, is deceptive. As we shall see, the institutional and procedural transformations promised by Fayyad's statebuilding agenda would not simply stand-by, but on the contrary, would begin to play an increasing role in deepening the OPT's conditions of de-development while nourishing the Palestinian investors in Palestine Ltd.

These plans received widespread political and financial support from donors,[2] particularly the Europeans, with more guarded support coming from the US. This should come as no surprise considering that undisclosed aspects of them were devised in concert with them. The PRDP for instance, received funding and technical assistance from the UK's DFID and the World Bank – though this is not explicitly mentioned in the document itself, with only a reference to 'consultation [...] with external development partners' (p. 14). The narrative voice of the PRDP also has a schizophrenic quality to it, with the PNA occasionally related to as an object, and other times, with the first person plural pronoun 'we.' In another revelatory elision, the English and Arabic versions of the document do not match up: in discussing relevant background information on the PRDP's implementation, the English version of the plan reads:

> The PNA was established as a transitional authority with a restricted mandate and limited powers. In essence, the PNA's task was to guarantee Israel's security in return for a gradual withdrawal from the OPT.
>
> (PNA, 2008, p. 15)

The Arabic version however, omits the frank admission of the second sentence (the guarantee of Israel's security) and suffices with 'it was expected that these powers would be expanded gradually with the gradual withdrawal of Israel from the OPT' (p. 8, Arabic version). So much for local ownership.

The statebuilding narrative and project would ultimately be deemed a great success by the international community, whose financial and technical assistance were instrumental in realizing it. By April 2012, a few months beyond Fayyad's initial two-year deadline, the IMF would assess the PNA statebuilding progress to definitively conclude that 'based on the track record of reforms and institution-building in the public finance and financial areas, IMF staff considers that the PNA is now able to conduct the sound economic policies expected of a future well-functioning Palestinian state' (IMF, 2012, p.3). The PNA appeared to have 'crossed the finish line' as the NDP had framed it, 'on the homestretch to freedom'

(PNA, 2011, p. 5). The IFIs appeared to be acknowledging that indeed the time had arrived for Palestinians 'to be the masters of our own density in a state of our own,' exposing thus 'the only remaining impediment' to a fully functioning state – 'the continued occupation and denial of our right to independence' (ibid., p. 5).

International Statebuilding

If the 'race' allegory was fitting for the PNA's statehood quest, the reality was figuratively closer to running on a treadmill as opposed to on a real road. Although statebuilding entailed the exertion of great amounts of resources and provided the impression of real progress in institution building, the PNA project was in fact running in place – perhaps even inadvertently pushing forward dynamics with deleterious consequences to its objectives overall.

While the above can only be an indicative and cursory overview of the PNA's statebuilding vision under the Fayyad leadership, it must be contextualized within a broader political and historical understanding to be fully comprehended. That is to say, the adoption of PWC tenets within the highest echelons of the PNA governance structure cannot be understood in isolation from the political and economic considerations of Western donors and dynamics taking place within the Palestinian body politic, in the context of the crises both faced as a consequence of the Al-Aqsa Intifada.

The Al-Aqsa Intifada forced Western donors to contend with a widespread Palestinian loss of faith in the peace process framework, including amongst substantial sections of Fateh. While Israel's military measures may have been successful in periodically pacifying the militant streams that emerged during the Intifada and which were attempting to develop an armed struggle component, this was no substitute for a political, economic and social project that could be relied upon to produce some form of meaningful stability in the long-term.

In fact, Israel's military onslaughts may have been too successful in so far as they radicalized Palestinian society further and threatened to collapse the PNA. Here we return to the words of World Bank country head Nigel Roberts' 2006 speech, which provides a helpful and candid account of the Bank's actions during this period:

The fabric of Palestinian governance was beginning to crack [. . .]
Internal anarchy, fragmentation of central governance, and the
ineffectiveness of governance throughout the Territories, was a
phenomenon that built up gradually over the five years of
compression that was caused by these closure measures [. . .] The
compression did not produce what I think many there [in Israel]
hoped it would, which was a rethinking in Palestinian society
about the value of confrontation. In fact, the polls at the time
suggested that support for Hamas and for continued confrontation
with Israel rose steeply in parallel with the closure measures, and
the actual impact of these on governance was clearly to begin to
weaken and fragment the capacity of Fateh to actually exercise
control over the Territories.

(Roberts, 2006)

Roberts' admission that the World Bank and its backers feared the total
undermining of Fateh and the PNA — which functionally would have
reversed more than a decade worth of international efforts — led it to
grappling with the problem of 'how do you balance Israel's security
requirements with Palestinian economic needs — the assumption
underlying that being that without a vibrant Palestinian economy
you will not be able to lay the foundations for reconciliation'
(Roberts, 2006).

Here Roberts acknowledges that the World Bank needed to revive
some variant of the 'peace dividends' rationale, however this time the
dividends needed to be distributed *in the absence of a political process*.
Moreover, it implied that the World Bank would again return to an
operational framework that assumed a neat separation between political
and economic considerations, and that it, and other donors, could resume
focusing on the latter, albeit in a more holistic PWC-like manner. The
proposed solution revolved around a distinctively econometric-like
Collierian reading of the conflict's motivations, in so far as the factors
contributing to conflict can be reduced to a combination of
quantifiable indicators.

Roberts:

The single indicator you need to target most actively when you are
looking at the economy is unemployment, because the way that

plays out into youth unemployment and the way youth unemployment is associated with radicalism. But to get at unemployment in general, you clearly have to go for a broad-based process of economic growth. It cannot be done by targeted programs of employment creation and intervention, because you do not create sustained employment on that basis. Essentially what one had to go after, was a combination of two factors: first of all, to open the economy up for trade, and second, to induce investment.

(Roberts, 2006)

With the departure of Arafat from the political scene by the end of 2004, and with Israel's military dominance largely asserted during this time within the West Bank (where Zionism's strategic interests lay, as opposed to Gaza), the donor community at large would now begin shifting gears searching for the possibility of creating some form of longer-term economic arrangement, irrespective of a renewal of political negotiations.

Within this operational logic, the World Bank began studying how such a venture might be realized in light of the much bloodier and more economically destructive Intifada that had just transpired – let alone the fact that the Oslo process and its underlying peacebuilding rationale had already failed once.

Unfazed, the World Bank set about exploring how the two factors it had identified as key to engendering 'sustained employment' could be realized.

As for opening up of the OPT economy for transport of goods and labor, the World Bank produced a series of technical papers exploring dimensions of movement and security (World Bank 2005b; 2005c; 2005d; 2005e and 2005f). These included how the 'back to back' system of cargo movement enforced by Israel upon Palestinian shippers using two trucks, could be transformed into a 'door to door' policy using one truck; how convoys between the West Bank and Gaza might be organized; whether a rail line linking the two might be a good solution; and what might be done in the short term to improve access and movement at select crossings, including the Karni crossing in Gaza and the border terminal with Egypt. These studies would lay the intellectual ground work for how various technical fixes, improved procedures and processes, infrastructural design, advance information gathering, and economic incentives, could all be combined to ensure packing and transport procedures were faster and more efficient. In a word, the World Bank was exploring how Israel's closure regime might be managed more efficiently to balance economic and 'security' needs.

Ignoring the political and moral effacement inherent in such studies, it is important to emphasize that the World Bank *did* see this balancing act as something that was fully realizable. From its perspective, opening up the OPT while preserving Israeli security was less a question of practicality, and more a matter of 'the degree of trust [the two parties] can achieve' – namely, whether Israel's political will existed to permit this (World Bank, 2005f, p. 6). Irrespective, the World Bank's intellectual groundwork in this domain, pushed behind the scenes for seven months by former World Bank president James Wolfensohn now acting as the Quartet Special Envoy, would be instrumental in forming the basis of what became known as the Agreement on Movement and Access (AMA), brokered by US Secretary of State Condoleezza Rice in mid-November 2005, sometimes referred to as the 'Rice Agreements' (World Bank, 2005g).

The AMA details a series of changes to Israel's closure regime that needed to take place if revitalizing the Palestinian economy was to be more than a theoretical jaunt.

It called for opening of the Rafah border crossing (with EU on-site monitoring, and Israeli distance monitoring); the opening of crossing points between Gaza and Israel; the opening of a link between Gaza and the West Bank, allowing for convoy passage; the removal of obstacles to movement in the West Bank; the facilitation of the construction of the Gaza seaport, and the re-opening of the Gaza airport. Every aspect of the agreement had associated timelines for implementation and quotas to be fulfilled. Had the AMA been fully implemented, it promised progressively significant transformations in the OPT's then-status quo – beginning to reconnect its fragmented parts with one another, Israel and the outside world. Furthermore, the fact that the World Bank had meticulously detailed how security could be balanced with economic exigencies, meant that at least in theory, the 'movement and access' aspect to economic revival had been fully worked out.

As to the issue of inducing investment, the challenges here were indeed daunting. The high levels of political risk and uncertainty characterizing the period (around 2005) made it an unwelcoming environment for capital. It has already been shown how during the Oslo period – when political hopes were a great deal more optimistic – Palestinian capitalists were only willing to invest under exceedingly profitable and favorable conditions and guarantees. But there were reasons to think that the investment climate of the OPT could be shifting. The Intifada's unorganized use of arms, and Arafat's death, posed serious questions for Palestinian society and leadership, and there was a general consensus that 2005 was to be an important transitional year in which reforms and elections should be given time to take shape. Militant factions agreed to a de-facto truce (*tahdi'a*) in March, brokered in Cairo, which Hamas was particularly keen to observe as it set its sights on local and national elections (Amayreh, 2005/06). Moreover, the Israeli military's anticipated unilateral redeployment from Gaza and the withdrawal of the settler population there ('the Gaza disengagement') in August 2005, was seen as an opportunity by the 'development first' wing of the donor community, led by Quartet Special Envoy James Wolfensohn, to shift the conflict's dynamics onto an optimistic forward footing. Despite its non-coordination with the Palestinian side, the Quartet and major European donors, as well as the UNDP, were intent on packaging the Israeli redeployment as a unique opportunity to 'bring about Palestinian economic recovery and to create an environment in which reconciliation and peace are once again possible.'[3]

Wolfensohn, who has deep familial ties to Israel[4] and considers himself a Zionist,[5] had imagined a scenario whereby former Israeli settler greenhouses could begin to serve as the basis for the mass employment generation schemes seen as needed by the World Bank, to seed hope in the donor community's longer-term strategy of economic regeneration. Despite initial complications related to paying-off the settlers for the greenhouses, Wolfensohn succeeded in securing $14.5 million in donations to permit their purchase and transfer to the Palestine Economic Development Company (PEDC), a newly founded company owned by the now reorganized PIF. The plan had all the elements of re-packaging a peacebuilding dynamic, after the international community witnessed the wholesale failure of this model previously. This time however, there were new political players (Abbas and Fayyad), new transparent mechanisms of accountability (an independently audited and consolidated PIF) and an emerging geopolitical context that could potentially be seized upon to decisively shift popular opinion in favor of turning their backs on the

Intifada and its 'radicalism.' As Wolfensohn himself had said 'when you talk about peace, you have to talk economics and hope' (Wolfensohn, 2005, p. 216).

That was at least what Wolfensohn, and behind him, the development-first wing of the donor community were hoping for.

It is significant noting in this regard that the task of repackaging such a peacebuilding step was designated to the Quartet in the first place. The Quartet is a multilateral body composed of the UN, US, EU and Russia that was only formally established in April 2002 (Tocci, 2013). Its formation represented what appeared to be a departure from US political control over the peace process, and was undertaken as an appeasement to internal criticism within the donor community after the collapse of negotiations and the start of the Al-Aqsa Intifada. 'Development firsters' had saddled the lion's share of the peace process' financial costs, but enjoyed almost no say in its political direction. Moreover, with the failure of US tutelage over negotiations, and with Israel's destructive attacks against PNA infrastructure largely targeting and damaging development firster investments, the pressure to create a multilateral diplomatic approach to the conflict emerged. This came on top of Palestinian reluctance to re-engage in negotiations with the US as the process' sole mediator, recalling that the latter was led by George W. Bush on a 'war on terror' footing. The failure of Oslo in this respect had forced the socialization of its costs and decision-making processes among Western government stakeholders, even though as we shall see, this was short-lived and manipulated to US advantage.

Quartet involvement in re-initiating peacebuilding is significant to note because once Wolfensohn exerted his efforts to put together the Gaza greenhouse deal, together with the intellectual and behind-the-scenes policy work that resulted in the AMA, the US and Israel both balked at the deal's implementation.

The initial deal Wolfensohn had crafted placed implementation oversight of the AMA within the Quartet's domain. But by the time US Secretary of State Condoleezza Rice negotiated the final deal personally between the parties – elbowing out Wolfensohn and EU Foreign Policy Chief Javier Solana – these powers were handed back to the US (see Wolfensohn, 2010, p. 429).

Thus, in the five months that ensued after Israel's redeployment from Gaza, and in the two months after the signing of the AMA, Gaza remained under lockdown, and most of the greenhouse's first harvest was left to rot at Israeli border terminals.[6] 'Instead of hope, the Palestinians saw that they were put back in prison,' Wolfensohn would recall (quoted in Smooha, 2007). Practically all the deadlines and expectations of the Rice Agreements had not materialized, with the exception of the functioning of the Rafah crossing under the EU's Border Assistance Mission (EUBAM).

Seething with antipathy, Wolfensohn would relate these events in his 2010 autobiography, attempting to record for history's sake what had transpired (see Wolfensohn, 2010, pp. 399–440). 'The Israelis and the Americans subsequently took apart our agreement piece by piece,' he writes (p. 429) openly blaming neoconservative elements within the US administration for torpedoing the initiative. He concludes by arguing that the Quartet was a useful foil to reassert US political control over the peace process:

> President Bush sought my help, and he seemed to treat me as a peace envoy, but that was not, in the end, the real appointment that I had received. I had been authorized to create and implement an economic program. The moment I extended this mission [by assuming a political role around the AMA], my head was cut off. I don't think President Bush was trying to undermine my efforts. But whatever he had in mind, [Condoleezza] Rice and [US Deputy National Security Advisor Elliot] Abrams did not view me as their partner. Rice and Abrams were the ones implementing Bush's policy. I was not useful, and I was going beyond my mandate. In the end, the Quartet was a necessary camouflage for US initiatives.
>
> (Wolfensohn, 2010, p. 438)

Precisely why the US allowed for the AMA and the Rice Agreements to be signed and then not followed through on is a question for future historians. Certainly Ariel Sharon's initial minor (18 December 2005) and then major (4 January 2006) strokes could be said to have contributed to their delay, though this does not explain why Sharon himself failed to uphold his commitment to allow passage of the seemingly innocuous bus convoys between Gaza and the West Bank due to have taken place before his first stroke, on 15 December, a full month after the AMA was signed. Nor does it explain why his successor (Ehud Olmert) and the US administration did not push this agenda in the interim period between strokes, or after Sharon's major stroke, and in the crucial three-week window before the 25 January 2006 election. Certainly Dov Weisglass' revelation from the previous year, that Israel's redeployment from Gaza was intended as a form of 'formaldehyde' such that 'there will not be a political process with the Palestinians', should not be taken lightly (quoted in Shavit, 2004). To add to this, it is worth reasserting the political, as opposed to military, objectives behind the closure policy overall, as determined previously.

With these considered, two additional elements deserve mention in light of later efforts by the US to facilitate a form of medium-term economic sustainability.

First, full implementation of the AMA would have meant that the Palestinians would have been able to assert a modicum of territorial and economic contiguity and connection to the outside world that had the potential to run counter to the fragmentationist politics of closure, which deepened de-development. Implementation of the greenhouse deal, together with implementation of AMA, would also have meant that a potentially significant productive sector could take root and grow, and that these profits would be directed back into PNA coffers (via PIF-PEDC). Gaza's settler greenhouses were said to generate $100 million in flower, soft fruit and fresh herb sales annually (Wolfensohn, 2010, p. 416).

On the other hand, non-implementation of the AMA functionally meant that matters of access and transportation remained unknown entities for any economic activity. Tradable goods produced for an international or even local market could not rely upon 'open' access to markets. In a word, non-implementation of the AMA meant the death knoll for a productive sphere in tradable goods – industry or agriculture – acting as the dynamo of a Palestinian economy. This must be kept in mind when we come to characterize the kind of economic development that would eventually emerge in the OPT encouraged by Western donors.

Second, a section of Israeli capitalists, some associated with the Labor party, was also interested in the deal succeeding. According to a wikileak, former Israeli Prime Minister Shimon Peres had discussed the matter with US representatives, indicating that his peacebuilding NGO, the Peres Center for Peace, was willing to build more greenhouses for the Palestinians.[7] Another wikileak describes Avi Kadan of the Adafresh agricultural export company speaking to US representatives expressing interest in teaming with Palestinian growers. His company, established only in 2005 when the disengagement was to take place, had partnered with the PIF-owned PEDC to export the greenhouse crops to European markets and developed the product's branding. Kadan described his motivations for the partnership as stemming from a logic that 'better ties with Palestinian producers' would 'open up opportunities for his company in Arab or Muslim countries. [. . .] He could use Palestinian produce to enter these markets initially, then eventually bring in Israeli-grown product, too.' Kadan had already begun using such maneuvers in his partnership with the PIF-owned PEDC in his Rotterdam subsidiary, 'to hide the Israeli connection and encourage Arab buyers.'[8]

Hani Dajani, head of the Palestinian office of the Portland Trust, also revealed in an interview that certain markets, including the US, had banned Israeli imports of fresh herbs, because of repeated infestation violations (Interview). The independent statistical nomination 'Palestine' however was not faced with the same export restrictions, despite the fact that products labeled as such were functionally grown and exported in the same geographical area.

These intriguing nuances point to how elements of Israeli capital still held hope for expanding into Arab markets under Palestinian cover. They also expose how the PNA was willing – or perhaps had no option but – to team with these elements to secure financial revenue, strengthening its economic and political rule, and perhaps even winning it some influence. Israel's larger political determination however – that Palestinian development and productive capacity still needed to be subverted and subsumed beneath a de-development logic – in the end over-ruled all other considerations. Additionally, the consensus that a form of economic recovery still needed to take place without a political track would fundamentally shape the new era in Palestinian development emerging in the wake of Arafat's death and the denouement of the Al-Aqsa Intifada.

The 2006 Election and Reform Rollback

These inconvenient details tend to be overlooked in light of the overwhelming victory of Hamas in the 25 January 2006 election.

The latter became a convenient excuse for the AMA's non-implementation *ex-posto*, setting the stage for Israel to engage with Gaza as the object of its 'scientific' besiegement. Moreover, for the next year and a half, the US, Israel and elements of Fateh, would plot a coup against Hamas, which once defeated in June 2007, sealed Gaza's fate as an open-air prison, and the victim of periodic devastating military blows (Rose, 2008).[9]

Here it is necessary to point to the all-too-obvious Western donor response to the elections – immediately imposing a financial and political blockade on the new government – sending a clear message to the Palestinian electorate regarding how genuine Western donors were in their demands for Palestinian reform or a liberal peace arrangment. Bush had explicitly called upon Palestinians 'to build a practicing democracy', using this as part of his political conditionality for sanctioning US support for provisional Palestinian statehood. If liberal political praxis was implicitly instrumentalized during the Oslo years, the response of the donor community to the 2006 elections explicitly underscored this.

Palestinian democracy was not the only victim of Western donor responses to the election results. The hard fought institutional reforms of the donor community built off of years of Palestinian struggle for reform, would equally fall victim to the apoplectic fears of Western donors of a Hamas-controlled PNA. The grand PWC theories undergirding Fayyad's public financial management reforms would promptly be done away with as the Western donor community hurried to redirect funds away from the centralized treasury account they had fought so hard to create, given that the incoming Hamas Minister of Finance was set to take control over it. Both wings of the donor community led by the EU would quickly work to establish a direct assistance mechanism known as the 'Temporary International Mechanism' (TIM) in May 2006 to provide cash assistance directly to the president. Though the mechanism was originally envisioned to only last three months, it would remain in place for another year and a half, until it expanded into a far larger mechanism known as PEGASE[10] established in 2008. It distributed €1 billion between 2008 and 2012 (ECA, 2013, p. 6).

PEGASE was established to pay for the Fateh-controlled PNA's recurrent costs, which included PNA civil servants in both the West Bank and Gaza, pensioners and vulnerable families. But its expenses also went to support 'essential public services' – namely, the provision of fuel to the Gaza power plant; 'private sector arrears' and; 'private sector reconstruction in Gaza'- that being, 'financial support for businesses destroyed or damaged during the Israeli "Operation Cast Lead" offensive of 2008' – 95 per cent of which were inoperational before the offensive (Amnesty International *et al.*, 2008), and with Hamas directing reconstruction anyway on the ground. In a word, TIM and PEGASE were mechanisms to keep Fateh and its appendages afloat as a 'polity', if it was realistically to be expected to pose a viable, less radical alternative to Hamas.

Control of the PNA's millions in the PIF also needed to be shifted from the jurisdiction of the MoF to a private individual – back to the PNA president himself.[11] Abbas would rely on issuing presidential decrees to give a veil of legality to these maneuvers, even though the Basic Law of 2003 – also passed at the behest of donor conditionality – had directly stipulated that such decrees could only be issued under a state of emergency. Though Abbas indeed declared such a state, Article 110 of the Basic Law also stipulated that it could not exceed 30 days, and if it did, needed a two-thirds majority of PLC members to support the extension. Of the PLC's 132 seats, 81 were considered loyal to Hamas. It goes without saying that the emergency government Abbas would bring to order, as convened by his appointed Prime Minister Salam Fayyad on 15 June 2007, would also not receive confirmation from the PLC as the Basic Law decreed.

The criteria of efficiency and accountability that donors had strenuously demanded only a few years earlier were now also belied by a bloating administration and wage bill.

After Arafat's death, Abbas needed to purchase the silence and loyalty of splinter Fateh militias who were acting autonomously ever since the Intifada began, actively participating in military operations, often in cooperation with opposition factions. With the denouement of the Al-Aqsa Intifada, Abbas would work to get these groups registered on the security services' payroll, and their leaders, Israeli amnesty. From 1 March 2005 to the end of the outgoing parliament's mandate (12 February 2006) more than 19,000 recruits were brought on to the security services, bringing their total numbers to 73,000 (Sayigh, Y., 2007).

An older generation of PLO security personnel, many of whom had been loyal to Arafat and were less trustful of Abbas, were also retired, and rewarded with generous pensions, providing coverage to all security personnel over the age of 45. Though the donor community described the situation as 'unsustainable' and warned 'that these not set unrealistic precedents', there was little it could do (Ball *et al.*, 2006). Donors were relying on yet another 'guesstimate' for what it would take to keep a Fateh-run PNA alive. A 2010 World Bank internal evaluation would acknowledge that 'civil service reform became a highly political issue' with many of the 180,000 public sector workers on the 2007 payroll employed to hide unemployment and 'to accommodate political allies and boost the security apparatus' (World Bank, 2010a, p. 20). It also complained that few, if any, achievements could be recorded in the sphere of pensions and civil service reform for the assessed period (2001–9).

Even though it was unable to exercise any control over governance functions there, the West Bank PNA continued to pay 70,000 public servants in Gaza, despite ordering them not to report for duty under Hamas (see Qarmout & Beland, 2012). The move forced the Gaza government to employ at least 40,000 new public servants, with the obvious waste in resources backed by the West Bank PNA's donors. A 2013 European Court of Auditor's investigation of PEGASE found that 22–4 per cent of the PNA Ministries of Health and Education employees were simply not showing up (ECA, 2013, p. 26). The report almost certainly selected these sectors (health and education) because they revealed the *least* amount of workers who were not showing up, with far higher rates of non-attendance amongst former security service personnel. Recall as well that 39 per cent of Gaza's labor force was on the PNA payroll, as opposed to around 16 per cent in the West Bank (22.7 per cent overall for 2013) (PCBS, 2013, p. 109).

By 2013, the West Bank government was spending 59.7 per cent of its total revenues on salaries alone (PMA),[12] representing 17 per cent of GDP. (To put this in perspective, Egypt spent 8 per cent and Jordan 5 per cent) (IMF, 2013).[13] About 30 per cent of this was spent on the security sector, compared to 9.6 per cent on health and 19.1 per cent on education (MoF).[14] To cover costs, the West Bank government received $1.36 billion in external budget support, of which less than a tenth ($106.8 million) was for development (PMA).[15] It ranked 135th out of 185 in IFC's 2013 *Doing Business Report* (World Bank, 2013).

Far from the model state that international statebuilding practitioners envisioned and claimed they wished to support, Western donors were politically supporting and financially backing yet another emergent neopatrimonial regime led by Abbas, who oversaw an even more bloated yet delimited institutional apparatus that enjoyed even less autonomy and held few if any means to raise itself out from its condition. Donors were also now paying more than double the amount of annual aid they had under the Oslo years, though the seat of governance they were supporting had halved after the 'loss' of Gaza.

Moreover, instead of the previous arrangement where it was Arafat who had selected the system's clients in relative secrecy, now the donor community was aware and sanctioning the benefactors of the new regime more directly through their backing of Abbas, his methods of governance, and their oversight of his books. They also remained in control of substantial rent allocation powers and an array of political, institutional, and legal levers to influence important elements of the OPT's investment climate and incentives regime – powers they would attempt to wield to their political advantage.

Palestinian Statebuilding

Before exploring the consequences of this arrangement it is necessary to further clarify transformations and dynamics within Palestinian political and economic spheres. Previous sections have looked at the political basis of the reformist currents as divided between maximalists and pragmatists. Setting aside the economic agendas of the maximalists, it is important to clarify the economic basis and social constituencies of the pragmatist reform impetus, given the kinds of privileging it would enjoy under statebuilding.

The new reality to arise after mid-July 2007 across the West Bank created opportune conditions in which the symbiotic dependencies of Fateh and the Western donor community would come together under the common agenda of neoliberal statebuilding. This only became possible however after the gestation and maturation of various socio-political and economic transformations underway.

For Fateh, the process of economic revival was crucial for the organizational and political task of reunifying its ranks after the death of Arafat, its defeat in elections, and the 'loss' of Gaza. Arafat's death had meant the death of the movement's patriarch. His charisma and legitimacy had animated the functioning of the original neopatrimonial model he led, and was the real force behind the PNA as an institution. In his absence, the institution lost its anchor, compass, and chief regulator, and the strings of control which had once collected in his hands, were now cut loose. The fallout of this untethering was seen in different spheres, threatening the organization as a coherent entity, if indeed it could still be characterized as such.[16]

There were clear splits amongst the elite. Abbas and his loyalists had to contend with elites formerly associated with Arafat, and others who had been built up by the apparatus of the PNA who had independent relations with Western and regional players as a result, and/or who potentially threatened Abbas politically regarding influence within Fateh. Bitter and often embarrassing public feuds emerged between Abbas and former Arafat investor Mohammed Rashid, as well as former head of Preventative Security in Gaza, Mohammed Dahlan. Both were accused of various misappropriations of Palestinian funds and other crimes: Rashid for involvement in an $800 million tourism village in the Jordanian city of Aqaba using money that was said to belong to the PLO; Dahlan for committing various assassinations, collaborating with Israel, and even a possible finger in Arafat's death (Rajjoub, 2014). Dahlan was expelled from Fateh in June 2011. Rashid was sentenced in abstention to 15 years of prison by a Palestinian court in 2012.[17]

Fateh's splintering was most visible in the 2006 election. Despite losing the overall popular vote to Hamas by a margin of 44 per cent to 41 per cent, the representation of Fateh in the PLC was far weaker – 45 seats (34 per cent) to Hamas' 74 (56 per cent) (NDI, 2006). This discrepancy emerged from the fact that Fateh split its votes among several candidates when voting for national lists, whereas Hamas was much more disciplined in only fielding one list of candidates.[18] This result was the consequence of the neopatrimonial organization of Arafat's power: unable to mediate their differences based upon clear political or ideological criteria in his absence, the number of Arafat's former 'clients' in each district outnumbered the fixed number of legislative slots. Fateh candidates bumped from the fixed slate still ran though, resulting in the split vote. Hamas took an absolute majority in the PLC even without the support of the 13 (10 per cent) Left and independent candidates who won the remaining seats (Haddad, 2007).

The unraveling of the PNA's first neopatrimonial model thus informed the political and economic decision-making environment in which Abbas needed to maneuver to assert leadership over Fateh and consolidate the political and economic base of the PNA as its formal institutional project. 'Statebuilding', led by the pristine resume of Fayyad, became the practical and logical best option for facilitating such maneuvering with the finance minister's expertise and orientation appearing to offer a more politically stable and economically profitable arrangement for the movement in the long term.

Part of making this determination stemmed from Abbas' historical managerial and financial role in Fateh, where he came to be known as a pragmatist. But the Al-Aqsa Intifada had also exposed and widened fissures amongst disaffected economic sectors within Palestinian society, with this disaffection extending into Fateh's own organizational base. These fissures needed to be addressed to consolidate Fateh's coherency and base to shore-up the PNA's intra-Palestinian political settlement.

Here the writings of Palestinian sociologist Jamil Hilal are helpful in guiding us through the shifts that were taking place in the OPT's socio-economic composition since the Authority's formation (Hilal, 2002).

Hilal describes a scenario during the Oslo years whereby native capitalists felt cut out from the lucrative spoils of 'peacebuilding' that the expatriate capitalists enjoyed. The early and most profitable of the economic deals cut between the PLO and the expatriate capitalists – the casino, the major tourism hotels, the telephone company, the power plant – had excluded native business elites entirely, and were allocated in non-transparent, non-competitive arrangements. In fact the precise details of many of these deals (telecom, electricity) have yet to be disclosed. Native capitalists were also initially excluded from setting up and sharing in state-run companies, as well as the main private investment portfolios which benefitted from PNA patronage. Even the public shareholding companies had limited amounts of floated stock, which anyway only became available for purchase after 1997. Hilal and Khan have suggested that the PNA leadership did not see smaller capitalists as critical growth leaders, and their capital anyway was limited in size and mobility (Khan and Hilal, 2004, p. 104).

The nature of this pact between the PNA's political elite and expatriate capitalists, operating through public and private shareholding companies and private corporations functionally also made the PNA a competitor in the domestic market to elements within the private sector itself, and native capital in particular, given the latter's involvement in the OPT's infant productive sector (textiles, pharmaceuticals, dairy production, food stuffs, furniture, and consumer goods), as well as import trade, deepening their animosity. The PNA's system of regulating consumer goods by requiring importers of certain goods to have a PNA-issued concessions license, particularly tipped market share power in certain sectors to the private shareholding company APIC – the Arab Palestinian Investment Company, which was 20 per cent owned by the PNA (initially PCSC, then PIF). Its subsidiary, UNIPAL flooded markets with consumer goods that only it was entitled to import. Although rationalized as a way to protect the Palestinian economy from Israeli product dumping and poor quality goods, the concessions-based import system allowed for UNIPAL to become the OPT's main supplier of a wide selection of consumer goods. It did this acting as the local subsidiary of multinational corporations and their regional Arab affiliates based in the Gulf, which APIC's Gulf-based shareholders (the Aggad Group, Khoury Group, Kingdom Group, Olayan Group) were major stakeholders in. UNIPAL's portfolio included products and services ranging from food to aluminum, with APIC subsidiaries forging strategic partnerships with multi-national companies including Philip Morris Tobacco, Procter & Gamble, Abbott International, Beiersdorf (Nivea), Eli Lilly, B. Braun, Hyundai Motors, GlaxoSmithKline, and Aventis (see APIC Annual Report 2012, p.11).

APIC also owned an affiliated advertising company, Sky Advertising, which promoted the products and services of a great many of the favored capital formations. Sky was managed by Mahmoud Abbas' son Tareq, who is also a board member of APIC. It is also worth noting that the company was established in the British Virgin Islands, and was registered as a foreign private shareholder company with the PNA Ministry of National Economy in 1996. In 2013, it changed its registration to a public shareholding company, but remained a foreign company, benefitting from the tax advantages this entailed (see APIC Annual Report, 2013, p. 8).

Economically, the PNA benefitted from this arrangement in different ways. As noted, it was a direct investor in many of the public and private shareholding companies. But the preferential treatment given to its patrons in trade through APIC, and the bias trade enjoyed during the Oslo years at the expense of local industry, also meant that larger VAT and customs revenues could be expected from Israel each month, providing the latter allowed their transfer. This method of revenue generation was also less complicated to rely upon and manage, as it was less risky than attempting to develop a productive economic potential (that could be destroyed militarily, through closure or prevention of access to land, water etc.), or alternatively, attempting to generate a local tax base. Taxation particularly would have raised thorny questions about the PNA's standing and legitimacy in the context of Israel's continued occupation. Palestinians anyway were reluctant to declare incomes or pay taxes, partly as a hold-over to its association with the Israeli Civil Administration, and partly because they were incentivized against doing so because of the differing geo-civic classifications (Areas A, B, and C) and the PNA's weak institutional/enforcement powers. Taxation also raised questions as to the competitiveness of the OPT as a site attractive to foreign direct investment, which the PNA sought to court.

All this to say nothing of the great majority of small- and medium-sized enterprises (SMEs) disenfranchised by this economic arrangement overall. 99 per cent of Palestinian businesses in the OPT were considered small and medium sized enterprises[19] (Abdelkarim, 2010). The World Bank's 2001 survey of the OPT's governance and business environment found strong discrepancies between how large firms and SME's experienced the economic dynamics of the Oslo years: large firms viewed policy instability and uncertainty as being a less serious constraint than small firms; corruption was also a less serious constraint than for medium size or small firms; and taxes were seen as a less serious constraint than for medium-size and small firms (Sewell, 2001). This points to the preferential treatment large capitalists enjoyed during the Oslo years in regards to taxation, fears of predation and representation of interests.

Productive sectors which native capitalists were invested in struggled to remain competitive under the Paris Protocol, with agriculture and industry's share of value added to GDP both witnessing declines over these years (see Graph 10.1).

The subcontracting industry for Israeli manufacturers in apparel for instance was particularly hard hit. According to the Hebron Chamber of Commerce, between 1970 and 1990, roughly 40,000 people – up to a third of Hebron's residents – had worked in 1,200 shoe workshops. By 2013, only 250 remained, employing 4,000 workers, with major competition coming from imported shoes from China (Abdalla, 2013).

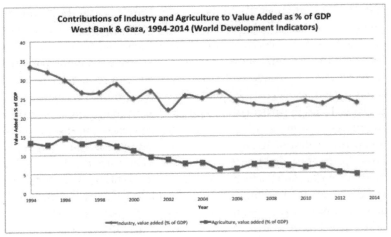

Graph 10.1 Contributions of industry and agriculture to value added as % of GDP, West Bank & Gaza, 1994–2014.

Trade remained the dominant Palestinian economic sector during the 20-year period covered in this research, never dipping below 71.1 per cent of GDP (year 2013), and sometimes reaching as high as 97.2 per cent (2007) (see Graph 10.2).

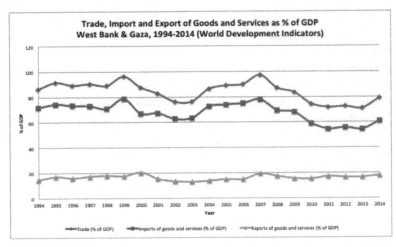

Graph 10.2 Trade, import and export of goods and services as % of GDP, West Bank & Gaza, 1994–2014.

These underlying economic concerns created the objective conditions that forced native capitalists to think of means to unify their vision regarding their role and interests (Hilal, 2002, p. 89). (To clarify – native capitalists refers to the few but significant capitalists who accumulated their wealth in the OPT, and were distinct from the petit bourgeoisie.) These capitalists began self-organizing through local chambers of commerce offices, businessmen's associations (Paltrade in particular, est.1998) and via PLC representatives, such as Azmi Shu'aibi, referred to earlier, who had been on the PLC's Economic Committee. Their concerns would also make their way to donor ears via these channels, contributing to the emergent concern for reform in the late Oslo period.

Though Hilal's analysis does not extend beyond the year 2002 when his study was published, he does refer to the phenomenon whereby sections of native capital and expatriate capital were beginning to find common cause, forming types of 'national' capital, through the shareholding companies and their projects, with these formations distinguished from family- or locally-owned businesses in so far as ownership and structure (ibid., p. 89). The interpermeation of interests through shareholding companies was facilitated by the creation of the Palestine Securities Exchange in 1995 which opened its doors to trading in February 1997. Interpermeation was also facilitated by the influx and creation of local, regional and international banks through credit provision and portfolio investment.

Hilal also highlights how this phenomenon was accompanied by the intermarriage between sections of the political and economic elite in its various forms. Likely because he writes in Arabic, he remains unspecific when referring to the phenomena whereby sons of the political elite from the PNA or PLO executive were seen to take up high-level positions in companies or became businessmen themselves. Although he believes this form of institutional corruption was limited to only the very top echelons of the political elite, it nonetheless pointed to emergent implicit interests between the ruling party, the upper echelons of the public sector (empowered with the executive authority to sign agreements, oversee project implementation, and to issue company registration and licenses), and/or the private sector.

These dynamics overall were taking place in an environment where the private sector began crystalizing a consciousness of its own interests, aided by the objective factors that the PNA has provided them for the first time: a nascent national market formed through the PNA's regulatory, political and institutional powers, however delimited, and an international climate encouraging of private sector-led development and growth (ibid., p. 91).

Nonetheless native West Bank capitalists tended to assert their independence from the PNA. As previously noted, native capitalists competed with the PNA in some sectors, feared potential predation and already felt on unequal terms in respect to how they were cut-out from the major initial deals of the Oslo years. Their involvement in some productive tradable export sectors also meant that they guarded their independence and needed to demonstrate more chameleon-like qualities in interacting with the real sovereign powers who controlled the destiny of their goods and businesses.

Expatriate capitalist also had their reasons for independence. A longer and more guarded history with the PLO existed between them, with several authors suggesting that Arafat was always cautious of the wealthy capitalists restoring the political pre-eminence of patrician families which had been lost after 1948, 'after having abandoned the national movement in favor of their business interests' (ibid., pp. 90–1; see also Nakhleh, 2012, pp. 37–129; Khan and Hilal, 2004, p. 102; Tamari, 2002). This despite courting their services once the PLO's political isolation increased in the 1980s, bringing them more on board through the Oslo process overall.

Several interviews also suggested that there were various rivalries between the expatriate capitalists themselves, partly to do with differences over their share of the OPT 'pie'. Locally, some of the 'sweetheart' projects expatriate capitalists benefitted from did not materialize as expected, while others were not able to take-off entirely: CCC (Said Khoury and Hasib Sabbagh) for instance was not able to move forward in the construction of the Gaza seaport, or to take advantage of the exploitation of its gas deal with British Gas. Alternatively, Munib and Sabih al-Masri, did very well with PADICO and Paltel Group respectively, with the former particularly expanding and diversifying holdings in select niches across the OPT.

Competition over the local OPT market however is likely to have been insignificant considering the regional competition these same actors were engaged in. The year 2012 witnessed a fierce rivalry exploding between Sabih al-Masri, Munib al-Masri and the Lebanese Hariri family on one side, vying for a commanding ownership stake in the Arab Bank from its then-control under the Shoman family on the other. Abdel Hameed Shoman's grandfather had established the bank in Jerusalem in 1930, but the bank was headquartered in Amman after the Nakba. Its 2012 balance sheet stood at $45.6 billion spread across 30 countries and five continents (Al-Khalidi, 2012). Separate interviews with individuals directly connected to the region's banking world affirmed that the struggle was tied to whether the Arab Bank would refinance loans which the Hariri-Masri wing needed for massive construction projects in Amman and Aqaba, Jordan. The bitter feud ended in the abrupt resignation of Abdel Hameed Shoman in August, and the election of Sabih al-Masri to the head of its board of directors.

In light of these gestating processes across and within Palestinian capitalists regionally and locally, we begin to see important shades of how the reform process and international statebuilding contributed to the consolidation and stabilization of the political settlement governing intra-Palestinian relations.

For Fateh and the West Bank PNA, reform and statebuilding created the institutional and economic means to re-forge an elite bargain between expatriate and native capitalists, the nomenklatura of the PNA executive and regulatory branches, Fateh leaders of different stripes, and traditional elites on the local level. This represented an expansion of the benefactors of the former political settlement, as well as a supposed more level playing field upon which their profit-seeking interests could advance individually and/or towards further inter-permeation. Statebuilding offered Fateh a means to reconsolidate its base through the apparatus of the PNA, with the principles of the PWC operationally substituting for Fateh's lack of an explicit ideological orientation or an inclusive, representational political and economic program for achieving Palestinian rights. Neoliberal statebuilding under Fayyadism claimed to offer the means to mediate differences based on established economic criteria for profit-rearing, and 'best practice.'

Alternatively, capitalists of all stripes looked positively to the reform period seeing it as an opportunity to expand their traction and leverage with the PNA, and their profits overall. As we shall see, the

PWC agenda was not a one-way street for Fateh to reconstitute itself through the PNA, but was also an opportunity for native and expatriate capitalists to empower themselves and assert their interests more aggressively, exploiting the fact that they were the constituency that both Fateh and the internationals needed to see succeed. Here, the 'stand-by' nature of statebuilding, was about to stand-up.

CHAPTER 11

INCENTIVIZING DE-DEVELOPMENT

The year and a half of instability caused by the election victory of Hamas, followed by the failed coup in Gaza, put many of these dynamics in limbo. However once the territorial-political division of 2007 was complete, and with renewed Western donor interest in reinvigorating the West Bank government, the conditions were prepared for 'statebuilding' to take off amongst the PNA and the private sector ensemble around it. In fact, it needed to take off quickly to ensure that Western donor states' then 14-year investment survived.

In so far as both donors and Fateh were keen to work towards creating a sustainable medium term economic arrangement, the key seemed to lie in realizing the missing link of private investment. However, because of the supremacy of the 'politics first' wing of the donor community over the donor agenda, Israel was given free rein to filter all development aid towards a de-development agenda. This, on top of the overall instability and risk associated with the investment climate right after the failed coup, when Fateh appeared particularly weak. The search for profitable investment and the encouraging of private sector interests as the core driving statebuilding activity thus inevitably led to the incentivizing of economic spheres where profit-making was considered least risky economically, while not violating any de-development agendas politically. This led to a situation we shall describe as the incentivization of de-development, which would provide the nourishing environment in which Palestine Ltd. could mature and become more pronounced.

Financialization

Incentivizing de-development arose from the confluence of donor policy orientations with the gestating political, economic, and social dynamics described above within OPT social relations. It also arose from a sense of political expediency and temporal exigency considering the circumstances.

Donors utilized three primary means to induce private sector investment with the hope of activating a sustainable OPT economy capable of performing the role outlined for it in terms of creating employment and administering social needs:

- continued provision of technical assistance within a neoliberal statebuilding model, concentrating particularly on the interaction between governance and economic actors;
- direct forms of aid and foreign direct investment at their disposal and through their influence amongst wealthy Gulf state donors, and;
- connected to both of the previous – particular forms of aid and policy that specifically targeted managing the risk investors faced operating in the OPT context.

All three means should be read as part of a broader dynamic that will be loosely described as inducing financialization across the OPT.

Here Gerald Epstein's broad definition of the term financialization is helpful in describing what is meant by this term, and the processes the West Bank was about to undergo:

> Financialization refers to the increasing importance of financial markets, financial motives, financial institutions, and financial elites in the operation of the economy and its governing institutions, both at the national and international level.
>
> (Epstein, 2001, p. 1)

It is also worth bearing in mind David Harvey's understanding of the role of financialization in so far as it facilitates the rise of finance capital, based on interest bearing capital (Harvey, 2006, pp. 284–6). Finance capital is by nature unable to solve capitalist crises 'because it can only deal with problems that arise in exchange and never with those in production' (ibid., p. 286). This has important ramifications for a context like the OPT, where de-development characterizes overall development conditions.

As Harvey explains, the credit system upon which much of financial capital rests and which financialization facilitates, acts as a kind of 'central nervous system through which the overall circulation of capital is coordinated' (ibid., p. 284). Credit is believed to have the potential to 'straddle antagonisms between production and consumption, between production and realization, between present use and future use, between production and distribution' (ibid., pp. 285–6). However in a context of de-development, where these antagonisms are politically generated and enforced as an outgrowth of Zionist settler-colonialism and its historical policies vis-à-vis Palestinian nationalism, the 'straddling impetus' abandons futile efforts to break out of conditions of de-development and instead works to focus on *accelerating exchange within de-development*, thus serving to break down the internal impediments to the efficiency of de-development overall. This leads to the *acceleration of the very de-developing character of de-development itself*, with crucial implications upon the national, political and social levels.

Donor Aid

The first means donors utilized towards this end was to continue the role of providing technical assistance to the PNA now under a Fayyadist statebuilding agenda.

Previous sections have already discussed Fayyadist statebuilding efforts, how they attempted to create the institutional basis for a functioning state, and how these efforts received recognition from IFIs as being successful at least on paper. These efforts were part and parcel of the overall impetus to create a functioning Palestinian economy within a PWC approach to generating growth in general, considering that now double the amount of aid was coming in for 'half' the geopolitical territory. The World Bank alone approved 47 projects after the failed coup (July 2007) to the end of 2013. This was more than half of the 91 projects it approved since arriving in the OPT in 1994. In six and a half years, the Bank committed itself to more projects than it did in the previous 13 and a half, totaling $959 million as opposed to $639 million for the other 44 projects. These were closely coordinated within the Fayyadist statebuilding visions, as articulated in the PRDP and the NDP.

There is no need to go into great detail regarding the legal and technical support Western donors continued to provide to the PNA under the Fayyad governments during this period, or to isolate those which dealt specifically with improving the economy by means of investment climate improvement schemes, trade facilitation, legal reform, microcredit and the like.[1] We have already established that statebuilding provided the opportunity to improve the economic and financial infrastructure of the OPT from a legal and institutional perspective, with these efforts building-off many private sector-oriented laws instituted during the Oslo period, and later, the reform wave of 2000 to 2005, which never had the political and economic conditions to bear fruit before 2007 due to political instability. The process of institutional reform would only continue apace in the post-2007 period, this time facilitated by the fact that such reforms were taking place through the issuing of presidential decrees, without oversight from the PLC or the input of a political opposition.

The West Bank-PNA's receptivity to this aid and technical support became more pronounced contrasting with the former strained relations of conditionality. For instance, an Arabic-language 2011 PECDAR publication that periodically reviewed Palestinian economic performance and developmental conditions in the OPT, describes an amicable and synergistic relationship between itself and the World Bank (PECDAR, 2011, p. 153). 'Tight cooperation' in regards to planning, preparing and implementing projects had led to enriched professional skills, the accumulation of valuable experience, and an increased overall trust beneficial to both parties. But this amicability starkly contrasted with PECDAR's own distrust of donors as voiced in a previous issue of the same series published years earlier (2003) at the height of the Intifada. Again, writing in Arabic (with the likely implication that the publication did not get back to its World Bank financiers), the publication openly expressed a conviction in a hidden agenda to international aid in the Palestinian context that aimed 'to achieve political goals' – 'protecting the security of Israel' – which was 'expected to occupy the place of spider' in 'a web of wide relations of a Middle East order' (PECDAR, 2003, p. 83).

Fayyadism cleared the cobwebs from within the PNA bureaucracy, bringing in and training a section of bureaucrats into the West Bank-PNA who demonstrated ideological fealty to the neoliberal agenda.

Ja'far Hdeibi, head of the Palestinian Investment Promotion Agency (PIPA) for instance, described the value of Western donor technical assistance to his agency as 'essential', singling out the particular contributions of the World Bank, USAID and DFID:

> I was one of these people who would say 'enough is enough – we don't need more experts here!' But after a while I discovered it is not easy [...] without having these experts and technical assistance. The world is improving, developing. But you don't know what's happening there. You know the titles but you don't know the techniques, the details – a lot of things. You need to exchange this knowledge through training, workshops, and experts.
>
> (Hdeibi Interview)

In another interview, Lena Ghabaisheh, Mortgages and Leasing regulator at the Capital Markets Authority, used the Arabic proverb 'give your bread dough to the baker!' as an explanation for why her agency allowed the International Finance Corporation to write its mortgage underwriting manual. Ghabaisheh explained that much of the economic activity being promoted and seen as strategic to the statebuilding mission, existed in financial sectors the PNA and its personnel had little experience in, particularly capital markets:

> Our sectors are nascent. We have to create a legal system and further develop our regulations. There is no legal framework, no sector, no culture, no awareness [about mortgages and leasing]. Everything coming into the market is new.
>
> (Ghabaisheh Interview)

The Palestinian economy already suffered from powerful financial tools transplanted to the OPT via the 'globalized' expatriate capital formations around the PNA. The Palestinian Securities Exchange (PSE) for example, currently equipped with a top-of-the-line Nasdaq OMX trading system, had experienced a bubble and crash in 2005–6, as investors rushed to buy, and then sell, PADICO stock. PADICO, which was the majority owner of the stock exchange itself, operated PSE since 1997 without government oversight, and local and global investors rushed to its market in the context of the exuberance generated over

Israel's Gaza redeployment, Wolfensohn's peacebuilding economic initiatives, and the overall impression that a period of major rebuilding and works could be around the corner with the denouement of the Al-Aqsa Intifada. 'Men were selling their wives' jewelry so they could buy PADICO stock, with some even thinking PADICO was a person,' noted Securities Regulator Burraq Nabulsi (Nabulsi, Interview). The Al Quds Index was one of the best performing markets in the world between 2003 and 2005, climbing more than 300 per cent in 2005. After the collapse of regional stock markets however, and with the Hamas election victory, market confidence collapsed from a high of 1336 points on 28 November 2005, to 494 by 16 July 2006.[2]

The importing of financial instruments, technologies and policies for economic revival and profit-making recalls the combined and uneven character to the kind of development taking place under neoliberal statebuilding throughout the OPT. It also recalls the notion that the OPT was undergoing a process of financialization immediately after the crisis conditions Israel created throughout the Intifada, which were now being selectively eased in the West Bank, while being tightened in Gaza. This cleared space for a local variant of Palestinian disaster capitalism to arise in collusion with donor policies.

Two key institutions were targeted to facilitate this process: the Palestine Monetary Authority (PMA) which oversaw the regulation of banks, money changers and microfinance institutions, and the Capital Market Authority (CMA) which oversaw the securities market, insurance companies and real-estate institutions (including mortgages and leasing). Improvements in the OPT's financial infrastructure are important to bear in mind considering the PWC mentality held them as key to giving investors and banks a sense that satisfactory conditions prevailed for investment capital to be injected into the local economy for profit and a more sustainable Palestinian economy.

OPT lending culture was considered exceedingly conservative with loans heavily collateralized (sometimes as much as 140 per cent), and banks demanding as many as three guarantors. Although banks were well capitalized with the value of total bank assets at the end of 2007 standing at just over $7 billion, the loan to deposit ratio stood only at 30 per cent ($1.63 to 5.37 billion).[3] Moreover, most Palestinian deposits ($3.74 billion) were being held or invested outside of the OPT.

We thus see the PMA working to establish a legal environment after the 2007 split that protected the Palestinian banking system's standing internationally, while encouraging a policy of loosening up credit provision locally, encouraging investment, and raising banking performance and standards overall.

The PMA benefitted from at least nine different presidential decrees between 2007 and 2013, including one against money laundering that was based on a draft written by the IMF. According to a wikileak, then-PMA president George Abed, speaking to US consul personnel, requested that two Gaza-based banks (Bank of Palestine and Palestine Islamic Bank (PIB)) transfer their headquarters to the West Bank. Abed had 'a lack of confidence in banking supervision in Gaza,' while speculating that PIB 'may be more susceptible to Hamas pressure than other banks.'[4] Such quotations illustrate how the West Bank-PNA colluded with donors to advance their project, protect the integrity of their financial system and international standing, and indirectly participated in the financial siege against the Gaza government, entrenching the overriding political division. Because the West Bank-PNA's political and economic model depended so heavily on the sanctity of its standing with Western donors and Israel, whether it was ideologically married or financially captive to the neoliberal agenda is inconsequential to the fact that unless such measures were taken, the West Bank PNA feared it would suffer a similar fate as the Gaza government.

Other reforms instituted by the PMA which advanced a financialization agenda included a bank instruction to raise loan to deposit ratios above 40 per cent; the launching of a Credit Registry System to track individual financial histories and; the issuing of an instruction allowing banks to grant loans for the purpose of investment financing of shares.[5] The PMA also ran hundreds of workshops to develop the skill set of local bank staff through its affiliated NGO, the Palestine Banking Institute (PBI). According to PBI's website, 659 workshops ran between 2007 and 2012 – more than double the amount of all eight previous years combined, while claiming to have trained 12,632 personnel of all grades.

Bank penetration across the OPT witnessed a phenomenal rise from the early days where two banks with 13 branches were in operation at the end of 1993 (Nasr, 2004). By 2007, the number of branches would reach 159 for 22 banks, and would only rise further to 238 branches for 17 banks by the end of 2013 (MAS 2008; 2013). These were five local

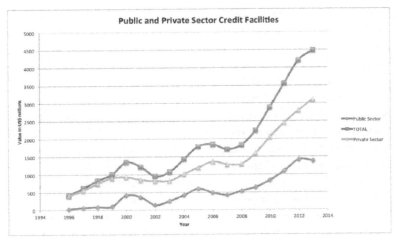

Graph 11.1　Public and private sector credit facilities.
(Based on statistics from 'Consolidated Balance Sheet of Banks Operating in Palestine, 1996–2013', PMA.)

Palestinian commercial banks, two Islamic banks (also local Palestinian), and 10 foreign commercial banks (one international, one Egyptian, the rest Jordanian).[6] Total assets and liabilities at the end of 2013 would amount to $11.1 billion, quintupling in size from total deposits in 1996 and which stood at $2.2 billion.

The wave of financialization would make 2007 a pivotal year in which the amount of public and private debt would begin to rise steeply (see Graph 11.1).

The amount of overall debt climbed from $1.63 billion in 2007 to $4.44 billion in 2013 – a rise of 172 per cent.

An examination of the allocation of credit facilities between 2008 and 2013 is revealing for deciphering what sectors were receiving these credit extensions.

The West Bank PNA owed 30.7 per cent of overall debt to local and foreign creditors, rising 226 per cent since 2007. The private sector exhibited slightly less, but still high rates of increasing indebtedness, with a 142 per cent increase for the same period. The majority of this credit was extended in the form of loans (69.6 per cent) and overdrafts (30.1 per cent).

Most debt was held in dollar (59 per cent) followed by shekels (29.5 per cent) and then Jordanian dinar (10.7 per cent), although public

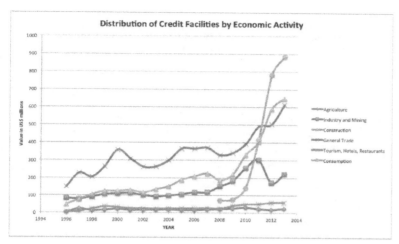

Graph 11.2   Distribution of credit facilities by economic activity. (Composed from PMA statistics on credit facilities by economic sector and activity.)[7]

sector debt was held primarily in shekels (54 per cent) and dollars (37 per cent) (PMA, 2012, p. 11).[8]

More than 70 per cent of all debt was financing four main sectors: consumption (including car and vehicular finance), 15.2 per cent; real estate, construction and land development, 13.9 per cent; trade, 13.9 per cent and; services (tourism, business and consumer, financial, and transport) another 13.9 per cent. Only 7.9 per cent of all debt was going to productive sectors, including 1.2 per cent for agriculture and food processing and 6.7 per cent for mining and manufacturing.[9]

The rise of private sector debt is captured by Graph 11.2 demonstrating the rise of various sector debt facilities.

Between 2008 and 2013, consumption, including for vehicle finance, increased an astonishing 820 per cent (from $110.4 to 1015.9 million), and debt in real estate and land development increased 218 per cent ($222.7 to 707.5 million).

This is reflected in another graph illustrating the type of capital formation and its transformation over time (see Graph 11.3).

Historically, the OPT's gross capital formation[10] has been overwhelmingly composed of fixed capital, with the only statistical difference between these two indicators being the net changes in levels

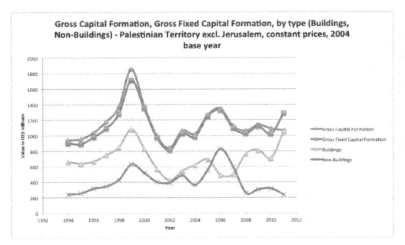

Graph 11.3   Gross capital formation, gross fixed capital formation, by type (buildings, non-buildings), Palestinian Territory excluding Jerusalem, constant prices, 2004 base year.
Source: 'Main Economic Indicators', PMA.[11]

of inventories and 'work in progress' (which are both only counted in the former). We thus see this consistent congruity between both lines on the above graph over time. Of this fixed capital formation, it was investment in buildings which composed the majority, excepting the years 2006 and 2007 when Hamas won the elections and the political and financial instability this entailed. The divergence in value starting in 2007 between building and non building-related fixed capital is telling. Investment in the built environment increased, while that in plant machinery and equipment clearly declined. Gross fixed capital formation was even able to outpace gross capital formation between 2010 and 2011, suggesting that either/or/both the push towards more building was generating more profit, while net inventories were being depleted and not restored. The latter suggests that traders felt more comfortable with supply conditions and didn't feel the need to buy and hold as much inventory – a likely possibility considering the loosening of trade within the West Bank post-2007.

Thus we see improved financial infrastructure and accelerated financialization of the OPT leading towards increased circulation of money for consumption and investment purchases, a good deal of

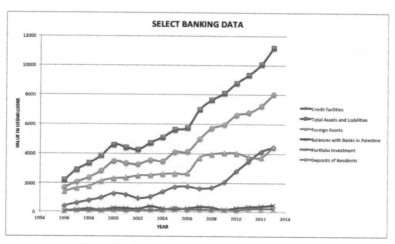

Graph 11.4 Select banking data.
Source: Consolidated balance sheet of banks operating in Palestine, PMA.[12]

which was debt financed and certainly with the overwhelming majority of it for non-productive purposes. Here it is worth pointing to how banks were managing the holding of their assets (see Graph 11.4).

Graph 11.4 reveals that while the total deposit of residents and total assets and liabilities of banks operating in OPT banks rose healthily from 2007, the holding of foreign assets by banks does not keep pace, but levels off around the $4 billion mark for several years, before slightly dipping, then rising. Alternatively after 2007 we observe a healthy increase in credit facilities until it appears to level in 2013. Throughout the entire period, the balance held by banks in Palestine together with portfolio investment, is stable and does not significantly rise from their low levels. The graph thus reveals that after 2007, banks refrained from holding the increased deposits in foreign assets. Instead, they allowed for parts of this money to go towards credit and to be invested locally. Credit holdings even eclipse foreign assets between 2011 and 2012, which might be considered the peak of Fayyadist statebuilding. This tells us that banks briefly saw the provision of credit for non-productive growth, as more profitable than holding foreign assets.

Finally, it is worth looking more closely at who precisely held the rising levels of OPT debt. Suleiman Abbadi and Sharif Abu Karsh's research on how Palestinian banks evaluate their credit risks, reveals that three major Jordanian banks – Arab Bank PLC, Cairo Amman Bank, and Bank of Jordan – accounted for about 50 per cent of commercial bank assets, more than 50 per cent of deposits, and more than 55 per cent of credit facilities (Abbadi and Abu Karsh, 2013). They also had large presences in almost all Palestinian cities, accounting for more than one-third of all branches by the end of 2013 (80 branches).[13]

PCBS gives an even clearer indication that it was Jordanian capital which was improving its market share under Palestinian statebuilding. At the end of 2012, total foreign liabilities of resident enterprises (stocks held by non-residents invested in resident enterprises) amounted to $2.6 billion.[14] Foreign direct investment (FDI) contributed 55.7 per cent, portfolio investments stood at 25.8 per cent, and other investments amounted to 18.5 per cent. More than half of FDI in resident enterprises was concentrated in financial intermediation activity, with investment from Jordan contributing nearly 80.4 per cent of total FDI stock in resident enterprises. 55.5 per cent of total portfolio investments was concentrated in services and transport, storage, and communications activities, while investments from Jordan contributed nearly 45.4 per cent of the total stock of portfolio investments.

Investment, Aid and Influence

'Getting institutions right' was not the only means by which donors attempted to get the Palestinian economy running.

The second means donors utilized to promote investment was through the provision of direct investment through infrastructure aid, and/or through the encouraging of direct investment by other potential donors and investors (particularly those in the Gulf), to look to the OPT as an emerging market.

Immediately after the failed 2007 coup, donors and the Fayyad government were anxious to portray the West Bank as a credible investment opportunity.

A Palestine Papers leak from the period relates a conversation between Quartet Special Representative Tony Blair (who replaced the resigned Wolfensohn) and Fayyad, in which Blair assures the latter he will be able to secure, via Israel, the safe passage of investors to a planned investment conference in May 2008. 'The Bethlehem [investment] conference is more important conceptually than substantively,' notes Fayyad. 'We want to show that despite immense adversity we are throwing a party. We want to show the other face of Palestine not only to the international community but to our people as well.'[15]

The need to demonstrate that the West Bank was indeed 'open for business' came in the form of support to the aforementioned investment conference, whose organization was handed at least partly to US contracting agency Booz Allen Hamilton, with USAID and DFID funding. In an interview, a principle consultant involved in conference organization complained of elementary problems whereby even the basic information investors needed to be able to formulate their decisions to invest or not, simply didn't exist. For example, potential investors in the OPT's large stone and marble stocks were dissuaded from investing because 'there was no one who could tell us [the sector's] export potential, because, how could you get it out? We were constantly stuck between what we wanted to do, and the reality of the situation, which was, you couldn't export anything anyway' (Anonymous, Interview).

The investment conference nonetheless was promoted as an enormous success by the donor community and the PNA, who boasted of 1200 private investors – the majority of whom were Palestinians from Jordan. Press releases claimed that over $1billion in investment commitments were realized through the conference, including two centerpiece deals in real estate and telecommunications: the building of the new city of Rawabi backed by the Qatari sovereign wealth fund, Qatari Diyar, and an investment for the second mobile telephone operator Wataniya Mobile, a Kuwaiti-owned holding company linked to the royal family that was bought out by Qatari company, Qtel (now Ooreedo), part owned by the Qatari government. Both investments however, were not new, but had been known for months prior to the investment conference. 'This is how the donors play the game all the time,' noted the consultant:

> If you want to talk business investment, business growth, business opportunities – you have got political realities that need to be dealt with. And what you didn't have attached to that conference was any kind of political momentum to say 'what are we doing to address the real blocks?' The blocks in Palestine are not lack of

education, they are not lack of enthusiasm, they are not lack of
engagement. Its lack of international access to growth markets,
and we didn't tackle that.

(Anonymous, Interview)

One wikileak reveals how Western governments wielded behind-the-
scenes influence to encourage OPT investments.[16] It describes a US
government representative's conversation with Shaykh Ali Al-Sabah
(Director of Economic Affairs at the Kuwaiti Ministry of Foreign Affairs),
and Rabah Al-Rabah, Deputy Director General of the Kuwait Chamber of
Commerce and Industry, at the beginning of May 2007. Both discussants
expressed skepticism about the planned investment conference with Al-
Rabah noting 'Iraq was a better investment destination than Palestine,'
with the latter seen as 'too gloomy.' Apparently the only interest the
Kuwaitis felt they could 'drum up' might come from Kuwaiti telecom
companies, which had already purchased the license for operating the
OPT's second mobile phone operator through their then-ownership of
Wataniya mobile, in March 2007.

Regardless of the overall tepid interest in investment, the US
representative nonetheless berated his Kuwaiti counterparts, '[decrying]
the lack of Arab investment in the Palestinian territories', and noted
'whatever security concerns remain, Arab countries could not wait for a
peace agreement to demonstrate economic support for the Palestinians.'
Investment according to the representative, 'constituted concrete
support for the PA and President Abbas, and we urged Kuwaiti
participation at the May conference.'

On top of encouraging wealthy Gulf donors to invest in the OPT,
some Western donors directly engaged in forms of investment
themselves. The US Overseas Private Investment Corporation (OPIC)
and the IFC were involved in supporting infrastructure projects that
specifically subsidized private sector interests. We have already seen
OPIC's involvement in the Gaza Power Plant and we shall see it again
in the area of mortgage finance. But USAID for example was also
directly involved in providing $5 million in infrastructure support
(roads and retaining walls) to the private sector initiative of the new
Palestinian city of Rawabi (Rawabi, 2011, p. 11), pushed forward by
Bashar al-Masri – a rising tycoon in the OPT's development, banking,
consultancy, stock market, services and high-tech sectors. It is

significant to note that the PNA's own housing development schemes being developed through the PIF – (Reehan, Jenan) applied for similar infrastructure support from Western governments, however according to PIF representatives interviewed for this research, these appeals were denied by Western donors, delaying their implementation for more than a year until funds were eventually found from the UAE (in the case of Reehan). The privileging of select, fully private initiatives is evidence of a residual distrust donors held of PNA investment initiatives, especially when they competed with the private sector. It also points to how donors retained the ability to tip market advantage to their private sector contacts. According to several developers discussed throughout the course of this research, infrastructure costs are seen as key to determining final cost and profit margins of their investments.

The IFC would also reactivate its portfolio in the West Bank after the failed coup, given its retreat from the OPT scene at the start of the Al-Aqsa Intifada. Between 2008 and 2013, it approved $204 million in investments, including $80 million for the Wataniya deal, and another $75 million for mortgage finance. It is worth pointing out that the Wataniya deal was a PIF-led initiative that would seem to contradict our previous claim that Western donors were not interested in supporting the PNA's own investment initiatives. While there may be relevance to this claim, it might also be argued that the Wataniya deal was primarily a Qatari investment (through Qtel's ownership of the former Kuwaiti company Wataniya) – with a 57–43 per cent Qtel-PIF equity spread. As such, it is also possible that their involvement in the deal would have been broached extensively with the US, as clearly this was both an investment opportunity, but also entailed forms of political and financial risk. This did not ultimately prevent Israel from delaying the release of frequencies for the project, resulting in Qtel almost pulling out, which would have greatly stymied the improved investment climate hype donors were pushing. 'If we cannot get the proper frequency and it cannot go forward then we don't have proper competition on mobile telephony and we don't get the investment and jobs,' noted Tony Blair who led international efforts to push the deal through (Rose, 2011).

In November 2009, Blair's interventions would finally bear fruit and a partial release of frequencies went through. Then PIF CEO Mohammad

Mustafa would relish Blair's success, which PIF stood to profit from, assured of its $354 million licensing fee, plus 7 per cent of Wataniya Palestine's annual revenue:

> This was a great economic achievement as well as having nationalist implications. We succeeded against all odds, brought in a foreign investor, and liberated some frequencies. One could even say we liberated a part of Palestinian space! This is what it means to control our natural resources: today it is frequencies, tomorrow it will be water, and next, land.
>
> (Mustafa, 2010)

Neoliberal statebuilding now enabled *pre*-state privatization of Palestinian frequencies to a majority Qatari company as a form of national liberation.

Two intriguing epilogues to this story are also worth noting.

Investigative reporter David Rose would later reveal that while Tony Blair was working in his capacity as Quartet Special Representative to secure the Wataniya deal, he was also retained as a consultant by J.P. Morgan investment bank and was paid £2 million annually for his services. This is significant because Qtel was a J.P. Morgan client at the time, which threatened to lose hundreds of millions of pounds if the frequencies did not go through (Rose, 2011).

Secondly, Israel's refusal to release the frequencies was later revealed to be the result of senior management at Jawwal – Wataniya's only 'Palestinian' competition – apparently bribing Israeli officials to not release them.[17] The scandal was briefly acknowledged by president Abbas, followed by Jawwal's then CEO Abdel Malik Jaber relocating to Jordan, where he became CEO of Jordanian mobile operator Zain in July 2009. Jaber had been involved in concomitant efforts around the same time (summer 2009), to merge Zain and Paltel, with the two companies already announcing a share-swap transaction. Zain Group would hold 56.5 per cent stake in Paltel while Paltel would own 100 per cent of Zain Jordan, essentially merging these two markets beneath one set of corporate interests (Zain, 2009). The deal was cancelled by November the same year.

Risk Management

The third means by which donors encouraged investment was through particular forms of aid and policy that specifically targeted managing investor risk.

Donors had attempted to use these schemes earlier during the Oslo years, but were largely unsuccessful. The World Bank's Multilateral Investment Guarantee Agency (MIGA) recorded only one investment of $5 million to support a tourism project in Bethlehem before 2000. However after 2008, MIGA offered risk insurance to nine more projects (at $18 million) and five more in 2014 for around $20 million. These projects supported domestic capitalist enterprises including dairy, soft drinks, and pharmaceutical production, specialized agriculture (date production, fresh herbs) and plastics. The insurance covered potential losses 'against the risks of transfer restriction, expropriation, and war and civil disturbance' and usually lasted for ten years. This insurance integrated well with a USAID trade facilitation project known as the 'Known Trader program,' intended to facilitate smooth passage of known traders through select checkpoints. USAID refused to be interviewed for this research.

In 2007, OPIC working through a later-day Bush administration project known as the Middle East Investment Initiative (MEII), establishing a Loan Guarantee Facility (LGF) to stimulate bank credit to SMEs. The project claimed to target the long-marginalized small and medium-sized enterprise (SME) sector, providing nine partner banks with insurance guaranteeing 70 per cent of the principal amount of loans extended. OPIC committed $110 million and PIF added $50 million, enabling a total of $230 million in extendable loans.

Although LGF claims to guarantee loans in the $10,000 to $500,000 range, the facility was criticized for veering away from the target constituency, and guaranteeing much larger projects associated with PIF's investment portfolio and that of PADICO (Entous, 2009). LGF provided PIF with $16 million in loan guarantees for its investment in Wataniya mobile. It also extended guarantees for $5 million of an $8 million syndicated loan put together by several local banks for Ramallah's only five-star hotel, managed by Mövenpick Hotels & Resorts. In both cases, the high employment potential of these investments was given as justification for their extensions.

By March 2013, LGF had disbursed 467 loans totaling $81 million (LGF, 2013). In 18 cases, LGF had to pay out a total of $1.7 million for losses borrowers incurred – 4 per cent of total monies disbursed. LGF is a non-revolving fund that exhausts itself once $230 million in loan guarantees have been disbursed. In that sense, once it ends, the businesses it hopes to sustain may only temporarily benefit from the increased production or employment they generate. This is worth noting in the context whereby many of the small and medium industries that LGF lent to were associated with the forward and backward linkages of the rising housing construction sector (such as carpentry for doors, furniture, etc.).

Mortgages

A similar formula of risk insurance would be used for mortgage finance. Mortgages never existed in the OPT with banks traditionally never extending loans beyond eight years. However, housing received heightened attention in the Western donor agenda because of its historically high contributions to private investment and the known shortage in low-cost housing supply. An 'antagonism' between supply and demand in housing had thus been identified by donors, which credit provision promised to be able to bridge through mortgages and mortgage risk insurance.

The demonstrated rise in credit provision for construction purposes witnessed throughout this period thus partly has its origins in early efforts by the World Bank to develop a mortgage market. As early as 1996, the World Bank began working with the Ministry of Housing to establish the Palestinian Mortgage and Housing Corporation (PMHC) as a secondary mortgage facility that encouraged bank lending by covering costs associated with mortgage lending risks. To get the project started, it provided PMHC with a $20 million loan on extremely favorable repayment terms (75 years at 0.75 per cent), and worked through the IFC and the Canada Mortgage and Housing Corporation to develop policy.

PMHC's formation took years to get off the ground and was only operational by the summer of 2000, just before the start of the Al-Aqsa Intifada. But by 2007, mortgage provision began benefitting from investment conditions, with both PMHC and the banking sector capitalizing on these, illustrated in the above graphs. PMHC offered

25-year adjustable-rate mortgages (adjusted every five years) while also allowing borrowers to purchase homes with a ten per cent down-payment. (Commercial banks usually demanded 15 per cent and adjusted rates every six months). Mortgage borrowers also needed to have life insurance policies and property insurance, which PMHC also offered through local partnerships with insurance agencies. In the event of default, properties would be repossessed and auctioned, with PMHC covering 70 per cent of bank losses. Banks were incentivized to begin foreclosure action – even after payment of an insurance claim – as they were to bear 30 per cent of the loss (Hannah *et al.*, 1999). Senior World Bank and IFC economists thus saw development of contract enforcement and foreclosure laws as crucial to the success of the project (ibid).

Just as the idea of industrial parks preoccupied the mindset of Western donors during the Oslo years, involvement in the housing market was seen as bundling together a host of economic, social and political issues whose alleviation were seen to have large net social benefits of stability and prosperity.

New housing construction throughout the OPT had been historically constrained by Israel's formal restrictions on land and housing development and by low and uncertain incomes. Before 1993, the Israeli Civil Administration impeded fund transfers, the development of local banking and credit institutions, access to land, and licensing, back-logging supply. A 1997 World Bank appraisal document of housing in the OPT notes that one third of Palestinian households lived in situations with more than three persons per room, and almost ten per cent lived with more than five per room (World Bank, 1997g, p. 2). One-quarter of all households had no running water, one fifth had no electricity, and one third had no sanitation facilities. The report also noted that informal norms also led to the creation of highly crowded nuclear household conditions because Palestinian families did not usually opt for informal housing such as squatting on public land or renting in slums.

Housing thus conformed to a larger transformative socio-political and economic vision of donors whereby improved social wellbeing was seen to have net peacebuilding effects. While this is implicit in the peacebuilding logic of donors overall, it was encouraged further by two broader historical trends: speculative housing markets were still rampant across many Western economies in mid-2007, while the culture of homeownership had also proven instrumental in stabilizing Western economies after World War II, and hence needed to be promoted for the political reason that 'debt encumbered homeowners do not go on strike!' (Harvey, 2012). Whether these were or weren't part of donor logic in their backing of this sector is inconsequential to the fact that donor aid vocally sponsored the OPT's construction boom.

In 2008, OPIC would approach PIF to propose the creation of a far larger $500 million mortgage finance facility in partnership with IFC, PIF, CCC and the Bank of Palestine as major shareholders. The 'Affordable Mortgage and Loan Corporation' (AMAL), was to be a signature project of the MEII, and promised to do very similar things in regards to mortgage finance that PMHC did/does. However the scale of the project dwarfed that of the latter (which only had $20 million in revolving capital), and if realized, promised to qualitatively change the penetration of finance capital throughout the OPT setting.

Mortgage provision throughout the OPT still encountered many obstacles to expanding, chief amongst them, the antiquated land registry system which limited the amount of land with clear title (*taboo*). Additionally informal norms throughout the OPT still looked with suspicion towards mortgages as a means of home finance, with some considering it 'unislamic', and others simply against the principle of being locked into a long-term financial arrangements that could easily double the amount paid for the property in mortgages of long-term tenor.

By the end of 2015, AMAL was yet to get off the ground, with the reasons for its delay unclear. Nonetheless, without speculating on the project and its prospects, a few words summing up some of the consequences of the enormous push in the real estate sector during the period of international statebuilding shall serve to tie-up this section, setting the stage for a fuller accounting of what the effects of neoliberal conflict resolution and statebuilding have been on the Palestinian national liberation movement overall.

International statebuilding created the grounds for both the Palestinian private sector and the West Bank-PNA, to turn towards investment sectors like real estate, telecommunications and trade, as the strategic sectors believed to harbor the potential to provide a sustainable economic arrangement for the OPT. PIF's investment in real estate in particular cannot be underscored enough given its $400 million Irsal Center development in Ramallah – a massive commercial complex designed to be the nucleus of new Palestinian economy. (The Irsal project is a joint development initiative with the Jordanian real estate company Arduna.) The joint public and private sector push into real estate, in a larger context of being prevented from engaging in productive, tradable export sectors, points to de-development indeed forming the basis of the Palestinian economy.

The incentivizing of de-development across the OPT appears to have repercussions that are far larger than simply promoting unproductive investment with low value added as the basis of a non-sovereign state, which benefits the propertied and the nascent financial-developer cartels around the PNA.

Geographically, land development is only taking place within the Areas where Palestinians are permitted to build (Areas A and B, roughly 40 per cent of the West Bank). This has resulted in steady rises in property prices as well as an increase in housing density. This disadvantages those unable to purchase these properties, while also fitting into Israel's geostrategic map for these areas, while unimpeded settlement expansion across Area C and Jerusalem continues.

The rise in land prices also gets incorporated into investment calculations as developers wait to gain a price that covers their costs and returns their expected profit margins, emphasizing the investment's 'lazy' characteristic. Implicit to this logic is a tendency to assume that no additional land in the OPT will become available for construction and that the potential for Palestinians to liberate more land (through negotiations or otherwise) is unlikely. This implicit 'bet' against the freeing-up of land lies behind multiple discussants expressing confidence that the value of land had 'never gone down in Ramallah', with inner-city tracts in Ramallah now valued well over $1 million per quarter acre (dunum), and rising 10 per cent annually (Abu Kamish, 2012).

This also raises questions around the vast majority of Palestinians priced-out of the rising cost of land, particularly in Ramallah's Area A. They are joined by Jerusalemites unable to find affordable housing within the city, leading to unlicensed construction of homes between these cities in areas on the eastern periphery of the 'separation barrier' (Kufr Aqab, Qalandiya, Shu'fat). These areas thus increasingly resemble emerging ghettoes of high density, unregulated housing, which are potentially threatened given the seismic geology of the region, prone to earthquakes. Demographically and politically this trend is aslo

significant as it contributes to the de-Arabization of Jerusalem, a
longstanding Israeli goal (see UNOCHA 2011; Cheshin *et al.*, 1999;
Badil, 2009).

A further question arises when one realizes that the rising cost of land
has led to a market whereby only highly-waged individuals have the
ability to purchase the homes being constructed by both private and
public sector real estate endeavors.

Developer Mohammed Shuman, interviewed by a local Arabic
economic bulletin, was asked why more low-income housing was not
being developed despite high demand:

> Providing homes for those with limited incomes is an honor we do
> not claim to make. You will not find amongst us [developers]
> anyone who can make available a home to those with limited
> incomes. The issue is simple: the average income in the country is
> $600 monthly. To be able to make available a home to those
> with limited incomes, the monthly premium cannot be more than
> 30–40 per cent of income. This means he would be required to
> pay around $250 monthly. You will not find any private sector
> company who is capable of selling homes to a citizen for a monthly
> rate of $250, not to speak of the down-payment.
>
> (Abu Kamish, 2012)

Thus, instead of meeting low-cost housing demand, a surplus of high-
value properties have entered the market, raising speculation of a
housing and commercial real estate bubble emerging, particularly in
Ramallah (Ghadban, Interview).[18] Rumors heard throughout the course
of this research also spoke of senior high-salaried Palestinian NGO
personnel, purchasing multiple apartments and deriving rent income
from the constant influx of international consultants and NGO
personnel in need of housing during their stays.

The speculative appetite of developers also appears to have been
whetted by the real estate boom, inducing some to lobby for further
legal reforms. A 1953 Jordanian rental law[19] still observed throughout
the West Bank currently protects the residency rights of long-term
tenants, while preventing raises to their rents. This functionally has
meant that while multi-million dollar properties are going up, long-
term tenant neighbors may be paying pennies on old rental contracts.

The pressure to gentrify is enormous. One developer interviewed during this research even expressed a desire to lobby the US Congress to withhold funding to the PNA, until it agreed to change the rental law.

The unscrupulous behavior of developers was witnessed in an interview with a property owner who was forced to sell to the Rawabi development, because the project's developer (Bashar al-Masri), had secured a presidential decree that his and Qatari Diyar's wholly private-sector initiative, was a 'national' project. This classification meant that the PNA had the right to appropriate the land 'in the public national interest' and force its sale.

'This is why there are revolutions in the Arab world', noted the former land owner Khalid el-Husseini (Interview). The latter accused al-Masri of being 'an economic hit man', empowered by the US, thanks to al-Masri's long history as a consultant for USAID, as well as other foreign donors.[20]

El-Husseini was no poor villager, but came from an elite Jerusalem family with centuries of land-holding across Palestine. This nonetheless does not mitigate the severity of the apparent strong-arm tactics used against him and others to secure the sale of his property, while also highlighting the nature of the aggressive profit-seeking incentives that have been unleashed across the OPT, and which can be harnessed by those with the know-how and networks to exploit these conditions.

These dynamics and others shall be discussed in the conclusion, reflecting upon the implications of incentivizing de-development and Palestine Ltd. on the Palestinian national movement. Needless to say, neoliberal statebuilding served to facilitate a whole range of economic dynamics, individual behaviors, and political implications that are a far cry from the utopian models of their proponents and the national aspirations of the Palestinian people.

CONCLUSION

Neoliberalism's impact on the Palestinian national liberation movement's quest for self-determination reflects features common to the impact of neoliberalism elsewhere, albeit its own specificities make these features more extreme. If neoliberalism is commonly accused of 'decentering' the state (Craig and Porter, 2006, pp. 103–4), and making 'the national level of government irrelevant for people in comparison to the local and supranational levels' (Laitin & Fearon, 2004), how might this tendency affect a formerly inexistent governance authority, with extremely delimited means of its own, under settler-colonial conditions? In fact, the tools of governance the PNA had at its disposal were so limited that most policy instruments of the Washington Consensus existed beyond the reach of Palestinian developmental policy powers, and hence could not even be applied directly by the PNA. In areas where the Palestinians had such regulatory powers, aspects of this agenda were indeed applied.

Instead, Israel's control over most aspects of Palestinian development, its commitment to de-development, and Western donor control over developmental purse strings, meant that developmental and governance arrangements were doubly filtered by these powers before Palestinians even gained the means to apply any given policy instrument.

This does not however mean that neoliberalism had no place in the OPT setting. The Western donor agenda led by the US and IFIs, still embraced a neoliberal orientation and mindset when it came to modeling their development, peacebuilding and statebuilding policies overall. The seductive appeal of neoliberal discourse and technologies, which promised prosperity and peace within a 'liberal peace' and 'peace dividends' framework, failed to provide the minimal governance and market conditions needed to succeed, even by their own standards. The OPT's lack of political sovereignty and basic discrepancies in the application of various civil and security regimes across different parts of its geography, strongly contrasted with the pretense of a 'free market' or the ability for Palestinians to regulate and enforce their affairs with any predictability and uniformity. Western donor demands for Palestinians to reform and improve their institutional governance arrangement thus cannot be understood as an instance where these powers were simply trying to get the Palestinians to exercise 'best practice', but instead speaks to the selective privileging of certain (secondary) agendas over other (primary) ones, which itself demands explanation.

Without assuming the reasons for this, the evidential track record established by both public and classified documentation paints an incriminating picture of how the Western donor community and Israel actually acted vis-à-vis Palestinian developmental and statebuilding aspirations since 1993.

Neoliberal peacebuilding during the Oslo years established a basic Palestinian governance framework animated by PLO Chairman Yasser Arafat as a willing and necessary neopatrimonial leader. Sufficient discretionary rent-seeking opportunities were allotted to him to distribute a peace-dividend and forge an intra-Palestinian political settlement that could conform to a neoliberal functionalist peace vision in alignment with Israel's long-standing Allon Plan.

After this basic model failed to reap a final peace accord however, Arafat was institutionally marginalized and 'statebuilding' was introduced as the operational framework justifying donor interventions, despite the fact that negotiations were no longer taking place. The PNA apparatus that only Arafat had the political legitimacy to construct under the given conditions of its birth would then be extracted from his grip through Western donor conditionality measures and Israeli military violence, thereafter undergoing extensive restructuring along post-Washington Consensus lines. These 'reforms' removed the limited discretionary powers of the PNA executive, reconfiguring them such that the donor community directly oversaw all finances. Measures to induce financialization together with reformed institutional arrangements that preferenced private-sector growth, subsequently led to incentivizing the economics of de-development. A weakened neo-patrimonial model was allowed to reconstitute itself under explicit donor oversight and heavy emphasis on 'security.' While the arrangement widened the benefactors of the previous political settlement forged amongst Palestinian political and economic actors undergirding the PNA regime, it prevented democratic oversight of this arrangement by the Palestinian parliament. In fact Palestinian democratic aspirations were brutally repressed and contained through direct military violence and the political and financial siege of the new Palestinian parliament. Nonetheless, this later model was unable to manage all the contradictions it generated and built off from, eventually resulting in the 'loss' of the geographic terrain of the Gaza Strip, which broke off from the control of Fateh's political patronage – the main 'polity' that the international community had been sponsoring.

Strong discrepancies between the theory and policy of donors on the one hand, and the actual applied policies in the OPT on the other, characterize the arrangement overall. Fairly strong evidence suggests that donors planned and actively sought to manipulate Palestinian powers and social relations in ways that advanced undisclosed political agendas. Conflict resolution modeling evidences the manipulation of temporal and jurisdictional elements, to realize a weak, fragmented and de-developed political arrangement conducive to Jordanian and Israeli influence. Though feigning a technical, apolitical agenda, Western donors also operated with finite assumptions regarding various aspects of social and economic policy (such as the ultimate scope of Palestinian governance arrangements, or how social policies should be run) and even touched upon final status issues (such as the refugee question). These policies attempted to gerrymander these issues in ways that circumvented international legal norms, thereby undermining Palestinian claims before they were tabled. In fact a great deal of peacebuilding and statebuilding activity can be read as efforts to engineer political, social and economic arrangements that conformed to undisclosed priorities of the donors and Israel, despite contradictions between and within these camps. This is what gives the OPT reality its particular deformity, irrespective of the deformities which arise from settler colonialism or neoliberalism itself.

Despite the empowering of a neopatrimonial arrangement, there is also consistent evidence of donor distrust in the neo-patriarch himself. Tensions over the degree of centralization and executive authority deemed appropriate by international actors, for the Palestinian leadership, remains a persistent feature of the arrangement.

Liberal political and economic practice was also belied by donor tolerance for undemocratic and illiberal economic arrangements from both Israel and the PNA. The donor community was deeply implicated in these policies through the funding of both versions of the neopatrimonial arrangement, and attempting to annul (and even overthrow) the results of democratic elections.

The fostering of elites within civil society and the private sector is also a consistent feature of the process overall. In respect to civil society, these served to buy-in certain political elites often associated with the political Left, creating and strengthening forms of upward vertical dependency and accountability to donors, as opposed to their grassroots base. Private sector buy-ins served to give confidence and help organize the interests of this constituency, vis-à-vis the PNA. Preference to the favored capital formations undergirding the political settlement was given at each stage, with early efforts targeting expatriate capitalists, while later efforts incorporated sections of native capital. Increasing interpermeation of interests among both wings helped to consolidate a strata of political and economic elites in the West Bank tied into the political economy of neoliberal statebuilding itself, while the majority of Palestinian society remained disenfranchised politically and economically.

Constantly vacillating between centrifugal and centripetal forces, the structurally disempowered PNA in the West Bank would be flanked by a strengthening elite private sector on the one hand, and civil society's networks on the other – with the latter two maintaining independent linkages with donors as well. Collectively this arrangement leads to the West Bank becoming enveloped in ever thickening webs of visible and invisible control that delimit the forging of a national consensus. The entire arrangement is enforced by Israel's military and bureaucratic regime buttressed by the discourse and funding of Western states. Alternatively, the Gaza Strip after 2006 would become functionally externalized to this arrangement, placed in political 'formaldehyde', its residents 'put on a diet' and with the periodic need for Israel to 'mow the grass.'[1]

Palestinians Negotiate Neoliberal Peacebuilding and Statebuiding

How are we to understand the response of the Palestinian leadership and society to this arrangement? Parts of the answer are implicit in our description itself though further elaboration of specific groups is in order.

The PLO/PNA Leadership

A basic contradiction existed between the PLO leadership's historically declared political positions on autonomy, settlements, and national liberation on the one hand, and the practical arrangement afforded by the Oslo Accords on the other.

Various political and historical exigencies were used to justify the leadership's acceptance of formerly eschewed political conditions related to self-governance under occupation and negotiations under continued settlement construction. A general 'statebuilding' narrative helped obfuscate the fact that the conditions of the Oslo arrangement failed to nominally secure statehood as the process' political endgame, or a reliable means of arriving there.

But the PNA/PLO was never able to admit to its base the consequences of accepting these conditions, which entailed getting a foothold on the ground in exchange for limited autonomy without enforceable guarantees that this would not be a permanent arrangement. Nor were the delimited policy instruments the PNA had sufficient to overcome these limitations overall. Instead, the PLO's degenerating diasporic bureaucracy was given new life through the financial streams of peacebuilding and statebuilding. The PNA's neopatrimonial rule consolidated the PLO's return to the OPT, albeit doing so on a weak political and economic footing: financially it relied upon expatriate elites, largely based in Jordan, who had accumulated their wealth through politically determined capital in the Gulf; socially it consolidated its base by buying in different sections of Palestinian society, often through formerly marginalized traditional elites, bypassing emergent political elites of the 1987 Intifada, including some within Fateh. Though this was not its only social basis, Arafat proved himself capable of being able to discipline the patron-client networks he constructed out of the porous and protean nature of Fateh. However after his death, the patronage arrangement lost parts of its integrity and disciplinary regulatory authority, resulting in various forms of splintering, both on a national level (the 2007 West Bank/Gaza territorial split) and within the movement itself (the deepened fragmentation of Fateh itself).

All the more dependent and vulnerable, the Fateh PNA leadership was forced to widen the sphere of the political settlement constituting its power base after the death of Arafat and the loss of the 2006 elections. International financial and technical backing of neoliberal statebuilding practices in this case served to partly mediate intra-elite frictions, substituting for Fateh's lack of a unifying national program or ideology, at least temporarily stabilizing its West Bank rule. This nonetheless came too late for the Gaza Strip, where Hamas and its orbit had become too powerful, and were ultimately able to displace and capture governance institutions from a fragmented, delegitimized Fateh in Gaza.

Throughout the whole process, the PLO leadership demonstrated a certain margin of autonomy although clearly it had accepted (through Oslo) and then was forced to accept (through Israel's military maneuvers and donor conditionality politics) a severe reduction of its discretionary potential.

Lacking virtually any recourse to alternative financial arrangements or independent arbitration, the leadership turned to capture the profit potential of an incentivized de-development, whether by directly investing in these sectors, or by investing in private entities doing the investing.

The PLO leadership relied upon its 'only game in town' status to consolidate its rule, while banking on an understanding that the cost for Israel to perform these duties was much higher. This was possible given the 'guesstimate'-based nature of donor support to the Palestinian 'polity' running the PNA.

Alternatively, through their reduction of the discretionary powers of the PNA, international donors attempted to transform the nature of the rents provided – from political transfer rents, to managerial and monitoring rents. Technocratic support along PWC lines, together with the promotion of financialization overall, aimed at strengthening the fiscal, technocratic and service provision functions of the PNA bureaucracy 'governing' the OPT Areas A and B, at the expense of the 'national' perspective that Fateh still nominally maintained. Fateh nonetheless was able to remain a force within the ministries and its hierarchies, benefitting from the continuation of political transfer rents to the PNA in terms of budget support, PEGASE, pension payment plans and utility provision.

The Private Sector

The private sector was clearly divided. Favoured capital groups benefitting from the first and second political settlements were able to lock-in and corner the few key economic opportunities of peacebuilding and statebuilding. These were the ultimate benefactors of de-development's incentivization. Though publicly professing their national capital role, backing the PNA leadership (not breaking from it at least) and fetishizing the statebuilding project and Palestinian nationalism overall, these economic elites demonstrated much more precautionary and deceptive behavioural traits.

Their companies were registered in tax havens paying limited local taxes. Based on an interview with former Minister of Telecommunications Mashour Abu Daqqa, they made significant gains in capturing strategic ministries like telecommunications, and bribed public officials not to regulate or legislate unfavourable laws (Abu Daqqa, Interview). The Paltel Group became the largest private sector corporation in the OPT employing 3000 employees and the largest publicly traded company on the Al Quds index. It also was reportedly involved in the bribing of Israeli officials to prevent the entrance of competition into the market – *competition which was economically-led by the PNA itself (through PIF)* in alliance with Gulf capital (the Wataniya deal). Although the liberalization of the telecom sector did lead to reduced rates for customers, the fact that the Paltel Group was brazen enough to attempt to stop the PNA from entering into its own market, speaks to the reduced disciplinary/regulatory potential of the PNA towards the elite of the private sector. Although the 'scandal' was eventually 'dealt with' via the relocation of the alleged guilty parties, as of 2015, Israel still prevents Wataniya from exercising its 3G licensing, which would also weaken the Paltel Group's market share. Thus, in the absence of sovereignty and its credible enforcement mechanisms, the OPT arrangement is open to other enforcers (Israel and donors) simply stepping in. The private sector intuitively understands this and changes its color to camouflage itself, allowing for continued accumulation. In responding to the 'real', 'credible' power structure, its political economy, and the credible threats and opportunities it harbours, chameleon capital pays its bribes to the Israelis with one hand, while literally handing out baseball caps with the company logo on it at national demonstrations with the other.

Though still too narrow to be considered a class, neoliberal statebuilding, financialization, securitization, Fayyadist reforms, and the incentivization of de-development overall have all helped to fuse chameleon capital and connect it in various ways with political power, the executive branches of the bureaucracy, and Western donors. Their competency in navigating the PNA apparatus on both political and technocratic levels using it to their advantage should also be seen as characteristic of the era. All the more so in light of the fact that the majority of 'statebuilding' activity that has taken place has happened after the 2007 political split, and hence with no oversight from the PLC's elected representatives.

Small and Medium Enterprises (SMEs)

The majority of private sector interests in the OPT remain stuck in their small workshops, unable to substantially expand or grow, and reliant largely upon family labor. Crushed by Israel's restrictive policies which prevent the taking root of modern productive sectors; unable to compete with the increasingly oligarchic favoured capital formations; lacking efficient formal means to resolve disputes – these sections of the Palestinian economy sought ways to mediate their conditions. It was not by accident that the three largest Palestinian cities where small industries had existed before Oslo – Gaza City, Nablus, and Hebron – would politically support Hamas during the 2006 elections. While the 1996 elections witnessed the much respected Dr. Heidar Abdel Shafi – a former communist and head of the Palestinian Red Crescent Society in Gaza – winning the largest number of votes in the entire election, in the 2006 elections, that honor went to Said Siyam – a former UNRWA teacher known and respected as a mediator in disputes, well-versed in tribal law and Islamic jurisprudence. Hamas selected Siyam as its Interior Minister – arguably the most sensitive political position in its government after the events of 2007. He was the most senior Hamas representative assassinated in Israel's 2008/9 Operation Cast Lead.

Not everyone turned to Hamas of course. Economic arrangements under statebuilding nonetheless increased personal debt and widened inequalities overall. Periodic economic revolts have occasionally arisen, including a 2012 OPT version of unemployed and indebted individuals attempting self-immolation in public spaces, akin to similar phenomena happening in other theatres across the Arab world. At the time, these revolts added to the pressure that would eventually see the resignation of the Fayyad government in April 2013. Sensitive to maintaining control and positioning over the West Bank, Fateh feared the brewing rebellion from below that was eating at its own base of support. It equally feared – largely correctly – that Fayyad's technocratic onslaught was directed at its control over ministries, and thus was happy to channel public pressure against Fayyad, who lacked a broad and popular organizational base.

SMEs nonetheless remain unable to compete in the OPT's variant of politically determined capital, creating an economic underclass, high unemployment, anomie, and the melding of traditional familial and gender roles to petit bourgeois market imperatives under de-development conditions overall.

Inducing Political, Economic and Social Transformations for 'Peace'?

The OPT's political, economic and social conditions produced by the overarching developmental conditions put in motion through neoliberal conflict resolution and statebuilding, hardly compose a constituency conducive to willfully accepting this arrangement. On the contrary, the eruption of the Al-Aqsa Intifada and the results of the 2006 election demonstrated wide-scale popular rejection of the neoliberal conflict resolution and statebuilding framework.

To answer whether these policies were capable of inducing the political, economic and social transformations for 'peace' to take root however entails first defining and interrogating what is meant by 'peace.'

Without getting caught in a lengthy discussion about the different types of peace, suffice it to say that if the question is posed around support for a 'positive peace' that 'seeks to go beyond the absence of violence and implies that the underlying resolution or causes and dynamics of violent conflict have been addressed to prevent a recurrence of violence and to build a peaceful future' (O'Gorman, 1988, p. 24; see also Galtung, 1969) – then there is no serious indication that neoliberal conflict resolution and statebuilding has demonstrated traction in inducing any significant section of Palestinian society towards leaning in this direction.

Despite its political tepidness, no one can seriously question that the PLO leadership still formally upholds the basic national political demands, and calls for their addressing through various avenues.

The private sector, both large and small, equally demonstrates no new-found appreciation for Israel, nor how it deals with them. Even fears of a peace process restricted to an 'economic peace', which some have warned Israel is pushing for – marked by a substantial and reliable peace dividend going to the private sector – even this, has no basis in reality. While some Palestinian economic elites may have no doubt benefited from the neoliberal conflict resolution and statebuilding arrangement, the OPT remains an unappetizing environment for capital investment, with numerous politically determined complications, transaction costs, risks etc. Even the lucrative deals of statebuilding pale in comparison to the accumulation offered in other regional arenas, including Jordan, not to mention the Gulf. Small and medium capitalists are doubly oppressed and equally demonstrate no new-found enthusiasm for a positive peace.

Alternatively, if peace is defined negatively however – as the absence of violence, and with the continued perpetuation of structural violence – a different picture may emerge.

Though it is impossible to quantify, support for not engaging in violent activity; for ensuring the smooth payment of VAT tax clearances; for the continuation of donor aid so that consumer and home debts can be paid etc. – support for a peace of this kind may indeed have social constituents that are gaining traction. It may not mean support for the structural violence of the occupation, but it also does not mean willingness to risk confronting this reality and to change it, considering especially the dangers this entails, as witnessed in Israel's periodic 'punishment' of Gaza under the Hamas government, attempting to convey a particular lesson both to Gazans and West Bankers.

Here the character and nature of the Palestinian development trajectory in the West Bank – the incentivizing of de-development – meant that the 'public' sector and the fairly narrow economic and political elites behind it – ministers, heads of the PNA bureaucracy, the heads of banks, developers, a few industrialists and consultants etc. – lead a broader public-private sector drive centered around unproductive, speculative and 'lazy' economic endeavors. These investments indeed tie their investors to aspects of a negative peace agenda insofar as accumulation is dependent upon prevalent political economic conditions, and the fundamental political aid transfers the Western donor community continues to supply while de-development continues.

In the case of real estate, investments implicitly 'bet' against a change in the status of land, bundling this assumption into the cost they are willing to pay to eventually return their profit. The real-estate developed ends up largely targeting middle- and upper-class Palestinians, often tied to the political economy of donor aid itself, while ignoring the majority of lower income families who need them most. The strengthening and aligning of interests among the benefactors of the statebuilding arrangement thus gets underway, facilitated by donor-sponsored financialization.

It is also worth noting that the PIF which leads this economic approach, liquidated its external assets, and invested them locally in the West Bank. This must be considered a major political and economic gamble by the PNA/PIF when considering the political context: only a decade earlier, the West Bank was an active violent 'conflict zone' where destruction to property was commonplace. Destruction to property continues to be meted out regularly to the undisciplined Gaza Strip, as just noted. Any migration of these political dynamics to the West Bank however would prove disastrous to the PNA's investment strategy. In this way, interests pushing for enforceable property rights and against any material destruction to real estate in the West Bank are being thickened daily, certainly amongst the elite who are purchasing, investing, and depending on these properties to yield profits as part of their long-term strategy to realize their vision of statebuilding.

Complex financial and political arrangements induced by neoliberal statebuilding and financialization have also begun to tie widening elements of Palestinian society in the West Bank directly or indirectly to the political economy of donor aid. Whether it be the 180,000 public sector employees, the private sector favored capital groups and their employees, and civil society organizations – a vertical aid dependency structure directly ties these actors to a specific political economic arrangement erected by Oslo that is fundamentally dependent on a political transfer rent that could stop if the arrangement were politically or militarily challenged. These sectors, thus embody the disassembled, unproductive, fragments denied 'rational structural transformation, integration and synthesis, where economic relations and linkage systems become, and then remain, unassembled [...] and disparate, thereby obviating any organic congruous, and logical arrangement of the economy or of its constituent parts' (Roy, 1995, pp. 129–30).

In this respect, one wonders whether dynamics are being fostered and cultivated around support for a negative peace, whereby incentivized de-development processes gain political, economic and social coherence and momentum, especially in the context of additional 'signaling' and the provision of 'commitment mechanisms', ensuring that the PNA has 'broken with the past' and that private sector needs are being listened to and addressed. The result is a gradual coagulation of a Palestinian constituency materially tied and politically dependent upon continuation of the status quo.

Here the true legacy of neoliberal conflict resolution and statebuilding may be found.

The Oslo years witnessed the creation of the PNA as the main institutional apparatus of this arrangement. In addition to the security role it would perform, its social service provision, its employment generation, patronage fostering, rent-seeking and priming of consumer demand — in addition to all these, the creation of the PNA brought with it the creation of a comprehensive statistical nomenclature composed of the economic and social indicators of 'the West Bank and Gaza Strip.'

This nomenclature was the product of the political consent and acknowledgement of Israel, the international donor community, as well as the Palestinian nationalist movement's own strategic desire to 'separate Palestine from Israel.' Previous to 1994, it did not exist in any publicly available, independently verifiable manner, with the little known about the OPT often needing to be deciphered and excavated from obfuscated Israeli data sources. But its independent emergence after 1994, and its linking to an institutional apparatus that could be tweaked, reformed, and manipulated in various coercive ways created new means of analysing the OPT reality that international and Palestinian actors had no previous access to.

With its political and legal status under military occupation elided, and with its statistical nomenclature consistent with that of other state entities, 'hard data' now existed in the hands of Western donor states to be used as tools of analysis and policy formulation to manage and influence unfolding political and economic dynamics. Without this nomenclatural and statistical conceptualization – nominally creating 'Palestine' – the world of Palestinian politics lacked sufficient definition and structure for international donors, and was seen to act too mercurially. Who reasonably amongst international donors could understand the complex world of the PLO, Palestinian political factions, clan structure, and the range of OPT elites – their rivalries, histories, and real and changing strengths in the tumultuous times of the Oslo years and ever since? 'Local ownership' was thus necessary though Israeli and international control attempted to ensure where, how and with who this took place.

The creation of the nomenclature itself did a service in organizing knowledge of the OPT, placing it in international hands. The PNA apparatus would now become a polity subject to delimited political economy modeling so as to conform to the economic principles and political interests (acknowledged and hidden) of its backers. These had various overlapping and divergent modeling ideas that shaped and informed the incentive regime and political decision making processes of Palestinian elites. They overlapped to the extent that they accepted to operate within a de-developed economic arrangement, characterized by increasing levels of Israeli-enforced asymmetric containment measures, towards a fragmented clientelist non-state model. They diverged in so far as each had independent political and economic interests they sought to fulfill through this aid, together with various priorities and understandings of policy sequencing dimensions regarding development, security and ultimately the ascendance of US and Zionist political imperatives. This was so, given the main donors' ultimate reliance upon US political and military hegemony on the broader international political economic chessboard, despite intra-state/imperial rivalries. These contradictions were hence not allowed to deviate significantly from the consensual parameters that the Oslo process established, ultimately determined by the US.

Fairly clear broad lines of economic and political interaction between the PNA and Western donors thus emerged, organized around the principle of ensuring the creation and survival of the PNA and its attending to basic needs of Palestinian society, while ensuring Israeli security. Donors consistently demonstrated willingness to pay for a 'guesstimate' of what it would take to realize these ends because costs were always going to be less than the marginal cost of paying for an alternative, especially if it meant the cost of threats to Western interests regionally. Ideally governance would evolve whereby the private sector would be given the opportunity to profit from the privatization of the economic and service provision aspects of denied political rights. Until then, close control and monitoring, now firmly in place, is necessary, enforced by Israel and the PWC-good governance agenda. In this way, the conflict is contained, wrapped in a web of intra-Palestinian political struggles and class dynamics while Israel selectively disengages and colonizes.

In one of the few international interviews conducted with a high-ranking diplomat from a major European country who agreed to speak anonymously, a remarkable confession was heard:

> Look to Iraq and Afghanistan – how expensive and costly it has been to try and set something up there, and it has failed. Here you have a willing political ally in Israel that you must support no matter what, as a foothold in the region, because look all around the region and see how it is crumbling.[2]

In this respect, a clear colonial and imperial dimension to neoliberal conflict resolution and statebuilding appears.

Support for the creation of the PNA was a crucial benefit to safeguarding an important Western ally in a geostrategic region. But it was an apparatus that needed to maintain the orientation of the powers who helped conceive, devise and pay for it. When the PNA's policy orientation was 'threatened' by a delimited national agenda, or even democratic elections, Israel and Western donors repelled these moves.

Neoliberal conflict resolution and statebuilding practices were also catalytic to deepening and entrenching the political/territorial division between Fateh and Hamas. The conditions created led to the consistent rise of Hamas, even though its institutional positioning before the DOP was considered 'modest' but 'far weaker' than 'any of the major PLO factions,' according to USAID internal reports. While this testifies to the improved sophistication, funding, and political appeal of Hamas since 1993, it is equally a testament to the failures of Fateh, the Palestinian Left and liberal voices in articulating an alternative to this arrangement.

The rise of Hamas in the shadow of Fateh's neo-patrimonial rule and its failures would lead to dual structures laying claim to the mantle of national liberation: two forms of legitimacy, linked to two sets of institutions, two political economies, two sets of elites, and two different political platforms come to govern two non-sovereign territories. The envelope of each political division would now be patterned onto separate geographical territories, shattering the former unity between geography, politics and political institutions. A unified political center to the movement was thus destroyed.

Though the pre-1993 PLO was hardly the most unified of organizations, it nonetheless was the only institution functioning as a national political framework for the displaced and dispersed Palestinian people, and had been so since the revolutionary guerilla groups took control over the body in the late 1960s. Neoliberal conflict resolution and statebuilding policies were instrumental in framing the lines of division that would destroy this unifying framework, deepening them, and strengthening political and economic forces that were vested in resisting reunification.

Whether the West Bank/Gaza division was a preplanned strategy on behalf of Israel or Western donor states is inconsequential to how its emergence has been exploited by these powers ever since. The different ways donors have dealt with each territory fundamentally reproduces the basic colonial tactic of 'divide and rule', though circumstances and reasons change, as necessarily they must. In this respect, one is authorized to assert that neoliberal conflict resolution and statebuilding – its discourse, policies and practices – function as a colonial tactic or technology – by design or by default. Moreover they partially succeeded in displacing the primary contradictions between the Occupation and the Palestinian national movement, into intra-Palestinian class and political conflicts.

Palestine Ltd.

The colonial dimensions to neoliberal conflict resolution and statebuilding cannot be seen in isolation from larger political and national implications of a divided and weakened Palestinian national movement under continued occupation and de-development.

Here the improved penetration of Jordanian capital in the shadow of these policies cannot be ignored. Jordan has been consistently raised by Israel and the US as a potential alternative administrator for the OPT, and is central to the original Allon Plan conception. Glenn Robinson's analysis of political institutions across the OPT, also singled out Jordan as a potential political benefactor to Oslo, if certain temporal and jurisdictional arrangements were met. Israel, backed by the donor community, indeed did impose these arrangements: limited autonomy was slowly implemented across the West Bank, leading to a Millet system model that was predicted to lead to another Intifada while leaving Israel and Jordan as its institutional benefactors. Though the Oslo years were too short, and Arafat too strong to allow for the creation of significant alternative patronage networks outside his dominion, successfully embedding his own brand of patrons and clients locally – the Robinson model and rationale remain objectively robust. 'Limited autonomy, slowly implemented' did force the PNA leadership to buy-in increasingly wider sections onto the PNA payroll using discretionary money supplies to assure political buoyancy and policy space.

After the Al-Aqsa Intifada however – where 'limited autonomy' became 'no autonomy' and 'slowly implemented' became 'slower implemented' – the reproduction of similar dynamics was witnessed and amplified. Increased injections of foreign aid, the expansion of Jordanian capital formations into the West Bank economy, and the expansion of the PNA bureaucracy overall, would all result as a consequence.

The PNA would expand to unsustainable, 'illogical' proportions, becoming a commanding actor within the Palestinian economy. Searching for means of profitable investment, and means to recapture some rent provision for the 'inclusive enough coalition' undergirding its political settlement, the Fayyadist agenda led to an economic program that oversaw increased Jordanian financial capital interests benefitting from the economic arrangements promoted. While, the expanded 'Jordanian influence' was gradual and derived from Palestinians of Jordanian origin – permitting its description as 'Palestinian' capital – its main seat of operations, regulation and accumulation is actually in Amman and indirectly, the Gulf, not Ramallah. The interpermeation of domestic elite interests with those of the expatriate, thanks to donor-driven financialization, served to bridge this extension across the Jordan River, and the subtle yet significant political and regulatory repercussions it entails.

Additionally it is worth noting that the OPT theatre represents only one sphere of its economic investments, with the bulk of its capital invested outside these areas.

It is not necessary to speculate on the particular political attachments of these economic interests to the OPT, or to question their national credentials and how 'brave' or 'cowardly' their capital is. What is more important to emphasize is the fact that we see here another division between the political and geographical patterning taking place. Financial capital interests nested and enforced via Jordan and indirectly the Gulf and US, have expanded their influence and presence in the OPT. These economic interests have also substantially benefitted from the liberalization process that Jordan itself witnessed throughout the course of the past 20 years. The same financial interests investing in the OPT are extended even more so in capital markets, telecom, services, real estate and contracting, and agricultural projects in Jordan. Despite its positioning in a sea of powerful neighbors, the elite within the Jordanian private sector, dominated by Palestinian capitalists, has nonetheless consistently benefitted from the rapid expansion of Amman during the years through the privatization of state companies and the liberalization of Jordan overall. It has also indirectly economically benefitted from regional instability, including the 2003 US-led invasion and occupation of Iraq, the 2006 Lebanon war, the destabilization of the OPT during the Intifada years, and today as a consequence of the Syrian uprising and civil war.

Thus we see a new form of disaster capitalism emerge with vulture-like qualities as well. While Naomi Klein warns at the end of *The Shock Doctrine* of how 'Israel has crafted an economy that expands markedly in direct response to escalating violence' and has 'built an economy based on the premise of continual war and deepening disasters' (see Klein, 2007, pp. 535–59), the flip-side of this arrangement is Jordan and the Palestinian capitalists at the center of its economy, who have assumed the 'Arab partner' to this arrangement – expanding and profiting from the regional crises and implosions, including into their own 'national' green pasture, the OPT.

The increased significance of Jordan throughout the West Bank raises questions as to whether this political outcome should have been foreseen earlier on. Political pundit David Makovsky of the conservative Washington Institute for Middle East Affairs related in 1995 that:

> Rabin is equally adamant that any future Palestinian entity should be linked to Jordan. The question remains whether the Oslo Accord, which was a pre-requisite for an Israeli-Jordan treaty, either ensured a Palestinian-Jordanian federation or foreclosed that option once and for all. In a post-Oslo interview, Rabin insisted that the [Oslo] Accord did not represent a betrayal of Jordan, and reiterated his vision of final status as two states, Israel and Jordan, with a less-than-independent Palestinian entity sandwiched between them. Rabin emphasized this message in private as well. He reportedly met King Hussein after Oslo on a yacht in the Gulf of Aqaba to assure him of Israel's continuing commitment to include Jordan in the final arrangements.
>
> (Makovsky, 1996, p. 123)

What makes Makovsky's quotation so relevant is not just the fact that he hints that this may have been Rabin's strategy from the beginning – to retain Jordan as the powerbroker of Palestinians in the West Bank – but the fact that this was only possible after a deal with the PLO. In this respect, the 26 October 1994 Wadi Araba Peace Treaty between Jordan and Israel may have been amongst the most significant of Israel's accomplishments from the Oslo Accord. Israel's pocketing of a Jordanian-Israeli agreement meant that Jordan's status as a 'buffer state' between Israel and Iraq, in the words of Yitzhak Rabin, was now strengthened, while Jordanian capital and political influence was eventually allowed to return to the West Bank (see Makovsky, 1996, pp. 122–3).

This sophisticated political and economic maneuvering facilitated by neoliberal conflict resolution and statebuilding, resonates with the experience of other developmental contexts, and are worth noting here. In particular it recalls the scholarly contributions of anthropologist James Ferguson (1994) who alludes to a 'euphemistic' tendency to 'development' practices (– *his* inverted commas) (p. xiii). Ferguson was concerned with not only the gaps between the declared aims and (failed) results of the development programs he studied in Lesotho, but particularly how the discourse used to legitimize these development interventions to begin with, constructs its subject as a particular object of knowledge. This knowledge then forms the basis of various developmental interventions, which irrespective of their successes or failure, produces kinds of effects and externalities that to Ferguson, compose the real reasons behind these interventions. In the case of Lesotho, while a road construction project failed to alleviate the poverty of certain rural farmers, its effect, together with that of other surrounding development projects, was to expand and entrench forms of bureaucratic state power. Moreover, the entire developmental game replete with its technical and scientific approach has a strong de-politicizing effect. Development becomes an 'anti-politics machine' that utilizes a kind of 'bait and switch' technique: 'depoliticizing everything it touches, everywhere whisking political realities out of sight, all the while performing, almost unnoticed, its own pre-eminently political operation of expanding bureaucratic state power' (pp. xiv–xv).

Parallels to the OPT context seem all but obvious. Fixation on 'peace' and 'Palestinian statebuilding' have constructed discursive objects of development and peacebuilding that then invite the de-politicizing, technicist approach of IFIs and Western donors. In reality however, a bait and switch maneuver may be taking place, obscured by the buzzwords and common sense appeal of development, peacebuilding and statebuilding. The initial peacebuilding model empowered Arafat to establish the PNA and forge a basic political settlement. Yet once this task was completed – a task deemed historically strategic to Israel's fulfilment of the Allon Plan – the apparatus was taken from under his control based on an appeal to good governance when it was donors themselves who funded his clientelism based on the need to 'clean up Gaza'. Advancing Palestinian national claims throughout the negotiations arrangement established thereafter became impossible. Moreover the incessant push to get the PNA to resemble and conform to utopian neoliberal proscriptions served to facilitate an equally significant maneuver: the DOP was the necessary first step for Israel to make peace with Jordan, which in turn was eventually given room to re-enter the West Bank through the advances of Jordanian capital formations penetrating the economic circuitry of the West Bank economy.

One wonders whether a third maneuver is in gestation in a context of incentivized de-development. David Harvey has emphasized that neoliberalization creates conditions for class formation and that as this class power strengthens, 'so the tendency arises (for example in contemporary Korea) for that class to seek to liberate itself from reliance upon state power and to reorient state power along neoliberal lines' (Harvey, 2005, p. 72). It is not difficult to read international statebuilding practices as preparing for a similar eventuality, considering how chameleon capital already implies an attempt for Palestinian capital to disassociate itself from its 'state' power. The improved legal and institutional position of private sector interests beneath Fayyadist reforms; donor 'tipping' of financial advantages to private capital at the expense of public (especially when in competition with PNA investments); and the processes induced by financialization overall, all imply how private interests are privileged over public/national. Were these interests to functionally displace the nominal national political logic which governs the PNA narrative and practice domestically, a third bait and switch maneuver of neoliberal development might be realized.

Of course speculating on these matters is delicate and need not be exaggerated. Furthermore it is specious to look retroactively back through history and impart direct linearity between where things started, and where they ended. At the same time, scholarship has the responsibility to interrogate larger questions of power and the interests at stake of the actors, and to assess as best as possible, the dynamics which brought about the situation we see today. Thanks to the availability of formerly de-classified documents and a critical approach to the actual policies devised and implemented in the OPT since 1993, a case can be made directly implicating Western donors in undemocratic, illiberal policies that sustain de-development, lead to inequality and fragmentation, and allow for a decades-old settler colonial occupation to manage its contradictions as Israel's larger geopolitical and ideological agendas are advanced.

While aspects of this agenda's realization were unquestionably premeditated, significant aspects of it should also be read as emerging from the implicit logic of neoliberalism itself and the Western states and IFIs that promote this agenda. The vision of the PNA that was given space to take form was not that of the PLO but was that of the hybrid fusion between Israel and Western donors and IFIs. While Zionist ideological and geopolitical considerations informed the Israeli side of this vision, Western donors and IFIs were informed by their own imperial/national visions, with particular neoliberal colorations specific to each state. The consensual mainstream of Western donors nonetheless was determined and carried out by the World Bank and the International Monetary Fund, which operate in accordance with a logic that demands preference of private sector interests over public, the cutting of transaction costs, the protection of private property, the provision of information, and the enforcing of security. This worldview similarly informs the interventions of these institutions in other arenas around the world, though rarely has the margin of their operations been so expansive as it has been in the OPT.

When we add the specific Palestinian contributions to this project: the neo-patrimonial model carried over from the PLO; the neoliberal visions and interests of Palestinian civil servants and the private sector; and the ways both attempted to shape and influence the character of the PNA within the framework established by Israel and donors – the specter of Palestine Ltd. emerges.

Palestine Ltd. is the dystopian product of an elaborate arrangement of political and economic actors operating within discordant visions and interests. The Western donor community, Israel, Fateh and Jordan each reap dividends in their currency of preference: power, money, security and logistical support, conducive to their interests and reproduction. It is also a particularly coercive, predatory and even cynical arrangement. The accumulation of profits and dividends relies upon the manipulation and appropriation of the dreams and hopes of an oppressed people for freedom, peace and justice. The emergence of the post-1967 Palestinian national liberation movement embodied in the PLO, invested enormous sacrifices to find its voice, win representation, root itself in communities and build institutions that attempted to service needs and win broader national claims.

Today these advances of the national movement are turned inside out and upside down as Palestine Ltd. 'encloses the commons' of Palestine the land, and Palestine the vision, which galvanized millions as a just struggle. A shambolic vision emerges in the ruin, where the former achievements of popular struggle are laundered through an anti-politics machine that disaggregates and cannibalizes them, converting them into commodities for the investors of Palestine Ltd. to reap dividends from. In this way, neoliberal conflict resolution and statebuilding functionally attempted to 'use greed to liquidate grievance', baiting and switching until a modicum of equilibrium emerges between the interests of its most powerful investors. Historical experience attests to the inherent instability and foolishness of this approach, as the contradictions generated will continue to rearticulate resistance in different forms and on different fronts, despite an admittedly destructive and divisive toll both visible and invisible.

APPENDIX 1

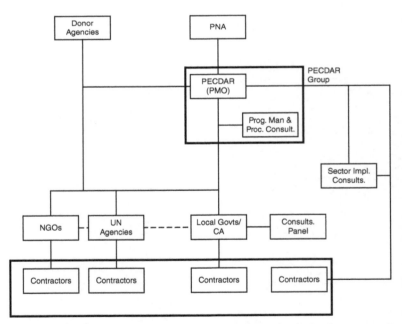

World Bank chart illustrating PECDAR's imagined role in donor overall program organization (World Bank, 1994, vol. 1, p. 121). License: Creative Commons Attribution License (CC BY 3.0 IGO).

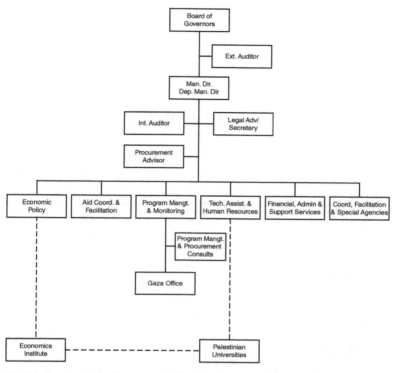

World Bank chart illustrating PECDAR's general organization (World Bank, 1994. vol. 1, p. 122). License: Creative Commons Attribution License (CC BY 3.0 IGO).

APPENDIX 2

Released on June 23, 2002, the PA's Reform Agenda expressed the commitment of the Palestinian Authority to a broad program of reforms. Because a number of specific measures were identified to be implemented within 100 days (while implementation of all other measures would be initiated so as to have a "tangible and visible" effect within three months of the plan's adoption), the entire agenda has come to be known as the "100 Days Plan." The agenda items are summarized below:

In the general domain:
- Reinforce separation of powers of the legislative, executive and judiciary branches of government
- Restructure and modernize ministries and government institutions
- Prepare for municipal, legislative and presidential elections
- Put into force all laws that have been passed
- Improve the standard of living, particularly of the unemployed and other segments of society that live in dire conditions
- Rebuild the infrastructure that has been destroyed by the occupation
- Tend to the needs of the wounded, families of those killed during the occupation, prisoners and detainees

In the domain of public security:
- Restructure and modernize the Ministry of Interior
- The Ministry of Interior is to be in charge of all matters relating to internal security
- Activate the role of the Ministry of Interior in the enforcement of court rulings
- Respond to the expectations of the people for safety, order and respect of law
- Improve discipline in the security services and strengthen social control
- Reinforce the loyalty of the security services to the job, the Authority and the country
- Raise awareness of the population of the measures above and secure their understanding, cooperation and support

In the financial domain:
- Reform operations in the Ministry of Finance
- Deposit all incomes of the PA in a single account of the treasury
- Manage all commercial and investment operations through a Palestinian Investment Fund, which is subject to stringent standards of disclosure and audit
- Limit expansion of employment in the public sector and unify payroll administration under the Ministry of Finance
- Modernize the pension scheme
- Strengthen internal and external auditing
- Develop the process of preparing the general budget to include recurrent and developmental expenditure
- Develop a monthly expenditure plan for the remainder of 2002
- Begin preparation of the 2003 budget
- Reorganize the financial relations between MOF and the municipalities/local authorities

In the judicial domain:
- Strengthen the judiciary, through appointment of judges and development of infrastructure
- Implement measures required by the Judiciary Law
- Prepare draft laws, decrees and decisions to accompany the Basic Law
- Establish the Government Legal Cases Administration to handle cases to which the government is party

In other domains:
- Reinforce the Palestinian values, including the spirit of democracy, enlightenment and openness
- Activate the role of the Ministry of Awqaf to serve national and religious objectives
- Resolve the financial crisis of the universities, schools and hospitals
- Review government institutions that operate outside the jurisdiction of the ministries with a view to attach or incorporate them with the ministries
- End the role of the security services in civilian affairs
- Improve employment policy, to prevent an inflated civil service
- Unify and develop institutions -- and promulgate laws -- that encourage investment
- Improve the training and conditions of employment of human resources
- Increase the effectiveness of the Palestinian diplomatic corps
- Rebuild the management boards of government institutions according to the law
- Pay special attention to the pollution of the environment

The 100-Day Reform Plan, as described by the World Bank (World Bank, 2003, p. 41).

NOTES

Introduction

1. The wording 'Marshall Plan' is mentioned in the DOP, Article XVI.
2. See Bush's 24 April 2002 speech (Bush, G. W. 2002) and Sharon's June 2003 Aqaba Summit speech (Jeffery, 2003).
3. See DARP database: http://darp.pna.ps/project/searchProject [Accessed: 19 September 2014].
4. Copy obtained by researcher.
5. http://web.worldbank.org/external/default/main?menuPK=294399&pagePK=141143&piPK = 399272&theSitePK = 294365 [Accessed 12 August 2014].
6. Tel Aviv Embassy files viewable at: http://www.wikileaks.ch/origin/41_0.html [Accessed 20 September 2014].
7. Jerusalem Consulate files viewable at: http://www.wikileaks.ch/origin/239_0.html [Accessed 20 September 2014].

Chapter 2   Getting to 'Peace': Survey of Historical, Political and Economic Factors Leading to the Oslo Peace Process

1. See the Pentagon's 18 February 1992 draft of the Defense Planning Guidance for the Fiscal Years 1994–1999, published in 'Excerpts from Pentagon's Plan: "Prevent the Re-Emergence of a New Rival"', *New York Times*, 8 March 1992. They were apparently penned by then US Deputy Defense Secretary Paul Wolfowitz, and can be accessed at: http://www.nytimes.com/1992/03/08/world/excerpts-from-pentagon-s-plan-prevent-the-re-emergence-of-a-new-rival.html?pagewanted=all&src = pm [Accessed 2 June 2013].
2. Not insignificant strands of Zionist ideology and political movements have always harbored the aspiration to transfer the Palestinians of the OPT, while forced dispossession has also remained a consistent theme to much of Zionist

practice since the founding of Israel in 1948, either via war or bureaucratic means (see Masalha, 1992; Badil, 2009). The accumulated colonization encouraged by the Allon Plan and the subsequent plans it inspired thus raises concerns that it parallels the strategy taken by the Zionist movement before 1948. Zionist colonies had formed the proto-state that secured a foothold in Palestine and served as the forward operating bases from which the great expulsion of Palestinians from their land took place during the events which became known as the Nakba, or Catastrophe, of 1947–9. The strategic framework outlined by the Allon Plan delineated the broad lines successive Israeli governments have taken towards the OPT from 1967 to the present, and raise serious concerns over what this harbingers for Israel's intentions vis-à-vis these territories and the 'non-Jewish' presence there in the long term.

3. ECCP – The European Coordinating Committee of NGOs on the Question of Palestine and NENGOOT – The Network of European NGOs in the Occupied Territories.

Chapter 3   Modeling a Resolution

1. For an assessment of resolutions pertaining to the Palestinian question at the United Nations, and the historical approach of the US, see Sarsar, 2004.
2. The World Bank Articles of Agreement, I (i) and III (Section Ia) stipulate that the resources and facilities of the Bank should be made available only to member countries. Given the fact that the OPT was not a member state, a special legal opinion needed to be written which argued that Bank assistance to the OPT (described therein as the Occupied Territories [OT], and later, the West Bank and Gaza Strip [WBG]) was acceptable on the basis that it was 'for the benefit of Bank members' (Shihata et al., 1992/94, p. 37).
3. All subsequent references in this section will relate to this study unless otherwise noted.
4. Referring to 'Occupied Territories', the term the World Bank then used for the OPT.
5. What constituted the public sector between 1967 and 1993 across most of the West Bank and Gaza Strip was the Israeli Civil Administration, which took over aspects of the former Jordanian and Egyptian government, albeit running affairs largely through military orders. East Jerusalem was annexed by Israel in 1967 and was administered under the city's 'united' municipality.
6. Glenn Robinson is an associate professor of defense analysis, and the co-director of the Centre on Terrorism and Irregular Warfare at the US Naval Postgraduate School. He has also worked at the Rand Corporation, helping to formulate their 'Arc study' of a Palestinian state. Robinson appears deeply involved in the mix of voices attempting to formulate US policy. According to a report summarizing the Naval Postgraduate School's Research for the year 2000, he participated in a project entitled 'Palestine Futures', directly sponsored by the CIA as part of a team of 10 scholars (see Naval Post Graduate School Summary, 2000, p.12)

7. All subsequent quotations in chapter shall derive from this report, unless otherwise stated. A copy can be retrieved at: http://pdf.usaid.gov/pdf_docs/ PNABY769.pdf [Accessed 12 March 2016].

8. Table I is very helpful for illustrating the alleged factional affiliations of various Palestinian service-related organizations, but could not be reproduced herein because of copyright issues.

9. Table II is a powerful illustration of how the scenarios were gamed, but could not be reproduced herein because of copyright issues.

10. Excepting Israel's unilateral redeployment from there in 2005, which was clearly unplanned and a consequence of the Al-Aqsa Intifada, not negotiations.

11. After the signing of the DOP, the incremental agreements reached between Israeli and Palestinian negotiators pertaining to the West Bank included: the Gaza–Jericho Agreement (the Cairo agreement) of 29 April 1994 or 4 May 1994, when including the Protocol on Economic Relations (Paris Economic Protocol); followed by the Early Empowerment Agreement of 29 August 1994; the Further Transfer Protocol (27 August 1995), the Israeli–Palestinian Interim Agreement (Oslo II, or Taba) of 24 September 1995; the Hebron Protocol of 7 January 1997; the Wye River Memorandum of 23 October 1998 to implement aspects of Oslo II; and the Sharm el-Sheikh Memorandum of 4 September 1999 to implement further aspects of Oslo II).

Chapter 4   The Voyage: Neoliberal Peacebuilding in Practice 1993–2000

1. The year 2000 is excluded because of the outbreak of the second Palestinian Intifada in September that year.

2. According to Shihata *et al.* (1992), the Ad Hoc Liaison Committee performed four crucial functions: 1. It facilitated the liaising with the Palestinian authorities 'to coordinate aid flow and to prioritize technical assistance programs and projects'; 2. It assisted the PNA in 'putting in place administrative and financial processes aimed at facilitating the disbursement of aid funds'; 3. It coordinated with donors and local and international non-governmental organizations; and 4. It maintained a data base on the aid flow.

3. This includes the Multilateral Investment Guarantee Agency (MIGA) and the International Finance Corporation (IFC).

4. This is the acronym used by the World Bank, and which excludes Jerusalem.

5. The PLC underwent four rounds of drafting a Basic Law which provided for parliamentary democracy, including oversight of the executive, and affirmed basic civil rights and freedoms, including independence of the judiciary. It also worked to establish a high constitutional court and promulgated laws dealing with political parties, NGOs, and the freedom of the press.

6. http://web.worldbank.org/WBSITE/EXTERNAL/COUNTRIES/MENAEXT/ WESTBANKGAZAEXTN/0,,contentMDK:22641181~pagePK:141137~p iPK:141127~theSitePK:294365,00.html.

7. The wording 'Marshall Plan' is mentioned in the DOP, Article XVI.

8. The date of the quotation is not noted, though the notion of Gaza as a future potential Singapore was bandied about with the arrival of the PNA to the Gaza Strip in mid-1994.

9. The Rocard Report was an Independent Task Report of the Council on Foreign Relations (CFR). It was uncharacteristic of the CFR to use this category of report towards its end – 'practical and detailed guidelines for the development of sound institutions and good governance' (see CFR, 1999, Forward). Its main co-authors were Yezid Sayigh and Khalil Shiqaqi.

10. Medium term economic outcomes depended on various policies, fiscal and institutional management assumptions, including capital inflows, and employment in Israel. Projected real per capita income in various scenarios was expected to fluctuate from an annual growth of 4 per cent to a decline of 3 per cent per year in the medium term (1994–98).

Chapter 5   The Enforcer: Structural Determinants of Palestinian Political Economy: The Israeli Contribution

1. See an overview of UNCTAD's work at: UNCTAD, 2011a.

2. See UNCTAD 2011a for a comprehensive view of these 'fiscal leakages' estimated between $166 and $275 million a year during the period from 1994 to 1996.

3. For accounts of the process of Israeli economic liberalization, see Hanieh, 2003a; 2003b; Shafir and Peled, 2002, pp. 231–59; and Beinin, 1998.

4. Indeed the Red-Dead and Dead-Med projects were conceived of as massive initiatives to bring sea water from the Red Sea to the Dead Sea. Energy was to be generated along the way, which could also be used domestically and potentially for desalination purposes.

5. The Noble Gas Consortium is composed of the Israeli firm Isramco, which holds a 28.75 per cent stake in Tamar; Houston-based Noble Energy Inc., operator of the field, controls 36 per cent; Israel's Delek Energy, through two subsidiaries, holds 31.25 per cent; and Dor Gas Exploration holds 4 per cent (McGrath, 2012).

6. Important leaders include Ahmed Abu Rish (Fateh Hawks leader, killed in November 1993); Ahmed Abu Ibtihan (Fateh Hawks leader, together with five other Hawks killed in March 1994 near Jabaliya Camp in Gaza); Fathi Shikaki (head of the Islamic Jihad, killed in Malta in October 1995); Yehiya Ayyash (Hamas military wing leader, killed in Gaza in January 1996). Netanyahu would continue this trend, assassinating Muhiyedin al Sharif (head of Hamas military wing in the West Bank, killed in Ramallah in March 1998); and the Awadalla brothers (Adel and Imad, Hamas military wing leaders, killed near Hebron in September 1998).

Chapter 6   The Guesstimate: Structural Determinants of Palestinian Political Economy: International Aid Contributions

1. Before becoming director, Nigel Roberts had extensive experience with the Palestine file, first acting as the World Bank's principal country officer for the OPT from 1993 to 1996, then as manager of the Bank's West Bank and Gaza assistance program between 1996 and 1998, based in Washington.

2. The Holst Fund closed in 2001 and was replaced by the Peace Facility Trust Fund (PFTF). This was replaced by the Public Financial Management Reform Trust Fund (PFMRTF), which closed in December 2004. The Emergency Services Support Program was another trust fund, established in 2002.

3. Note how an internal USAID document refers to 'well-intentioned democratic initiatives.'

4. According to the US Justice Department's Enron document, other investors included the Arab Bank; Al Aggad Group – 'billionaire Saudi-based investor'; the Arab Palestinian Investment Holding Co (APIC); the Palestinian Commercial Services Company – 'Arm of Palestinian Government', and PADICO.

5. See http://www.treasury.gov/FOIA/Documents/04142003opic.pdf [Accessed 23 September 2014].

6. Enron Corporation used a series of questionable and illegal accounting practices to cover loses and make investments look more profitable than they were. After experiencing astonishing growth in the late 1990s and the year 2000, the company was forced to declare bankruptcy in November 2001. See Healy and Palepu, 2003.

7. See http://www.justice.gov/archive/enron/exhibit/03-08/BBC-0001/OCR/EXH001-01734.TXT [Accessed 5 April 2014]. The document has lost its original formatting when placed on the web, but a coherent reading of its material is still possible. All quotations related to Enron derive from this document unless otherwise stated.

8. See Ferrara and Rabinowitz, 2013.

9. The USAID contractor was The Services Group, Inc. based in Arlington, Virginia.

10. http://www.pcbs.gov.ps/Portals/_Rainbow/Documents/e-BOP-time-2012.htm [Accessed 5 May 2014].

11. The latter is a British-based non-profit 'action tank' specifically focused on encouraging Israeli–Palestinian private sector cooperation chaired by British venture capitalist Sir Ronald Cohen, author of the book *The Second Bounce of the Ball: Turning Risk into Opportunity* (Cohen & Ilott, 2007).

Chapter 7   Palestinian Political Actors Negotiate Neoliberal Peacebuilding

1. Interview conducted July 2012.

Chapter 8   Rents, Rent-Seeking and the Political Settlement of the Oslo Years

1. Notably, the demonstrations after the Ibrahimi Mosque massacre (Feb–March 1994); the 'Tunnel Uprising' (September 1996); the demonstrations against the construction of Har Homa settlement (February–April 1997) and the prisoners strike demonstrations of May 2000.

Chapter 9   Reform and Statebuilding

1. The Special Cash Facility and the Direct Budgetary Assistance Program (Phases 1–5).
2. See 2003 Amended Basic Law http://www.palestinianbasiclaw.org/basic-law/2003-amended-basic-law [Accessed 12 July 2014].
3. http://www.islah.ps/new/index.php?page=viewThread&id=128 [Accessed 20 September 2014].
4. CFI was founded in 1995 by the NDI. The latter was created in 1983 as one of four core institutes of the National Endowment for Democracy, itself established by the US Congress 'to act as a grant-making foundation, distributing funds to private organizations for the purpose of promoting democracy abroad.' See https://www.ndi.org/frequently_asked_questions.
5. *Loya Jerga* is Pashto for 'grand assembly' or 'grand council.' A jerga is a common Pashtu tribal institution to formulate consensual decisions and resolve disputes. Jamil Hanifi notes that the Loya Jerga was invented by the governments of Afghanistan in 1922 and derived from the colonial reconstruction of events in 1747 surrounding the foundational moment of the Afghan monarchy. After the US-led occupation of Afghanistan in 2001, a Loya Jerga was convened in Bonn, Germany attended by 30 hand-picked expatriate Afghans, naming Hamid Karzai as the head of a newly founded 'Interim Authority.' The Loya Jerga model was also suggested for Iraq by US politicians. As Hanafi writes 'It seems as though this exotic Afghan mechanism for the production of the hegemony of the bourgeoisie has become the favorite consent-producing tool of American neocolonialism' (Hanifi, 2006).

Chapter 10   'Fayyadism'

1. Fayyad was first appointed Minister of Finance by Arafat in June 2002, holding the post until 2006. He assumed the role again during the short-lived National Unity government from 17 March–14 June, 2007. After the latter's dissolution, he immediately accepted the post of Prime Minister beginning 15 June 2007, but never received confirmation for doing so from the PLC. He briefly resigned in March 2009, only to re-accept the post in May, under similar non-PLC confirmed circumstances. He resigned once again in April 2013.

2. The Council of the EU, the Union's highest foreign policy decision making body, stated on 8 December 2009, 'The EU fully supports the implementation of the Palestinian Authority's Government Plan [...] and will work for enhanced international support [...]' The Quartet also 'welcomes the Palestinian Authority's plan for constructing the institutions of the Palestinian state within 24 months as a demonstration of the PNA's serious commitment to an independent state' (24 September 2009).

3. Letter from Wolfensohn to Sharon and Abbas, 20 November 2005, Palestine Papers.

4. In a speech made at Ben Gurion University, Wolfensohn would credit his father for having recruited Israel's first prime minister David Ben Gurion to the Zionist labor commune, *Gedud Ha'Avodah* (Labor Battalion) in 1917 (Wolfensohn, 2005, p. 216).

5. In an interview with the Israeli daily *Ha'aretz*, Wolfensohn was asked if his experience with the Quartet changed the way he perceived Zionism and Israel, to which Wolfensohn replied, 'No. I still believe in that [...]' (Smooha, 2007).

6. The Israeli export company Adafresh which had secured the deal to export and distribute the greenhouse products, was only able to export 500 of 7000 tons planned for the season, before the Karni crossing experienced lengthy closure. See https://wikileaks.org/plusd/cables/06TELAVIV4272_a.html [Accessed 20 September 2014].

7. See https://wikileaks.org/plusd/cables/05TELAVIV2722_a.html [Accessed 20 September 2014]. It is worth noting that the Peres Center for Peace was also involved in investing in Palestinian telecommunications through the Peace Technology Fund, and had taken a $60 million stake in the Palestinian Telecommunications company, Paltel.

8. https://wikileaks.org/plusd/cables/06TELAVIV4272_a.html [Accessed 20 September 2014].

9. Interestingly, Mohammed Rashid would also explicitly acknowledge that this was in fact, what was attempted against Hamas: 'I've heard a lot of the terminology that is used in regards to "the Hamas coup" [an expression used often by Fateh personnel to describe Hamas' takeover of Gaza in June 2007.] Let me tell you honestly, I grew up within Fateh and was raised around Yasser Arafat. Hamas [...] a coup was conducted against them. I know this talk is going to upset a lot of my friends [...]' (Al-Arabiyya 2012).

10. The PEGASE acronym derived from its expanded name, Mécanisme Palestino–Européen de Gestion et d'Aide Socio-Économique.

11. https://www.wikileaks.org/plusd/cables/06JERUSALEM585_a.html [Accessed 20 September 2014].

12. See PMA website, 'Main economic indicators' for 2012.

13. IMF urges the Palestinian Authority and Donors to reassess priorities. See: https://www.imf.org/external/country/WBG/RR/2013/071013.pdf [Accessed 24 June 2014].

14. http://www.pmof.ps/documents/10180/460525/GFS.TABLES.2013.pdf/
    5f212b82-706d-4f90-9e83-a1428891b2f7.
15. See PMA website, 'Main economic indicators' for 2012.
16. Yezid Sayigh argues that Fatah had 'long ceased to be a coherent organization, but this was obscured by its command of political assets and material resources so long as it was in power' (Sayigh, Y., 2007).
17. See http://www.alarabiya.net/articles/2012/06/09/219611.html [Accessed 20 September 2014].
18. The amended Elections Law No 9 of 2005 introduced a mixed electoral system whereby half of the legislative seats were to be filled from closed national lists using a minimum threshold of two per cent of the total number of valid votes. The remaining 66 legislators were to be elected under a multiple-member district-based majoritarian system, commonly called the 'Block Vote System' (see NDI, 2006).
19. Over 90 per cent of businesses in the OPT were defined as 'very small' with four or less employees; 'small business', with five to nine employees, composed 6.7 per cent of enterprises and; 2 per cent were considered medium in size, employing between 10 and 19 employees.

Chapter 11   Incentivizing De-Development

1. On trade facilitation, see Taghdisi-Rad, 2011. Also see Hamdan, 2011 for a general overview.
2. See trading data at PSE: http://www.pex.ps/psewebsite/English/Default.aspx [Accessed 26 September 2014].
3. See 'Consolidated Balance Sheet of Banks Operating in Palestine' from the PMA, retrieved at: http://www.pma.ps/Portals/1/Users/002/02/2/Time% 20Series%20Data%20New/Annual_Banking_Data/7_banks_assets%20.xls [Accessed 24 September 2014]. All deposit data will derive from this database unless otherwise noted.
4. https://www.wikileaks.org/plusd/cables/07JERUSALEM1995_a.html.
5. See PMA instructions: http://www.pma.ps/Default.aspx?tabid=193&language = en-US [Accessed 20 September 2014].
6. See http://www.pma.ps/Default.aspx?tabid=379&language = en-US [Accessed 20 September 2014].
7. See http://www.pma.ps/Portals/1/Users/002/02/2/Time%20Series%20Data %20New/Annual_Banking_Data/17_facilities_by_economic_sectors.xls and; http://www.pma.ps/Portals/1/Users/002/02/2/Time%20Series%20Data %20New/Annual_Banking_Data/17a_facilities_by_economic_sectors.xls [Accessed 20 September 2014].
8. Total debt figures come from PMA database for years 2008–13 inclusive. Public debt is for year 2012.
9. 'Consolidated Balance Sheet of Banks Operating in Palestine', 1996–2013, PMA.

10. The World Bank defines gross capital formation as outlays on additions to the fixed assets of the economy plus net changes in the level of inventories. Fixed assets include land improvements (fences, ditches, drains, and so on); plant, machinery, and equipment purchases; and the construction of roads, railways, and the like, including schools, offices, hospitals, private residential dwellings, and commercial and industrial buildings. Inventories are stocks of goods held by firms to meet temporary or unexpected fluctuations in production or sales, and 'work in progress.'

11. Retrieved at: http://www.pma.ps/Portals/1/Users/002/02/2/Time%20Series%20Data%20New/Palestinian_Main_Indicators/main_indicators_palestinian_economy.xls [Accessed 20 September 2014].

12. Retrieved at: http://www.pma.ps/Portals/1/Users/002/02/2/Time%20Series%20Data%20New/Annual_Banking_Data/7_banks_assets%20.xls [Accessed 20 September 2014].

13. See http://www.pma.ps/Default.aspx?tabid=379&language = en-US [Accessed 20 September 2014].

14. http://www.pcbs.gov.ps/site/512/default.aspx?tabID=512&lang = en&ItemID = 950&mid = 3171&wversion = Staging [Accessed 20 September 2014].

15. Palestine Papers, 'Meeting Minutes – Salam Fayyad Tony Blair', 11 March 2008.

16. https://www.wikileaks.org/plusd/cables/08KUWAIT497_a.html [Accessed 20 September 2014].

17. See See 'Paltel Executives on Gaza Operations, Wataniya, and the Troubled Zain Merger', wikileaks 22 September 2009. Retrieved at: https://wikileaks.org/plusd/cables/09JERUSALEM1711_a.html [Accessed 12 March 2016].

18. Shadi Ghadban, Director of Engineering- City Architect, Ramallah, Palestine, December 2012.

19. Jordanian Law 62 of 1953 applicable in the West Bank maintains tenant rights to continue occupation of a rented property after the lease has ended, and at the same level of rent.

20. Masri is CEO of Massar International, which has as one of its affiliates, Massar Consulting and Technical Services. See http://www.massar.com/consulting/.

BIBLIOGRAPHY

Abbas, M. (1995). *Through Secret Channels*. Reading: Garnet.

Abdel Jawad, S. (2013). A Palestinian Sociocide? Russell Tribunal on Palestine, 8 January. New York. Retrieved at: https://www.youtube.com/watch?v= L_LkdzZsVlA.

—— (2002). The Question of Reform, *Between the Lines*, #16, pp. 17–20.

Abdalla, J. (2013). 'Palestinian Shoe Industry Declines in Hebron.' *Al-Monitor*, 13 March.

Abdel Shafi, K. (1992). General Social Services in the Occupied Palestinian Territories, in NENGOOT (1992). A. Brown, R. Heacock & F. Torre (Eds) *Palestine – Development for Peace* [Network of European NGOs in the Occupied Territories-NENGOOT] The Proceedings of the ECCP-NENGOOT Conference, Brussels 28 September–1 October 1992, pp. 85–90.

Abdelkarim, N. (2010). *Towards Policies that Stimulate Adequate Financing to Small and Medium Size Enterprises*. Palestine Economic Policy Research Institute (MAS).

Abed, G.T. (1986). Israel in the Orbit of America: The Political Economy of a Dependency Relationship *Journal of Palestine Studies*, Vol. 16, No. 1 (Autumn), pp. 38–55.

—— (1988). *The Palestinian economy: Studies in development under prolonged occupation*. London: Routledge.

—— (1990). The Economic Viability of a Palestinian State. *Journal of Palestine Studies*, Vol. 19, No. 2 (Winter), pp. 3–28.

Abourahme, N. (2009). The Bantustan Sublime: Reframing the Colonial in Ramallah. *City*, 13:4, pp. 499–509.

Abu Kamish, I. (2012). Shuman: The private sector cannot make homes available to those on limited incomes. *Hayat wa Souq*, 8–14 April, #49, 2–3.

Abu Karsh, S., & Abbadi, S. (2013). Methods of Evaluating Credit Risk used by Commercial Banks in Palestine. *International Research Journal of Finance and Economics* (111).

Abu Sitta, S. (2004). *Atlas of Palestine, 1948* London: Palestine Land Society.

Abualkhair, A. (2007). Electricity Sector in the Palestinian Territories: Which Priorities for Development and Peace? *Energy Policy*, 35:4, pp. 2209–2230.

Abujidi, N. (2009). The Palestinian States of Exception and Agamben. *Contemporary Arab Affairs*, 2(2), April–June, pp. 272–91.

Aburish, S.K. (1998). *Arafat: From defender to dictator.* London: Bloomsbury.

Achcar, G. (1994). The Washington Accords: A Retreat Under Pressure. *International Viewpoint*, 252 (January). (Available in Achcar 2004.)

——— (1995). Zionism and Peace: From the Allon Plan to the Washington Accords. *New Politics* 5, 3 (Summer), pp. 95–115.

——— (2004). *Eastern cauldron: Islam, Afghanistan, Palestine and Iraq in a Marxist Mirror.* London: Pluto.

——— (2013). *The People Want: A Radical Exploration of the Arab Uprising.* London: Saqi.

Adams, B. (1993). Sustainable Development and the Greening of Development Theory, in F.J. Schuurman (Ed.) *Beyond the Impasse: New Directions in Development Theory,* London: Zed Books, pp. 207–22.

Ahern, M. (2012). The West Bank and Gaza Mark. In R.P. Beschel & M. Ahern Jr. *Public Financial Management Reform in the Middle East and North Africa An Overview of Regional Experience.* Washington D.C., pp. 165–76.

Ahmad, A. (2004). Imperialism of Our Times. *Socialist Register.* 40, pp. 43–62.

Ajluni, S. (2003). The Palestinian Economy and the Second Intifada. *Journal of Palestine Studies*, 32:3, pp. 64–73.

Akram, S.M. (2002). Palestinian Refugees and Their Legal Status: Rights, Politics, and Implications for a Just Solution. *Journal of Palestine Studies*, 31:3, pp. 36–51.

Al-Arabiyya. (2012). Interview with Mohammed Rashid. *Al Arabiyya* – Four-part interview for 'The Political Memory'. Retrieved at: http://www.youtube.com/watch?v=Hs30jfafvrU&list=PL9A397DA55AC8764D [Accessed: 20 September 2014].

Al-Ayyam (2006). Fayyad: Everything can be Privatized Except Security Which is the Responsibility of the Authority. *Al-Ayyam*, 7 January, Ramallah.

Al-Khalidi, S. (2012). Arab Bank board appoints new chairman, *Reuters*, 26 August. Retrieved at: http://www.reuters.com/article/jordan-arabbank-chairman-idUSL5E8JQ5ZK20120826 [Accessed: 12 March 2016].

Allon, A. (1977). *Israël: la lutte pour l'espoir.* Paris: Stock.

Amayreh, K. (2005/06). A Decisive Year. *Al Ahram.* 775. Retrieved at: http://www.almubadara.org/new/edetails.php?id=303 [Accessed 12 March, 2016].

Amin, S. (2003). Geostrategy of Contemporary Imperialism and the Middle East. *Kasarinlan: Philippine Journal of third World Studies* 18(1–2), pp. 5–41.

——— (2004). US Imperialism, Europe, and the Middle East. *Monthly Review*, November, vol. 56, #6, pp. 13–33.

——— (2012). Liberal capitalism, crony capitalism and lumpen development. 11–21, Issue 607. Retrieved at: http://pambazuka.org/en/category/features/85513 [Accessed: 20 September 2014].

Amnesty International *et al.* (2008). The Gaza Strip: Humanitarian Implosion. A joint publication of a coalition of aid and human rights organizations comprised of Amnesty International UK, CARE International UK, Christian Aid, CAFOD, Medecins du Monde UK, Oxfam, Save the Children UK and Trócaire. March. Retrieved at: https://www.amnesty.ie/sites/default/files/report/2010/04/AI%20britain%20report%20on%20Gaza%20March%202008.pdf [Accessed: 10 March 2016].

Amr, N. (2002). Letter to President Arafat. *Al-Hayat.* 2 September.

Annan, K. (1999a). Report of the Secretary-General on the Work of the Organization. UN document no. A/51/4 (31 August). Retrieved at http://www.un.org/depts/german/gs/gsb99/gsb99.htm [Accessed: 12 March 2016].

——— (1999b). Message to the Business Humanitarian Forum, Geneva (Jan. 27) <http://www.bhforum.ch/ report/mesage.htm> [Accessed: 20 September 2014].

——— (2000). We the Peoples: The Role of the United Nations in the 21st Century. UN Doc. A/54/2000. Retrieved at: http://www.un.org/en/events/pastevents/pdfs/We_The_Peoples.pdf [Accessed 12 March 2015].

Arnon, A. (2007). Israeli Policy towards the Occupied Palestinian Territories: The Economic Dimension, 1967–2007. *Middle East Journal*, 61:4.

Aruri, N. (2003). *Dishonest Broker: The Role of the United States in Palestine and Israel.* South End: Cambridge (Rev. ed.).

AP. (2011). IMF: Palestinian economic bodies ready for state. 5 April.

Aspen Institute (2009). In conversation with Salam Fayyad. 4 July. Retrieved at: http://www.aspenideas.org/sites/default/files/transcripts/01%20In%20Conversation%20with%20Salam%20Fayyad.pdf [Accessed: 4 September 2014].

Asseburg, M. (2009). European Conflict Management in the Middle East: Toward a More Effective Approach, Stiftung Wissenschaft und Politik, *German Institute for International and Security Affairs, Carnegie Endowment for International Peace*, RP 4, February Berlin.

Awartani, H. and Kleiman, E. (1997). Economic Interactions among Participants in the Middle East Peace Process, *Middle East Journal*, 51:2, pp. 215–29.

B'Tselem. (2002). *Land Grab: Israel's Settlement Policy in the West Bank*. May.

——— (2010). *By Hook and By Crook: Israeli Settlement Policy in the West Bank.* July.

Badil (2009). *Survey of Palestinian Refugees and Internally Displaced Persons 2007–2009*. Badil Resource Center for Residency and Refugee Rights, Bethlehem.

Baldwin, D.A. (1985). *Economic Statecraft*. Princeton, N.J. Princeton University Press.

Ball, N.J., Friedman, D. & Rossiter, C.S. (1997). The Role of International Financial Institutions in Preventing and Resolving Conflict, in Cortright, D. *The Price of Peace: Incentives and International Conflict Prevention*, Rowman & Littlefield Publishers.

Ball et al. (2006). Squaring the Circle: Security-Sector Reform and Transformation and Fiscal Stabilisation in Palestine Report prepared for the UK Department for International Development Nicole Ball, Peter Bartu and Adriaan Verheul Consultants 16 January.

Barnett, M. (2006). Building a Republican Peace: Stabilizing States After War. *International Security*, 30(4), pp. 87–112.

Bateman, M. (2008). Microfinance and Borderlands: Impacts of 'Local Neoliberalism', in Pugh, M.N. Cooper and M. Turner (Eds) *Whose Peace?: Critical Perspectives On The Political Economy Of Peacebuilding*, Palgrave Macmillan, Basingstoke, pp. 245–86.

——— (2010). *Why Doesn't Microfinance Work?: The Destructive Rise Of Local Neoliberalism*, London: Zed Books.

Beath, A., Christia, F., and Enikolopov, R. (2012). *Winning Hearts and Minds through Development? Evidence from a Field Experiment in Afghanistan*, Policy Research Working Group, World Bank, East Asia and the Pacific Region, Office of the Chief Economist, July, Washington.

Behrendt, S. (2007). *The secret Israeli-Palestinian negotiations in Oslo: Their success and why the process ultimately failed.* London: Routledge.

Beinin, J. (1998). Palestine and Israel: Perils of a Neoliberal, Repressive 'Pax Americana'. *Social Justice*, 4: 74, pp. 20–39.

——— (2005). Forgetfulness for Memory: The Limits of the New Israeli History *Journal of Palestine Studies*, 34: 2, pp. 6–23.

Beit-Hallahmi, B. (1992). *Despair and deliverance: Private salvation in contemporary Israel.* Albany: State University of New York Press.

Ben-Porat, G. (2006). Markets and Fences: Illusions of Peace, *Middle East Journal* (60(2)), pp. 311–28.

——— (2008). *The Failure of the Middle East peace process?: A comparative analysis of peace implementation in Israel/Palestine, Northern Ireland and South Africa.* Basingstoke; New York: Palgrave Macmillan.

Benvenisti, M. (1993). Border conflict. *Ha'aretz*, 16 December.

Birch, K., & Mykhnenko, V. (2010). *The rise and fall of neoliberalism: The collapse of an economic order?* London: Zed.

Bouillon, M. (2004). *The peace business: Money and power in the Palestine-Israel conflict.* London: I.B.Tauris.

Boyce, J. (2002). *Investing in peace: Aid and conditionality after civil wars.* Oxford: Oxford University Press.

——— (2007). *Peace and the public purse: Economic policies for postwar statebuilding.* Boulder, Colo.: Lynne Rienner.

Brown, A. Heacock R. & Torre, F. (Eds) (1992). *Palestine – Development for Peace* [Network of European NGOs in the Occupied Territories-NENGOOT] The Proceedings of the ECCP-NENGOOT Conference, Brussels, 28 September–1 October.

Brown, R. (2005). Reconstruction of Infrastructure in Iraq: End to a means or means to an end? *Third World Quarterly* (4), pp. 759–75.

Brynen, R. (1996). International Aid to the West Bank and Gaza: a primer. *Journal of Palestine Studies*, 25:2, pp. 46–53.

——— (2000). *A very political economy: Peacebuilding and foreign aid in the West Bank and Gaza.* Washington, D.C.: United States Institute of Peace Press.

——— (2005). Donor Aid to Palestine: attitudes, incentives, patronage and peace. In: M. Keating, A. Le More and R. Lowe, eds *Aid, diplomacy and facts on the ground: the case of Palestine.* London: Chatham House, pp. 129–42.

Cammack, P. (2004). What the World Bank Means by Poverty Reduction, and Why It Matters. *New Political Economy* 9(2): 23, pp. 189–211.

CARE International (2002a). Preliminary Findings: Humanitarian Situation in the Occupied Palestinian Territory?

——— (2002b). *Health Sector Bi-Weekly Report* Johns Hopkins University/Al-Quds University CARE International, ANERA and the Maram Project (3:16) 6 September.

——— (2002c). Nutritional Assessment of the West Bank and Gaza Strip Johns Hopkins University/Al-Quds University, September 2002 (financed by USAID through CARE International). 65.

———— (2002d). Survey finds high rates of malnutrition and anemia in the West Bank and Gaza Strip. 5 August.

Caruso, R & Klor, E.F. (2012). Peace Economics, Peace Science and Public Policy 18, 2. Political Economy Studies on the Israeli-Palestinian Conflict.

Cavatorta, F. (2007). Normative foundations in EU foreign, security and defence policy: The case of the Middle East peace process – a view from the field. *Contemporary Politics* (4), pp. 349–63.

CBS (2003). Arafat's Billions', CBS News, *Sixty Minutes*, 9 November. Retrieved at: www.cbsnews.com/stories/2003/11/07/60minutes/main582487.shtml. [Accessed: 20 September, 2014].

CFR [Council on Foreign Relations] (1999). Strengthening Palestinian Public Institutions. Retrieved at: http://i.cfr.org/content/publications/attachments/pal instfull.pdf [Accessed: 20 September 2014].

Civic Forum Institute (CFI) & Friedrich Naumann Foundation (2003). *Reform – A Palestinian Perspective – Between Reality and Aspirations*. Retrievable at: http://www.cfip.org/publications/reform.pdf]. [Accessed: 20 September 2014].

Challand, B. (2008). The Evolution of Western Aid for Palestinian Civil Society: Bypassing Local Knowledge and Resources, *Middle Eastern Studies*. 44, 3.

———— (2009). *Palestinian civil society: Foreign donors and the power to promote and exclude*. London; New York: Routledge.

Chandler, D. (2004). *Constructing global civil society: Morality and power in international relations*. Basingstoke; New York: Palgrave Macmillan.

———— (2006). *Empire in denial: The politics of state-building*. London; Ann Arbor, MI: Pluto Press.

———— (2008). Post-Conflict Statebuilding: Governance Without Government. In M. Pugh, N. Cooper and M. Turner (Eds) *Whose Peace? Critical Perspectives On The Political Economy Of Peacebuilding*, Palgrave Macmillan, Basingstoke, pp. 337–55.

———— (2009). EU Statebuilding: Securing the Liberal Peace through EU Enlargement. In R. Mac Ginty and O. Richmond (Eds), *The Liberal Peace and Post-War Reconstruction Myth or Reality?* Routledge, pp. 103–18.

Chang, H. (2000). An institutionalist perspective on the role of the state: towards an institutionalist political economy in Chang, H. *Institutions and the role of the state*. Cheltenham: Edward Elgar.

Cheema, G.S. (2003). Strengthening the Integrity of Government: Combating Corruption Through Accountability and Transparency. In Rondinelli, D.A. and G.S. Cheema (Eds) *Reinventing Government For The Twenty-First Century: State Capacity In A Globalizing Society*; foreword by President Vicente Fox of Mexico. Kumarian Press, pp. 99–120.

Cheshin, A., Hutman, B., and Melamed, A. (1999). *Separate and unequal: The inside story of Israeli rule in East Jerusalem*. Cambridge, MA: Harvard University Press.

Chomsky, N. (1999). *The fateful triangle: The United States, Israel, and the Palestinians* (Updated ed.). London: Pluto.

———— (2003). *Middle East illusions: Including Peace in the Middle East?: Reflections on justice and nationhood*. Lanham, Maryland: Rowman & Littlefield.

Clout, Z. (2011). Why I blew the Whistle About Palestine. *The Guardian*. 14 May.

Coase, R. (1937). The Nature of the Firm. *Economica* 4: 16, pp. 386–405.

———— (1992). The Institutional Structure of Production. *American Economic Review*. 82, 4, pp. 713–17.

Cobban, H. (1984). *The Palestinian Liberation Organisation: People, power and politics*. Cambridge: Cambridge University Press.

Cobham, D. and Kanafani, N. (eds) (2004). *The Economics of Palestine*. London: Routledge.

Cockett, R. (1995). *Thinking the unthinkable: Think-tanks and the economic counter-revolution, 1931–1983*. London: Harper Collin.

Cohen, R., & Ilott, T. (2007). *The second bounce of the ball: Turning risk into opportunity*. London: Weidenfeld & Nicolson.

Collier, P. (1999). Doing Well out of War. Paper prepared for Conference on Economic Agendas in Civil Wars, London, pp. 26–27 April, The World Bank.

———— (2004). Development and Conflict. Centre for the Study of African Economies, Department of Economics, Oxford University 1 October. Retrieved at: http://www.un.org/esa/documents/Development.and.Conflict2.pdf [Accessed: 20 September 2014].

———— (2009). The Market for Civil War, *Foreign Policy*, 2 November. Accessible at: http://foreignpolicy.com/2009/11/02/the-market-for-civil-war/ [Retrieved 5 March 2016].

Collier, P. and Hoeffler, A. (1998). *On Economic Causes of Civil War*. Oxford Economic Papers, 50(4), pp. 563–73.

———— (2004) *Greed and Grievance in Civil War*. Oxford Economic Papers, 56(4), pp. 563–95.

Cooper, R. (2002). The New Liberal Imperialism, *The Guardian*, 7 April.

Cordesman, A.H. (2000). Peace and War: Israel Versus the Palestinians, A Second Intifada? A Rough Working Draft. Center for Strategic and International Studies (CSIS). 9 November. Washington, DC. Retrieved at: http://csis.org/files/media/csis/pubs/israelvspale_intafada%5B1%5D.pdf [Accessed: 12 March 2016].

Coren, O and Feldman, N. (2013). US aid to Israel totals $233.7b over six decades *Ha'aretz*, 20 March.

Corr, E. (2007). *The search for Israeli-Arab peace: Learning from the past and building trust*. Brighton; Portland, OR: Sussex Academic Press.

Cortright, D. (1997). *The price of peace: Incentives and international conflict prevention*. Lanham, Md.: Rowman & Littlefield.

Cousens, E.M., Kumar, C., and Wermester, K. International Peace Academy (2001). Peacebuilding as politics: Cultivating peace in fragile societies. Boulder, Colo; London: Lynne Rienner Publishers.

Cox, R. (1999). Civil Society at the Turn of the Millennium: Prospects for an Alternative. *Review of International Studies*. (25:1), 12.

Craig, D. (2006). *Development beyond neoliberalism?: Governance, poverty reduction and political economy*. London: New York; Routledge.

Cramer, C. (2006). *Civil War is Not a Stupid Thing: Accounting for Violence in Developing Countries*. London: Hurst.

———— (2008). From Waging War to Peace Work: Labour and Labour Markets in Pugh, M. (2008). *Whose peace?: Critical perspectives on the political economy of peacebuilding*. Basingstoke, UK; New York: Palgrave Macmillan, pp. 121–38.

———— (2009). 'Trajectories of Accumulation through War and Peace' in Paris, R. and T. Sisk, *The Dilemmas Of Statebuilding: Confronting The Contradictions Of Postwar Peace Operations*, Routledge, pp. 129–48.

Critchlow, D. (1985). *The Brookings Institution 1916–1950: Expertise and the Public Interest in a Democratic Society*. North West Illinois University Press.

Curtis, M. (1994). Gaza Police Fire on Militants; 12 Dead in Clashes. *Los Angeles Times*. 19 November.

Da'na, T. (2014). Disconnecting Civil Society from its Historical Extension: NGOs and Neoliberalism in Palestine. In S.Takahashi (ed.) *Human Rights, Human Security, and State Security: The Intersection*, Vol. 2 Praeger Security International, Oxford, Praeger.

Davidi, E. (2000). Globalization and Economy in the Middle East, *Palestine/Israel Journal* – The Search for Regional Cooperation. 7:1&2. Retrieved at: http://www.pij.org/details.php?id=278 [Accessed: 20 September 2014].

Deacon, B. *et al.* (1997). *Global Social Policy: International Organisations and the Future of Welfare*. London: Sage Publications.

Deranyiagala, S. (2005). Neoliberalism in International Trade: Sound Economics or a Question of Faith? In A. Saad-Filho and D. Johnston (Eds) *Neoliberalism: A Critical Reader*, Pluto Press, London, pp. 99–105.

DFID (2009). Building the State and Securing the Peace – Emerging Policy Paper. London. Retrieved at: http://www.gsdrc.org/docs/open/CON64.pdf [Accessed: 20 September 2014].

DiJohn, J.& Putzel, J. (2009). Political Settlements: Issues Paper, Governance Development Resource Centre (June) Retrieved at: http://www.gsdrc.org/docs/open/EIRS7.pdf [Accessed: 20 September 2014].

Diwan, I. (1999). *Development under adversity: The Palestinian economy in transition*. Washington, DC: World Bank.

Doumani, B. (1995). *Rediscovering Palestine: merchants and peasants in Jabal Nablus, 1700–1900*. Berkeley: University of California Press.

Dreizen, Y. (2004). The Impact of Desalination Israel and the Palestinian Authority. Paper presented in the 2nd Israeli-Palestinian International Conference on Water for Life in the Middle East, Antalya Turkey, pp. 10–14, October 2004. Retrieved at: http://www.yemenwater.org/wp-content/uploads/2013/03/desalination-palestine.pdf [Accessed: 12 March 2016].

Druker, R and Shelah, O. (2005). *Boomerang*. Jerusalem: Keter Publishing House.

Duffield, M. (2001). *Global Governance and the New Wars*, Zed Books, London.

———— (2005). Getting savages to fight barbarians: development, security and the colonial present. *Conflict, Security & Development*. 5:2.

Duffield, M. and Waddell N. (2006). Securing Humans in a Dangerous World *International Politics*, 43, pp. 1–23.

Dumènil, G. and Lèvy D. (2004). *Capital Resurgent Roots of the Neoliberal Revolution* (translated by Derek Jeffers). Cambridge, MA: Harvard University Press.

Edwards, M. & Hulme, D. (1996). Too Close for Comfort? The Impact of Official Aid on Nongovernmental Organisations. *World Development*, 24, pp. 961–73.

EIR (1995). A Six Year Plan for Developing Palestine. 22, 4. Retrievable at: http://www.larouchepub.com/eiw/public/1995/eirv22n04-19950120/eirv22n04-19950120_024-a_six_year_plan_for_developing_p.pdf [Accessed: 20 September 2014].

El Erian M. & Fischer S. (2000). Is MENA a Region? The Scope for Regional Integration. in Wright, J. (2000). *Economic and political impediments to Middle East peace: Critical questions and alternative scenarios.* Basingstoke: Macmillan.

El Naggar, S. and M. El Erian (1993). 'The Economic Implications of a Comprehensive Peace in the Middle East', pp. 205–225, in S. Fischer, D. Rodrik, and E. Tuma (eds), *The Economics of Middle East Peace: Views from the Region.* Cambridge and London: MIT Press.

Elam, S. (2000). Peace with Violence or Transfer. *Between the Lines.* 2, pp. 11–15.

Eldar, A. (2002). The Constructive Destruction Option. *Ha'aretz.* 25 October.

————— (2005). A State Inquiry into Sharon et al. *Ha'aretz,* 4 July.

Elizur, Y. (2014). Over and drought: Why the end of Israel's water shortage is a secret. *Ha'aretz.* 24 January.

Entous, A. (2009). US aid goes to Abbas-backed Palestinian phone venture. *Reuters.* 24 April.

Epstein, G. (2001). Financialization, Rentier Interests, and Central Bank Policy. *manuscript,* Department of Economics, University of Massachusetts, Amherst, MA, Retrieved at: http://www.peri.umass.edu/fileadmin/pdf/financial/fin_Epstein.pdf [Accessed: 20 September 2014].

Escobar, A. (1995). *Encountering Development: The Making and Unmaking of the Third World,* Princeton, Princeton University Press.

EU (2005). OLAF finds 'no conclusive evidence' to link EU funds and terrorism: European Commission welcomes final report on assistance to the Palestinian Authority – 17 March. Retrievable at: http://unispal.un.org/UNISPAL.NSF/0/C6D3A9F772113EB285256FC70065DC63sthash.20xM6aQe.dpuf [Accessed: 10 July 2014].

Evans, M. (2006). Clear, Hold, and Build: The Role of Culture in the Creation of Local Security Forces – A Monograph. Army National Guard of the United States. School of Advanced Military Studies, United States Army Command and General Staff College Fort Leavenworth, Kansas.

Farsakh, L. (1998). *Palestinian Employment in Israel: 1967–1997. A Review,* Palestine Economic Policy Research Institute (MAS), Ramallah.

————— (2002). Palestinian Labor Flows to the Israeli Economy: A Finished Story? *Journal of Palestine Studies,* 32:1, pp. 13–27.

Faucon, B. (2010). *West Bankers.* Mashrek Editions Ltd., London.

Fayyad, S. (2009). A Palestinian State in Two Years: Interview with Salam Fayyad, Palestinian Prime Minister. *Journal of Palestine Studies,* 39: 1, pp. 58–74.

Fearon, J.D. & Laitin, D. (2004). Neotrusteeship and the Problem of Weak States. *International Security.* 28(4), pp. 5–43.

Ferguson, J. (1994). *The anti-politics machine: 'development', depoliticization, and bureaucratic power in Lesotho.* Minneapolis: University of Minnesota Press.

————— (1995). From African Socialism to Scientific Capitalism: Reflections on the Legitimation Crisis in IMF Ruled Africa. In D. Moore and G. Schmitz (Eds), *Debating Development Discourse,* Palgrave, pp. 129–49.

Ferrara, C. & Rabinowitz, A. (2013). Gaza's gas: the EU's burned millions. Investigative Reporting Project Italy, 25 March. Retrievable at: https://irpi.eu/italiano-il-gas-di-gaza-e-gli-sprechi-dellunione-europea/ [Accessed: 12 March 2016].

Fine, B. (2010). Zombieconomics: the Living Death of the Dismal Science. In K. Birch K. & V. Mykhnenko (Eds) *The Rise And Fall Of Neoliberalism: The Collapse Of An Economic Order?* Zed Press, London, pp. 153–70.

Fine, B. and Van Waeyenberge, E. (2006). Correcting Stiglitz: From Information to Power in the World of Development. *Socialist Register.* 42.

Fischer, S. (1993). *The economics of Middle East peace: Views from the region.* Cambridge, Mass: MIT Press.

————— (1993/94). Building Palestinian Prosperity. *Foreign Policy* (93), pp. 60–75.

————— (1994). Economic Transition in the Occupied Territories. An Interview with Stanley Fischer with Sadek Wahba, *Journal of Palestine Studies*, 23: 4, pp. 52–61.

Fischer, S., Alonso-Gamo, P. & von Allmen, U.E. (2001). Economic Developments in the West Bank and Gaza since Oslo. *The Economic Journal*, 111: 472, F254–F275.

Friedman, M. (1962). *Capitalism and Freedom!* with the assistance of Rose D. Friedman, Chicago: University of Chicago Press.

Fritz, V. and Menocal A.R. (2007). Developmental States in the New Millennium: Concepts and Challenges for a New Aid Agenda. *Development Policy Review*, 25:5, pp. 531–52. Retrieved at: http://www.odi.org/sites/odi.org.uk/files/odi-assets/publications-opinion-files/1979.pdf [Accessed: 20 September 2014].

Fukuyama, F. (2001). Social Capital, Civil Society and Development. *Third World Quarterly*, 22:1, pp. 7–20.

————— (2004). *State-Building: Governance And World Order In The 21st Century* Profile Books, London.

Gad, E. (2005). Egyptian-European relations: from Conflict to Cooperation. In Nonneman, G (ed.) Analysing Middle East Foreign Policies and the Relationship with Europe, Oxon: Routledge, pp. 64–81.

Galtung, J. (1969) 'Violence, Peace and Peace Research', *Journal of Peace Research* 6(3), pp. 167–91.

Gavron, D. (1994). The Business of Peace *Palestine-Israel Journal* – Peace Economics. 1:1.

German–Arab Chamber of Commerce (1995). Trade for peace in the new Middle East. Cairo: Commission for the European Communities.

Gerson, A. (2001). Peacebuilding: The Private Sector's Role. *American Journal of International Law*, Jan. 95:1, pp. 102–19.

Gill, S. (1995). The Global Panopticon? The Neoliberal State, Economic Life, and Democratic Surveillance. *Alternatives: Global, Local, Political* (1), pp. 1–49.

————— (2002). Constitutionalizing Inequality and the Clash of Globalizations. *International Studies Review* (2), pp. 47–65.

Gisha (2011). A Guide to the Gaza Closure: In Israel's Own Words. September http://gisha.org/publication/1659 [Accessed: 20 September 2014].

————— (2012). Food Consumption in the Gaza Strip – Red Lines. Position Paper, October. Retrieved at: http://www.gisha.org/UserFiles/File/publications/redlines/red-lines-presentation-eng.pdf [Accessed: 20 September 2014].

Goldsmith, A. (1992). Institutions and Planned Socioeconomic Change: Four Approaches. *Public Administration Review*, 56(6), 583.

Goodhand, J. (2002). Aiding violence or building peace? The role of international aid in Afghanistan. *Third World Quarterly*, 23(5), pp. 837–59.

————— (2004). From War Economy to Peace Economy? Reconstruction and Statebuilding in Afghanistan. *International Affairs* 58(1), pp. 155–74.

————— (2006). *Aiding peace?: The role of NGOs in armed conflict* Boulder, Colo.: Lynne Rienner.

————— (2008). War, Peace and the Places in Between: Why Borderlands are Central. In M. Pugh, N. Cooper and M. Turner (Eds) *Whose Peace? Critical Perspectives On The Political Economy Of Peacebuilding*, Palgrave Macmillan, Basingstoke, pp. 225–44.

Goodhand, J. & Sedra, M. (2006). Afghanistan Peace Conditionalities Study. Department for International Development (DFID). London.

Gresh, A. (1988). *The PLO: The struggle within: Towards an independent Palestinian state* (Rev. ed.). London: Zed.

Grindle, M.S. (2004) 'Good Enough Governance: Poverty Reduction and Reform in Development Countries', Governance: An International Journal of Policy, Administration and Institutions, Vol. 17, No. 4, October, pp. 525–48.

Haberman, C. (1992). Shamir Is Said to Admit Plan to Stall Talks 'for 10 Years. *New York Times*, 27 June.

Haddad, T. (2001). Tayyar el Moqawama. *Between the Lines*. 8.

————— (2007). The Hamas Victory and the Future of the Palestinian National Movement in T. Honig-Parnass, & T. Haddad. *Between the lines: Readings on Israel, the Palestinians, and the US 'war on terror'*. Chicago IL: Haymarket Books, pp. 317–34.

Haley, P. (2006). *Strategies of dominance: The misdirection of US foreign policy*. Washington, D.C.: Baltimore, Md.: Woodrow Wilson Center Press; Johns Hopkins University Press.

Halper, J. (2000). The 94 Percent Solution: A Matrix of Control. *Middle East Report*. 216, pp. 14–19.

————— (2005). Victims of war are not like victims of earthquake: the conflict between humanitarianism and political work. In M. Keating, A. Le More and R. Lowe (Eds), Aid, Diplomacy and Facts on the Ground: The Case of Palestine, London: Royal Institute of International Affairs. Chatham House, pp. 186–89.

Hamdan, A. (2011). Foreign Aid and the Molding of the Palestinian Space. Bisan Center for Research and Development Bisan Center for Research and Development, Ramallah, Palestine. Retrieved at: http://www.campusincamps. ps/wp-content/uploads/2012/07/Forgin-Aid-final-with-cover.pdf [Accessed: 20 September 2014].

Hammami, R. (1995). NGOs: the Professionalization of Politics. *Race and Class*. 37(2).

————— (2000). Palestinian NGOs Since Oslo: From NGO Politics to Social Movements? *Middle East Report*, 214.

Hamed, O. (2008). The continued de-development of the Palestinian economy in the post-Oslo period, *The Economics of Peace and Security* 3(2), 25.

Hamed, O. and Shaban, R. (1993). One sided customs and monetary union: the case of the West Bank and Gaza Strip under Israeli occupation. In S. Fischer, D. Rodrik, and E. Tuma (Eds). *The Economics of Middle East Peace*. Cambridge, MA; MIT Press, pp. 117–48.

Hanafi, S. (2009). Spacio-cide: colonial politics, invisibility and rezoning in Palestinian territory. *Contemporary Arab Affairs*. 2:1, pp. 106–21.

Hanafi, S. and Tabar, L. (2005). *The Emergence of a Palestinian Globalized Elite: Donors, International Organizations and Local NGOs*. Jerusalem, Institute of Jerusalem Studies and Muwatin, the Palestinian Institute for the Study of Democracy.

Hanieh, A. (2003a). Global Capitalism and Israel, *Monthly Review.* 54(8).

———— (2003b). From State-led Growth to Globalization: the Evolution of Israeli Capitalism. *Journal of Palestine Studies.* 32(4), pp. 5–21.

———— (2008). Palestine in the Middle East: Opposing Neoliberalism and US Power, Parts 1 & 2, *MR Zine.*

———— (2011). The Internationalisation of Gulf capital and Palestinian Class Formation *Capital & Class*, 35, pp. 81–106.

———— (2013). *Lineages of revolt: Issues of contemporary capitalism in the Middle East.* Chicago, Illinois: Haymarket Books.

Hanifi, M. (2004). Editing the past: Colonial production of hegemony through the 'Loya Jerga' in Afghanistan. *Iranian Studies* (2), pp. 295–322.

Hannah, L. Lansky, T.& Lea, M. (1999). Creating a Housing Finance System in West Bank and Gaza. *Housing Finance International*, 13–4, pp. 33–39.

Harrigan, J. & El-Said, H. (2010). *Globalisation, democratisation and radicalisation in the Arab world.* Basingstoke: Palgrave Macmillan.

Harriss, J. (2002). *Depoliticizing development: The World Bank and social capital.* London: Anthem Press.

———— (2006). Social Capital. In K.S. Jomo and B. Fine. (Eds) (2006). *The New Development Economics: After the Washington Consensus,* Zed Books: London, pp. 184–99.

Harriss, J., Hunter, J., & Lewis, C.M. (1995). *The new institutional economics and Third World development.* London: Routledge.

Harrison, G. (2004). *The World Bank and Africa: The construction of governance states.* London: Routledge.

———— (2010). *Neoliberal Africa: The impact of global social engineering.* London; New York: Zed Books.

Harvey, D. (2003). *The new imperialism* Oxford: Oxford University Press.

———— (2005). *A Brief History of Neoliberalism,* Oxford: Oxford University Press.

———— (2006). *The Limits to Capital.* London: Verso.

———— (2012). The Urban Roots of Financial Crises: Reclaiming the City for Anti-Capitalist Struggle, *Socialist Register.* 48.

Haskell, T. (ed.) (1984). *The Authority of Experts: Studies in History and Theory,* Indiana University Press, Bloomington.

Hass, A. (1999). *Drinking the sea at Gaza: days and nights in a land under siege* New York: Metropolitan Books.

———— (2002). Israel's Closure Policy: an Ineffective Strategy of Containment and Repression. *Journal of Palestine Studies,* 31(3), pp. 5–20.

———— (2012). 2,279 calories per person: How Israel made sure Gaza didn't starve October. 17. Retreived: http://www.haaretz.com/news/diplomacy-defense/2-279-calories-per-person-how-israel-made-sure-gaza-didn-t-starve.premium-1.470419 [Accessed: 20 September 2014].

Healy, P.M. & Palepu, K.G. (2003). The Fall of Enron. *The Journal of Economic Perspectives,* 17(2), pp. 3–26.

Hearn, J. (2007). African NGOs: The New Compradors? *Development and Change* 38(6), pp. 1095–1110.

Hemmer, C. (2010). Balancing, Bonding, and Balking: The European Union, the United States, and the Israeli-Palestinian Peace Process. *Mediterranean Quarterly* (2), pp. 47–60.

Hermann, C. (2007). Neoliberalism in the European Union. FORBA Discussion Paper *Studies in Political Economy* 79, 3.

Hever, S. (2010). *The political economy of Israel's occupation: Repression beyond exploitation.* London; New York, NY: Pluto.

Hilal, J. (2002). *The formation of the Palestinian elite: From the emergence of the national movement to the establishment of the National Authority.* Ramallah and Amman: Muwatin and al-Urdun al-Jadid.

Hiltermann, J.R. (1991). *Behind the Intifada: Labor and women's movements in the Occupied Territories.* Princeton: Princeton University Press.

———— (2000). Al-Haq: The First Twenty Years. *Middle East Report.* 214, pp. 42–4.

Hindness, B. (2002). Neoliberal Citizenship. *Citizenship Studies.* 6, 2, pp. 127–43.

Hirschman, A.O. (1980). *National Power and the Structure of Foreign Trade.* University of California Press: Berkeley.

Hoff, K and Stiglitz, J. (2001). Modern economic theory and development. In Meier G. and J. Stiglitz (Eds). *Frontiers of Development Economics: The Future in Perspective*/OUP/World Bank, pp. 419–20.

Honig-Parnass, T. and Haddad, T. (Eds) (2007). *Between the Lines: Readings on Israel, the Palestinians and the US 'War on Terror'.* Chicago, Ill.: Haymarket.

Howard, M.W. (2000). *The Invention Of Peace: Reflections On War And International Order* London: Profile Books.

Hroub, K. (2006). A 'New Hamas' through Its New Documents. *Journal of Palestine Studies*, 35(4), pp. 6–27.

Hunter, J. (1987). *Israeli Foreign Policy: South Africa and Central America*, Nottingham (Britain): Spokesman.

IEG (2000). Utilization of Project Implementation Units (PIUs) Independent Evaluation Group (IEG). Retrieved at: http://lnweb90.worldbank.org/oed/oeddoclib.nsf/24cc3bb1f94ae11c85256808006a0046/adf4b0ad4ae0bb25852569ba006e34b4?OpenDocument {Accessed: 15 March 2014}.

Ignatieff, M. (2003). America's Empire Is an Empire Lite. *New York Times.* 10 January.

Inbar, E and Shamir, E. (2014). Mowing the Grass in Gaza BESA Center Perspectives Paper No. 255. 20 July.

International Monetary Fund (IMF) (1995). *West Bank and Gaza Strip – Recent Economic Developments and Prospects and Progress in Institution-Building,* Washington DC.

———— (1997). *Recent Economic Developments, Prospects, and Progress in Institution Building in the West Bank and Gaza Strip.* Washington DC.

———— (1998). *The Economy of the West Bank and Gaza Strip.* (S. Barnett, N. Calika, D. Chua, O. Kanaan and M. Zavadjil), Washington DC.

———— (1999). *West Bank and Gaza Strip: Economic Developments in the Five Years since Oslo* (P. Alonso-Gamo, M. Alier, T. Baumsgaard and U. Erickson von Allmen), Washington DC.

———— (2000). *West Bank and Gaza Economic Policy Framework Progress Report.* The Secretariat of the Ad Hoc Liaison Committee. May 31, Prepared by the Palestinian Authority in collaboration with the staff of the International Monetary fund Lisbon, pp. 7–8 June.

———— (2001). *West Bank and Gaza: Economic Performance, Prospects, and Policies.* (R Valdivieso, U Erickson von Allmen, G. Bannister, H. Davoodi, S. Fischer, E. Jenkner and M. Said), Washington DC.

——— (2003). *West Bank and Gaza: Economic Performance and Reform under Conflict Conditions*, Washington DC.

——— (2011). Macroeconomic and Fiscal Framework for the West Bank and Gaza, Seventh Review of Progress, Staff Report for the Meeting of the Ad Hoc Liaison Committee, Brussels, 13 April. Retrieved at https://www.imf.org/external/country/WBG/RR/2011/041311.pdf [Accessed: 10 March 2016].

——— (2012). Overview Note, West Bank and Gaza, 27 April. https://www.imf.org/external/np/country/notes/pdf/WestBankGaza.pdf [Accessed: 20 September 2014].

——— (2013). IMF urges the Palestinian Authority and Donors to reassess priorities. Retrieved at: https://www.imf.org/external/country/WBG/RR/2013/071013.pdf [Accessed: 20 September 2014].

ISEPME (Institute for Social and Economic Policy in the Middle East) and Fischer, S. (1994). Securing peace in the Middle East: Project on economic transition. Cambridge, Mass.: MIT Press.

Israeli Water Authority (2012). Master Plan for the National Water Sector: Main Points of the Policy Paper, Powerpoint presentation, March. Retrieved at http://www.water.gov.il/Hebrew/ProfessionalInfoAndData/2012/09-Israel-Water-Sector-Master-Plan-2050.pdf [Accessed: 8 March 2015].

Jacoby, T. (2009). Hegemony, Modernisation and Post-war Reconstruction. In Mac R. Ginty, and O. Richmond (Eds). *The Liberal Peace and Post-War Reconstruction Myth or Reality?* Routledge, pp. 31–48.

Jamal A. (2007). *Barriers To Democracy: The Other Side Of Social Capital In Palestine And The Arab World*. Princeton, Princeton University Press.

Jeffery, S. (2003). Sharon Endorses Palestinian State. *The Guardian*. 4 June.

Jihan, A. (2013). Palestinian Shoe Industry Declines in Hebron, Al Monitor. *Al Monitor*. 13 March.

JMCC (1998). PLC Special Committee Report Concerning the Annual Report of the General Comptroller Office for 1996. Reprinted in English in *The Palestinian Council*, 2nd Edition (Jerusalem: Jerusalem Media Communication Center).

Johnson, J. and Wasty, S. (1993). *Borrower Ownership of Adjustment Programs and the Political Economy of Reform*. World Bank, Discussion Paper, 199., Washington D.C.

Jomo K.S. and B. Fine. (eds) (2006). *The New Development Economics: After the Washington Consensus*. Zed Books: London.

Kadri A. and M. MacMillen (1998). The Political Economy of Israel's Demand for Palestinian Labour. *Third World Quarterly*, 19(2), pp. 297–311.

Kahler, M. (2009). Trajectories of Accumulation through War and Peace, in R. Paris and T. Sisk (eds), *The Dilemmas of Statebuilding: Confronting the Contradictions of Postwar Peace Operations*. London: Routledge, pp. 287–303.

Kamat, S. (2004). The Privatization of Public Interests: Theorizing NGO discourse in a Neoliberal Era. *Review of International Political Economy*, 11 (1), pp. 155–76.

Kanafani, N. and Cobham, D. (2007). The economic record of the World Bank and the International Monetary Fund in the West Bank and Gaza: an assessment. Paper presented in *Proceedings of MAS' Annual Conference 2007 Palestinian Economy: Forty Years of Occupation … Forty years of Arrested Development*, pp. 4–5 December, Ramallah, pp. 33–80. Retrieved at: http://www.mas.ps/files/server/20141811150825-1.pdf [Accesed: 12 March 2016].

Kattan, V. (2012). The Gas Fields off Gaza: A Gift or a Curse? *al-Shabaka Policy Brief* 25 April.

Kauzya, J-M. (2003). Strengthening Local Governance Capacity for Participation. In D.A. Rondinelli, and G.S. Cheema (Eds) *Reinventing Government For The Twenty-First Century: State Capacity In A Globalizing Society*, Kumarian Press, pp. 181–95.

Kaya, T.O. (2012). *The Middle East peace process and the EU: Foreign policy and security strategy in international politics*. London: I.B.Tauris.

Keating, M., Le More, A. & Lowe, R. (eds) (2005). *Aid, Diplomacy and Facts on the Ground: The Case of Palestine*. London: Royal Institute of International Affairs. Chatham House.

Keohane, R. (2002). Ironies of Sovereignty: The European Union and the United States. *Journal of Common Market Studies*, 40(4), pp. 743–65.

———— (2003) Political Authority after Intervention: Gradations in Sovereignty. In J.L. Holzgrefe and R.O. Keohane (Eds) *Humanitarian Intervention: Ethical, Legal and Political Dilemmas*, Cambridge, Cambridge University Press.

Khalidi, R. (2005). Reshaping Palestinian Economic Policy Discourse: Putting the Development Horse before the Governance Cart. *Journal of Palestine Studies*, 34 (3), pp. 77–87.

———— (2014), The Economics of Palestinian Liberation, *Jacobin*, October 15. Retrieved at: https://www.jacobinmag.com/2014/10/the-economics-of-palestinian-liberation/ [Accessed: 12 March 2016].

Khalidi R. and Samour, S. (2011). Neoliberalism as Liberation: The Statehood Program and the Remaking of the Palestinian National Movement. *Journal of Palestine Studies*. 2, pp. 6–25.

Khan, M.H. (1995). State Failure in Weak States: A Critique of New Institutionalist Explanations. In J. Harris, J., Hunter, and C. Lewis (Eds). The New Institutional Economics and Third World Development. London: Routledge, pp. 71–86.

———— (2000a). Rents, Efficiency and Growth. In Khan, Mushtaq H. and K.S. Jomo (Eds) *Rents, Rent-Seeking and Economic Development: Theory and Evidence in Asia*, Cambridge: Cambridge University Press, pp. 21–69.

———— (2000b). Rent-Seeking as a Process: Inputs, Rent-Outcomes and Net Effects. In M. Khan and K.S. Jomo (Eds), *Rents, Rent-Seeking and Economic Development*. Cambridge: Cambridge University Press, pp. 70–144.

———— (2004). Evaluating the Emerging Palestinian State: 'Good Governance' versus 'Transformation potential'. In Khan, *et al. State formation in Palestine: Viability and governance during a social transformation*. London: RoutledgeCurzon, pp. 13–63.

———— (2006). Corruption and Governance. In Jomo K.S. and B. Fine. (Eds) (2006). *The New Development Economics: After the Washington Consensus*, London: Zed Books, pp. 200–21.

Khan, M.H., Giacaman, G., & Amundsen, I. (2004). *State formation in Palestine: Viability and governance during a social transformation* (Routledge political economy of the Middle East and North Africa series). New York; London: RoutledgeCurzon.

Khan, M.H. and Hilal, J. (2004). State formation under the PNA: Potential Outcomes and their Viability. In M. Khan *et al.* (2004). *State formation in Palestine: Viability and governance during a social transformation* (Routledge political economy of the Middle East and North Africa series). New York; London: RoutledgeCurzon, pp. 64–119.

Khan, M.H. and. Jomo, K.S (Eds) (2000). *Rents, Rent-Seeking and Economic Development: Theory and Evidence in Asia*, Cambridge: Cambridge University Press.

Kimmerling, B. (2003). *Politicide: Ariel Sharon's wars against the Palestinians*, Verso London.

Kleiman, E. (1997). The Waning of Israeli 'Etatisme'. *Israel Studies*, 2(2), pp. 146–71.

Klein, N. (2007). *The Shock Doctrine: The Rise of Disaster Capitalism*, Metropolitan Books, New York.

Knox, C. and Quirk P. (2000). *Peace Building In Northern Ireland, Israel And South Africa: Transition, Transformation And Reconciliation*, Basingstoke, Palgrave Macmillan, Houndmills.

Krasner, S. (2004). Sharing Sovereignty: New Institutions for Collapsing and Failing States. *International Security*, 29(2), pp. 5–43.

Kubursi A. & Naqib, F. (2008). The Palestinian economy under occupation: Economicide. *The Economics of Peace and Security Journal*. 3(2), 16.

Kurtzer, D. C., Lasensky, S. B., Quandt, W. B., Spiegel, S. L., & Telhami, S. Z. (2013). *The peace puzzle: America's quest for Arab-Israeli peace*, 1989–2011. Ithaca: Cornell University Press.

Lagerquist, P. (2003). Privatizing the Occupation: The Political Economy of an Oslo Development Project. *Journal of Palestine Studies*, 32(2), pp. 5–20.

Lapavitsas C. (2005). Mainstream Economics in the Neoliberal Era. In S. Saad-Filho and D. Johnston. *Neoliberalism: A Critical Reader*, London, Pluto Press.

Lasensky, S. (2004). Paying for Peace: The Oslo Process and the Limits of American Foreign Aid. *Middle East Journal*. 58(2), pp. 210–34.

Lazzarato, M. (2009). Neoliberalism in Action: Inequality, Insecurity and the Reconstitution of the Social. *Theory Culture Society*. 26.

Le More, A. (2005). Killing with kindness: funding the demise of a Palestinian state. *International Affairs*, 81(5), pp. 981–99.

———— (2008). *International assistance to the Palestinians after Oslo: political guilt, wasted money*. Abingdon: Routledge.

Leenders, R. (2012). *Spoils of Truce: Corruption and Statebuilding in Postwar Lebanon*. Ithaca, Cornell University Press.

Lerner, D. (1958). *The passing of traditional society: Modernizing the Middle East*. Glencoe, Ill.: Free Press.

LeVine, M. (2009). *Impossible peace: Israel/Palestine since 1989*. Black Point, N.S.: Fernwood Pub.

Lloyd, J. (1996). Eastern Reformers and Neo-Marxist Reviewers. *New Left Review*, I:216, pp. 119–24.

Loan Guarantee Facility [LGF] (2013). Progress Report 1st Quarter. Retrieved at: http://www.meiinitiative.org/uploads/file/Other%20MEII%20articles/LGF_Progress_Report_Q12013.pdf [Accessed: 20 September 2014].

Lockman, Z. (1996). *Comrades and Enemies: Arab and Jewish Workers in Palestine. 1906–1948*. Berkeley, University of California Press.

Long, W.J. (1996). *Economic Incentives and Bilateral Cooperation*. Ann Arbor, University of Michigan Press.

Looney, R. (2003). The Neoliberal Model's Planned Role in Iraq's Economic Transition. *Middle East Journal*, 57(4), pp. 568–86.

Lowe, R. (2005). *Aid, diplomacy and facts on the ground: The case of Palestine*. London: Chatham House.

Lugard, Lord (1965) [1922]. *The Dual Mandate in Tropical Africa*. London, Frank Cass.

Mac Ginty, R. & Richmond, O. (Eds) (2009). *The Liberal Peace And Post-War Reconstruction: Myth Or Reality?* London: Routledge.

Makovsky, D. (1996). Making peace with the PLO: The Rabin government's road to the Oslo Accord. Boulder: Westview Press.

Malik, K & Wagle, S. (2010). Building Social Capital Through Civic Engagement. In K. Birch & V. Mykhnenko (Eds) *The Rise and Fall of Neoliberalism: The Collapse Of An Economic Order? London*, London, Zed Press, pp. 143–62.

Malley, R. (2001). Fictions About Camp David. *New York Times*. 8 July.

Malley, R. and Agha, H. (2001). Camp David: Tragedy of Errors. *New York Review of Books*. 9 August.

Manna', 'A. (1986). Palestinian Notables in the Ottoman Period, Jerusalem: Arab Studies Society.

Masalha, N. (1992). *Expulsion of the Palestinians: The concept of 'transfer' in Zionist political thought, 1882–1948*. Washington: Institute for Palestine Studies.

McGrath, J.J. (2012). Noble Energy-Led Consortium Signs $680 Million Natural-Gas Deal in Israel. *International Business Times*. 12 February.

Meiksins Wood, E. (2006). Logics of Power: A Conversation with David Harvey *Historical Materialism*, 14(4), pp. 9–34.

Mendus, S. (1989). *Toleration and the Limits of Liberalism*, London, Macmillan.

Miller, M. (1995). 'Israelis, Arabs Get Down to Business at Conference' *Los Angeles Times*, 1 November.

Miskin, A. (1992). AID's "Free Market" Democracy *Middle East Report*, 179, pp. 33–4.

———— (1994). Chemonics Revisited. *Middle East Report*. 186, 28.

Mosco, V. (2009). *The political economy of communication* (2nd ed.). Los Angeles: Sage Publications.

Murphy, E. (1995). Stacking the Deck: The Economics of the Israeli-PLO Accords: *Middle East Report*, 194/195, pp. 35–8.

———— (2000). The Arab-Israeli Peace Process: Can the Region Benefit from the Economics of Globlaization Wright, J.W. and Drake, L. (2000). *Economic and Political Impediments to Middle East Peace, Critical Questions and Alternative Scenarios*, Macmillan Press Ltd. London.

Mustafa, M. (2010). The Palestinian economy and future prospects: Interview with Mohammad Mustafa, head of the Palestine Investment Fund. *Journal of Palestine Studies*. 39(3), pp. 40–51.

Nachtwey, J. & Tessler, M. (2002). The Political Economy of Attitudes toward Peace among Palestinians and Israelis. *The Journal of Conflict Resolution*. 46(2), pp. 260–85.

Nakhleh, K. (2012) *Globalized Palestine: The National Sellout of a Homeland*. New Jersey: Red Sea Press.

Naqib, F. (2003). Economic Aspects of the Palestinian-Israeli Conflict: The Collapse of the Oslo Accord. *Journal of International Development*. 15, pp. 499–512.

Narten, J. (2008). Dilemmas of Promoting 'local ownership': the case of postwar Kosovo. In R. Paris, and T. Sisk, *The Dilemmas Of Statebuilding: Confronting The Contradictions Of Postwar Peace Operations*, Routledge, pp. 252–84.

Nasr, M. (2004). Monopolies and the PNA. In M.H. Khan (2004). *State formation in Palestine: Viability and governance during a social transformation* (Routledge political economy of the Middle East and North Africa series). New York; London: RoutledgeCurzon, pp. 168–89.

Naval Postgraduate School (2000). *Summary of Research*, Department of National Security Affairs, Faculty of the Naval Postgraduate School. Monterey, California. Retrieved at: http://www.dtic.mil/dtic/tr/fulltext/u2/a408377.pdf [Accessed: 12 March 2016].

NDI (2006). *Final Report on the Palestinian Legislative Council Elections* National Democratic Institute January 25. Retrieved at: https://www.ndi.org/files/2068_ps_elect_012506.pdf [Accessed: 28 September, 2014].

NENGOOT (1992). The Proceedings of the ECCP-NENGOOT Conference, Brussels 28 September–1 October 1992. Brown, A., Heacock, R. & Torre, F. (Eds) Palestine – Development for Peace [Network of European NGOs in the Occupied Territories-NENGOOT.

New York Times (n.a.) (1992). Excerpts From Pentagon's Plan: 'Prevent the Re-Emergence of a New Rival'. 8 March.

Nitzan, J. and Bichler, S. (1996). From War Profits to Peace Dividends: The New Political Economy of Israel. *Capital & Class*. 60, pp. 61–94.

——— (2002a). *The global political economy of Israel*. London: Pluto.

——— (2002b). Global accumulation and the New-Middle East Wars, July. Retrieved from: http://bnarchives.yorku.ca/84/ [Accessed: 29 September 2014].

——— (2002c) War Profits, Peace Dividends and the Israeli-Palestinian Conflict. *News From Within*. XVIII, 4, pp. 14–19.

North, D.C. (1981). *Structure and Change in Economic History*. New York: Norton.

——— (1990). *Institutions, Institutional Change and Economic Performance*. Cambridge: Cambridge University Press.

——— (1995). The New Institutional Economics and Third World Development. In Harriss, J. Hunter, J. and Lewis, C. *The New Institutional Economics and Third World Development*. London: Routledge, pp. 17–26.

North, D.C., Wallis, J.J., and Weingast, B.R. (2009). Violence and the Rise of Open-Access Orders. *Journal of Democracy*, 20(1), pp. 55–68.

——— (2012). *In the shadow of violence: Politics, economics, and the problems of development*. Cambridge: Cambridge University Press.

OECD/DAC (1995). *Participatory Development and Good Governance*. Development Cooperation Guideline Series.

——— (1997). *Guidelines on Conflict, Peace and Development Cooperation*. Paris.

——— (2007). *The principles for good international engagement in fragile states and situations*. Paris.

——— (2008). *Concepts and dilemmas of state building in fragile situations: From fragility to resilience*. Paris.

——— (2010). *DAC guidelines and reference series: Supporting statebuilding in situations of conflict and fragility: Policy guidance for good international engagement*. Paris.

——— (2011). *Conflict and Fragility From Power Struggles to Sustainable Peace: Understanding Political Settlements*, Economic Surveys Series. Paris.

Offshore Technology Web. (n.d.). Gaza Marine Gas Field, Palestine. Retrieved at: http://www.offshore-technology.com/projects/gaza-marine-gas-field/ [Accessed: 14 September 2013].

O'Gorman, E. (2011). *Conflict and development: Development matters*. London: Zed Books.

Ottaway, M. (2002). National Building, *Foreign Policy*, 132.

PADICO (2011). Padico Announces USD 38.1 Million Profits in 2010. Press release, 16 February.

Paige, J.M. (1998). Coffee and power: Revolution and the rise of democracy in Central America (1st Harvard University Press pbk. ed.). Cambridge, Mass.: Harvard University Press.

Palley. T.I. (2007). Financialization: What It Is and Why It Matters, Washington, D.C.: The Levy Economics Institute and Economics for Democratic and Open Societies, Working Paper. 525.

Pappé, I. (2006a). *A History Of Modern Palestine: One Land, Two Peoples* Cambridge, New York: Cambridge University Press.

——— (2006b). *The Ethnic Cleansing of Palestine*, Oxford: Oneworld.

Paris, R. (1997). The Limits of Liberal Internationalism. *International Security*, 22(2).

——— (2002). International Peacebuilding and the 'Mission Civilisatrice'. *Review of International Studies*, 28: 4, pp. 637–56.

——— (2004). *At War's End: Building Peace after Civil Conflict*. Cambridge: Cambridge University Press.

Paris, R. & Sisk, T. (2008). *The Dilemmas Of Statebuilding: Confronting The Contradictions Of Postwar Peace Operations*, Routledge.

PECDAR (2003). The Palestinian Economy in the Transitional Period (Second edition). Shtayyeh, M. (Ed.). Ramallah.

——— (2011). The Palestinian Economy in the Transitional (Third Edition). Ramallah.

Peck, J. and Tickell, A. (2002). Neoliberalizing Space. *Antipode* 34(3), pp. 380–404.

Peled, Y. (2008). Who Was Afraid of Decolonization. In G. Ben-Porat (ed.) (2008). *The Failure Of The Middle East Peace Process? A Comparative Analysis of Peace Implementation in Israel/Palestine, Northern Ireland and South Africa*, Palgrave Macmillan.

Pelham, N. (2012). Gaza's Tunnel Phenomenon: The Unintended Dynamics of Israel's Siege. *Journal of Palestine Studies* 41:4, pp. 6–31.

Peres, S. (1993). *The New Middle East*/with Arye Naor, Shaftesbury, Dorset: Element.

Peteet, J. (1991). *Gender in Crisis: Women and the Palestinian Resistance Movement*. New York: Columbia University Press.

PMA (2012). Public Debt Sustainability Report 2012, Palestine Monetary Authority, Ramallah.

Polakow-Suransky, S. (2010). *The unspoken alliance: Israel's secret relationship with apartheid South Africa*. New York: Pantheon Books.

Pugh, M. (2008). Employment, Labour Rights and Social Resistance. In M. Pugh, N. Cooper & M. Turner (eds) *Whose Peace? Critical Perspectives On The Political Economy Of Peacebuilding*, Palgrave Macmillan, Basingstoke, pp. 139–56.

Pugh, M. & Cooper, N. (2004). *War Economies in a Regional Context: Challenges of Transformation*/ with Jonathan Goodhand, Lynne Rienner, Boulder.

Pugh, M. Cooper, N. & Turner, M. (eds) (2008). *Whose Peace? Critical Perspectives On The Political Economy Of Peacebuilding*, Palgrave Macmillan, Basingstoke.

Putnam, R. (1993). *Making Democracy Work: Civic Traditions in Modern Italy*, Princeton, N.J.: Princeton University Press.

Qarmout, T. & Beland, D. (2012). The Politics of International Aid to the Gaza Strip. *Journal of Palestine Studies*, 14:4, pp. 32–47.

Quandt, W. (2005). *Peace process: American diplomacy and the Arab-Israeli conflict since 1967* (3rd ed.). Washington, D.C.: Berkeley: Brookings Institution Press; University of California Press.

Qurei, A. (2006). *From Oslo to Jerusalem: The Palestinian story of the secret negotiations.* London; New York: New York: I.B.Tauris.

Rajjoub, A. (2013). Abbas Hints at Dahlan's Responsibility in the Death of Arafat, Aljazeera net. March 13. Retrieved at: http://www.aljazeera.net/news/arabic/2014/3/13/%D8%B9%D8%A8%D8%A7%D8%B3%D9%8A%D9%84%D9%85%D8%AD%D9%84%D9%85%D8%B3%D8%A4%D9%88%D9%84%D9%8A%D8%A9%D8%AF%D8%AD%D9%84%D8%A7%D9%86%D8%A8%D9%88%D9%81%D8%A7%D8%A9%D8%B9%D8%B1%D9%81%D8%A7%D8%AA%D8%AA%D8%AA [Accessed: 29 September 2014].

Rawabi (2011). Rawabi home. Spring. Retrieved at: http://www.rawabi.ps/newsletter/2011/download/en/rawabi_spring_2011_en.pdf [Accessed: 28 September 2014].

Razin, A. & Sadka, E. (1993). *The economy of modern Israel: Malaise and promise.* Chicago: University of Chicago Press.

Reinhart, T. (2001). Out now! A simple and human step. *Yediot Aharonot*, 8 July.

———— (2006). *The Road map to Nowhere: Israel/Palestine since 2003.* London: Verso.

Reiter, Y. The Palestinian-Transjordanian Rift: Economic Might and Political Power in Jordan. *Middle East Journal*, 58:1, pp. 72–92.

Richmond, O. (2002). *Maintaining order, Making Peace*, London: Palgrave.

———— (2008). Welfare and the Civil Peace: Poverty with Rights? in Pugh, M.N. Cooper and M. Turner (Eds) *Whose Peace?: Critical Perspectives On The Political Economy Of Peacebuilding*, Palgrave Macmillan, Basingstoke, pp. 287–336.

———— (2011). *A Post-Liberal Peace*, London: Routledge.

Roberts, N. (2005). Hard Lessons from Oslo: foreign aid and the mistakes of the 1990s. In M. Keating, A. Le More and R. Lowe (Eds), *Aid, Diplomacy and Facts on the Ground: The Case of Palestine*, London: Royal Institute of International Affairs.

———— (2006). International Aid, Diplomacy and the Palestinian Reality. Transcript of Remarks by Nigel Roberts For the Record No. 244 (10 February). Retrieved at: http://www.thejerusalemfund.org/ht/display/ContentDetails/i/2604 [Accessed: 28 September 2014].

Robinson, G.E. (1993). The Role of the Professional Middle Class in the Mobilization of Palestinian Society: The Medical and Agricultural Committees. *International Journal of Middle East Studies*, 25:2, pp. 301–26.

———— (1997a). *Building A Palestinian State: The Incomplete Revolution*. Bloomington: Indiana UP.

———— (1997b). The Politics of Legal Reform in Palestine. *Journal of Palestine Studies*, 27(1) pp. 51–60.

———— (2000). Civil Society and Local Government: An Assessment of Civil Society in Relation to Prospects for Local Government Decentralization in the West Bank and Gaza Strip. In ARD, Inc., *Shaping Local Government Decentralization: Prospects and Issues for Local Government Decentralization in the West Bank and Gaza Strip*, Report to the US Agency for International Development, April.

———— (2001). Israel and the Palestinians: Bitter Fruits of Hegemonic Peace. *Current History: A Journal of Contemporary World Affairs*, 100 (642).

Roemer, J.E. (1982). A General Theory of Exploitation and Class. Cambridge, MA: Harvard University Press.

––––––– (1988). Free to Lose: An Introduction to Marxist Economic Philosophy, London: Radius Hutchinson.

Rondinelli, D. and Cheema, G.S. (eds) (2003). *Reinventing government for the twenty-first century: State capacity in a globalizing society*. Bloomfield, CT: Kumarian Press.

Rosecrance, R. (1987). *The Rise of the Trading State*. New York: Basic Books.

––––––– (2008). The Gaza Bombshell. *Vanity Fair*. April.

––––––– (2010). Special investigation: How Blair rescued Palestine deal worth $200m to his £2m-a-year paymasters. *The Daily Mail*. 11 September.

Rothstein, R.L. Ma'oz, M. and Shikaki K. (eds) (2002). *The Israeli-Palestinian peace process: Oslo and the lessons of failure: perspectives, predicaments and prospects*, Brighton: Sussex Academic, 2002.

Roy, S. (1995). *The Gaza Strip: The Political Economy Of De-Development*, Washington, DC: Institute for Palestinian Studies.

––––––– (1999). De-development Revisited: Palestinian Economy and Society Since Oslo. *Journal of Palestine Studies*, 28: 3, pp. 64–82.

––––––– (2004). The Palestinian-Israeli Conflict and Palestinian Socioeconomic Decline: A Place Denied. *International Journal of Politics, Culture, and Society*, 17, 3.

––––––– (2006). *Failing peace: Gaza and the Palestinian-Israeli conflict*. London: Pluto.

––––––– (2011). *Hamas and civil society in Gaza: Engaging the Islamist social sector*. Princeton, N.J.: Princeton University Press.

Ruggie J.G. (1983). International Regimes, Transactions and Change: Embedded liberalism in the postwar economic order, in Krasner, S. (1983). *International regimes*. Ithaca: Cornell University Press, pp. 195–232.

Saad-Filho, A. (2005). 'From Washington to Post-Washington Consensus: Neoliberal Agendas for Economic Development' in A. Saad-Filho & D. Johnston *Neoliberalism: A Critical Reader*, London: Pluto Press, pp. 113–19.

––––––– (2011). Crisis In Neoliberalism Or Crisis Of Neoliberalism? *Socialist Register*, 47.

Saad-Filho, A. and D. Johnston. (2005). *Neoliberalism: A Critical Reader* London: Pluto Press.

Sabet A.G.E. (1998). The Peace Process and the Politics of Conflict Resolution. *Journal of Palestine Studies*. 27:4, pp. 5–19.

Sabri, N. (2003). The Palestinian Public Sector in the context of the Palestinian economy, Muwatin. Ramallah.

Sadan, E. (1991). A policy for immediate economic-industrial development in the Gaza Strip. *Ben-Ezra Consultants*. August.

––––––– (1993). Durable employment for the refugee-populated region of Gaza. April.

Said, E. (1993). "The Morning After", *London Review of Books*, 15, pp. 20–1. 21 October.

––––––– (1995). *Peace and its Discontents: Gaza-Jericho 1993–1995*. London: Vantage.

––––––– (2001). *The End of the Peace Process: Oslo and after* New York: Vintage books.

Salinas, M., & Abu Rabia, H. (2009). *Resolving the Israeli-Palestinian Conflict: Perspectives on the Peace Process*, Amherst: Cambria Press.

Samara, A. (2000). Globalization, the Palestinian Economy, and the 'Peace Process': *Journal of Palestine Studies*, 29:2, pp. 20–34.

———— (2001). *Epidemic of Globalization: Ventures in World Order, the Arab Nation and Zionism*, Glendale: Palestine Research and Publishing Foundation.

Samuels, W.J. and Mercuro, N. (1984). A Critique of Rent-Seeking Theory. In D.C. Colander (ed.) *Neoclassical Political Economy: The Analysis of Rent-seeking and DUP Activities*, Cambridge, MA: Ballinger Publishing Company.

Sarsar, S. (2004). The Question of Palestine and United States Behavior at the United Nations. *International Journal of Politics, Culture, and Society*. 17: 3, pp. 457–70.

Sasson, A. (2010). Has Israel turned into a natural gas superpower? *Haaretz*. 27 September.

Savir, U. (1998). *The process: 1,100 days that changed the Middle East* (1st edn). New York, NY: Random House.

Sayigh, Y. (1997). Armed struggle and the search for state: The Palestinian national movement 1949–1993. Oxford: Oxford University Press.

———— (2007). Inducing a Failed State in Palestine, *Survival: Global Politics and Strategy*, 49:3, pp. 7–39.

Sayigh, Y.A. (1986). The Palestinian Economy under Occupation: Dependency and Pauperization. *Journal of Palestine Studies*. 15:4, pp. 46–67.

Schiavo-Campo, S. (2003). Financing and Aid Management Arrangements In Post-Conflict Situations. The World Bank: Social Development Department Environmentally and Socially Sustainable Development Network. CPR Working paper No. 6, Washington D.C.

Schiff, Z. (1990). *Intifada: The Palestinian uprising – Israel's third front*. New York: London: Simon and Schuster.

Sciolino, E. (2000). Violence Thwarts C.I.A. Director's Unusual Diplomatic Role in Middle Eastern Peacemaking. *New York Times*, 13 November.

Segal, R. and Weizman, E. (2003). (Rev. Ed.) *Civilian Occupation: The Politics of Israeli Architecture*, Verso Books.

Segev, T. (2007). *1967: Israel, The War And The Year That Transformed The Middle East* London: Little, Brown.

Selby, J. (2008). The Political Economy of Peace Processes. In Pugh, M.N. Cooper and M. Turner (Eds) *Whose Peace?: Critical Perspectives On The Political Economy Of Peacebuilding*, Palgrave Macmillan, Basingstoke, pp. 11–29.

Sewell, D. (2001). Governance and the Business Environment in the WBG. The World Bank: Middle East and North Africa Working paper series 23, Washington D.C.

Shaban, O. (2013). Fixing Gaza's Electricity Crisis, *Al-Monitor*. 19 November. http://www.al-monitor.com/pulse/originals/2013/11/gaza-electricity-crisis-sewage-power-israel-egypt.html# [Accessed: 5 April, 2014].

Shafir, G. (1989). *Land, labor and the origins of the Israeli-Palestinian conflict 1882–1914*. Cambridge: Cambridge University Press.

Shafir, G. and Peled, Y. (2002). *Being Israeli: The dynamics of multiple citizenship*. Cambridge: Cambridge University Press.

Shavit, A. (2002). The Enemy Within: interview with IDF Chief of Staff Moshe Ya'alon. *Ha'aretz*, 29 August.

———— (2004). Top PM aide: Gaza plan aims to freeze the peace process. *Ha'aretz*. 6 October.

Shihata, I., Abushakra, H., and Gruss, H-J. (1992/94). Legal aspects of the World Bank Assistance to the West Bank and Gaza Strip'. In *The Palestinian Yearbook of International Law*, vii, pp. 19–43.

Shlaim, A. (2005). The Rise and Fall of the Oslo Peace Process. In L. Fawcett (ed.) *International Relations of the Middle East*, Oxford, Oxford University Press, pp. 241–61.

Shlaim, A. (2009). *Israel and Palestine: Reappraisals, revisions, refutations*. London; Brooklyn, NY: Verso.

Smooha, S. (2007). All the dreams we had are now gone. *Ha'aretz*. 19 July.

Sourani, G. (2009). Social and Class Transformations in the West Bank and Gaza. Critical Vision. Gaza. [*Attahawulat alijtima'iyya wa-ttabaqiyya fi ad-diffa algharbiyya wa qita' ghazza*] Retrieved at: http://www.doroob.com/wp-content/library/changes_sourani.pdf [Accessed: 29 September 2014].

Stein, H. (2008). *Beyond the World Bank agenda: An institutional approach to development*. Chicago; London: University of Chicago Press.

Stiglitz, J.E. (1998). Towards a New Paradigm for Development: Strategies, Policies, and Processes. Paper given at 1998 Prebisch Lecture. Geneva: UNCTAD; 19 October.

——— (2001). *Joseph Stiglitz and the World Bank: The rebel within*. London, England: Anthem Press.

Stocker, J. (2012). No EEZ Solution: The Politics of Oil and Gas in the Eastern Mediterranean. *The Middle East Journal*. 66:4, pp. 579–97.

Suhkre, A. (2009). The Dangers of a Tight Embrace: Externally Assisted Statebuilding In Afghanistan. In R. Paris, and T. Sisk, *The Dilemmas Of Statebuilding: Confronting The Contradictions Of Postwar Peace Operations*, Routledge, pp. 227–51.

Swain, A.V. Mykhnenko and S. French (2010). The Corruption Industry and Transition: Neoliberalizing Post-Soviet Space? In Birch K. and V. Mykhnenko (Eds) *The Rise And Fall Of Neoliberalism: The Collapse Of An Economic Order?* Zed Press, London, pp. 112–32.

Swisher, C. (2011). *The Palestine Papers: The End of the Road?* Hesperus Press Ltd.

Taghdisi-Rad, S. (2011). *The Political Economy of Aid In Palestine: Relief From Conflict Or Development Delayed?* London: Routledge.

Tal, A. (2008). Water Management in Israel: The Conspicuous Absence of Water Markets. Water and Sustainable Development: Water Economics and Financing, Expo Zaragosa 2008. Retrieved at: http://www.zaragozaciudad.com/contenidos/medioambiente/cajaAzul/21Conferencia_Magistral-2-Alon_TalACC.pdf [Accessed: 12 March 2016].

Tamari, S. (2002). Who Rules Palestine? *Journal of Palestine Studies*, 31:4, pp. 102–13.

Taraki, L. (2008). Enclave Micropolis: the Paradoxical Case of Ramallah/al-Bireh. *Journal of Palestine Studies*. 37:4, pp. 6–20.

Taylor, I. (2009). What Fit for the Liberal Peace in Africa? In R. Mac Ginty, R. & O. Richmond (Eds). *The Liberal Peace and Post-War Reconstruction Myth or Reality?* Routledge, pp. 63–76.

Thompson, J.B. (1984). *Studies in the Theory of Ideology*. Berkeley and Los Angeles: University of California Press.

Tocci, N. (2013). The Middle East Quartet and (In)effective Multilateralism. *The Middle East Journal*, 67:1, pp. 29–44.

Tuma, E.H. (1989). The Economies of Israel and the Occupied Territories: War and Peace – A Panel Discussion. *Economic Quarterly*. (139), pp. 593–606.

————— (2000). Will an Arab–Israeli Peace Bring a Trade Dividend? In J.W. Wright Jr., and L. Drake, *Economic and Political Impediments to Middle East Peace, Critical Questions and Alternative Scenarios*, London, Macmillan Press Ltd.

Turner, M. (2009). The Power of 'Shock and Awe': the Palestinian Authority and the Road to Reform. *International Peacekeeping*, 16(4), pp. 562–77.

————— (2011). Creating 'Partners for Peace': the Palestinian Authority and the International Statebuilding Agenda. *Journal of Intervention and Statebuilding* 4(1), 121.

————— (2012). 'Completing the circle: peacebuilding as colonial practice in the occupied Palestinian territory', *International Peacekeeping*, 19(5), pp. 492–507.

————— (2015). Peacebuilding as counterinsurgency in the occupied Palestinian territory. *Review of International Studies*, 41:3, pp. 647.

Turner, R. (2007) The 'rebirth of liberalism': The origins of neo-liberal ideology. Journal of Political Ideologies.12:1, pp. 67–83.

United Nations (UN) (1987). World Commission on Environment and Development Report of the World Commission on Environment and Development: Our Common Future. Retrieved at: http://www.un-documents. net/our-common-future.pdf [Accessed: 29 September 2014].

————— (1992). An Agenda For Peace: Preventive Diplomacy, Peacemaking And Peace-Keeping, UN Doc. A/47/277- S/24111, at 22 (1992), UN Sales No. E.95. I.15. Retrieved at: http://www.un-documents.net/a47-277.htm [Accessed: 12 March 2016].

————— (2000). United Nations Millennium Declaration, GA Res. 55/2. 18 September. Retrieved at: http://www.un.org/millennium/declaration/ares552e.htm [Accessed 12 March 2016].

UNCTAD (United Nations Conference on Trade and Development) (1994). *Prospects for Sustained Development of the Palestinian Economy in the West Bank and Gaza Strip: 1990–2020*. UNCTAD/ECDC/SEU/6, Geneva, UNCTAD, 11 November. Retrieved at: http://unctad.org/en/PublicationsLibrary/ecdc-seud6a1_en.pdf [Accessed 12 March 2016].

————— (1996). Prospects for *Sustained Development of the Palestinian Economy*. UNCTAD/ECDC/SEU/12, Geneva, UNCTAD, 21 August. Retrieved at: http://unctad.org/en/Docs/poecdcseud12.en.pdf [Accessed 12 March 2016].

————— (1998). *The Palestinian economy and prospects for regional cooperation*. UNCTAD/GDS/SEU/2. 30 June. Retrieved at: http://unctad.org/en/Docs/pogdsseud2.pdf [Accessed 12 March 2016].

————— (2004). *Transit trade and maritime transport facilitation for the rehabilitation and development of the Palestinian economy*. UNCTAD/GDS/APP/2003/1. New York and Geneva. 22 March. Retrieved at: http://unctad.org/en/Docs/gdsapp20031_en.pdf [Accessed 12 March 2016].

————— (2006). *The Palestinian war-torn economy: Aid, development and State formation*. UNCTAD/GDS/APP/2006/1. New York and Geneva. 5 April. Retrieved at: http://unctad.org/en/Docs/gdsapp20061_en.pdf [Accessed 12 March 2016].

————— (2009). *The Economic dimensions of prolonged occupation: Continuity and change in Israeli policy towards the Palestinian economy* UNCTAD/GDS/2009/2. Retrieved at: http://unctad.org/en/Docs/gds20092_en.pdf [Accessed 12 March 2016].

————— (2011a). *Paris Protocol on Economic Relations (PER) Between Palestine (PLO) and Israel – Critical analysis, historical failings, future options: An extract of relevant UNCTAD reports and studies since 1998*. 1 October.

———— (2011b). *Rebuilding the Palestinian Tradable Goods Sector: Towards Economic Recovery and State Formation* UNCTAD/GDS/APP/2010/1. Retrieved at: http://unctad.org/en/PublicationsLibrary/gdsapp2010d1_en.pdf [Accessed 12 March 2016].

UNDP (United Nations Development Programme) (1994). Human Development Report 1994. Retrieved at: http://hdr.undp.org/sites/default/files/reports/255/hdr_1994_en_complete_nostats.pdf [Accessed: 29 September 2014].

———— (1997). Governance for Sustainable Human Development, New York, UNDP Policy Document, Management Development and Governance Division, Bureau for Policy and Programme Support. Retrieved at: http://www.pogar.org/publications/other/undp/governance/undppolicydoc97-e.pdf [Accessed 12 March 2016].

UNOCHA [United Nations Office for the Coordination of Humanitarian Affairs] (2010a). West Bank and Gaza Strip Closure Map. Retrieved at: http://www.ochaopt.org/documents/ocha_opt_opt_closure_maps_booklet_july_2010_a3.pdf [Accessed: 28 September 2014].

———— (2010b). *Between the Fence and a Hard Place, The Humanitarian Impact of Israeli Imposed Restrictions on Access to Land and Sea in the Gaza Strip* – Special Focus August, Jerusalem. Retrieved at: http://www.ochaopt.org/documents/ocha_opt_special_focus_2010_08_19_english.pdf [Accessed 12 March 2016].

———— (2011). *East Jerusalem – Key Humanitarian Concerns*, Special Focus, March Jerusalem. Retrieved at: http://www.ochaopt.org/documents/ocha_opt_jerusalem_report_2011_03_23_web_english.pdf [Accessed 12 March 2016].

Urqhart, C. (2006). Gaza on brink of implosion as aid cut-off starts to bite. *The Guardian*, 16 April.

USAID (United States Agency for International Development). (1993a). Palestinian Institutional Configurations in the West Bank and Gaza under Four Autonomy Scenarios. Democratic Institutions Support Project, 18 May. Retrieved at: http://pdf.usaid.gov/pdf_docs/PNABY769.pdf [Accessed 12 May 2016].

———— (1993b). *An Overview of Palestinian Institutional Capabilities and Development Requirements in the Health Care, Agricultural, Industrial and Educational Sectors of the West Bank and Gaza Strip.* Democratic Institutions Support Project, 1 September. Retrieved at: http://pdf.usaid.gov/pdf_docs/pnaby770.pdf [Accessed 12 March 2016].

———— (1993c). *First Annual report for the period 21 September 1992–20 September 1993*, The Democratic Institutions Support Project, 29 October.

———— (1995). *West Bank and Gaza: Industrial Estate Development. Next Steps and Possible Roles For USAID Support – Final Report.* September.

———— (1996a). *USAID Democracy and Governance Strategy, The West Bank and Gaza.* Center for Governance and Democracy. March.

———— (1996b). *The Democratic Institutions Support Project – Final Report.* 21 August.

———— (1996c). *Environmental Assessment for the Gaza Industrial Estate Project.* Bureau for Asia and the Near East. Activity Report 28.

———— (1998). *Palestinian Industrial & Free Zone Authority (PIFZA): Business Plan for the Initial Twelve Months* – Final Report. May.

———— (1999). *Investor Targeting Strategy for Industrial Estates in the West Bank and Gaza.* November.

———— (2000). *PIEFZA Corporate Plan.* February.

———— (2002a). *Palestinian Investment Promotion Agency Promotional Materials May. Promoting Industrial Zones and Investment Mobilization, Expanding Economic Opportunities.*

———— (2002b). *Assessment of the Humanitarian Situation in Palestine: Key Findings.* July.

———— (2011). *Statebuilding In Situations Of Fragility And Conflict Relevance For Us Policy And Programs.* Statebuilding Strategy Workshop, Office of Conflict Management and Mitigation. February.

US Geological Survey (2010). Assessment of Undiscovered Oil and Gas Resources of the Levant Basin Province, Eastern Mediterranean, March.

USG (1996). Free Trade Area Extended To West Bank And Gaza Strip [Office of the United States Trade Representative, Press Release, 3 October, 1996. Retrieved at: http://www.clintonlibrary.gov/assets/storage/Research%20-%20Digital%20Library/ClintonAdminHistoryProject/101-111/Box%20101/1756308-history-ustr-press-releases-september-october-1996.pdf [Accessed: 25 September 2014].

Usher, G. (1996). The Politics of Internal Security: The PA's New Intelligence Services *Journal of Palestine Studies.* 25:2, pp. 21–34.

———— (1999). *Palestine in crisis: the struggle for peace and political independence after Oslo.* London: Pluto Press.

———— (1999). *Dispatches from Palestine: The rise and fall of the Oslo peace process.* London; Sterling, Va.: Pluto Press.

Uvin, P. (1999). *The Influence of Aid in Situations of Violent Conflict.* Paris: Organization for Economic Cooperation and Development, September.

Van Waeyenberge, E. (2006). From Washington to Post Washington Concensus: Illusions of Development. In K.S. Jomo and B. Fine. (Eds) (2006). *The New Development Economics: After the Washington Consensus,* Zed Books: London, pp. 21–45.

———— (2010). 'Tightening the Web: the World Bank and Enforced Policy Reform' in Birch K. and V. Mykhnenko (Eds) *The Rise And Fall Of Neoliberalism: The Collapse Of An Economic Order?* Zed Press, London, pp. 94–112.

Vitalis, R. (1994). The Democratization Industry and the Limits of the New Interventionism. *Middle East Report.* 187/188, Intervention and North-South Politics in the 90s, pp. 46–50.

Von Mises, L. (1936). *Socialism: An Economic and Sociological Analysis.* London: Bradford and Dickens, pp. 31–2.

Waage, H.H. (2004). Peacemaking Is a Risky Business: Norway's Role in the Peace Process in the Middle East, 1993–96. PRIO. Report commissioned by the Norwegian Ministry of Foreign Affairs.

———— (2005). Norway's Role In The Middle East Peace Talks: Between A Strong State And A Weak Belligerent *Journal of Palestine Studies,* 34: 4, pp. 6–24.

Wade, R.H. (2011). Emerging world order? From multipolarity to multilateralism in the G20, the World Bank, and the IMF *Politics and Society,* 39 (3), pp. 347–78.

Wallensteen, P. & Sollenberg, M. (2001). Armed Conflict, 1989–2000. *Journal of Peace Research* 38:5, pp. 629–44.

Weber, M. (1978). *Economy and Society.* 2 vols, Berkeley: University of California Press.

Wigglesworth, R. (2010). Qtel consortium buys Orascom Tunisia's stake. *Financial Times.* 22 November.

Williams, D. (1996). Governance and the Disciple of Development. *European Journal of Development Research* 8, 2, pp. 157–77.

——— (2008). *The World Bank and Social Transformation In International Politics: Liberalism, Governance And Sovereignty*, London: Routledge.

Williamson, J. (1990). What Washington means by Policy Reform. In J, Williamson (Ed.) *Latin American Adjustment: How Much has Happened?* Washington D.C.: Institute for International Economics.

Williamson, O. (1985). *The Economic Institutions of Capitalism: Firms, Markets, Relational Contracting.* New York: Free Press.

——— (1994). The Institutions and Governance of Economic Development and Reform. In *Proceedings of the World Bank Annual Conference on Development Economics 1994*, Washington, DC: World Bank, pp. 171–208.

Wolfensohn, J.D. (2005). *Voice for the world's poor: Selected speeches and writings of World Bank president James D. Wolfensohn, 1995–2005.* Washington, D.C.: World Bank.

——— (2010). *A global life: My journey among rich and poor, from Sydney to Wall Street to the World Bank* (1st ed.). New York: Public Affairs.

Work, R. (2003). Strengthening Local Governance: Participation and Partnership in Service Delivery to the Poor, in D.A. Rondinelli, and G.S. Cheema (Eds) *Reinventing Government For The Twenty-First Century: State Capacity In A Globalizing Society*; foreword by President Vicente Fox of Mexico. Kumarian Press, pp. 195–218.

World Bank (1993). *Developing the Occupied Territories- An Investment in Peace*, 6 vol. Washington, DC.

——— (1994). *Emergency Assistance to the Occupied Territories*, 2 vol. Washington, DC.

——— (1996). People and Development. Annual Meetings Address, James D. Wolfensohn, President, The World Bank, 1 October.

——— (1997a). *The State in a Changing World. World Development Report 1997.* New York: Oxford University Press.

——— (1997b). *Role of the World Bank in Post-Conflict Reconstruction.*

——— (1997c). *Legal Development Project West Bank and Gaza.* January.

——— (1997d). *West Bank and Gaza Community Development Project*, Middle East North Africa, Report No. PIC4676.

——— (1997e). *Project Appraisal Document For A Proposed Trust Fund Credit In The Amount Of $10.0 Million Equivalent To The West Bank And Gaza For The Gaza Industrial Estate Project.* 10 December.

——— (1997f). *West Bank and Gaza Update.* The World Bank Group, September.

——— (1997g). *West Bank And Gaza Housing Project*, WBGZ Staff Appraisal Report. 18 March.

——— (1998). *Post-Conflict Reconstruction: Role of the World Bank.*

——— (1999). *West Bank and Gaza: Strengthening Public Sector Management.* Social and Economic Development Group. Middle East and North Africa Region.

——— (2000). *Implementation Completion Report on a Trust Fund Credit In The Amount of $10 Million to The West Bank And Gaza For The Community Development Project (CDP).* 30 June.

——— (2001). *One Year of Intifada, West Bank and Gaza Update* (quarterly publication of the West Bank and Gaza Office).

——— (2002a). *West Bank and Gaza: An Evaluation of Bank Assistance.* Operation and Evaluation Department, Report No. 23820. Washington. 7 March.

────── (2002b). *Fifteen months – Intifada, closures and Palestinian economic crisis – an assessment*. Washington, DC.

────── (2002c). The Palestinian Authority's (PA) Reform Agenda, *West Bank and Gaza Update*, August.

────── (2003). *Twenty-Seven Months – Intifada, Closures, and Palestinian Economic Crisis: An Assessment*.

────── (2004a). West Bank and Gaza Proposed Public Financial Management Reform Trust Fund. April, Report 28260.

────── (2004b). *Country Financial Accountability Assessment Report* No. 28990-GZ West Bank and Gaza Country Financial Accountability Assessment West Bank and Gaza (MNCA4) June.

────── (2004a). *Four Years-Intifada, Closures and Palestinian Economic Crisis: An Assessment*. West Bank and Gaza Resident Mission, World Bank, October.

────── (2004b). *Disengagement, the Palestinian Economy and the Settlements*. West Bank and Gaza Resident Mission, June.

────── (2004c). *Stagnation or Revival? Israeli Disengagement and Palestinian Economic Prospects*. December.

────── (2005a). *West Bank and Gaza Update*. November.

────── (2005b). *Linking Gaza and the West Bank: convoys*. Washington, DC.

────── (2005c). *The Gaza/West Bank Link - Rail vs. Road*. 19 June.

────── (2005d). *Short Term Improvements for Trade Facilitation and Passages: Improvements to the Karni Border Crossing, Gaza–West Bank Link and Internal Closures*. 8 July.

────── (2005e). *Rapid Development of the Egyptian Border: A Role for a Third Party*. (Customs and Immigration Technical Assistance) Staff Technical Note. 1 October.

────── (2005f). *The 'Door to Door' Movement of Goods*. 5 July.

────── (2005g). *The Agreement on Movement and Access of November 15, 2005 The Passages – Technical Elaboration*. 2 December.

────── (2005h). *Implementation Completion Report On A Credit In The Amount Of $17.4 Million To The West Bank And Gaza For A Housing Finance*, Report No: 33721. 29 September.

────── (2007). *West Bank and Gaza Energy Sector Review*. Report No. 39695-GZ. May.

────── (2010a). *The World Bank Group in West Bank and Gaza, 2001–2009 Evaluation of World Bank Group Program*. Independent Evaluation Grou., 27 September.

────── (2010d). A Unique Challenge: Commitment in an Uncertain Environment. June. Retrieved at: http://web.worldbank.org/WBSITE/EXTERNAL/COUNTRIES/MENAEXT/WESTBANKGAZAEXTN/0,contentMDK:22626587~pagePK:1497618~piPK:217854~theSitePK:294365,00.html [Accessed: 28 September 2014]

────── (2011a). *The State and Peacebuilding Fund: Addressing the Unique Challenges of fragility and Conflict*.

────── (2011b). *World Development Report: Conflict, Security and Development*.

────── (2011b). *Building the Palestinian State: Sustaining Growth, Institutions, and Service Delivery*. Economic Monitoring Report to the Ad Hoc Liaison Committee. 13 April.

────── (2012). The West Bank and Gaza Mark. In R.P. Beschel & M. Ahern Jr. *Public Financial Management* Reform in the Middle East and North Africa An Overview of Regional Experience. Washington D.C., pp. 165–76.

—————— (2013). *Doing Business Report 2013.*

World Bank and CSAE (1999). Justice-Seeking and Loot-Seeking in Civil War. Paper presented by P. Collier & A. Hoeffler, at Conference on Civil Conflict, Crime and Violence World Bank: Washington D.C., February.

World Bank and Japan Aid. (2000). *Effectiveness in the West Bank and Gaza*, June.

World Bank and MAS (1999). Development under Adversity – The Palestinian Economy in Transition, By I. Diwan and R. Shaban (Eds). World Bank and the Palestine Economic Policy Research Institute (MAS), Washington and Ramallah.

World Bank and UNDP (2010). *State-building – Key Concepts and Operational Implications in Two Fragile States.* A Joint Initiative by the World Bank's Fragile and Conflict-affected States Group (OPCFC) and United Nations Development Programme's Bureau for Crisis Prevention and Recovery (BCPR). Retrieved at: http://siteresources.worldbank.org/EXTLICUS/Resources/statebuilding.pdf [Accessed: 12 March 2016].

Wright, J.W. (2002). *Structural flaws in the Middle East peace process historical contexts.* Houndmills, Basingstoke, Hampshire; New York: Palgrave.

Wright, J.W. and Drake, L. (2000). *Economic and Political Impediments to Middle East Peace, Critical Questions and Alternative Scenarios*, Macmillan Press Ltd. London.

Wuyts, M. (2003). The Agrarian Question in Mozambique's Transition and Reconstruction. In *From Conflict to Recovery in Africa*, T. Addison (ed.) Oxford: Oxford University Press, pp. 141–54.

Yetiv, S.A. (1997). Peace, Interdependence, and the Middle East. *Political Science Quarterly*, 112, 1, pp. 29–49.

Yftachel, O. (2000). 'Ethnocracy' and Its Discontents: Minorities, Protests and the Israeli Polity. *Critical Inquiry*, 26:4, pp. 725–56.

Zagha, A. and Zomlot, H. (2004). Israel and the Palestinian Economy: Integration or Containment? In Khan, M.H., with Giacaman, G. and Amundsen, I. (Eds) *State Formation in Palestine: Viability and Governance During a Social Transformation*. London: Routledge.

Zain (2009). Zain enters into agreement to merge Jordan operation with Palestinian operator Paltel – 18 May. Retrieved at: http://www.zain.com/media-center/press-releases/zain-enters-into-agreement-to-merge-jordan-operation-with-palestinian-operator-paltel-2/#sthash.8PQzvWhB.dpuf [Accessed: 15 September 2014].

Zanotti (2010). US Security Assistance to the Palestinian Authority Jim Zanotti Congressional Research Service. 8 January. Retrieved at: https://www.fas.org/sgp/crs/mideast/R40664.pdf [Accessed 12 March 2016].

Zaum, D. (2007). *The Sovereignty Paradox: The Norms and Politics of International Statebuilding*. Oxford: Oxford University Press.

Zeitoun, M. (2008). *Power and water in the Middle East: The hidden politics of the Palestinian-Israeli water conflict*. London, New York: I.B.Tauris.

Zertal, I. (2007). *Lords of The Land: The War Over Israel's Settlements In The Occupied Territories, 1967–2007*. New York: Nation Books.

Zoellick, R. (2009). Securing Development, United States Institute of Peace 'Passing the Baton' Conference, 8 January, Washington D.C. Retrieved at: http://web.worldbank.org/WBSITE/EXTERNAL/EXTABOUTUS/ORGANIZATION/EXTPRESIDENT/EXTPASTPRESIDENTS/EXTPRESIDENT2007/0, contentMDK:22029111~menuPK:64822311~pagePK:64821878~piPK:64821912~theSitePK:3916065,00.html [Accessed: 12 March 2016].

Primary source websites

Bush, G.W. (2002). Full text of George Bush's speech. *The Guardian* 25 June. Retrieved at: http://www.guardian.co.uk/world/2002/jun/25/israel.usa [Accessed: 9 September 2014].

Berlin Declaration (1999). Berlin European Council. Presidency Conclusions, 24 and 25 March. Retrieved at http://www.consilium.europa.eu/ueDocs/cms_Data/docs/pressData/en/ec/ACFB2.html [Accessed: 11 March 2014].

Casablanca Declaration (1994). Middle East/North Africa Economic Summit, 30 October, pp. 30–1, November. http://www.mfa.gov.il/mfa/foreignpolicy/peace/guide/pages/casablanca%20declaration%20-%20mideast-nafrica%20economic.aspx [Accessed: 19 April 2014].

Declaration of Principles On Interim Self-Government Arrangements, 13 September 1993. Retrieved at: http://www.nad-plo.org/etemplate.php?id=62 [Accessed: 28 September 2014].

Enron web (1999). Agenda Meeting Of The Board Of Directors Enron Corp. June 28. Enron Building, Houston, Texas (Via Teleconference), http://www.justice.gov/archive/enron/exhibit/03-08/BBC-0001/OCR/EXH001-01734.TXT [Accessed: 5 April 2014].

European Court of Auditors (ECA) (2013). European Union Direct Financial Support to the Palestinian Authority, Special Report No. 14, http://www.eca.europa.eu/Lists/ECADocuments/SR13_14/SR13_14_EN.pdf [Accessed: 28 September 2014].

European Union (EU) (1997). Euro-Mediterranean Interim Association Agreement On Trade And Cooperation, Official Journal of the European Communities, 16 July, 1997, http://trade.ec.europa.eu/doclib/docs/2004/june/tradoc_117751.pdf [Accessed: 28 September 2014].

IEG web. (n.d.) Utilization of Project Implementation Units (PIUs), http://lnweb90.worldbank.org/oed/oeddoclib.nsf/DocUNIDViewForJavaSearch/ADF4B0AD4AE0BB25852569BA006E34B4 [Accessed: 28 September 2014].

Israel Water Authority (2012). State of Israel, Master Plan for the National Water Sector – Main Points of the Policy Paper. March 2012 Power Point Presentation http://www.water.gov.il/Hebrew/ProfessionalInfoAndData/2012/05-Israel-Water-Sector-Master-Plan-2050.pdf [Accessed: 9 April 2014].

Israeli MFA web (1993). Foreign Minister Peres Meeting with Foreign Journalists, Israeli Ministry of Foreign Affairs. 28 June. Retrieved at: http://mfa.gov.il/MFA/MFA-Archive/Pages/FM%20PERES%20BRIEFING%20TO%20FOREIGN%20JOURNALISTS%20-%2028-Jun-.aspx [Accessed: 8 April 2014].

Israeli-Palestinian Interim Agreement on the West Bank and the Gaza Strip, Washington D.C. 28 September 1995. Retrieved at: http://old.paltrade.org/en/about-palestine/agreements/Paris%20Protocol.pdf [Accessed: 28 September 2014].

Palestine Development Program (PDP) (1993). *Programme for development of the Palestinian national economy for the years 1994–2000.* Report On The United Nations Seminar On Assistance To The Palestinian People, Paris. Papers And Statements, pp. 26–29 April. Retrieved at: http://unispal.un.org/UNISPAL.NSF/0/5E8AC6417D605B968525610F0051CA1Csthash.Ytw8l9WQ.dpuf [Accessed: 19 April 2014].

Palestine Gazette (*For laws, amendments and decrees are published*): http://muqtafi. birzeit.edu/en/pg/ Accessed: 28 September 2014].

Palestine Papers, http://www.aljazeera.com/palestinepapers/ [Accessed: 28 September 2014].

Palestine Stock Exchange – Reports, http://www.pex.ps/PSEWebSite/english/ Default.aspx# [Accessed: 28 September 2014].

Palestinian Central Bureau of Statistics [PCBS] (2012). Balance of Payments in Palestine 2000–2012 (Preliminary Results) http://www.pcbs.gov.ps/Portals/ _Rainbow/Documents/e-BOP-time-2012.htm [Accessed: 9 September 2014].

———— (2013). Labor Force Survey: annual Report 2012, April Retrieved at: http:// www.pcbs.gov.ps/Portals/_PCBS/Downloads/book1972.pdf [Accessed: 4 August 2014].

Palestinian National Authority [PNA] (2008). *Palestinian Reform and Development Plan 2008–2010*, Palestinian National Authority, Ramallah. English version retrieved at: http://www.mopad.pna.ps/en/index.php?option=com_content& view=article&id=2:palestinian-reform-and-development-plan-prdp-2008-2010&catid=10&Itemid=137 [Accessed: 28 September 2014].

———— Arabic Version retrieved at: http://www.mopad.pna.ps/attachments/article/ 5/PRDP%202008-2010-1.pdf [Accessed: 19 July 2014].

———— (2009) – *Palestine: Ending the Occupation establishing the State*. Program of the Thirteenth Government August. Retrieved at: http://www.un.int/wcm/ webdav/site/palestine/shared/documents/Ending%20Occupation%20Establishing %20the%20State%20(August%202009).pdf [Accessed: 28 September 2014].

———— (2011) National Development Plan 2011–2013 – Establishing the State, Building our Future, April 2011. Retrieved at: http://www.mopad.pna.ps/en/ attachments/article/5/EstablishingtheStateBuildingourFutureNDP202011-13. pdf [Accessed: 28 September 2014].

Silver, C. (2012). Leaked Documents Show PA outsources Palestinian land and Rights to Turkish Firm. *The Electronic Intifada*. September 19, http://electronicintifada. net/content/leaked-documents-show-pa-outsourced-palestinian-land-and-rights-turkish-firm/11680 [Accessed: 13 April 2014].

The Agreement on Movement and Access of 15 November 2005, The Passages – Technical Elaboration Prepared by the World Bank Technical Team, 2 December, 2005. Retrieved at: http://www.ochaopt.org/documents/AMA_ The_Passages_Technical_Elaboration.pdf [Accessed: 25 September 2014].

World Bank Projects and Operations – WBGS: http://web.worldbank.org/external/ projects/main?pagePK=217672&piPK=95916&theSitePK=40941&menu PK=223661&category=regcountries&regioncode=6&countrycode=GZ [Accessed: 25 September 2014].

World Bank web (n.d.) Improving the Quality and sustainability of Palestinian NGO Social Service Delivery, http://web.worldbank.org/WBSITE/EXTERNAL/ COUNTRIES/MENAEXT/WESTBANKGAZAEXTN/0,contentMDK:2264 1181~pagePK:141137~piPK:141127~theSitePK:294365,00.html [Accessed: 25 September 2014].

World Bank web-NGOs, World Bank project website: http://web.worldbank.org/ WBSITE/EXTERNAL/COUNTRIES/MENAEXT/WESTBANKGAZAEXTN/ *0,contentMDK:22641181~pagePK:141137~piPK:141127~theSitePK: 294365,00.html [Accessed: 25 September 2014].

Annual reports

Generally all publicly disclosed financial information on Palestinian private and public-private corporations can be accessed via their listings on the Palestine Stock exchange, retrieved at: http://www.pex.ps/PSEWebSite/english/Default.aspx [Accessed: 25 September 2014].

APIC
Arab Bank
Bank of Palestine
Cairo Amman Bank
PADICO Holding
Palestinian Mortgage and Housing Corporation (PMHC)
Palestine Investment Fund
Paltel

Human Rights reports and websites

B'tselem: http://www.btselem.org/.
Palestinian Center for Human Rights – Gaza: http://www.pchrgaza.org/.
United Nations Office of Coordination of Humanitarian Affairs – Occupied Palestinian Territory http://www.ochaopt.org/.

INDEX

conspiracy theories
about, 15
establishment of Palesti-
nian state, 150–8
Interim Agreements, 86,
98–9, 151
Joint Liaison Committee,
97–8
Millet system, 76, 275
Palestine Liberation
Organization (PLO)
finances, 41
reasons for failure, 57,
156–8
rents/rent-seeking,
161–2, 164
role of Israel in, 41–6,
58–60, 95–8, 157
role of Jordan in,
95–8
role of Palestine Liber-
ation Organization
(PLO) in, 1, 46–9,
95–8, 264
role of US in, 36–41,
58–60, 95–8
secret negotiation
channel, 57–60, 85
signing, 1, 36–7, 95–8
statehood, 72
Ottoman Empire, 43, 77

PADICO, 134–8, 171, 174,
234, 241–2, 253,
289n4
Paige, Jeffrey, 150
Palestine Banking Institute,
243
Palestine Economic Devel-
opment Corporation
(PEDC), 219, 222–3
Palestine Electricity Company (PEC), 135–6,
173
Palestine Industrial Estate
Development and
Management Com-
pany (PIEDCO),
134–8

Palestine Investment Fund
(PIF), 176, 193, 195,
219, 222–3, 225, 230,
251–3, 256, 266, 270
Palestine Islamic Bank, 243
Palestine Liberation
Organization (PLO)
Allon Plan, 44
armed struggle, 46
Department of Economic
Affairs and Planning,
155
in elections, 130–2
exile in Tunis, 39
finances, 41, 47–8, 233
and First Intifada, 39
and institutional reform,
182, 198, 202–7
intertwining with Fateh,
47
leftist factions within, 79
and Madrid Conference,
40–1
negotiations with Rabin
government, 103–5
and neoliberal peace-
building policies,
3–9, 23–31, 85–91
'pragmatist' phase,
150–1
Program for Develop-
ment of the Palestinian
National Economy
(PDP), 155–6
relations with US, 38–9,
170
role in Oslo Accords, 1,
46–9, 95–8, 264
and secret Oslo nego-
tiation channel, 58–9
security personnel,
225–6
services and infrastruc-
ture, 41, 52–3
two-state solution, 38–9
Palestine Monetary
Authority, 141, 242
Palestine Papers, 11, 111,
248–50

Palestine People's Party
(PPP), 74, 78
Palestine Securities
Exchange (PSE), 174,
233, 241–2,
266
Palestine Standards
Institute, 141
Palestinian Banking Association (PBA), 143
Palestinian Capital Markets
Authority, 141,
241–2
Palestinian capitalists
Gulf War, 48
industrial estates, 132
influence on Arafat, 48,
126
as intermediaries between
Gulf and Western
capital, 51, 168–70
investments in Palestine,
168–77, 219
and Jordan, 79,
276–9
native vs. expatriate, 228,
233–4, 264
neoliberalism, 4
oil industry, 48–9
rents/rent-seeking, 5,
166, 168
and Saudi Arabia,
48–9
Palestinian Commercial
Services Company
(PCSC), 137, 173–4,
176, 230, 289n4
Palestinian Economic
Council for Recon-
struction and Devel-
opment (PECDAR),
84, 119–25, 144, 151,
156, 240, 282–3
Palestinian Energy Authority
(PEA), 135
Palestinian Higher Agency
for the Promotion of
Investment (PHAPI),
138–9